The Jews of Moslem Spain

2

THE JEWS OF MOSLEM SPAIN

by

ELIYAHU ASHTOR

VOLUME 2

Translated from the Hebrew by

Aaron Klein and Jenny Machlowitz Klein

The Jewish Publication Society of America
PHILADELPHIA 1979/5739

Originally published in Hebrew by
Kiryat Sepher Ltd., Jerusalem
Maps by DESIGN KARTA, JERUSALEM
ISBN 0-8276-0100-X
Library of Congress catalog card number 73-14081
Manufactured in the United States of America
Designed by
Sol Calvin Cohen

The translation of this book into English
was made possible through a grant from

THE ADOLF AMRAM FUND

CONTENTS

LIST OF MAPS

The Jews of Moslem Spain

2

1

THE DISRUPTION OF THE SPANISH CALIPHATE

I

Winter days are short and cold in Andalusia in southern Spain. The sun hides behind clouds, and bitter winds penetrate the gates of the courtyards. The inhabitants of the cities lock themselves inside their homes, and traffic diminishes in the streets. So they do in our own time, and so they did in the remote day when Arabs ruled the land.

February 15, 1009, was one such wintry day. Even inside the houses one could feel the chill, and the number of passersby waned, until by late afternoon, the streets of Cordova were almost empty. The peasants who had come in the morning from the surrounding villages to buy and sell had already left; the merchants in the bazaars stood idle, while the artisans exercising their crafts in their narrow stalls waited impatiently for the time when they, too, could return home.

Unexpectedly, there was a sudden burst of noise which drew closer and closer. Here and there people left their work to go see what happened, but even before anyone returned with news, voices on all sides were heard crying: "A rebellion," "To arms, to arms." Many of those in the marketplace were terror-stricken. All the workers put down their tools and went into the streets, but the men sounding the alarm had already moved on. However, there were people who appeared to explain the significance of the turmoil; they were privy to the event and continued to goad the populace.

At this samé moment about thirty conspirators stood on the large terrace in front of the big gate of the palace of the caliph, Hishām II. They pretended to be merely strolling, for it was the custom of the Cordovans to stroll for pleasure on this terrace, which overlooked the *raṣīf,* the highway running the length of the river and over a wide stretch of ground on the other side.

But they did not come for a stroll. They had swords and daggers concealed under their garments and were waiting for a signal. Near the Gate of the Bridge, southeast of the palace, an armed group also waited tensely. The leader of the conspirators was himself in the suburb of Shaḳunda, on the other side of the river. He was an Omayyad prince, tall though slightly stooped, his face essentially white, but tanned, his red hair falling on a rather average brow. His name was Muḥammad b. Hishām, a great-grandson of caliph ʿAbdarraḥmān. He had a long account to settle with the caliphal government—particularly with the brutal manner in which it put his father to death—and this was the moment for which he had waited. Impatient, biding the appointed hour, he at last gave the order to initiate action. Muḥammad b. Hishām sent one of his men, the one who excelled in physical strength and unusual courage. He ascended the terrace swiftly, signaled to his companions by winking his right eye, in a flash struck a guard, and slew him with the one blow. His fellowmen killed the rest and broke into the courtyard of the palace, searching for the governor of the city, Ibn ʿAskalādja. When they found him sitting as two young women sang to him, they slew him on the spot too.

They beheaded him and toured the streets of the city with his skull impaled on a spear.

This sight sent the city into an uproar. On first hearing the cry of revolt, Cordova's inhabitants were amazed and dumbfounded, but the sight of Ibn 'Askāladja's severed head impelled them to close their stores and workshops. From every district, groups swarmed to the center of the city: the butchers from east of the Great Mosque, the cobblers from the south, the fishmongers from the east—all poured tumultuously toward the palace. Meanwhile a stream of people from the north of the city began to arrive—the brickmakers and the potters from Kūta Rāshō, the shopkeepers from the Sharḳīya. Most of them were dressed in sleeveless tunics of lambskin, went bareheaded, or wore small caps, and in the manner of simple folk, their feet were shod with boots made from rabbitskins. They bore no arms, but many waved cudgels and the butchers had brought their long knives.

Members of the higher classes also emerged into the streets: officials wearing voluminous garments trimmed in fur, finely lined jackets, and silken hats *(ḳalansuwa)* shaped like tall sugar loaves. Turbaned theologians joined the throng. And soon, from nearby villages, the peasants appeared, wearing their multicolored short shirts of rough wool, their cone-shaped hats on their heads.

The crowd beat upon the gates of the palace (which by now had been locked by court servants), but it was unable to open them. Still, Muḥammad b. Hishām urged the throng on, and after bringing ladders and strong beams, it succeeded in breaking into the palace.

At the same time, Muḥammad sent a band of his men to open the large jail so that the culprits imprisoned there could join the revolt. When they reached the palace, they at once began to grab the spoils, and all the lowest classes of the people, who looked forward to this, joined them. Naturally they hungered after the women in the caliph's harem, and it was with great difficulty that Muḥammad b. Hishām prevented them from carrying out their evil intentions. Even though they were frustrated for the time being, there was much gaiety in Cordova that evening. Truly, the revolt was altogether successful; the government, which most of the citizens hated, was overthrown. Hishām II (who in fact had never been the ruler) was ousted that very night from his office as caliph, his place taken by Muḥammad b. Hishām, who assumed the title of al-Mahdī.

As was customary during great events, the caliph's palace was brilliantly illuminated that night. From bronze chains hung hundreds of vessels containing burning wicks in oil, set in varicolored glass cups which glistened in a multitude of hues, and as these lamps illuminated the streets with their clear light, companies of singers traversed Cordova giving forth their joyous melodies.

On that evening a long epoch in Spain's history ended. Cordova's inhabitants exulted because they had overthrown the government of al-Manṣūr and thought they had restored the greatness of the Omayyads. Several decades had passed since dominion had been wrested from the Omayyad caliph, and the subjects of the kingdom laid the blame for every problem upon the rulers whom they regarded as illegitimate and as tyrants.

The revolt of Cordova's inhabitants began seven years after the death of al-Manṣūr, who had supplanted Hishām II, allowing him the royal title in name only. Al-Manṣūr died in 1002 in the city of Medinaceli, as he was mounting a military campaign against one of the provinces of Old Castile. Later Christian chroniclers relate that the doughty Moslem warrior was vanquished in this last venture and died in anguish over his defeat, but this account is simply a legend. Al-Manṣūr had been ill for some time, and it was his malady that sent him to the grave. His death during war against the Christians of northern Spain is symbolic of his life's achievements. With a strong hand he defended an advanced civilization against attacks by peoples whose cultural level was much lower—an "external proletariate." His forceful rule also prevented the enemies within the kingdom from tearing it apart. He supplied "bread and circuses" to the lower classes, which derived little benefit from his victorious campaigns beyond the country's boundaries and which was always ready to cast off the yoke of the government—an "internal proletariate," having no part in the splendid culture of the Omayyad kingdom.

This kingdom achieved its apogee with the reign of al-Manṣūr. After its first flourishing in the days of 'Abdarraḥmān I and his heirs it experienced a temporary breakup in the second half of the ninth century, but 'Abdarraḥmān III again succeeded in uniting and converting it into a powerful state. Al-Manṣūr surpassed him in his military attainments, and his government was unshaken from within, but his death marked the waning of the glory of the Omayyad kingdom.

Before his death, al-Manṣūr designated his son, 'Abdalmalik, as his successor, and Caliph Hishām II, who had never aspired to dominion, readily concurred in his choice. To be sure, some opposition among the courtiers did develop; however, 'Abdalmalik easily crushed it and thereafter ruled the kingdom as chief vizier *(ḥādjib)*, as had his father before him. 'Abdalmalik inherited much of his father's ability and sought to follow in his path. Like him, he made annual forays into the Christian kingdoms of northern Spain, returning crowned with victory and laden with spoils. On returning in 1007 from a military campaign in the region of the Duero River, he received the honorary title of al-Muẓaffar (he who won victory with the help of God) from the caliph.

The political security which Moslem Spain enjoyed also set its stamp upon its economic life. The years of al-Muẓaffar's rule were marked by prosperity and abundance. The Jews of Andalusia also benefited from this efflorescence, and immigrants from lands across the Straits of Gibraltar joined their communities. There were Jews among the Near Eastern merchants who came to Spain in those days; people of other groups came to Andalusia from the many communities of Babylonia, Egypt, and North Africa. A Hispano-Arabic writer of the eleventh century tells about a Jewish wizard from Bagdad who settled in Cordova at that time; a contemporary Hebrew philologist mentions a meeting with Abū Ibrāhīm Isaac b. Sahl of Tlemcen, who tarried in Egypt and later came to Spain.[1] Many Jews from Babylonia, who had migrated from their ancient birthplace, reached Spain at this period, either directly or after first settling in some intermediate way station. It is reported in a letter from the renowned Geniza at Fostat that an authorization was sent to Spain by Fardjōn al-parnās al-Battānī, empowering someone "to receive a bill of divorcement from Ibn Bānūḳa for his wife, the daughter of Ḥazūm b. ar-Raḥbī." Thus we learn about a woman who came from the city of ar-Raḥba on the Euphrates and was married in Spain (or at least she married a man living in Spain). Indeed, from another document discovered in the Geniza we learn, too, that Jews from that same city had settled in Kairawan.[2] The flow of immigrants from distant lands was a result of the security and flourishing economy of Moslem Spain. The Cordovans had never enjoyed such pampered living. Men and women dressed in splendid garments of the finest silk and adorned themselves in costly ornaments of gold and precious gems. But the splendor and serenity were no more than a thin veneer; underneath, cracks in the Andalusian society upon which this great state depended grew progressively deeper.

Al-Muẓaffar's reign did not last long. Toward the end of 1008 his younger brother poisoned him and took his place. The name of this brother was 'Abdarraḥmān, but the people called him Sanchol (the small Sancho), the name his mother, a Navarese princess, had called him, after her father, King Sancho Abarca. It was not without reason that the Cordovans called him by that name, for they meant thereby to refer to his descent from a Christian mother and thus to indicate that he was an offshoot of alien stock. His way of life did actually provoke much anger among the pious Moslems, for this new *ḥādjib* lacked both understanding and ability. He was a young man, twenty-five years old, who pursued pleasure and openly broke Moslem commandments; resentment against him increased from day to day. All Cordovans knew that he loved wine and it was also reported that he held Moslem worship in derision. Further, and beyond all bounds, although his father and brother were satisfied to rule in fact, 'Abdarraḥmān aspired to the title of caliph, and shortly after becoming chief vizier to Hishām II, he had the caliph name him heir presumptive to the throne. This ill-considered step was the match which lighted the fire of revolt.

For some time now there had been many Andalusians who were filled with outrage against the heads of the government and who kept zealous watch upon their actions, voicing criticisms aloud. The arrogance of the Berber troops, the mainstay of al-Manṣūr and his successors, and the luxury of the rich dazzled the proletarian masses in the big towns of Andalusia. But the general apathy of a satiated bourgeoisie which no longer had faith or ideals, or which indulged in heretical and conspiratorial movements, was even more dangerous. Clearly all these factors stimulated the Spanish inclination to rebelliousness and their natural joy in combat. At all events, the revolt that erupted in February 1009 in Cordova was the outcome of a ferment among various strata of the Hispano-Moslem population, one of those revolts which is carried on waves and ripples of dissatisfaction and social antagonism and whose end cannot be predicted. Even the recognized leaders who manipulate these movements do not have the power to control them, so that after a while the helm of leadership slips from their hands.

The Omayyad prince Muḥammad b. Hishām was the leader of the revolt in Cordova, but those who held the conspiratorial reins behind the scenes were other members of the Omayyad family. Indeed, the mother of al-Muẓaffar put large sums of money at its disposal in an attempt to avenge her son's death.

The well-to-do classes in Cordova, though sympathetic to the revolt, took no prominent part in it, but the lower strata among the city's inhabitants participated in it enthusiastically. Muḥammad b. Hishām's revolt was a revolt by artisans and laborers. The Arabic chroniclers, who were accustomed to armies compounded of several tribes, to regiments of mercenaries and feudal militia, describe with surprise and wonder the revolt of Muḥammad al-Mahdī and the establishment of his rule. The artisans and laborers who stormed the palace of the caliph and placed Muḥammad al-Mahdī in it did not return to their occupations; instead they became a body of militia, taking the preservation of order and security upon itself. This was a real people's army, composed of butchers, dealers in charcoal, weavers, and street cleaners. According to chroniclers, in those days Cordova's inhabitants had difficulty in finding workers to take care of their needs, but in the initial stages even affluent merchants, physicians, and theologians joined the army of the new caliph.

Naturally, the masses were eager for spoliation, and indeed, immediately after the rebels seized control of Cordova, several bands left Cordova for al-Madīna az-Zāhira, the governmental seat of al-Manṣūr and his sons, east of the city. Unbridled looting, lasting several days, began after the militia had cleared the area. Even within Cordova itself the mob looted the houses of those who had supported the former government. The new caliph did not restrain the rioters but instead spurred them on; and so that his government would be popular among the various strata of the people, he remitted some of the taxes with which they had been burdened. Small wonder, then, that the enthusiasm of the masses steadily mounted. When Sanchol, who was on a military campaign, heard about the revolt in Cordova, he decided to return in the hope that he would be able to crush it. But his army deserted him, and when he neared the city he was slain by followers of the new caliph. Meanwhile, the governors of the various provinces made known their support of Muḥammad al-Mahdī; among them was Wāḍiḥ, the governor of the Middle Marches, whose seat was in Medinaceli.

However, al-Mahdī's lack of ability and the behavior of his Berber guards aroused discontent.

This change in attitude toward him was noticed, of course, by the caliph, and he tried to regain the confidence that the masses formerly reposed in him. He well knew that the Cordovan populace elevated him to the royal throne because they preferred the rule of the ancient Omayyad dynasty. Therefore he was apprehensive that, after a change in mood, the deposed caliph, Hishām II, would be brought from his palace and crowned once again. Now, at that very time, a Jew died in Cordova who closely resembled the deposed caliph. When Muḥammad al-Mahdī and his followers heard about this, they immediately decided to use the dead body for their purpose. First they removed Hishām II from his palace and transferred him elsewhere; then they brought the Jew's corpse to the caliph's palace and showed it to some of the courtiers, enjoining them to testify before the multitudes that they had indeed seen the body of Hishām II and that he had died a natural death. Whether the courtiers believed this or were afraid to reveal the truth, they did as they were ordered to do: They went forth and testified before the people that they saw the caliph's body, which bore no overt marks of a wound or violent treatment.

The chief judge of Cordova, the prominent theologians, and the notaries, together with groups of the common people, were summoned to enter the palace; they recited prayers over the corpse and interred it in the Omayyad burial ground in the palace garden.[3]

But al-Mahdī's machinations availed him nothing, and shortly thereafter the Omayyad prince Hishām b. Sulaimān began preparing a fresh revolt. He had no difficulty finding supporters and helpers among the poor from the suburbs of Cordova—especially those who had been dismissed from al-Mahdī's army. Even many Berbers, who had been al-Mahdī's most enthusiastic followers, joined Hishām willingly. Moreover, since they were professional soldiers and included many officers, they obviously filled a leading role in this revolt. After proclaiming Hishām to be the caliph, they erupted into the middle of Cordova—it occurred at the beginning of June 1009—and for a day and a night a terrible battle developed between them and al-Mahdī's followers. In the end the Cordovan supporters of al-Mahdī decided the outcome—not because they loved him, but because they loathed the Berbers. Hishām b. Sulaimān was captured and slain, and his Berber followers fled Cordova. After the revolt had been crushed the inhabitants of Cordova wreaked vengeance upon the Berbers, plundering their homes and taking their women. Muḥammad al-Mahdī announced that he would reward anyone who slew a Berber and brought him his head. When this information was publicly proclaimed, the violence increased. Even soldiers and decent citizens joined in, killing Berbers who had come to Spain to take part in the *djihād,* the holy war, against the Christians; they ravished the Berber women, sold some into slavery, killed those who were pregnant.

The early Arabic historians who report on those confused times speak of "Cordovans" generally. But in that large metropolis Moslems, Jews, and Christians, Arabs and *muwalladūn* (the Spaniards who had converted to Christianity) lived side by side. Did all these religious and national groups really take the same stand? And, specifically, what was the position of the Jews in Cordova and the other cities of Moslem Spain in those fateful days when the caliphate was about to be overthrown? Apparently the same emotions really did stir within the hearts of all Andalusians. The Jews were as much repelled by the boorishness and arrogance of the Berbers as were the Moslems. Irrespective of religious distinctions, the Andalusians belonged to an old, refined culture and detested the Berbers, who were accustomed to domineering the tranquil citizenry, daily perpetrating offenses against them and their possessions. The Jews called them "Philistines," because they and the Arabs thought that the biblical Philistines went to North Africa after being vanquished by King David, and that the Berbers were their descendants; this appellation carried with it both contempt and reproach.

But even more than they scorned the Berbers, the Andalusians feared them. Both the Jews and the Moslems were afraid of what the Berbers would do to them should they succeed in completely dominating the country. Although this hatred and fear united the people of the entire country, the opposition shown to the Berbers by the various religious and national groups was undoubtedly for dissimilar reasons. The Arabs fought the Berbers on the matter of domination, whereas the Jews had no such aspirations. These basic differences were destined to reveal themselves, but in the summer of 1009, and especially in Cordova, they had not yet found expression. As one man, the inhabitants of the capital of Moslem Spain rose against the Berbers.

Those Berbers who had supported Hishām b. Sulaimān did not despair of attaining their goal: to dominate Moslem Spain completely. When they returned to the camp outside Cordova after their defeat in battle with the troops of Muḥammad al-

Mahdī, they began to plot their next steps. Opinions among them were divided, not a few arguing that they ought to bring down the rule of the Arabs, impose their dominion openly, and not merely place on the royal throne an Omayyad prince who would serve as their tool. But the most important Berber leader, Zāwī b. Zīrī, a prince of the royal house of Tunisia, dissuaded them from carrying out this plan and advised them to choose as caliph an Omayyad who would be malleable in their hands. Acting on this advice, the Berbers chose a nephew of Hishām b. Sulaimān—his name was Sulaimān b. al-Ḥakam—and went north with him. They hoped that the garrisons in the center of Spain would join them, but they were disappointed in this. Wāḍiḥ, the governor of the Middle Marches, attacked them with the help of reinforcements sent him from Andalusia; but although Wāḍiḥ was defeated, he succeeded in blocking the supply routes of the Berbers, so that they suffered from a lack of food and ultimately from actual starvation.

At the same time both factions sent emissaries to Sancho García, the duke of Castile, seeking his aid. The Christian prince decided to support the Berbers but demanded a solemn oath that after his victory the fortresses on the Duero, which al-Manṣūr had captured, would be restored to him. On securing this assurance he provided the Berbers with whatever they needed, delivered them from the blockade, and together with them, went forth at the head of a Castilian force to Andalusia. Muḥammad al-Mahdī and his militia joined battle with them, but as could have readily been foreseen, his cobblers and shopkeepers could not cope with the onslaughts of the Berbers and Castilians, who were well-trained, professional soldiers. During the ensuing panicked flight many men were trod on and crushed by their fellow soldiers and many drowned in the waters of the Guadalquivir. Arabic chroniclers report that ten thousand Cordovans died in this battle, which took place at Ḳanṭīsh, east of Cordova, at the beginning of November 1009.

The victors entered the city and al-Mahdī went into hiding. Sulaimān b. al-Ḥakam settled down in the caliph's palace and the inhabitants of the city had to submit. To be sure, they had already become accustomed to the behavior of the Berbers, but the appearance of a Castilian army in the streets of the capital of Moslem Spain was an entirely new phenomenon. Since the Moslems conquered the country three hundred years before, a Christian force had never been seen in Cordova; now, only a few months after the fight over al-Manṣūr's succession and that of his sons, the Castilians were called in to help and entered the capital of Andalusia as conquerors and rulers. The residents of the city were witness to most extraordinary spectacles.

Four days after the battle of Ḳanṭīsh, Sulaimān staged a reception in the caliph's palace for the duke of Castile to express his gratitude for the duke's help. But even as the throne of 'Abdarraḥmān an-Nāṣir was occupied by his hapless great-grandson, who uttered flattering words into the ears of the Castilian prince, mobs of Cordovans gathered in front of the palace gates, pondering the changing times.

On the following day the Cordovans swarmed to the Great Mosque to behold yet another spectacle—the coronation of Sulaimān as caliph of Moslem Spain. The large hall of the mosque was full to capacity. Masses of people flocked to its doors but were unable to enter, and it was with considerable difficulty that the Berber soldiers maintained a narrow passageway by which notables and officials could enter. In front of the *miḥrāb,* at the eastern end of the prayer hall, a royal throne had been placed, with broad rugs spread before it. On the throne sat Sulaimān b. al-Ḥakam, and at his side stood chiefs and Berber soldiers, swathed in immense burnooses; opposite them a space was left for the groups of people who came successively to swear fealty to the new caliph, Sulaimān al-Musta'īn. First the Omayyad princes approached, and as the caliph put forth his hand, each man clasped it as a sign and a token of his loyalty to the "Ruler of All the Faithful." After them came high officials called viziers, courtiers, judges and prominent theologians, notaries and representatives of the various districts of the city, and the rest of the honorable citizens of Cordova, each in his particular garb. Opposite them, amid the maze of columns topped with golden capitals, stood the multitude of the people; behind them the walls glistened with marble slabs forming a varicolored mosaic.

Thus was crowned a new caliph, the majority of whose subjects despised him from the first day. In the eyes of the Andalusians, Sulaimān was not qualified because they held him to be the "caliph of the Berbers."

While the inhabitants of Cordova and the other cities of Andalusia groaned beneath the yoke of the savage Berbers, Muḥammad al-Mahdī fled to Toledo, where he was welcomed as the lawful caliph; the other provinces, except Andalusia, also recognized his authority as before. Al-Mahdī's right-hand man, Wāḍiḥ, the commander of central Spain, deceived Sulaimān by making a spurious peace with him. Wāḍiḥ was reappointed to his post and even given increased authority; thus he gained time to prepare for a fresh struggle. Neither Muḥammad al-Mahdī nor Wāḍiḥ were blind to the fact that their forces were insufficient for them to overpower the Berbers. Therefore they, too, decided to enter into a compact with one of the Christian principalities in the north of the Iberian peninsula. They sent messengers to the princes of Catalonia, Ramón Borrel III, count of Barcelona, and his brother, Armengol, count of Urgel, pleading with them to intervene in their behalf.[4] However, the Catalonian princes laid down conditions: They demanded that they be compensated for the expenses of the campaign, that their provisions be supplied to them, and that all spoils remain in their hands. After al-Mahdī had agreed to all these stipulations, the counts mobilized a force of nine thousand men. This certainly was not a large force, but it consisted of select units which included the finest knights of Catalonia. Priests and bishops of high rank also joined the counts, for in those days it was the custom of the Spanish clergy to take part in military campaigns and even to join in the actual fighting. Nor were Jews absent from the Catalan army; one such was the finance minister of the count of Barcelona.

The Christian army went by way of the Ebro Valley and, on reaching Saragossa, treated its inhabitants with wanton cruelty, behaving as if it were a conquering army of aliens. As they moved southward they were joined by a large Moslem host from those provinces that were loyal to Muḥammad al-Mahdī. The rulers at Cordova prepared to repel the attack, but when Sulaimān called on the inhabitants of the capital to fight, they refused. So it happened that when the two armies clashed on the battlefield near ʻAḳabat al-baḳar, north of Cordova, the forces of al-Mahdī enjoyed a decisive numerical superiority. According to Arabic historians his army—not counting the Catalan units—numbered thirty thousand men. But the Moslem troops did not take an active part, and the brunt of the battle with the Berbers fell upon the Catalans; one of their rulers, Armengol, count of Urgel, was killed in the fighting. However, Sulaimān, who did not understand Berber tactics, fled before the outcome was decided, and when the caliph fled, there was a general rout.

The battle, which was waged in the first half of June 1010, thus ended with a Catalan victory. They forthwith entered Cordova; Muḥammad al-Mahdī became caliph at Cordova once again. Although he imposed heavy tribute on the citizenry in order to fulfill the Catalan demands, all the Cordovans, no matter what their religion, were satisfied—the Berbers, who had ruled them tyrannically and haughtily, were removed.

After the capture of Cordova by the Catalans, additional vicissitudes time and again overtook the inhabitants, altering the character of authority and bringing disaster upon the densely populated city. Its entire population—Moslems, Jews, and Christians—suffered bitterly.

The Catalans did not linger at Cordova after entering the city, but pursued the Berbers, who had fallen back to southern Andalusia. They overtook them in the valley of the Guadiaro, near the city of Ronda; but in the battle that took place there on June 21, 1010, they suffered a critical defeat. Many Catalan nobles were slain, among them Adalbert, who had formerly been the governor of Barcelona. The bishop of Barcelona and the bishop of Gerona were slain, while the bishop of Vich was severely wounded and later died of his wounds. The Jewish finance minister of the count of Barcelona was also among the fallen.[5]

The Catalans returned to Cordova and wreaked their anger upon its inhabitants. They pillaged some quarters of the city, rampaging and slaying anyone who even resembled a Berber. The Arabic chroniclers report that a Cordovan would say of his enemy: "He's a Berber"—and thereupon kill him. Women and children were not spared; the bellies of pregnant women were ripped open on the main streets. The Catalans made a mockery and a derision of the Islamic faith. They reviled the name of Mohammed and wantonly affronted the Moslem sanctuaries in various ways. When they left the city to return to their own country at the beginning of July, the Cordovans, despite all that had been inflicted upon them, regretted this departure, for the future looked dark if they had to stand alone against the Berbers.

With the departure of the Catalans, the Slavs became the

sole rulers in Cordova. By the end of July 1010, they had murdered the caliph, Muḥammad al-Mahdī, severed his head, impaled it upon a spear, and paraded it through the market-places. They crowned Hishām II anew as caliph; but Wāḍiḥ, their military commander, became the chief vizier and, in actuality, the ruler. At the same time, however, the Berbers were preparing to avenge themselves upon the inhabitants of Cordova and to restore their rule once again. In the fall of 1010, they began a siege of the city which lasted about three years and resulted in unimaginable anguish for its inhabitants.

During the winter of 1010–11, bands of Berbers pillaged the villages around Cordova and prevented food supplies from reaching the city. This not only reduced the city to want but also led to another dire consequence. The villagers, who by now were in total privation, came to the besieged city hoping to find food there, and of course the multitude of starving peasants only increased the city's distress. Costs rose daily. The famine increased. But the Berbers did not revenge themselves upon the Cordovans alone. They entered Elvira, Jaén, and the other cities of Andalusia; and wherever they entered, they pillaged, murdered, tortured the women (if they suspected them of hiding money, they hung them by their breasts). In Algeciras they perpetrated a frightful slaughter taking the children as slaves; later, when Sulaimān set them free, most of them died because of the hardships they endured.

Epidemics spread throughout besieged Cordova during that period. In the spring of 1011 the Guadalquivir overflowed its banks; many houses in the city's suburb on the left bank were demolished, leaving a great number of homeless victims. In the summer of that year pestilence again erupted within the city, claiming many lives.

Meanwhile, differences of opinion among the Slavs who dominated the city began to surface. Wāḍiḥ, in despair over the prolonged struggle, opened negotiations with the Berbers against the wishes of a faction of his officers and in consequence was slain by them in the fall of 1011. Once more the inhabitants of the city beheld a former governor being borne through the streets, his decapitated head impaled on a long spear. Nor did Wāḍiḥ's followers go unscathed; their homes were plundered and their property seized. The Slav chieftain, Ibn Wadā'a, became the governor of the city, conducting its defense with strength and vigor.

The siege continued throughout the year 1012. Even though various attempts were made to bring the struggle to a peaceful end, there was no letup in the fighting. The Cordovans mounted sorties which were, for the most part, unsuccessful; meanwhile, the distress inside the city reached indescribable proportions. Yet the hatred for the Berbers and, even more, the fear of them gave the city's inhabitants strength. They refused to hear of surrender and severely punished anyone who dared to mention it.

During those unsettled days the Jews bore their share of the burden. A tattered and faded letter which found its way into the Geniza at Fostat tells of the intense suffering of the Cordovan populace and of the destruction wrought by the siege. The author of the letter, which was sent to the Jewish merchant Abu 'l-Faradj Joseph b. Jacob Ibn 'Aukal, mentions the Slavs who hold sway in the city in the name of Caliph Hishām and writes that the Cordovans, notwithstanding their difficult circumstances, have decided that it is better to be slain than to come under Berber domination.[6] But in May 1013 their resistance was broken, and they had to send emissaries to the Berbers informing them of their submission.

The Berbers imposed heavy tribute upon the Cordovans, but this payment, though oppressive, was as nothing compared with what the victors did to them on entering the city. That which they dreaded befell them. Great indeed was the misery of Cordova. The savage Berbers plundered, ravished, and murdered in every section of the city. They spared neither the aged notables nor the young children. Theologians advanced in years, who had never borne arms, and ascetics who had withdrawn from society were killed on the main thoroughfares. Infants were slain in the arms of their mothers. Cries pierced the air every hour. Mourning and grief were everywhere. When the magnificent houses of Cordova's wealthy were looted of money and gems, jewels and precious articles, they were put to the torch. One of the greatest writers of Moslem Spain, who was driven from Cordova, his birthplace, relates that a man came to him and described vividly the destruction of the suburban villas to the west of the city, where his family's house was located. This eyewitness account tells of how the palaces were razed to their foundations, destroying every trace of the grand salons and lovely balconies; the entire suburb was turned into a wilderness for the jackals to roam.

When dominance over Cordova was restored to the Berbers they once more crowned Sulaimān al-Musta'īn, and he occupied the throne of the caliphate for three more years. Sulaiman himself was a well-intentioned person. He was a man of refinement, an intellectual who wrote verse in polished Arabic. But real power was exercised by the Berbers, who did as they pleased in Cordova and the other cities of Andalusia. They tyrannized the populace mercilessly, taking the large estates for themselves and living the life of wealthy feudal lords.

Neither Sulaimān nor his Berbers wielded any influence outside of Andalusia. Yet the civil strife which preceded the siege of Cordova showed that the political disintegration of Moslem Spain had already begun. Various provinces broke away from the Omayyad kingdom, becoming independent principalities; and with the conquest of the city, the severance of the ties was complete. Then even those provinces which remained faithful to it throughout all those unsettled times separated from the kingdom. Only central and southern Andalusia remained a part of it. After three years a prince of the Idrīsī dynasty in Morocco (which had intermingled with the Berbers to such a degree that it was difficult to discern that they were of Arab stock) revolted against Sulaimān al-Musta-'īn. This prince, whose name was 'Alī b. Ḥammūd, was appointed by Sulaimān as governor of Ceuta and the stretch of seacoast surrounding it, but he had high aspirations—and his revolt was indeed crowned with success. He crossed the Straits of Gibraltar with a small force, but as soon as he arrived in Andalusia he obtained help from all sides and reached Cordova without encountering serious opposition. He dethroned Sulaimān, had him executed, and he himself mounted the throne of the caliphate.

This marked the end of Omayyad rule in Moslem Spain, even though the many princes of the dynasty made some attempts to restore and renew their dominion. In Andalusia and the other provinces of Moslem Spain which had become independent states a new period in the history of Moslem Spain was initiated, the era of the "provincial kings" *(Mulūk aṭ-ṭawā-'if;* in Spanish, *Reyes de Taifas).*

II

The great change which occurred in Spain at the beginning of the eleventh century also wrought discernible alterations in the Jewish communities there, which at that time constituted one of the most important groups among all the Jewish people.

When the Omayyad caliphate disintegrated and those small kingdoms were established in its place, the social structure also changed and a new spirit permeated the ruling circles.

While the Omayyad caliphs occupied the throne and held dominion in Cordova, certain factors—conceptual, emotional, and social—operated among the ruling classes, stabilizing and shaping the large Moslem kingdom on the Iberian peninsula. Of all these factors the most important was the tradition of the Eastern caliphate: both adherence to the principles of the Omayyad dynasty which had formerly ruled over all the Moslem lands and the conscious will to maintain the customs developed at Damascus, the capital of the caliphate from bygone days. The emirs and the caliphs at Cordova, who claimed to be the successors of the caliphs at Damascus, acted with some discretion in their relations with the non-Moslem communities. Although they patterned themselves after the Omayyad caliphs in Damascus by giving important posts in their government even to non-Moslems who were outstanding in their administrative and political skill, to be sure, they generally refrained from conferring upon them the status of high dignitaries or from becoming intimate with them. In their view they could not act otherwise: They were rulers who professed to be heads of the Moslem community and, moreover, competitors of the Abbasid caliphs, who stressed their own religious zeal and enacted discriminatory laws against Christians and Jews. It was no mere chance that Ḥasdai Ibn Shaprūṭ was never appointed vizier; it was a consequence of the tradition of the caliphs.

Further, the national tradition of the Arabs, the dominant class during the time of the Omayyad rule, operated toward this end. Those who held the high posts in the army and in civil administration were almost all members of noble Arab families, who prided themselves on their descent from the chiefs of past generations. These particular families fostered the Arabic national spirit, treating all members of other nationalities with antipathy and disrespect. But in the tenth century, the desire to work toward the unification of the national and religious groups and to bring the various sectors closer to each other dominated the government of the

Omayyad caliph in Cordova. The caliphs and their officials were careful not to receive help from or to depend on any one group in order to oppress another. The place occupied by the Jews in this system of government was, in consequence, relatively modest.

This characteristically Omayyad approach by the rulers to the non-Moslem changed entirely when they were replaced by the "provincial kings." These kings were officers who rose to dominance because of their personal ability or because of the sensitivities of tribal national groups; many of them had not been reared in the age-old traditions, nor had they carried on the practices of princely families in every respect. Most were not Arabs, but were Berbers or "Slavs" from various European national backgrounds who had achieved high rank after liquidating members of Arab nobility. They were completely without national pride. These usurpers generally had no great aspirations; they did not set themselves far-reaching goals but instead only wanted to widen the scope of their dominion by conquest of their neighbors' territories. To achieve their aims with the limited forces under their authority they always needed help, and with a characteristic lack of principles they did not hesitate to depend on anyone who was prepared to assist them. Thus it happened that, shortly after the disintegration of the Hispano-Omayyad caliphate, Jews began to occupy a prominent role in the courts of the rulers.

Jews of ability obtained various posts in the service of the Moslem kings, both in the seat of government and elsewhere. Writing in or about 1040, a Hebrew poet composed a laudatory poem for a Jew who held an eminent position in the court of one of the rulers, had influence over Moslem and Christian dignitaries, and defended Jewish communities from their enemies. The poet did not forget to note that the father, too, held office in the service of a prince.[7] Most of those Jews who were intimates of the princes used their power to defend their brother Jews. In a poem composed by this Jewish poet in honor of the "chief" Isaac—who was one of that group of courtiers—he states in his flowery style that "with his sword he cut down every arrogant man who acted presumptuously against his people."[8]

Now and then court Jews would meet a bitter, speedy end. At about the time he wrote the poem in honor of that Jew who achieved a measure of authority, the poet composed an elegy for a Jew who had been one of the aides of a Moslem king, and when he was sent to give succor to besieged cities, he was murdered in a forest by a band of Christians. The murder of this Jewish courtier made a strong impression and more elegies were composed for him. One of these avowed, among other things, that his enemies made the malicious suggestion to the king to send him on that mission in the hope that the Jew would fall into the hands of the Christians.[9]

But despite the intrigue and the perils lurking for them in the politics of the royal courts, the Jews were filled with great hope. They were like one for whom a magnificent drawing room opened which till now he could only gaze upon from his own threshold. The change in the social climate did, indeed, open completely new portals to the Jews of Spain.

Even though the establishment of the small kingdoms was a turning point in the historical development of Spain and was accompanied by a break in the sociopolitical continuity, the new rulers endeavored to copy the practices of the Omayyad caliphs to a considerable extent. Many of them did their utmost to give their courts the cultured character of those of other kings and even to make them centers of literary creativity. But in the courts of these rulers, who were free from the bonds of tradition of the caliphs, the tendency toward secular culture grew more pronounced, and most of them championed scholars preoccupied with the exact sciences. Consequently, they did not hesitate to favor Jews who showed ability and to give them their support.

Release from the fetters of orthodox piety is a characteristic thread running through the history of Moslem Spain, particularly in the eleventh century. The Ibero-Roman inhabitants of the Iberian peninsula, who constituted an overwhelming majority among the subjects of the Moslem rulers, were, like the other peoples of southern Europe, extremely pious but nonetheless had a bent for the secular and for the high life. That extremism which is the stamp of the Spaniard, which is in his blood, impelled these people throughout the generations to religious zealotry and at the same time to throwing off all the restraints of religion. Orthodox Islam, based on Semitic monotheism, strict, opposed to any artistic similitude, dry and devoid of any mysticism, negating all embellishments of gold and silk as well as divertisement through music—this religion laid a heavy burden upon Spain for many generations, and when the Omayyad caliphs were deposed, it apparently threw off this entire weight without delay. Certain classes among the Moslems in Spain, it seemed, waited for this moment to discard a tradition which was oppressive to them, even though outwardly they still gave it recognition. Points of view which had been held among closed and limited circles throughout the tenth century now spread throughout entire classes; and, as was customary with Spaniards, the change occurred swiftly and in extreme measure.

This was a mass rejection of the higher classes—one measure of distance along the road taken by the spirit of Mediterranean man in the Middle Ages, who had been tossed between blind faith (nurtured in part by insecurity) and the serenity of devoutness, and the affirmation of this world and the aspiration to enjoy it to the fullest possible degree. But it was also one step on the long road from simple faith to the new times in which the sublime ideas of freedom of thought and the liberation of mankind would dominate men's minds and when science would take the place of superstition. To be sure, a regression was destined to come. But progress along with some backsliding has always been the path of the human spirit as it frees itself. For this is the stuff of history.

The Spanish Jews in those days were riven in spirit, and the intellectuals, whose hearts were torn by doubts, were prepared to rise against the traditional faith, which to them seemed overly simple and not based on intellectual foundations. As a result, these intellectual Jews took part quite willingly in that ballet of agnosticism in thought and deed which is the chief characteristic of the culture of Spain in those times, an interim period between the dominance of the *faḳīhs* and that of the Christian clergy and the monks. But the Jews benefited no less from their propinquity to the Moslems. When a bridge was suddenly erected over the chasm which had once separated them and the Moslems, the intellectuals and wealthy among the Jews walked across it with joyous celerity. They believed they were leaving behind them an obscure past and going toward a future glowing with expectations. Hence their strong desire to strike roots in Moslem society, to participate in the affairs of the government, and to collaborate with its intellectuals in cultural endeavors.

So began that period in the life of the Jews of Moslem Spain which historians have named the "Golden Age." This period lasted three generations—long enough to allow the large Jewish community on the Iberian peninsula to reinforce its economic and social position and to reach cultural achievements unlike any other in the annals of the Jews. But this blossoming and their closeness with their non-Jewish neighbors had a decisive influence on the religious outlook of the upper strata among the Jewish community—and this imperiled their absolute existence.

Before the changes in the history of Moslem Spain set their imprint upon the Jews in that big country, however, other changes occurred which were, in effect, the direct and immediate results of a certain decisive development.

III

The Arabic chroniclers report that even while the siege was in progress, the inhabitants of Cordova began to leave the city in order to seek refuge in other parts of Moslem Spain. According to these writers the Cordovans were beset by famine, oppression, and terror. But one must also remember that during the successive revolts in the city, people had ample opportunity for private vengeance behind the mask of political activity, and the relatives and friends of such slain chiefs suffered too. When the Berbers did take Cordova and the frightful massacres began, many citizens fled, now to preserve their lives.

But even this wave of fugitives was not the greatest one to leave Cordova. After the anger of the conquerors subsided somewhat and they began to make their authority secure, they issued a stringent decree against the city's inhabitants: They ordered them to evacuate all neighborhoods except the inner city *(al-Madīna)* and a small part of those sections in the east of the city—which to this day are called *ash-Sharḳīya.* Then a new stream of exiles poured into all sectors of Spain, among whom were numerous Jews. Although the old Jewish quarter near the caliph's palace was within the inner city, and therefore the decree of expulsion did not affect it, the Jews dwelt not only in this neighborhood but also in the northern part of the city. Moreover, the Jews of Cordova had taken part in the struggle with the Berbers as had the other inhabitants of the city, and they could not look for better treatment than their neighbors. Thus political upheaval in Andalusia resulted in an internal migration within the large Jewry gathered in Moslem Spain.

Many Cordovan Jews migrated to various cities in southern Andalusia where the power of the Berbers was still unfelt, such as Almería, where the Slavs held sway. Not only were these cities nearby and the living conditions there familiar to the Cordovans, but many of the migrants, apprehensive lest conditions worsen so much that they would have to leave Spain altogether, preferred to go to a port city where seagoing ships were available.

Others preferred to flee to the north, in order to be as far from the savage Berbers as possible. A Jewish writer living in Spain in the twelfth century reports that many Cordovan Jews migrated to Toledo and faraway Saragossa, and he stresses that even in his own time descendants of those immigrants constituted separate congregations of their own.[10] There is good reason for him to mention Toledo and Saragossa, for these cities absorbed large bodies of migrants, writers among them. According to reports, the poets Isaac Ibn Khalfōn and Abū Zakarīya Ibn Ḥanīdjā went to Toledo.[11] One of the important cultural leaders of that epoch relates how he, together with other Cordovans, migrated to Saragossa.[12]

These writers speak only of the emigration from Cordova, but the migratory movement which inundated all of the provinces of Spain did not issue alone from the capital of Andalusia. In other areas of Spain, too, Arabs, Berbers, and Slavs fought for dominance in cities large and small, in provinces and districts. The atrocities of war prompted many Jews from Andalusia and other provinces in southern Spain to take the wanderer's staff in hand and to seek new homes. The uprooting of masses of people from their origins always involves monstrous suffering, especially since it is often sudden, even panicky. Families are scattered. People who have lived within a large family circle suddenly find themselves alone. A Spanish poet of that era relates how the "times made him a lone individual." Many of the migrants wandered from place to place until they finally settled somewhere or reached their destination by tortuous paths after long journeys. The poet expresses it thus:

I measured the face of the earth with my feet
As though they were two measuring rods.[13]

Many decided to quit totally the Moslem districts in Spain, where civil war had played havoc with them and where turmoil and revolts followed one upon the other. Others migrated to the Near East. Eleventh-century documents mention Spanish Jews who settled in Egypt. Lists preserved in the Geniza which deal with the distribution of alms by the community of Fostat contain appellations such as "the Spanish youth" or "the Spanish orphan" or "the man from Spain." Some of the migrants were religious functionaries who are also mentioned in Geniza documents.[14] Even though many of these "Spaniards" probably arrived in Egypt in the second half of the century, some of them were no doubt among those who left Spain at the time of the immense troubles at the start of the century.

Much more numerous than the migrants who crossed the sea were those who went to the Christian kingdoms and principalities in northern Spain. This was the second wave of migration which changed the demographic map of the Jews of Spain. To be sure, the civil and juridical status of the Jews in the Christian principalities of northern Spain was still generally inferior in those times. They were regarded as dependents of the rulers, as unfree people; anyone who killed a Jew or hurt him had to indemnify the ruler, and this indemnity was larger than the usual.[15] Their security was shaky, since the rulers and the knights were not always able to defend them. But they had ample opportunities for earning livelihoods because the Christian states needed urbanities like them as skilled craftsmen and as traders who would import manufactured products from Andalusia and other Moslem countries.

Various documents of Christian Spain indicate that there was a sizable Jewish migration which, at the beginning of the eleventh century, flowed from the Moslem regions of the Iberian peninsula to the Christian principalities in the north.

Growth of the Jewish population was especially pronounced in Castile and Navarre. By the first half of the eleventh century the Jews already constituted a significant element in the economic life of those kingdoms and apparently filled positions in the royal service. Sancho al Mayor, king of Navarre (1004–35), at that time was supreme among the rulers of Christian Spain—he had succeeded in imposing his dominance over all the Christian provinces between the Ebro and the Pyrenees, over Castile and León. The retinue of this Christian king included Jews, as seems to be indicated in a document from the year 1032. On a bill of sale of a village which was acquired by Princess Urraca for the convent of Covarrubias, in which she sojourned, the king and queen and twenty-three Castilian nobles set their seals, and these are followed by three Jewish signatories—Scape Levi, Bueno, and Jacob.[16] Don Scape Levi is mentioned in another document as a person of considerable property. In 1028 Donna Jimena, the mother of King Sancho, gave the monastery of San Milan de la Cogolla two villages which formerly belonged to Scape Levi and were apparently confiscated by the king and bought from him by her for a large sum of money.[17] Scape Levi was, as we see, affluent, and had close contact with the rulers of Castile.

At that time Jews were to be found in most of the districts of Old Castile, even in small cities and villages—either staying briefly as traders or residing there permanently as settlers. In a writ of privileges which was given in 1039 by Sancho el Mayor's son, Fernando I, king of Castile, to the inhabitants of Villafria, Orbaneja, and San Martín, reference is made to a payment of indemnity for killing and wounding Jews.[18] Even if this is no proof that Jews actually lived in those villages (which are in the vicinity of Burgos), it is still clear that they were to be found in that district. In any case, there is no doubt that during the reign of King Sancho el Mayor a Jewish settlement was based in Nájera, west of Logroño, which then belonged to the kingdom of Navarre.[19]

The population of this portion of the country grew substantially at the end of the first third of the eleventh century as a result of the efforts of King Sancho el Mayor. Roads were improved, measures were taken to secure the safety of wayfarers, and new settlements were established.[20] We can safely assume that the number of Jews also increased steadily and they struck roots in places where they formerly could not gain footing. In a document listing the property which King García gave to the monastery of San Julian in the village of Sojuela, southwest of Logroño, in 1044, mention is made of the village of Medrano, with its fields and vineyards to the Jews' Road in the south.[21] The vineyard of a Jew of Sojuela is referred to in a document from the year 1056.[22] The Jews of Belorado are mentioned in a document from the time of Sancho, prince of Castile, who reigned from 995 to 1017. This was no doubt a new Jewish settlement because only in the 1070s did Belorado change from a village to a market town.[23]

Even in the region which later became the kingdom of Aragon, Jews could already be found. The city of Jaca, which after the death of Sancho el Mayor and the division of his kingdom became the capital of Aragon, was then but a small village with perhaps two or three streets; in a document of that period there is note of Belito, the influential Jew from the fortress called Jaca, and his brother, Isḥāḳ (Azaka).[24]

There is much more information about the Jews in the kingdom of León of that period. In sales documents drafted in the city of León in the eleventh century many Jews are cited whose names (or the names of their fathers) are Arabic, an indication that they were recent immigrants from Moslem Spain or were children of immigrants. Among the Jews who had vineyards in the vicinity of León in 1015 mention is made of Vita Habiz (Khabbāz), which means a baker in Arabic.[25] The name Yūsuf appears in documents of the years 1021, 1022, 1026, and 1049,[26] the name Marwāh in a document dated 1028,[27] and the names of Sulaimān and his wife Sayyida (Cida) in documents dated 1029 and 1032.[28] In 1053 Joseph bar Joab Eshkafat sold a vineyard to a woman of the royal family. The family name of the seller means shoemaker in Arabic.[29] In Puente del Castro, today a suburb of the city of León, an important Jewish settlement existed in the Middle Ages, and among the monuments discovered in its cemetery is a memorial inscription for Ḥiyyā bar Joseph b. 'Azīz, a goldsmith who died in 1100 at the age of sixty-five.[30] The name 'Azīz indicates that this was a Jewish family which had migrated from Moslem Spain to the kingdom of León. The grandfather of the deceased, who still bore this Arabic name, lived at the beginning of the eleventh century. A decree by King Fernando I points toward the occupations and the origin of the Jewish community of Puente del Castro, which because of the great number of Jewish inhabitants was also called the Fortress of the Jews *(Castrum Judaeorum);* it obligates the Jews to pay five hundred solidi and three well-tanned hides annually to the cathedral of León. This decree, promulgated about 1060,[31] demonstrates that tanning was a characteristic occupation of the Jews of Puente del Castro. Indeed, for many generations this was one of the renowned export industries of Andalusia and, in particular, of Cordova. Even then there were Jewish communities—as is revealed by monuments with Hebrew letters inscribed on them which were found at La Coruña.[32]

This large migration, which took Jews from southern Spain to other areas and especially to the northern part of the country, was vitally important in shaping the cultural mold of the Jewish community on the Iberian peninsula and in crystallizing the social tendencies operating within it. The total number of Jews in all of eleventh-century Spain was still low; no more than fifty or sixty thousand.[33] Until the migration northward most Spanish Jews dwelt in a relatively small area of Andalusia, and now they were scattered throughout the peninsula. Up to this time most Spanish Jews lived in compact areas within large and small communities. No great distances separated the Jews, but now many of them emigrated to towns and villages containing few Jews and far from big city communities.

In the big cities (or, more accurately, in the cities which then were considered big) Jews constituted a sizable portion of the population, about five to fifteen percent, but the distances between these cities were great. From this it follows that the Jews had more constant contact with the non-Jews than heretofore. These new circumstances forced them into a greater degree of adaptability, which resulted, for many, in assimilation. For some, on the other hand, greater contact with non-Jews resulted in an intensification of devotion, an emphasis on their personal selves, a strengthened awareness of difference. Migration and the geographic dispersal thus polarized Spanish Jewry.

Moreover, from the time that the Jews of Andalusia first began to scatter over the whole Iberian peninsula, their influence in shaping Spanish culture as a whole continued to grow. Through steady contact with non-Jews of diverse origins, they passed on perceptions and concepts, tenets and approaches that were enduring characteristics of the Jewish people. In the eleventh century a "Spanish" civilization did not yet exist; the name *Español* was unknown. The process of crystallization and the molding of the Spanish entity was only beginning, and it is certain that even a small religioethnic group, properly defined in substance and possessing an ancient, viable cultural heritage—as the Jews—could make a significant contribution to the developing society. Precisely because they were few in number, the Jews stressed their lineage, their descent from the heroes of the Bible, from the patriarchs and the prophets, and they reiterated to themselves and to others that they were members of a chosen people bearing a message for all humanity. Their awareness heightened in reaction to servitude and in opposition to non-Jews. But they bequeathed these concepts to Gentiles, and ultimately these ideals became the bases of the non-Jews' national consciousness. Thus did the Jews fill a critical role for Christians and Moslems in shaping that Spanish culture which was destined to be the culture of a vast continent across the ocean.

IV

The big political shift resulted also in changes in the direction of the spiritual life of Spanish Jewry.

In the course of two generations, during the era of Rabbi Moses b. Ḥanōkh and of his son, Rabbi Ḥanōkh, the religiocultural ties between the Jews of Moslem Spain and the Babylonian academies had weakened, but these ties were not completely severed—there were, after all, merchants going from the one country to the other in both directions. The Jews living between these points sent the writings of Spanish authors to Babylonia, and copies of the responsa of the heads of the Babylonian academies (in which they commented on complete tractates of the Gemara) were brought to Spain. Nonetheless, by the time of Rabbi Moses and his son they no longer turned to the *g'ōnīm* of Babylonia with every difficult problem, which earlier was the practice of Andalusian Jewry; they also sent fewer contributions. Certainly the existence of noted rabbis in Andalusia was a factor, but this situation also resulted from a desire to follow the policy of the Omayyad caliphs who reigned at Cordova. There is no doubt that the Omayyads looked favorably upon the burgeoning of Spain as a Jewish cultural center and the consequent break in the close ties with the Babylonian schools. They were not opposed to such ties per se; but, in former times, the relations between their Jewish subjects and the *g'ōnīm* in Babylonia had distinctly implied an acknowledgment of another authority—and this was not to their liking.

As the first decade of the eleventh century ended, various factors again altered the direction of the religiocultural life of Andalusian Jewry. In the fall of 1014, Rabbi Ḥanōkh b. Moses, who for several decades was the recognized religious leader of the Jews in Spain, died, and a rabbi of his authority could not be found among them.[34] The Omayyad dynasty meanwhile departed from the political stage and its kingdom disintegrated. It seems Spanish Jewry renewed its contacts with the Babylonian academies in the last years of al-Manṣūr's descendants. When their dominion toppled and Moslem Spain no longer was a unified kingdom competing with the Abbasid caliphate in the East, no further obstacle remained to a renewal of contacts with Babylonian Jewry. The rulers of the small principalities who supplanted the Omayyads were not opposed to their Jewish subjects contacting the heads of the academies in Babylonia. Therefore, during that period, the communities in Moslem Spain once more sent their questions on legal and religious matters to the Babylonian schools and provided them with financial support.

In those days, the ancient *y'shībhōt* in Babylonia were headed by eminent men who were the spiritual leaders of world Jewry.

The *gāōn* of Pumbedita, which was then located in Bagdad, was Rabbi Hai b. Sh'rīra, a brilliant scholar and a man of imposing authority. The name of this *gāōn* is symbolic of that period known in Jewish history as the Geonic Era—his achievements marked its glory as well as its end. When still a youth, Hai served as a teacher in the *y'shībha* and in 986, when he was nearly fifty, he was appointed president of the court. Rabbi Hai assisted his father, Rabbi Sh'rīra Gaon, then very old, in the conduct of the academy and together with him responded to the questions which were addressed to it. This accounts for decisions bearing the names of both Rabbi Sh'rīra and Rabbi Hai as joint signatories. In 1004 Rabbi Sh'rīra resigned in favor of his son, and thereafter Rabbi Hai served in the post thirty-four years; he died in 1038 at the age of ninety-nine. Throughout his long life he labored indefatigably to elevate the reputation of the academy and to restore it to the position of seniority it held formerly, before major academies were established in other countries.

The *gāōn* Rabbi Hai, a foremost teacher of halakha, was distinguished for his skill as an educator, his powerful logic, and his clear exposition. These traits are conspicuous in his numerous responsa to individuals and to communities, as well as in his halakhic writings. The number of his responsa constitutes more than one-third of what has been preserved of all the responsa of the *g'ōnīm* of the two great academies in Babylonia over a period of four hundred years. He wrote several halakhic treatises dealing with various aspects of Jewish law, most of them in Arabic. He also wrote commentaries on the Bible and on certain tractates of the Babylonian Talmud, a Hebrew-Aramaic lexicon, and liturgical hymns.

However, Rabbi Hai was not only a talmudist. He also was well-grounded in secular learning: He read the writings of Arabic scientists and philosophers, and in general did not confine himself to the "four ells of the halakha," as did most of his geonic predecessors. In his time Karaism reached its fullest flowering, and the members of this sect severely attacked Orthodox Jews because the folklore of the Talmud includes tales of miracles and other matters of dubious merit. In addition, among Jews in various countries there were a number of mystics who had a marked influence upon the community. Rabbi Hai took a moderate and compromising stand between the opposing currents of thought. He endeavored to exonerate the scholars of the Talmud from accusations that they held anthropomorphic beliefs, and time and again he restated the principle that authority must not be ascribed to folklore. He also upheld the principle of freedom of choice and was most decidedly opposed to belief in fatalism. The influence of the *gāōn* Rabbi Saadya and of the Moslem theologians of the Mutazilite sect is discernible in this approach. On the other hand, Rabbi Hai did not negate the miracles wrought on behalf of the righteous, and he was unable to free himself entirely of the belief in spirits and demons.

Because of Rabbi Hai's impact on his contemporaries and on succeeding generations, he was generally referred to merely by the title "the *Gāōn.*" His rich personality, his inclination to encompass wide areas of learning, and his moderate approach in religious matters captured the hearts of the Jews of Moslem Spain. But, of course, primarily they saw him as an authoritative master of halakha, and therefore they addressed their questions on religious and juridical practice to him. Whereas the letters of the *gāōn* Rabbi Sh'rīra to Rabbi Ḥanōkh remained unanswered, strong ties were maintained between the Jews of Andalusia and Sh'rīra's son, Rabbi Hai.

In one of his responsa Rabbi Hai counts Spain among those countries where Jews turn to him "in the matter of their questions and doubts."[35] Halakhic works of later generations cite many decisions laid down by the *gāōn* in Bagdad in reply to queries from Spain; but from the language of the authors of these texts it is clear that, despite the great respect they accorded this *gāōn,* they did not always accept his opinion since in their view local practice took precedence.[36]

Rabbi Hai's commentaries on various tractates of the Babylonian Talmud were available in Spain in the first half of the eleventh century, and scholars perused them and learned from them. One renowned Hebrew grammarian who lived in Spain at that time quotes copiously from the responsa and commentaries of the *g'ōnīm* Rabbi Sh'rīra and Rabbi Hai on the tractates *B'rākhōt, Shabbat, Bēṣa, Giṭīn, Ḥūlīn,* and others.[37] The most important among Rabbi Hai's halakhic works is his treatise on buying and selling, and this book (which, like his other writings, is in Arabic) was translated into Hebrew in Spain in the second half of the eleventh century.[38] The extent of Spanish Jewry's admiration for Rabbi Hai can be deduced from the elegies composed by Hebrew poets in Spain after his death.[39] In these poems Rabbi Hai is depicted as the teacher of all Jewry par excellence, a man who had no equal.

But the Jews of Spain also had broad contacts with the heads of the Academy of Sura, which reopened in Bagdad at the end of the tenth century. At the outset of the eleventh century this academy was headed by Rabbi Samuel b. Ḥofnī (died 1013), who was remarkably similar to Rabbi Hai. He too was not exclusively a scholar of Talmud. In addition to halakhic monographs, he wrote commentaries on the Bible; he was familiar with, and influenced by, the writings of Arabic philosophers. His theological views were rationalistic, and therefore they aroused suspicion and anger among many of his contemporaries; even the *gāōn* Rabbi Hai was provoked to wrath against him. As the head of an academy, Rabbi Samuel wrestled with the heavy material difficulties which had been the lot of the heads of the Babylonian academies since the middle of the tenth century. He too was obliged to send pleading letters to

Jewish communities all over the world and to entreat them to remember the scholars of his academy in their contributions. There is no doubt that he communicated by letter with Spanish Jewry.[40]

Because of the particular sense of kinship that Spanish Jews felt toward Babylonian Jewry, they expressed their renewed contact in another way too. Touching on both their well-being and on their sorrows, the Spanish communities kept the Jewish center in Babylonia informed of the diversified events in their lives. In keeping with the spirit of that epoch, they often resorted to verse, and more than one lyrical creation of the celebrated Spanish Hebrew poets was written primarily for this purpose.[41]

The resumed communication between the Jews of Andalusia and the academies in Babylonia was one of the signs of the great change that was then occurring in every circumstance of the life of the Jews in Moslem Spain. This was a concomitant of the great change in the politicosocial situation after the fall of the Omayyad kingdom and the establishment of the small principalities which replaced it.

2

SAMUEL THE *NĀGĪD* AND HIS SON

I

Early in July 1013 a small group wended its way down the hills near the city of Ossuna. Even though the morning was still young the heat was intense, and the men, women, and children, twenty or twenty-five of them, advanced slowly, notwithstanding the prodding of the villager who was their guide. Their fatigue enveloped them. They did not use paved and well-traveled paths. Instead of moving along the broad highway which would take them eastward to the city of Antequera, they turned south, directing their footsteps toward the eastern slopes of the Sierra de Veguas, to reach the Guadalhorce Valley. As they made their way along, overcome by exhaustion, they continually sent frightened looks in every direction. From time to time, at a short distance, they could see two or three horsemen, wrapped in white burnooses, galloping hurriedly by; at this the group would hold up to hide behind tall bushes.

They were refugees from Cordova. When they left the city they headed southwest, where a broad plain spreads out and there are no mountains to climb. Near the city of Écija they crossed the Genil River, continuing their journey southward till they came to the hill country between Estepa and Morón. Generally the distance between Cordova and Málaga—their destination—was then a four-day journey, but although they had started out four days earlier, they had only covered half the route.

Among them was a young man, about twenty years old, blind in one eye. His mien was one of refinement and sensitivity, an indication that he probably was not a manual laborer. He seemed absorbed in the immensity of the calamity which had befallen him, and his face was marked by pain and sorrow. Yet he obviously did not despair and made his way confidently.

The fleeing Cordovans were seeking refuge in Málaga because the citizenry of that city, headed by their Slavic governor, ʿĀmir b. Futūḥ, had made a pact with the Berbers. When the detachment of Berber warriors had raided the southern districts of Andalusia, they had carried on their depredations in the villages on the outskirts of the city; however, they did not harm Málaga. Instead they attacked Elvira, wreaking havoc throughout that city. They destroyed scores of houses and seized the women; if a woman was reported to be rich, they hung her by her breasts until she disclosed where she had hidden her wealth. Later the Berbers returned to Málaga. When its populace heard what had been done to the inhabitants of Elvira, they offered the Berbers seventy thousand dinars to go and leave them in peace. The Berbers accepted and then attacked Algeciras, where they carried on their unbridled spoliation and slaughter. Some of the captives from this foray, set free by Caliph Sulaimān al-Mustaʿīn, found refuge in Málaga. Two years went by, the Berbers honored their pact, and did no harm in Málaga.[1]

Málaga had always been a precious gem in the ring of settlements running the length of the southern coast of the Iberian peninsula. The strong waves of the sea lap against the white

MOSLEM MÁLAGA

1. Calle Santiago
2. Poso del Rey
3. Al-Katsvilya Street
4. Calle Granada
5. Bāb-al-baḥr
6. Bāb-al-wādī
7. Bāb-Antequera
8. Great Mosque
9. al-Ḳaisarīya
10. Citadel
11. al-Kitzbah

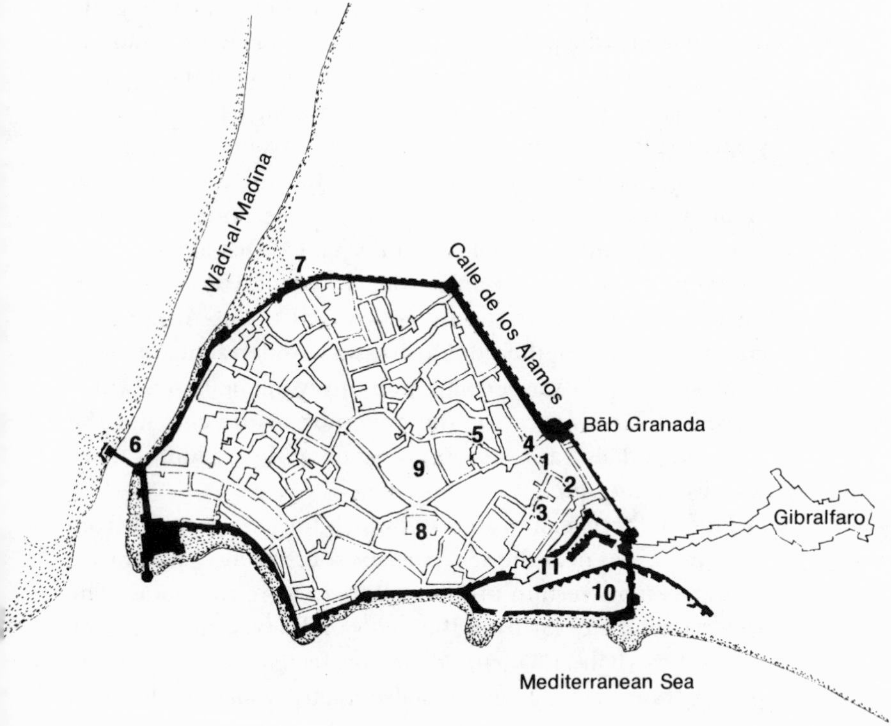

houses, and the fortress seems to ascend from the clear blue waters. The flat white roofs gleam in the sunlight, and behind them extends a wide area of blooming gardens and green fields. It was not for naught that the writers in the Middle Ages were stirred by the city's beauty and never wearied of extolling its enchanting buildings and its markets alive with the noise of humankind.

But in those days Málaga was still quite small. *Al-Madīna,* the city between the walls, extended from the fortress in the east to the Guadalmedina River in the west and from the sea to the Plaza San Pedro in the north. The sea covered a large segment in the southern part—today the city is built up—including the broad avenue which turns east from the Tetuan Bridge and the streets south of it. The most prominent section of the city was the fortress, al-Ḳaṣaba. This stands on a high hill on whose slopes the Phoenicians, who founded the city, first settled; they gave it the name it bears to this day, after the idol Malak (in Hebrew, *melekh*—king). East of al-Ḳaṣaba a second fortress was built on a mountain which the Arabs named Djabal Faro (now Gibralfaro) because of the lookout tower located there; both fortresses were connected by double walls. The Arab rulers continued to strengthen the fortresses, 'Abdarraḥmān I especially. The *ḳaṣaba* was a compound of several buildings which served as a residence for the governor of the city and the garrison and also as a storehouse; among the buildings there was also a mosque.

The southern wall of the city, which turned westward from the *ḳaṣaba,* was near the sea, perhaps some twenty paces away. In the western section of this wall there were two gates. The western gate, not far from the wall's end, was called the Gate of the Sea (Bāb al-baḥr) and was protected by a strong and protuberant tower. There was also a jetty, which the Romans had erected; two coves served as a harbor for the Moslems. At the very edge of the wall was a fortified structure in which weapons and military stores and spare parts for ships were kept. From there the wall ran north the length of the east bank of the river, and on this side too there was a gate, the Gate of the River (Bāb al-wādī), which is in the southern part of the wall. Where De la Compañia Street (formerly known as De las Guardas) now reaches the riverbank the wall turned to the northeast, running the length of the street presently called Carterias; on reaching the beginning of Mariblanca Street it turned again to the southeast, parallel to the street now known as Calle de los Alamos, until it reached the slopes of the hill of the *ḳaṣaba.* In the northwest was the Bāb Antequera, where the Square of the Convent of Catalina now is located; and in the east, at the end of the slope of the hill of the *ḳaṣaba,* is the Granada Gate. This gate, which was also called Bāb al-mal'ab, because of the remains of a Roman theater in its vicinity, was at the end of Granada Street. The wall continued from this gate in a more easterly line, encircling the fortress from the north.[2] The wall had many turrets, some being square and some shaped like horseshoes. In the middle of the southern wall there was a protrusion on which stood a particularly strong turret which actually overhung the seashore.

West of the fortress the Great Mosque, a magnificent structure having five porticos, rose in splendor. North of the mosque, in the center of the city, were the markets with covered roofs called *al-Ḳaisarīya,* which were bolted at night. To this day the streets in this sector of the city are narrower and more winding than elsewhere, and shops, small but opulent with wares, crowd upon each other. Threading its way among them to the Granada Gate runs Granada Street, which the Christians, after the conquest of the city, called Calle Real. Somewhat before the place where the gate was located, Santiago Street winds to the right. This street, once known as Barrio Nuevo, was the street of the Jews during Moslem rule.[3] The Jews' houses also stood on the other side of Alcazabilla

Street, atop a hill upon which Pozo del Rey Street ascends to the walls of the fortress. The Jewish neighborhood was not far from the focal point of the city's activities. Not only was it a residential area, but it also contained business shops (the Jews sold their wares in the *al-Ḳaisarīya* as well); outside the Granada Gate, on the slopes of the Gibralfaro, was their cemetery.[4] The number of Jews in the city was not great: The community numbered about thirty families.[5]

The Jews were not the only non-Moslem community in the city.[6] Málaga (or as it was then called, Mālaḳa) also had a settlement of Christians whose community was not inconsequential, since it was headed by bishops until the beginning of the twelfth century.

When the refugees from Cordova, both Moslems and Jews, reached Málaga, its governor was still 'Āmir b. Futūḥ, the manumitted slave of one of the courtiers of Caliph al-Ḥakam. He, like other Slav governors, became independent at the end of the civil war. However, before long the city and the surrounding region fell under the dominance of 'Alī b. Ḥammūd, who governed Ceuta and Tangier in the name of Caliph Sulaimān al-Musta'in. When 'Alī b. Ḥammūd determined to rebel against the caliph, he entered into negotiations with the chief of the Slavs and in particular sought to win the support of Khairān, the ruler of Almería. 'Amir b. Futūḥ also sided with the rebels, and when 'Alī b. Ḥammūd crossed the Straits of Gibraltar he handed him the city.[7]

After 'Alī attacked Cordova and became caliph there, he appointed his young son, Idrīs, as governor of Málaga, a role he filled for three years. He was an able governor, strong in character and deliberate in his actions. As the Arabic chroniclers describe him, he endeavored to improve the lot of the city's inhabitants, particularly by giving his support to men of learning. In 1019, after 'Alī was murdered and his brother, al-Ḳāsim, succeeded him as ruler in Cordova, Yaḥyā, the oldest son of ʻAlī, came to Málaga from the African coast to instigate a revolt against al-Ḳāsim.[8] The two brothers, Yaḥyā and Idrīs, began to mobilize a force and made other preparations, no doubt giving the craftsmen and merchants plenty of work. In general the city's inhabitants thus enjoyed a good living. Málaga was even merry in those days. An Arabic scholar from the Near East who came to Málaga in 1015 bitterly deplores his misfortune in having fallen ill but being unable to sleep throughout the night because of music that rent the air at all hours on all sides.[9]

But the Cordovan refugees did not regret having gone to Málaga.

One young man in the group was a Jew. His name was Samuel b. Joseph ha-lēvī, whose family surname was Ibn Nagrīla.[10] When he arrived in Málaga, he naturally headed for the Jewish quarter. Shortly thereafter he began to engage in trade, but he did not have any clear goal in mind; he was hesitant and indecisive. He also went to Almería, at the southeastern end of the peninsula, because it was a large city involved in commerce and, being in the hands of the Slavs, was secure against Berber invasion. But he did not tarry in that city very long and soon returned to Málaga, where he continued in trade.[11] Since he was endowed with ability and knew how to conduct his affairs, he not only made a decent living, but was able to save a little money. And as the entire city flourished, he too prospered.

Nevertheless, he derived no satisfaction from all this and happiness seemed beyond his grasp. The young man had ambitions of achieving great things, and success in business was not his goal. He came from a prominent family—it could not boast of a genealogy connected with the nobility—but his father was a well-respected man, a merchant who made a good living even though he was not overly affluent.[12] The family came originally from Mérida, but when that city lost its importance in consequence of the wars and revolts which enveloped its district, they moved to Cordova, where Samuel was born in the spring of 993.[13] His father had sired another son, named Isaac, who was surnamed Abū Ibrāhīm.[14] Samuel studied at school with this brother,[15] and all his life he was bound to him with truly strong bonds of love. Because Isaac was a true scholar and also knowledgeable in practical matters, he won Samuel's admiration from an early age.

Samuel's parents spared no effort in giving him a superior education[16] since he showed a keen and fundamental grasp even when a child. He was sent to study with preeminent teachers, among them Rabbi Ḥanōkh, and the disciples of Rabbi Moses b. Ḥanōkh and his sons. Rabbi Ḥanōkh was already old at that time, but Samuel ha-lēvī listened eagerly to his teaching, remembering with admiration what he learned from his distinguished tutor.[17] As was customary in Spain, his parents also ascribed importance to the study of language, and they sent him to study under the guidance of the leading Hebrew grammarian of his generation, Judah Ḥayyūdj.[18] Since the latter died when still young, however, Samuel spent only a short time studying under him. Inasmuch as the instructors informed his father of the exceptional abilities of the youngster, he encouraged Samuel to apply himself diligently to his studies and took pains to clear every obstacle from his son's path. Similarly, he introduced Samuel to his business affairs so that he became a capable, practical, and self-sufficient man. Once he sent Samuel on a business trip, and while he was at sea in a rickety ship a dangerous storm developed. On returning from this journey Samuel composed a long poem of thanksgiving to commemorate his escape.[19]

But most of his time was dedicated to study and reading. As was the practice among scholars in Moslem lands, Samuel spent considerable time in the company of friends and frequented the homes of his teachers. It must be borne in mind that in these countries higher studies did not have the fixed patterns of those that existed in the Christian world, and this was especially so in Spain at the beginning of the eleventh century. Scholars would meet at set times in private homes, in various types of study halls, and in bookshops; they would discuss topics of literary concern and would debate new ideas propounded by one scholar or another; they would also listen to poetry recitations and express their own views. Such gatherings of Jewish scholars occurred frequently, particularly on the Sabbath and on the long summer days, when excessive heat made study difficult. One of the scholars whom he visited was a judge, Rabbi Isaac.[20] He also associated a great deal with a youth as ambitious as himself, Abū Ḥasan, a member of a distinguished Jewish family in Cordova.[21]

All these young men tried their hands at composing verse, metered and unmetered, but Samuel ha-lēvī excelled over them all. On various occasions his verses elicited the admiration of his acquaintances and friends—not only for their form or content—but primarily for his command of a vocabulary culled from biblical Hebrew. He applied himself diligently to the study of other languages and to general sciences. In just a short time he acquired a perfect knowledge of Arabic and could write letters in the ornate and flowery style of Arab writers, employing all the veiled allusions and linguistic embellishments in which they delighted. His mastery of Arabic was so marvelous that even the boastful Arabs were forced to admit it.[22] He also studied Latin and was fluent in the Romance and Berber tongues.[23] His desire for learning was boundless and his absorptive capacity was truly amazing.

While he was applying himself to the study of languages, he delved into the exact sciences, astronomy especially; he also had a considerable grounding in geometry and logic. Moreover, this young Jew read the Koran and the works of Moslem theologians and obtained the commentaries of the Church fathers on the Bible, seeking to learn from them whatever he could. He was noted for his cogent remarks when in a discussion with a circle of friends; his rivals were obliged to admit that in the clarity of his expression and the logic of his assertions none among his peers could equal him.

But even while he dedicated himself to study and reading and engaged in discussions with friends and with proud Moslems, his heart was preoccupied with other thoughts. Discerning that all his friends and acquaintances recognized his incomparable abilities and respected him, and convinced of his own superiority in discussions with both Jews and non-Jews, a question began gnawing at him—was it within his power to rise above the status of a mere scholar in the Talmud school? The Jewish neighborhood in Cordova was near the palace of the caliphs and the Great Mosque, and the young man often saw the Moslem dignitaries who came and went astride their horses while youths ran before them to clear the path. As he gazed at their coarse visages he would ask himself how these men merited their authority, prominence, and wealth. Then civil war erupted, and there was one coup d'etat after another. Samuel ha-lēvī witnessed the ease with which relatively small groups could seize power and saw how incompetent men became viziers and governors, while the Jews, like the rest of the Cordovans, were crushed and downtrodden, suffering under the rod of the Berber and Slav oppressors.

When in the grip of these meditations, he would recall hearing his parents tell of the eminence of the Jew Ḥasdai Ibn Shaprūṭ, a leading figure in the court of the illustrious Caliph ʿAbdarraḥmān III. He then began to indulge himself in reveries: It seemed to him that he too was destined to play such a role and that God had endowed him with resplendent qualities so that he could perform noble deeds. He toyed with these fancies, dreaming of the greatness to which he would rise and of the dominion and glory which awaited him in the fullness of time; then, so he told himself, he would do good in behalf of the Jews, raising them from their lowly estate among the Arabs and Berbers. Even as he bent over his beloved books, these fantasies never left him.

The conquest of Cordova by the savage Berbers marked the end of Samuel ha-lēvī's happy youthful years. Who could carry on studies while bands of the Zenāta and Ṣinhādja tribes rioted in the streets of the city, pillaging and raping, destroying houses, setting shops and storehouses afire? In such violent times a person had no other concern except his own existence. Yesterday's rich man became today's pauper, and the daily problem of eking out a living troubled everyone. Bonds of friendship were severed: Some of Samuel's close friends, such as Joshua and Yaḥyā b. Aḥiya, were imprisoned[24] or taken captive by the Berbers; some hid or fled. As so many Cordovans were doing, Samuel ha-lēvī decided to leave the unfortunate city. This was neither simple nor easy. The roads were overrun by soldiers and bands of robbers. Leaders of caravans demanded huge sums, and he had no money. It was therefore necessary to consider his destination carefully and to seek sound advice and help. In parlous times a person reveals his true self: erstwhile friends betrayed him, turned their backs, and refused to aid him;[25] but he also had steadfast friends. One of them, M'naḥem, encouraged and cheered him with kind words—an act he never forgot.[26] Ultimately Samuel departed from Cordova, leaving behind his family, with whom he had lived till now.[27] Parting was difficult for him and for them, especially since he was going to seek his fortune where he was a stranger. But he always knew how to proceed, and he did not yield to dejection at this critical hour. Because he had confidence in his abilities and exceptional qualities, he was less dispirited than the other members of the group he joined on leaving Cordova. He was determined not to spare any effort in reaching the goal of his fantasies and then—so he wrote—he would not betray his friends as they had betrayed him.[28]

But as he sat in his shop in Málaga he was overcome by depression and struggled powerfully with himself. This was a city whose economy was one of commerce: the only ambition of its inhabitants was to make profit, and their conversation revolved around the prices of merchandise. The Jewish community was small, consisting mainly of merchants and craftsmen. A poor refugee just beginning to engage in trade had no weight and commanded no respect among the established, wealthy traders who sent their wares overseas. There were no circles of young scholars or writers, like himself, with whom he could discourse and benefit thereby from their erudition, nor could he learn of or discuss new developments in literature and science. Sometimes he would make his way to the courthouse of Rabbi Judah, who was also a teacher, but there, too, he did not find the atmosphere he was accustomed to in Cordova, nor did he feel especially at home. He suffered all the pain of one abruptly removed from his birthplace and all the misery of loneliness.

At such dismal moments he took heart from the many aphorisms he had collected: A fool "suffers in the land of his birth, whereas a wise man prospers even in a foreign land," or that one who wanders far away "will find treasure in a strange city." When assailed by doubt as to whether he had done well to leave his native city, he would find courage in his observation that it is better "to eat herbs in security rather than meat attended by peril."[29] But he also recalled other proverbs and composed new ones expressing another view: "It is better to suffer in one's homeland than to find benefit in a foreign country" and "A man strives in vain to find happiness for himself, for everything is in the hands of God."[30]

During those stringent times Samuel ha-lēvī had only one meeting with a writer of considerable talent—a meeting which stirred Samuel to think and meditate and which made a lasting impression upon him. In the first year of his exile from Cordova he met 'Alī b. Aḥmad Ibn Ḥazm, one of the renowned intellectuals of his generation. Although Ibn Ḥazm was still young, about one year younger than Samuel ha-lēvī, he was already famous for his erudition. Samuel had heard about him while still in Cordova, but had never met him, for they belonged to very different classes. 'Alī Ibn Ḥazm was the son of a high official in al-Manṣūr's government, albeit he was a supporter of the House of Omayya. When Muḥammad al-Mahdī ousted the family of al-Manṣūr from power, Ibn Ḥazm's father was dismissed and expelled from the court. When the Slavs were in power and Wāḍiḥ, the commander of the army, headed the government in Cordova, 'Alī's father was imprisoned and some of his property was confiscated.

But in spite of the misfortunes of his family during those years in which the personality of an individual is set, 'Alī Ibn Ḥazm continued to devote himself with exceptional diligence to his studies. He did, indeed, acquire a broad foundation in all branches of Arabic literature; he was well versed in Arabic philology and in the theory of logic; he composed beautiful poetry. But he delved most particularly into theology, and apparently he was unsurpassed in his knowledge in this discipline. In 1013 he too left Cordova and shortly thereafter met Samuel ha-lēvī.[31]

Throughout his life Ibn Ḥazm was a controversial figure. He argued extensively concerning literary subjects and on religious matters particularly with both Moslems who held differing religious views and with non-Moslems. He mentions that among others he maintained an ongoing dispute with the chief priest of the Christians of Cordova.[32] Ibn Ḥazm also arranged debates, mainly with heretics and all sorts of philosophers; he was therefore glad to have the opportunity to carry on discussions with a celebrated Jewish scholar. For Samuel ha-lēvī, too, this meeting was an experience. The debate was fierce: Ibn Ḥazm was outstanding in his thorough grasp of theological problems and a master in the art of debate—the polished barbs he directed at his opponents were honed with an acridity and sarcasm which resulted from the traumatic experience of his youth. His father's downfall, indeed that of his entire family—a descent from zenith to nadir—grieved him all his life. But, in any case, it is in the nature of a Spaniard to become excited during a discussion, particularly one dealing with religious matters—and Ibn Ḥazm was, after all, of Hispano-Christian origin.

The discussion pivoted around those topics on which most of the debates among Jews, Moslems, and Christians in the Middle Ages hinged. As was usual among Moslem theologians, Ibn Ḥazm sought to demonstrate that the Torah of the Jews was fraudulent and was not the Holy Book of God. Among the various verses he cited as unethical, and thus proof of fraudulence, is the phrase in Genesis 12:13, "Say, I pray thee, thou art my sister"; he added that according to the text in the Torah, Abraham took his sister to wife. Samuel ha-lēvī replied that "sister" in Hebrew can also mean a kinswoman. Whereupon Ibn Ḥazm further cited the verse in Genesis 20: 12, "And moreover she is indeed my sister, the daughter of my father, but not the daughter of my mother."[33] (Ibn Ḥazm returned again and again to this phrase throughout his life; expanding it as his own education broadened.)

The Moslem theologian did not fail to introduce an old argument employed in all such debates—Ibn Ḥazm asked how Samuel would explain Genesis 49:10—"The sceptre shall not depart from Judah." If the Torah by which the Jews abide is indeed God's Holy Book, he declared, it has been proved false: for many generations Jews have neither had authority nor has a redeemer appeared in their behalf. Since the days of Nebuchadnezzar they have had no kingdom, a matter of over fifteen hundred years, except for the short interval of the rule of Zerubabel ben Shealtiel.

To refute this argument, Samuel ha-lēvī pointed to the exilarchs in Babylonia who ruled over the Jews for hundreds of years, but Ibn Ḥazm endeavored to prove that such an argument was essentially without merit because these princes were never given real dominance. His view was that the title was merely honorary and nothing more. The rebuttals advanced by Samuel so vexed Ibn Ḥazm that he overreacted, countering that even before Nebuchadnezzar "the sceptre had departed from Judah" and that after the reign of Zedekiah ben Josaiah seventy-two years passed before Zerubabel achieved dominance; and he was, no doubt, the last of the tribe of Judah to hold the reins of government.[34] Indeed, after him—the Moslem theologian argued—kings who had descended from Aaron ruled over the Jews for hundreds of years without leaving a trace of authority to the descendants of Judah. It is true, he added, that certain historians state that Herod, his two sons, and his grandson, Agrippa ben Agrippa (it should be Agrippa ben Aristobulos), were of the tribe of Judah, but in truth they were Romans. Such were the arguments that Ibn Ḥazm voiced to Samuel Ibn Nagrīla; and he himself asserts, in his book on this controversy between them, that Samuel was the most accomplished debater he ever knew.[35]

Discussion with this outstanding Moslem scholar at first impressed Samuel ha-lēvī greatly and expanded his own philosophic thought, but his response lessened as again and again he was overcome by depression. He was already approaching his thirtieth year and the point had come—so ran his musings—for him to occupy a position he felt worthy of him.

He could not foresee that his time of eminence was drawing ever nearer.

II

Gradually it was becoming known in Málaga that Samuel ha-lēvī was a man of broad erudition as well as an excellent Arabic stylist. In those days this skill was especially valued in Spain. Everyone was careful to produce letters with language free of errors and with a grammatically accurate style; anyone who was unable to write with clarity sought the help of an expert. Such experts occupied special shops, headquarters for the composition of correspondence and letters of request, and they had plenty of work. Samuel ha-lēvī was not engaged primarily in the composition of letters, but if requested to do this by neighbors or acquaintances he would not refuse them, be they Jews or Moslems.

Among the people who called upon him from time to time with such requests were the stewards of a Moslem official named Abū 'l-'Abbās Ibn al-'Arīf. He was one of the viziers of the principality which the Berbers of the Ṣinhādja tribe had established in the province of Granada; because of this Ibn al-'Arīf stayed there most of the year, but he had a house and property in Málaga from which he derived some income. There were no problems in this arrangement since the Berbers of Granada recognized the Ḥammūdite caliphs (who had supplanted the Omayyads); their principality was regarded as a loyal province of those caliphs just as Málaga was loyal to them. On occasion Ibn al-'Arīf would come to Málaga, but usually he had to be satisfied with the written reports of his stewards and underlings on matters relating to his house and property. Since the house was near the shop where Samuel ha-lēvī was engaged, the stewards occasionally would ask him to write letters for them, to be forwarded to Granada. The style of the letters amazed the Arab dignitary, and on his return to Málaga, Ibn al-'Arīf wanted to know who had written them. Samuel was introduced to him, and in the course of the ensuing conversation Ibn al-ʿArīf became convinced that the Jew was also skillful in practical affairs; Samuel ha-lēvī's quiet but confident manner of speaking added to the deep impression he made. Ibn al-ʿArīf requested Samuel to enter his service and he willingly assented. Samuel Ibn Nagrīla then left Málaga for Granada.[36]

On arriving there he once again found himself in an entirely different milieu. Whereas practically no alteration in the mode of life and in the government had occurred in Málaga despite the change in rulers, Granada was in flux. The Berbers of the Ṣinhādja tribe who governed this province of southeastern Spain had come to the Iberian peninsula fifteen years earlier with the other mercenaries of the rulers from the House of al-Manṣūr. At their head was Zāwī b. Zīrī, a prince of the dynasty which then ruled Tunisia, although he belonged to a branch which had been excluded from the government. This prince later became one of the loyal officers of Sulaimān al-Mustaʿīn—in fact, the power behind this caliph, who was no more than a cat's-paw of the Berbers. Sulaimān rewarded him for his services by giving him the province of Granada so that he and his men could maintain themselves. Zāwī also succeeded in establishing friendly ties with the Ḥammūdites while they occupied the caliphal throne at Cordova. But he really had his heart set on ruling in the land of his birth and dreamed of the day when he would return there at the head of his troops. The future of the Ṣinhādja in Andalusia was clouded. The struggle over the caliphal throne was not ended, and the new rulers—who tore segments from the Omayyad domain by creating principalities in the eastern part of the peninsula—had their eyes on the province of Granada. When Samuel ha-lēvī arrived, the Ṣinhādja had not yet established their own governmental apparatus and had no organized administration. The sole function of the native officers whom they appointed was to collect taxes as high as they could get away with.

Samuel ha-lēvī also had to function as tax collector in some districts of the Granada principality.[37] It was a difficult task since in most of the Spanish provinces at that time all governmental functions were in disarray; however, his ability and character stood him in good stead. His assignment, eased by his cleverness, his alertness, his quick grasp, and his fundamentally balanced judgment, brought him success. He not only delivered the required sums to the exchequer on time, but he even was able to retain a decent profit. Tax collecting was performed by tax farmers, and as long as the collector honored his obligations and did not keep too much for himself, the Berber rulers did not interfere.

Meanwhile, Samuel ha-lēvī learned from certain Jews that a quarrel had arisen in the Málaga community and that false accusations were being leveled against the *dayyan* (judge), Rabbi Judah, with whom Samuel had established a relationship while he was in Málaga. When this report reached him he sent a letter of encouragement, couched in the form of a poem, to the *dayyan.*[38] Now that it appeared to him that he was on the way to success—that his star was in the ascendancy—Samuel ha-lēvī desired to fulfill the vow he made when he was spiritually distressed. To be sure, for various reasons he never found contentment in his visits to the *dayyan* when he dwelt in Málaga; nevertheless he longed to aid a scholar who was being attacked. Simultaneously, however, he fostered a thought that was self-serving and strongly purposeful. He therefore suggested to Rabbi Judah that he too enter the service of the Ṣinhādja principality; since passions at Málaga had not been quelled, Rabbi Judah promptly accepted the offer.

Rabbi Judah and some members of his family who joined him engaged for a time in tax collecting, meeting with success in their labors and collaborating in good spirit with Samuel. But before long his lot turned—instead of success, Samuel now faced disappointment.

Among the Jews living in Granada who had witnessed the rise of Samuel Ibn Nagrīla, there were some who insisted that his position as a tax collector constituted encroachment. When the dissidents now learned that he brought Jews in from Málaga who also engaged in the lucrative occupation, their resentment increased. It is true that initially they had close ties with Samuel, but they believed that as natives of Granada, they had prior claim to this occupation. Finally they decided to act. To be sure, they were afraid to harm Samuel directly since he held a high office and was an intimate of the vizier. They therefore turned to Moslem dignitaries, influential officers in the government whom they had known a long time. Carrying evil reports of Samuel to them, they asserted that this alien Jew collected unduly large sums and was becoming exceedingly rich; as a consequence Samuel was arrested and, in 1020, thrown into prison. At the same time his enemies hired thugs who attacked and murdered Rabbi Judah and his nephew while they were on a journey.

After a brief period Samuel was released from prison, but a heavy fine was imposed upon him and he was deprived of his post.[39] His friend Isaak Ibn Khalfōn sent him a letter of encouragement, written both in verse and in prose, when he was freed.[40] In like manner, on his release Samuel attempted to hearten Rabbi Judah's family with comforting words. But he was unsuccessful—they had sustained a double blow. For some time Samuel had sought the hand of Rabbi Judah's daughter; however, the family was opposed, preferring the slain nephew. And then, after the father's tragic death, they held that the marriage of the daughter would be inappropriate because of the mourning period.[41]

Notwithstanding the large fine he had to pay, Samuel ha-lēvī was still financially secure. He remained in Granada because his political instincts told him that a gratifying future still awaited him in that country. Since he well knew that in Moslem governments officials rose and fell with astonishing rapidity, he believed that—particularly in a new state such as the Ṣinhādja principality, which had no stability—his condition was likely soon to change. Actual hostility prevailed between the Berbers and the native Andalusians, and yet the latter could not be disregarded because of the service they rendered in conducting governmental affairs—the Berbers themselves only knew the art of war and almost none of them could read or write. Málaga was one of the cities under the rule of the Ḥammūdites who traced their genealogy to Mohammed; therefore there was no deep hostility there. Even though they depended upon Berber troops, the rulers here could employ Andalusians without apprehension. The Ṣinhādja, however, feared treachery and mistrusted all Andalusians serving them as officials and effectuating their orders; they viewed them as both invaders and barbarians.

These considerations led Samuel ha-lēvī to hope that once again the Berber officers would need a person with his ability to conduct their affairs. Samuel also sensed that the vizier who first sponsored him still viewed him with some kindness and that he had not lost favor.

And indeed Samuel was right. From his youth he had been endowed with an ability to establish ties with people of varied circles and to acquire friends, an aptitude which one does not readily lose. People who met him immediately perceived his unusual talents and wide knowledge, even though Samuel made no effort to assert them. He knew that people usually dislike one who is superior to them, that they envy him and are apprehensive of him. Knowing this human weakness, Samuel often affected humility. Because of these traits and the ties he fostered, influential people eventually championed his cause and persuaded Ibn al-'Arīf to remember his initial esteem for him. The vizier, who was still the first minister in the principality of Granada, called Samuel back and again took him into service.

Samuel ha-lēvī learned from his mistakes and from his agonizing experience. More than ever he sought to behave modestly and to make no display of his ambitions, doing his best to overcome them. Throughout his life he wrestled with his impulse to achieve prominence and also to refrain from provoking the anger of his fellowman. Now he made a special effort: He rarely expressed his opinions or overtly showed initiative, since such openness does not make one who holds an official position popular with his superiors. It is true that with his own enterprising judgment he inaugurated activities that he regarded as necessary; but he succeeded in giving the impression that the impetus stemmed from the vizier. When Samuel offered a suggestion to a minister, his manner made it appear that the Jewish official was merely supporting the minister's own opinion. The vizier, pleased with him, began to advance him in the hierarchy of the principality's administration. In 1027 Samuel Ibn Nagrīla was appointed to collect taxes from all Jews in the Ṣinhādja dominions and from then on he was known among them by the title "the *Nāgīd.*"[42]

As success and good fortune shine upon a man, people also favor him. When Samuel rose to prominence in the royal service he was given the daughter of the slain *dayyan,* Rabbi Judah, for a wife. Thus, at long last, he could establish for himself a household befitting one with an important office in the state and among its Jewish communities.

But Samuel was still far from occupying a position in the highest echelons of government—and this is what he craved. He was also apprehensive about the Jews of Granada, for he was keenly aware of the grudge against him—the Jewish stranger who now had achieved some prominence. Yet his advancement and that of Abū 'l-'Abbās, the vizier with whom he was associated, depended on the pleasure of the Berbers, who were apt to change their governing staff on pure whim. The Ṣinhādja principality had a number of viziers who bore the title of *kātib,* a designation also given to lesser officials.[43] Vizier was the title given to high-ranking officials, as was the custom in the Omayyad caliphate whose practices were imitated by all the small kingdoms which replaced it. There were rivalries, intrigues, and envy aplenty among these viziers. The majority were Andalusians, slippery and wily, lauding a person while thrusting the proverbial dagger in his back. The Berbers themselves were fierce soldiers of barbaric practices in warfare and acknowledged cruel behavior in governmental administration.

What capricious administrators they were was demonstrated by the Ṣinhādja during a troubled period in 1025. Zāwī b. Zīrī, who had led the Berbers from triumph to triumph and had established a principality for them, decided to leave Spain and to return to Tunisia. Two factors prompted him. One was that he was concerned about the Slavs in eastern Spain and the Berbers of the Zenāta tribes who had settled in the central districts of southern Andalusia; not only did these Berbers outnumber the Ṣinhādja, but they sustained a long-standing, active hostility to the Ṣinhādja. Zāwī feared that the Ṣinhādja would not be strong enough to protect their principality from attack. The other motive for his return was that reports which reached him from Tunisia roused his hopes, that despite all the disappointments he had suffered, he would at long last ascend the throne which his forefathers had occupied.

But he was cautious. When he decided to return to Tunisia and found that even with all his urging only a few joined him, he did not relinquish his position as prince of the Ṣinhādja in Granada—he wished to avoid losing either way. Before departing for Tunisia he assembled the Ṣinhādja chiefs and adjured them by the life of God and by the life of their Prophet and by the holy Koran not to choose another prince, and especially not to appoint his nephew Ḥabbūs b. Māksen. At first his son acted in his stead, but after a brief period the Ṣinhādja changed their minds, violated their solemn oath, and gave Zāwī's position to Ḥabbūs. This new prince did not take the title of king, but after the manner of the Berber princes called himself *ḥādjib,* as the illustrious al-Manṣūr had. (*Ḥādjib* was the title of the grand vizier in the kingdom of the Omayyad caliphs.) Like al-Manṣūr, who had left the title of caliph to al-Ḥakam's unfortunate son, the Ṣinhādja recognized the Ḥammūdites as caliphs but in practice hardly took notice of them. Ḥabbūs, who learned of Zāwī's failure in Tunisia and of his death, tried to strengthen his own position and to buttress the dominion of the Ṣinhādja. He commenced acting as a king and gave himself the ringing sobriquet of "Saif ad-daula—Sword of royalty."[44]

Continuing the practice of the Berber kings, he appointed an Andalusian secretary to head the government office. His name was Abū 'Abdallāh al-Biziliānī, a scholar and a scribe, who, as was common among those in his position, plied his craft with one prince after another, serving them with his pen. He was well regarded at the court of Ḥabbūs and for a time acted somewhat as his foreign minister, wielding great influence over him.[45]

Abū 'l-'Abbās was the minister of finance. Because his duties eventually expanded into numerous areas, he required the help of his Jewish aide, Samuel ha-lēvī, in an ever-increasing measure. The ascent of Ḥabbūs to dominance brought a dramatic change in Granada. Recognition of the Ḥammūdites as caliphs and sovereign rulers became almost meaningless, since those princes were expelled from Cordova. Yaḥyā b. 'Alī, who reigned in Málaga till 1035, was invited to return to Cordova after being compelled to leave it in 1023, but his rule over the city of the caliphs was short; thereafter he had to be satisfied with the province of Málaga.

The Ṣinhādja principality became at that time a strong kingdom. Whereas in the days of Zāwī they had held sway only over the mountain country west of the Sierra Nevada (the valley of the Genil and the mountains north of it), Ḥabbūs annexed the hill country north and west of the Granada mountains. In the north his kingdom included the province of Jaén, reaching into the environs of Andujar up to the Guadalquivir Valley, and in the west he added the district of the city of Cabra.[46] The troops of Ṣinhādja soldiers that Zāwī commanded were few; in a decisive battle in 1018 his horsemen numbered less than one thousand, but Ḥabbūs increased his army by mobilizing Berbers of other tribes. When his forces were strengthened, Ḥabbūs, together with other rulers, initiated an offensive against the kingdom of Seville in 1038, penetrating to its capital and putting the suburb Triana (which is across the Guadalquivir) to the torch.[47] Of course the enlargement of his army and his expansionist policy required huge expenditures; the revenue Ḥabbūs required had to be provided by the minister of finance and his subordinates.

But it was not just because of these needs that the minister and officers absorbed additional functions. Ḥabbūs organized his administration in the accepted pattern of the developed Moslem states. He appointed judges who were paid from the government exchequer, he was concerned for safety on the highways. Time and again, as the demand for funds mounted, Abu 'l-'Abbās, Ḥabbūs's finance minister, imposed additional responsibilities on his staff and on Samuel ha-lēvī in particular. However, as close as Samuel was to the minister he was never given an opportunity to come into direct and regular contact with Ḥabbūs himself.

When Abu 'l-'Abbās Ibn al-'Arīf died, leaving two sons, Ḥabbūs appointed his oldest son to take his place as vizier. But as the father suited his function, in like measure the son did not. He was a young man not only without experience in the complex matter of operating the treasury but also lacking the necessary dedication. He was preoccupied with mundane pleasures and not government business.

This was the opportunity for which Samuel ha-lēvī had been waiting. He took advantage of the situation with consummate shrewdness, acting with the caution necessary for one who was walking through the morass that was a royal Moslem court. (Once, when the vizier was summoned before the king but was away from his office, Samuel appeared before Ḥabbūs; he did not malign the young vizier. On the contrary, he shielded him and, as it were, justified his absence.) At any rate, Samuel gained access to the king and could demonstrate his efficiency and diligence in financial affairs.[48] Ḥabbūs and the other Berber and Slav princes achieved greatness because of their abilities as rulers and soldiers. They had no special devotion to religious principles—in their ethic the ends justified all means. Therefore they had no hesitation in awarding high offices to non-Moslems; and indeed the Berber king ultimately did appoint Samuel ha-lēvī as minister of finance, giving him the title of vizier.[49]

Thus, by virtue of his abilities, the persevering refugee attained a status never before reached by a Jew in Spain. For even Ḥasdai Ibn Shaprūṭ did not receive this resounding title from the Omayyad caliph; officially he only administered one of the several bureaus in the finance ministry. It may well be that Samuel Ibn Nagrīla succeeded in endearing himself to the people and winning the friendship and appreciation of the Berbers to a greater degree than Ḥasdai did in his time. Abū Ibrāhīm Ismāʿīl, as he was called, was a beloved and honored personality among the Ṣinhādja. He was economically secure, and when he became a vizier and minister of finance his personal income automatically increased. In that period he delighted in the felicity of his homelife, and when his first son, Joseph, was born in 1035, his happiness was great indeed.

But despite all this, he was troubled and insecure. The wealthy Jews of Granada, the old-time inhabitants of the city, were unreconciled to his rise to eminence. Such was the nature of Jews in the Diaspora—anyone who struck roots in a country thought of it as his true fatherland. A Jew coming from another land was considered an alien who disturbed the serenity of relations between the local Jews and the non-Jews; and if he made a charitable contribution for the alien Jew, he felt his obligation to all his fellow Jews discharged. Those Jews of Granada could not forgive Samuel ha-lēvī his success, and inasmuch as they had access to the Berber chiefs, he had ample reason for his anxiety. He well knew that they were waiting for the opportune moment to strike him down. Meanwhile, a crisis in the Berber kingdom was approaching . . . a crisis whose development had long been apparent.

Samuel ha-lēvī was appointed vizier in the 1030s. Ḥabbūs had already reached middle age, and the question of his successor consumed the Ṣinhādja nobles, not only because of their concern for the young kingdom but also because of their preoccupation with their own futures. True, Ḥabbūs did appoint members of his family as governors of provinces, but when he wanted to assemble them for a consultation, he nevertheless treated them respectfully. Ḥabbūs did not invite them to his palace but met them elsewhere to avoid the impression that they were his servants and subordinates. Naturally they became accustomed to this and did not want a king who would deviate from the ways of Ḥabbūs. Many of them were followers of Yaddair b. Ḥubāsa, Ḥabbūs's nephew. This prince, whose sole desire was to usurp the place of Ḥabbūs's sons, Bolug-gīn and Bādīs, spoke eloquently and was a persuasive flatterer of the chiefs—even of the king himself. Yaddair was a relatively learned person who perused books and associated with the *faḳīhs* to educate himself—but especially did he wish to appear zealous in the Moslem faith. Ḥabbūs valued his cleverness and constantly sought his advice on important questions. He asked Yaddair to negotiate with emissaries from other governments and would make him responsible at various times for dealing with various royal affairs.

Yaddair also fostered good relations with the vizier Abu 'l-'Abbās and with other estimable Andalusians in his campaign to succeed his uncle. Some time earlier, as a result of long consultations by Yaddair's faction, a highly regarded Berber chief presented himself before Ḥabbūs, petitioning him to designate a successor to avoid disputes after his death. Following a prearranged plan, he was promptly joined by Abu 'l-'Abbās who proposed that the king designate his nephew Yaddair. Abu 'l-'Abbās explained that there was no one more deserving than Yaddair—he was popular and did not covet what did not belong to him; thus only good could result from his rule. Thereupon a Berber chief arose and, defending the right of Bādīs to succeed, argued that Bādīs was well versed in governmental matters and heaped abundant praises upon him. Moreover, he advised Yaddair publicly not to vie with Bādīs. Ḥabbūs said nothing on that occasion and the question of the succession remained suspended. Samuel was uneasy, for Yaddair had treated him with coolness since he removed the son of Samuel's friend, the vizier; he knew, too, that Yaddair's faction was uncommonly active.

Nor did Bādīs sit idly by. He attempted to lure the Berber chiefs to his side, lavishly distributing money and gifts among them and assuring them that he would follow his father's path and would treat them as had his father. Ultimately his efforts succeeded. Ḥabbūs was persuaded to appoint him heir designate to the throne. Ḥabbūs also publicly admonished his nephew Yaddair to desist from undermining his son Bādīs.

But the problem of succession was far from solved. The majority of the chiefs did not want Bādīs. They were convinced that his strong will and fearlessness would vitiate their own influence. Bādīs was not one to exchange pleasantries but spoke his mind plainly and directly; he relied on his own merits and abilities. Although Bādīs did weigh his actions and was wary of offending the Ṣinhādja chiefs, it was foreign to him to hide his views and mask his intentions.

Such an heir to the throne was distinctly undesirable and therefore a powerful bloc sprang up which supported Boluggīn, Bādīs's younger brother. If a son must succeed Ḥabbūs, it held, then it should be the younger prince, who was markedly different in character from his brother. He had no compulsion to rule. Neither shrewd nor crafty, he was slow in recognizing intrigue. Boluggīn was a good soldier and well disposed toward people. While most of the chiefs inclined toward making Boluggīn king after his father died, the Berber masses leaned to Bādīs. They were apprehensive of the chiefs' obduracy, which would increase if a feeble king occupied the throne. Even Yaddair, who had not yet relinquished his ambitions, supported Boluggīn. He became an intimate of his and attempted to persuade him to kill his older brother, Bādīs. Yaddair was certain that he could effortlessly depose this weakling once his forceful sibling was out of the way.

Just as the Jews of Spain were always involved in Moslem and Christian governmental affairs over the centuries, the Jews of Granada were drawn into this maelstrom. They, too, were marked by the factionalism similar to that prevalent among the Berbers. The affluent group which had ties with the Berber chiefs were predisposed toward Boluggīn. This circle included Joseph Ibn Migash, Isaac b. Leon, and Nehemiah Eshkafa, all of them among the wealthiest and most distinguished men of the Granada community. The establishment of a strong central government would limit the scope of activity of these Jews, who benefited from their link with the chiefs. But should the power of the chiefs increase, it would be possible to distribute the function of tax farmers, purveyors, and bankers to a greater number of rich merchants. The masses among the Jews of Granada preferred the rule of Bādīs, however, who was more likely to defend them from the iniquitous acts of tyrannical officials.

Notwithstanding being a vizier and an influential man, Samuel ha-lēvī clearly found himself in an uncomfortable position. The party which supported Bādīs, was weak, and it was plain to him that if Boluggīn ascended the throne, those Granadan Jews would hasten to settle their accounts with him.

Samuel ha-lēvī, then, had more than enough enemies within the kingdom of Granada impatiently waiting for his downfall. But even outside the government of the Ṣinhādja, enemies rose against him, seeking to lay a snare for him. The vizier of the kingdom of Almería was foremost.

In the provinces east of the kingdom of Granada, whose chief city was Almería, the Slav general Khairān had established his own kingdom at the time of the dissolution of the Omayyad caliphate. He was involved in numerous cabals and succeeded in imposing his authority on all the provinces along the coast of southeast Spain, as well as on the hill and mountain country behind it. In the north his domain reached beyond Orihuela. After Khairān died in 1028 he was succeeded by the eunuch Zuhair, who became even more powerful than Khairān. Zuhair broadened his dominion: He absorbed the province of Xativa, which is south of Valencia, and also the district of Baeza, between the Segura Mountains and the Guadalquivir; for a time he also held sway over Cordova. Because Khairān's kingdom was, therefore, substantially larger and more powerful than that of the Ṣinhādja, the question of their relations with the Slavs was of utmost importance for them. For a time the two kingdoms were allies, and when the ruler of Seville attacked Zuhair in 1036, Ḥabbūs went to his aid and they invaded Seville together. But when Samuel ha-lēvī was appointed the vizier for Ḥabbūs, the vizier of Almería began to undermine this alliance.

This vizier, whose name was Abū Dja'far Aḥmad b. 'Abbās, was a young man of great opulence. His knowledge of Arabic literature was outstanding; his epistolary skill the finest; he was an excellent orator of quick perception—and withal he was quite handsome. Arabic writers recount the marvels of his character and wealth, and among other things, they report that he had five hundred women of wondrous beauty in his harem. But they assert also that none could compare to him for miserliness and egotism.

His most conspicuous trait was his conceit. He boasted of his genealogy, which he traced to the first Moslems in Medina who welcomed the Prophet when he fled from his birthplace, Mecca; he flaunted the immense wealth he inherited from his father; and he was especially proud of his scholarly achievements. Pride is a characteristic trait of the Arabs; anyone who mortifies them is never forgiven.

This particularly haughty Arab was now compelled to witness the degradation of his people and to resign himself to subjugation by mercenary slaves once sold in the market—those Slavs, those eunuchs, toward whom he harbored contempt and hostility. Many of the Arabs in Spain were of like mind, but having lost their militant disposition long ago, they were powerless and unable to combat their adversaries. But although he and those like him could not wreak vengeance upon the regnant Slavs and Berbers, they could further humiliate those with less strength than they—namely, the Jews.

Throughout generations, Moslems believed that the Jews and Christians living among them must be humbled. While it is true that in Moslem Spain not all of the debasing laws enacted by zealous theologians in the Near East were implemented, even here it was recognized and accepted that a non-Moslem must not be given an office having any measure of authority; even as enlightened a caliph as 'Abdarraḥmān had to take this view into consideration. Now a Moslem ruler had disregarded Arab sentiments and the principles laid down by the theologians: He had designated a Jew as vizier. The appointment of Samuel ha-lēvī demonstrated the decline of their nation to Aḥmad b. 'Abbās and those sharing his feelings. It seemed to them that there was no longer any difference between them and those infidels who, according to the commandment of the Koran, ought to be crushed to dust. The Jewish vizier of Granada was a symbol of their abasement, and this accounts for the bitterness with which they began their struggle against him.

The vizier of the kingdom of Almería addressed a missive to the king of Granada asking him to dismiss his vizier, the Jew. At the same time he sent letters to some of the Ṣinhādja chiefs, indicating to them that it was a great sin to let the Jew retain his post since this was contrary to the laws of the Koran. Although he stressed that he was not only referring to the vizier but to other Jews who held posts in the service of the Berber kingdom, he was particularly vehement in his accusations against Samuel ha-lēvī, whom he regarded as the root of the evil.

Aḥmad b. 'Abbās knew the ways of the Berbers. Many of them broke Islamic law without restraint—they drank wine and made light of fasting—but wanted to appear to be devoutly observant Moslems to the Andalusians; this led the Arab to hope they would assent to his request. But Ḥabbūs and the Ṣinhādja acted as other Moslem rulers did when they had to choose between their own interests and theological considerations: they retained the Jewish vizier because he was more diligent and loyal than others.

The Almerían vizier also petitioned the Ḥammūdite government in Málaga. He exploited the fact that the Ṣinhādja acknowledged the Ḥammūdite prince as their caliph, and thus the prince had the authority to require the king of Granada to dismiss his Jewish vizier. Indeed, Aḥmad b. 'Abbās found attentive ears at Málaga. The Ḥammūdite vizier, whose name was Aḥmad Ibn Baḳanna and who was also called Ibn Abī Mūsā, fully supported the Almerían zealot, and together they devised their perfidious scheme.[50]

When Aḥmad b. 'Abbās saw that the king of Granada would not honor his request, he persuaded his king, Zuhair, to renounce his pact with the Ṣinhādja. Zuhair followed his advice, ignoring the assistance that the king of Granada had but recently extended to him, and entered into a pact of friendship with Muḥammad b. 'Abdallāh, the Berber prince who reigned at Carmona. The principality of Carmona belonged to Berbers of the Zenāta tribe, who were ancient enemies of the Ṣinhādja. Had the Almerían vizier succeeded in his plan, he would have surrounded the kingdom of Granada with an alliance of hostile states.

King Ḥabbūs died in July 1037.[51] The question of succession now had to be decided, and the fate of Samuel ha-lēvī hung on its outcome. The hours after the death of the king who had raised him to the high rank of vizier were some of the most difficult in his life, and time seemed to creep by. If Bādīs's opponents succeeded in crowning Boluggīn, Samuel was likely to come to a bad end.

The attempt was made: A band of Ṣinhādja chiefs tried to place Boluggīn on the throne and to do it before the courtiers assembled to swear fealty to Bādīs—as was the ritual in Moslem states—and thus present them with a fait accompli. After the king's death they went without delay to Boluggīn to shake his hand. This act was tantamount to a pledge of allegiance, for it was their method of avowing their loyalty. But they suffered a disappointment, for the prince did not disobey his father's wishes. He refused to accept the declaration of fealty and proclaimed his intention to remain loyal to his brother

Bādīs; the chiefs were compelled, against their wishes, to do likewise. Thus Bādīs became king in his father's stead.[52]

III

Samuel ha-lēvī was relieved. He was sure that he would be retained by the king and that no evil would befall him. The new ruler was well aware that Samuel had worked in his behalf when a majority of the chiefs opposed him, and he respected Samuel's talents and devotion to duty.

Yet Samuel had sufficient ground for apprehension regarding new dangers, even after Bādīs occupied the throne: Samuel's foes—both manifest and secret—continued to weave their evil designs. The path of a vizier at a royal Moslem court had never been easy, especially at a Berber court, where Andalusians and Arabs, Berbers and Slavs—who hated and envied each other—struggled for influence. Bādīs appointed as viziers two men of the Ibn al-Ḳarawī family; this was a Christian family that converted to Islam and had become aides of the Ṣinhādja chiefs. They were intimate with them and spent much of their time with these leaders. The new viziers, the brothers 'Alī and 'Abdallāh, had studied with Bādīs at the school for chiefs' sons and from that time were on friendly terms with him. The king gave the two brothers high posts in the army.[53] Samuel ha-lēvī had to adapt his ministerial agenda to theirs, and once more he had serious misgivings.

Meantime the vizier of Almería, Aḥmad b. 'Abbās, renewed his attempts to overthrow Samuel. After Ḥabbūs's death, Ibn 'Abbās hoped that things would change in the Ṣinhādja kingdom and that he would be able to convince the new king to remove the infidel vizier. He sent Bādīs a strongly worded letter pointing to the sin involved in giving high office to a Jew and demanded that Samuel be purged. If the king would dismiss Samuel Ibn Nagrīla, he wrote, peace would obtain between his kingdom and that of Almería. Should he refuse, however, he would have to face the opposition of allied kings —a clear reference to the pact between Zuhair and the prince of Carmona, a pact that did indeed seem highly dangerous to the rulers of Granada. But again Ibn 'Abbās's hopes were dashed, for the new ruler of Granada rejected his request. His reply was clear and unequivocal: He would not dismiss the loyal vizier.[54]

But Bādīs considered good-neighborly relations with the kingdom of Almería essential for his own safety. His main opponent was the king of Seville, and as long as Bādīs was at peace with the king of Almería his rear border was secure and there was no threat of a war on two fronts. Zuhair's army was relatively strong. It was composed of troops of Slavs, Arabs, Negroes, and Christian mercenaries; when it became necessary, it was not difficult for the king of Almería to mobilize additional troops from among the Catalans, who were always ready to hire themselves out to Moslem rulers in eastern Spain and to participate in their military ventures.

Bādīs was especially perturbed by the pact between Zuhair and the prince of Carmona. This Berber principality bordered his kingdom on the west, and its rulers had blood ties with the Berbers who had settled in southern Andalusia. He feared that one day they would unite to destroy the rule of the Ṣinhādja. Bādīs therefore sent an emissary to Zuhair, the king of Almería, to ask him to renew the pact between their neighboring kingdoms. For this mission he chose a judge of Granada, Abū 'l-Ḥasan 'Alī b. Muhammad Ibn Thauba, hoping that such a respected theologian would know how to address the Arab vizier as one person of stature to another and that Zuhair would give the proposal serious consideration.

But Zuhair, heady with his own accomplishments, toyed with the idea of annexing Granada for his own dominions, believing that Bādīs would be unable to withstand his attack. Encouraged in this by his vizier, Aḥmad b. 'Abbās, Zuhair did not accede to the proposal by Bādīs—which his emissary reported to him.

In the beginning of August 1038 Zuhair suddenly appeared at Granada. For a ruler of another kingdom to visit—uninvited and without prior announcement—was against all accepted rules of etiquette and was, as it were, a provocation and an insult. Not only had he come to Granada uninvited, he had arrived at the head of a column of many soldiers. His intent was to frighten the Ṣinhādja by a demonstration of strength and thus lay the groundwork for the conquest of Granada. Explaining his most unusual visit, he stated that he had come to pay his respects at the grave of his friend Ḥabbūs (even though he did not find it necessary to offer condolences to Bādīs when his father died). Nevertheless, the ruler of Granada welcomed him graciously, and Zuhair pitched his tent on a hill near Granada. Bādīs dined him with ceremony and festivity, as befit a king, and of course presented him with the customary gifts.

When, however, they began to discuss the problems involving relations between their two governments, Zuhair was not at all courteous; his entire demeanor was one of arrogance. The ruler of Granada asked him to annul his pact with the prince of Carmona, but Zuhair, boasting of his military strength, proclaimed that it lay within his power to act as he pleased. He even hinted that the kingdom of Granada was actually dependent upon him. Aḥmad b. 'Abbās was the most prominent of the high officials from both kingdoms who participated in these conversations. What the king merely alluded to the vizier stated explicitly, leaving no doubt about the real intent of Almería's ruler. The Ṣinhādja chiefs were greatly irritated. The king of Almería had pleaded with them for help only two years before, and now here he was, in their kingdom, presumptuously challenging them.

The debate was hot; Aḥmad b. 'Abbās was particularly outspoken. He brought up the matter of the Jewish vizier and, in the presence of the king and of Samuel ha-lēvī himself, incited the Ṣinhādja chiefs to act against Samuel. To be sure, Bādīs frequently consulted him when the discussions were over and showed no sign of doubt, but Samuel was once again full of misgivings.

Meanwhile, the king set upon a course of action. Having despaired of a renewal of the pact with his neighbors, he was bent on war. Bādīs had already made preparations and contacted the Negro troop in his army, when a Berber officer named Boluggīn came to the king asking permission to make one last effort at reconciliation with Zuhair to prevent the war whose end could not be foretold. Bādīs granted his request. In the depth of the night the officer went to the tent of the vizier of Almería and, with unrestrained emotion, urged him not to renounce the old pact with the kingdom of Granada but to forsake the prince of Carmona. Aḥmad b. 'Abbās was adamant. With scorn and irony he told Boluggīn that as long as Samuel Ibn Nagrīla remained in service there would be no peace between the Ṣinhādja and the rulers of Almería. The Berber alternately raged and pleaded, but he failed.

Bādīs waited impatiently for the reply; Samuel ha-lēvī and other officers waited with him. On his return, however, Boluggīn told them that hope was useless. The other side intended to destroy the Ṣinhādja kingdom. The Berber chiefs, headed by Bādīs's brother, Boluggīn, were convinced. Then and there it was decided to give battle, and Prince Boluggīn was given command of the army.

Not far from Granada, there was a bridge near a village named for a spring, Alfuente. Zuhair, on his way back to Almería, had to pass through a defile over this bridge; Bādīs ordered it destroyed. The Almerían troops would then have to cross the mountains to reach the plain behind them, and they would be caught in an ambush by the detachments of soldiers stationed in the passes. But after all the commands had already been given, Bādīs wavered. He still hoped that Zuhair might reconsider—and, after all, it was better to secure the eastern border of his kingdom through a pact of amity than by war. Indeed, should Zuhair be defeated and perhaps slain, he might be replaced by a ruler even more dangerous. Better that a Slav rule in Almería than that an Arab acquire dominance there—so ran the king's thoughts. He sent emissaries to Zuhair apprising him of the peril he faced and counseling Zuhair to traverse the mountains before the Granadan army took its positions.

Zuhair was inclined to accept the advice, but his vizier proved a stumbling block; Aḥmad b. 'Abbās prevented his escape. According to reports in the Andalusian cities, his advice was not trustworthy since his ambition was to become king of Almería himself. In fact, the Arab vizier despised the Slav ruler. In his eyes the king was only a slave who had attained dominion, whereas he—Aḥmad b. 'Abbās—boasted ancestral merit as well as high station. His father was a man of status in Almería, and many inhabitants of the city owed him their gratitude. As for intellectual attainments and personal standards, surely in these respects too he was more worthy to rule than the eunuch. In the coming battle, which would rage in the mountains, he would rely on luck. He was convinced that his own good fortune would not desert him and that even if his king was entrapped, he himself would escape.

Zuhair hearkened to his vizier, and when he reached the bridge of Alfuente on the following day, Friday, August 4, he found it demolished. Having no choice, his soldiers began to ascend the mountains where the Granadans lurked behind the cliffs. Arrows and missiles rained down on them. Wherever they were forced to advance in rows, troops of horsemen sallied forth and wreaked havoc upon them. Notwithstanding, the Granadans did not feel secure—their forces were smaller than those of Almería, and they also feared that desperation might embolden the enemy.

Samuel ha-lēvī, who ventured onto the battlefield with his sovereign, beheld for the first time the horror that is war. In a whisper he uttered a supplication to the Creator of the universe, praying that the merit of his ancestors come to his aid. Zuhair meantime had succeeded in setting his surprised army in battle array. And all the while his vizier screamed against the Jewish vizier—incredibly, the voice of Aḥmad b. 'Abbās dominated the battle sounds.

The actual fighting did not last long. The Negro foot soldiers in the Almerían army, who numbered some five hundred men, were venal. They quickly turned traitor, plundered Zuhair's store of weapons, and went to the side of the Ṣinhādja. The commander of the Slav cavalry, Hudhail, fell from his horse and was taken captive. The rout began. First the horsemen fled, then Zuhair himself, and after them the remainder of the army. As the Granadan forces pursued, the horses of the Almeríans stumbled, falling into the gorges below, carrying their riders with them—among them the king of Almería himself. Many were slain by the Granadans and many were taken captive. Among the prisoners was the vizier, Aḥmad b. 'Abbās, and it was Samuel's lot to bring him in fetters to Granada. The other captives were quickly released, but the arrogant vizier—who had led his king astray and brought destruction upon him—was imprisoned.

Aḥmad b. 'Abbās knew that his life was in danger, but he relied on his wealth to save him, offering Bādīs a huge sum in ransom. The Berber king postponed his decision, wanting to consult with his chiefs. On the one hand he realized that if he released the vizier, Aḥmad b. 'Abbās would conspire with yet greater vigor in retaliation for his disgrace. Bādīs understood well the thinking of the Arabs and knew what revenge meant to them. But on the other hand he was avid for the money the vizier had offered. It was difficult for Bādīs to resolve.

Meanwhile, the kingdoms and principalities in Andalusia and eastern Spain sent emissaries to him in order to intervene some spoke in his favor, others against him. Once again Samuel ha-lēvī was overcome by apprehensions. What if the king decided to accept the ransom and to free the vizier? Aḥmad b. 'Abbās would never rest until his avengement was complete. Samuel was uneasy from Rosh Hashana through Yom Kippur; his gladness during Succot was marred by worry. On the eve of Simḥat Torah, September 24, Bādīs, strolling with his brother Boluggīn, passed the house in which the Almerían vizier was being held. Bādīs at last ordered Aḥmad b. 'Abbās brought before him. Again the vizier pleaded for himself and, sensing that his fate was about to be decided, doubled the sum he was offering for his redemption. However, Boluggīn had convinced Bādīs that it was better to forgo the ransom and to earn tranquillity by liquidating the scheming vizier. Bādīs plunged his spear into Aḥmad b. 'Abbās. Boluggīn and the vizier 'Alī Ibn al-Ḳarawī, who accompanied them, did likewise. Seventeen times Aḥmad b. 'Abbās was stabbed before he died.

When this news was brought to Samuel ha-lēvī his gratitude was boundless, and he gave full expression to his joy. With the slaying of this bitter foe a stone was removed from his heart. He wrote a long poem with as many stanzas as the Book of Psalms and sent it, with a letter, to the Jewish communities in the Near East, to Egypt and Tunisia, apprising them of the victory which was his own triumph too; he also requested that they remember the day each year, establishing it as the Purim of Granada.[55]

Those were days of satisfaction and rejoicing for Bādīs and the Ṣinhādja chiefs, for their victory over Zuhair was an important political achievement. Not only did their prestige and esteem increase greatly in the eyes of the neighboring princes, but they also annexed some provinces of the kingdom of Almería which included several fortified cities. The kingdom of Granada gained an outlet to the sea, for it imposed its sway over the seacoast south of the Sierra Nevada, near the city of Almuñecar. Samuel ha-lēvī felt that his position had been greatly strengthened, and he looked forward to a more secure future.

Yet a few months later a crisis erupted among the highest echelons of the kingdom that placed the government of Bādīs in question and, as a matter of course, affected the fate of his Jewish vizier.

Bādīs, who bore the surname al-Muẓaffar ("to whom the Lord gave victory"), did not succeed in winning the affection of the Ṣinhādja. Although the hands of his soldiers were filled with the spoils of conquest, they had misgivings about Bādīs which he did nothing to dispel. His cousin, Yaddair, always attentive to the prevailing mood, perceived the unsympathetic climate surrounding the new king, and he resumed his undermining activities.

Meanwhile, an adventurer who had traversed many countries chanced to come to Granada from the Near East. When he came into contact with Yaddair and sensed the disquiet within the Ṣinhādja kingdom, he goaded Yaddair on and he himself took up subverting operations. This man, Abū 'l-Futūḥ Thābit b. Muḥammad al-Djurdjānī, was a learned writer and a warrior—a man of both the book and the sword. And, as it so often happens in the drama of history, he appeared but once on its stage. Yaddair and his followers lavished money upon the soldiers and gave some of them writs of appointment to high office, on the assumption that their scheming would succeed; and it did indeed seem that their activities assured them of success.

This time Yaddair's faction attempted to remove all opposition from the outset, so even Samuel ha-lēvī was brought into the cabal, even though Yaddair disliked him. Their intent was to involve Samuel in such a way that he would be prevented from taking action against them. Since they were sure that he would learn about the plot anyway, they preferred to make him one of their circle. They asked his permission to call a meeting in his home; Samuel ha-lēvī granted it but shrewdly duped them. Not only did he reveal the matter to the king, but he also invited Bādīs to listen in on the meeting from the attic of his house. A plan to murder the king was openly discussed, but unsure of the Jewish vizier, the conspirators refrained from giving the precise details of their scheme in his presence.

Bādīs, deeply moved by his vizier's loyalty, grew even closer to him than before. Naturally Bādīs now was on guard, and he soon learned the details of the schemers. A Berber officer revealed to him that the assassination would take place at the horse races in the vicinity of Granada at which he intended to appear. As the cabal waited for Bādīs, and it became clear that their plan was made known to the king, they realized that one of their number had betrayed them and imperiled their lives. Yaddair and his cohorts fled from Granada to Seville, and among them were the affluent members of the Jewish community who had earlier supported the candidacy of Boluggīn. It is certain that Samuel hal-lēvī was not unhappy to learn that he was rid of them. Boluggīn himself, who had known of the plot but did not impart it to his brother, now came to Bādīs seeking his forgiveness.[56]

But the machinations of Yaddair were not yet over. This ambitious prince was determined to fight to the end for the throne. Knowing that many of the Ṣinhādja who remained in

Granada still sided with him, he continued his activities and maintained contact with his supporters; his emissaries visited Granada from time to time and emissaries from Granada reciprocated. When his agents revealed that no less than two hundred warriors from among the Ṣinhādja were corresponding with Yaddair, Bādīs, appalled by the strength of the hostile faction, resolved to execute all of Yaddair's followers. The moderate and cautious Samuel ha-lēvī, however, restrained him from this step which might considerably weaken the army of Granada. On Samuel's advice the king endeavored to win over Yaddair's supporters with sumptuous gifts, while trying at the same time to stir dissension among them by various means.[57]

Yaddair made new plans in which he was supported by the king of Seville, who was less than pleased with the growing strength of the Ṣinhādja kingdom. After Zuhair's defeat, Granada was the most powerful state in eastern Andalusia. The conflict between Granada and Seville was the axis around which the politics of all of Andalusia revolved, and a new conflict was practically unavoidable. Whereas Granada was a Berber kingdom, Seville was an Arabic realm—a state which sprang out of a struggle with the Ḥammūdite caliphs who drew their support from the Berbers. When the inhabitants of Cordova rebelled against the rule of the Ḥammūdite al-Ḳāsim' driving him from their city in 1023—just as they had forced his nephew Yaḥyā to flee to Málaga two years earlier—the Sevillians rose against those bogus caliphs.

Seville then became a quasi-republic, and the judge of the city, Abu 'l-Ḳāsim ibn 'Abbād, was appointed as its head. This wealthy man was a scholar who had far-reaching ambitions. He established an armed force and warred upon the neighboring states. After he frustrated the attempt of Yaḥyā to take his city in 1027, the kadi became the sole ruler. Eight years later he took a step shrewdly designed to bolster his position. At that time a rumor had spread through Spain that the hapless caliph Hishām II had not died, as was claimed by the Omayyad princes who succeeded him to the caliphal throne, but had appeared in the city of Calatrava. The truth is that a man who resembled the caliph did reside in this city. His name was Khalaf and he was a poor laborer, a weaver of mats. The kadi, now governor of Seville, brought Khalaf to the city and inveigled some of the women who were once inmates of the caliph's harem to testify that the man was indeed the caliph. After thus confirming his identity, the kadi proclaimed the weaver to be the caliph and "Ruler of all the Faithful" (Amīr al-mu' minīn), calling upon all the princes of Moslem Spain to take the oath of allegiance to him. The pseudo-Hishām was to fill the same role as the real Hishām had formerly in Cordova: He was to be a puppet for the kadi, who intended to rule in his name and thus give his government the seal of legality.

But besides bolstering his position in Seville itself, the wily kadi sought a further goal. He planned to unite all the Arab and Slav princes around the puppet caliph and to form an alliance of Arab-Slav states in opposition to the Berber princes, whom he despised even as did the other Arabs of Andalusia. The kadi was wholly successful. Not only the Arab and Slav princes but even some of the Berber princes recognized his caliph, whereas the Ṣinhādja found themselves eclipsed. However, this was only the more immediate of the kadi's objectives. Just as the Ṣinhādja were striving to enlarge their kingdom, the kadi's ultimate goal was his dominance over all of Andalusia.

The publicity given to the naming of the "caliph" was therefore an important phase in the struggle between Seville and Granada; in a certain measure, it was a struggle between two nations. It is true that the long, enduring war between the two kingdoms was, for practical purposes, no different from those wars on which all the kings and princes who replaced the Omayyad caliphate in Moslem Spain spent their days. The national antagonism was not, however, the decisive factor. More immediate were the personal motives, the capabilities, the ambitions of the rulers and the viziers.

To be sure, in each state the government was in control of one national group, but men of several nations and various religions served in their armies. The army of Seville contained Arabs, Christians from what is present-day Portugal, and Berbers. The armies of the Slav princes were a mix of various nationals, including mercenary troops who went from prince to prince, hiring themselves out for a fixed period of time or for specific ventures. These armies were small, numbering a few thousand at most. Battles in which only a few troops took part decided the fate of broad regions. In general the states of Moslem Spain at that time were unstable, and this was even more true of their regimes. Rulers and boundaries changed frequently. Each state coveted growth; the warfare among them was seemingly endless.

Indeed, not even a year passed since the Ṣinhādja won their splendid victory over Zuhair when they were forced to war against the kingdom of Seville. In the summer of 1039 the ruler of Seville, embroiled in a dispute with the prince of Carmona, dispatched his army to invade its borders. The subjugation of this principality and its annexation to the state of Seville appeared to the kadi to be the first indispensable move in his expansion to the east, since it lay between Seville and central and southern Andalusia. Its rulers were the Berbers, whom he fully intended to remove from the Iberian peninsula; the prince himself, Muḥammad b. ʿAbdallāh, had proved to be an ingrate who did not repay the kadi for past kindnesses. The kadi therefore mobilized his forces, placed his son, Ismāʿīl, at their head, and enjoined him to spare no effort in seizing this small state. The expeditionary force occupied the two important cities in the eastern sector of the principality, Écija and Ossuna, as well as several other towns; and Muḥammad b. ʻAbdallāh was forced to insulate himself in his capital city, Carmona. When he perceived that the troops of Seville were closing in, he dispatched emissaries to Bādīs and to Idrīs b. ʻAlī, the Ḥammūdite ruler of Málaga (who had been named caliph), pleading that they hasten to his aid.

These two rulers had already grasped the intentions of the kadi of Seville and realized that their aid to the prince of Carmona would be not merely an act of national fraternity but a necessity prompted by diplomatic sagacity. Idrīs, who was quite ill, sent his force under the command of his vizier, Ibn Baḳanna, whereas Bādīs went himself, accompanied by Samuel ha-lēvī. When the combined Berber corps attacked, the Sevillian army was forced to lift its siege of Carmona and march against them. This permitted Muḥammad b. ʻAbdallāh to join forces with Granada and Málaga. When the troops of Seville confronted the Berber armies, they did not engage in open battle, and the Berbers, assuming that they had already achieved their objective by their rescue of Carmona, returned to their own country.

But the army of Seville pursued, blocking the road eastward against Bādīs's forces. The Granadans wanted to reach the region of Cabra, the westernmost province of their kingdom, by the shortest route, which necessitated crossing the Genil River. But before they even arrived there they learned that the kadi's forces were assembled at the ford; and by now the Málagan army had already departed. When they immediately called upon their allies, who were not yet too far away, to rejoin them, the allies responded with alacrity. The kadi's troops, to their amazement, ran into the Berbers—reunited and prepared for battle. On October 3 the armies engaged on the banks of the

Genil. Bugles were sounded and drums were beaten—the clash of swords began. Amid the neighing of horses the squadrons of horsemen attacked, shouting their battle cries.

In this turmoil stood Samuel ha-lēvī, uttering a prayer. With all his heart he hated the ruler of Seville and his companions, those haughty Arabs who despised the Jews; but their armies were powerful and this filled Samuel with misgiving.

However, the Berber contingents in the army of Seville had no desire to war with their fellow nationals and withdrew. When Ismā'īl, the kadi's son, fell, his soldiers fled from the battlefield. They quit Écija and Ossuna and returned to their country, highly disappointed. The severed head of Ismā'īl was sent to the caliph at Málaga. While the Ṣinhādja were occupied in assembling their spoils and removing precious articles from the corpses, the Jewish vizier remained in his tent composing a hymn of praise to the God of heaven and earth—a hymn which contains 149 lines, almost equaling the number of the Psalms.[58]

The rout of the army of Seville was complete. The death of his son Ismā'īl, a skilled commander and the successor to his throne, grievously affected the kadi. For some time he ceased his attempts to enlarge his kingdom, although he endeavored to replenish the ranks of his forces, which did suffer losses, and to raise their morale. The kadi refrained from dispatching his troops into neighboring states, but he supported the activities of the conspirators in those countries.

As a parched man thirsts for cool water, after the slaying of his son the kadi thirsted for revenge against the Ṣinhādja, and he saw his opportunity in Seville. Prince Yaddair, who was consumed by his desire to supplant Bādīs, dwelt there and the ruler of Seville abetted him. Yaddair mobilized a small force of Slav mercenaries,[59] and in the summer of 1041 he penetrated the kingdom of Granada from the north. It was difficult to speed reinforcements to the northern province because between it and Granada stood a buffer—a ring of high mountains. For an army to go around them from the west would require much time, so Yaddair was optimistic about his chances. And he did indeed succeed in capturing the city of Arjona, south of Andujar; after slaying its garrison he pushed on southward past Jaén, the chief city of the province, subduing more fortresses in the hill country which stretched to this city.

At the beginning of August an expeditionary force, assembled in the capital of Granada, approached Yaddair's troops. At its head was Samuel ha-lēvī. Yaddair shut himself up in one of the high, mountain fortresses, not daring to clash with Samuel in the open field. The Granadans had to lay siege to the fortress, and this was not easy; whenever the besieged ventured forth severe battles ensued. Finally the Granadans launched a general onslaught and seized the stronghold. Yaddair himself took advantage of the attendant confusion and escaped. But two of his loyal aides were taken captive, one of whom was put to death while the other died immediately from his wounds. Yaddair and a small number of his supporters headed for nearby Cordova, then an independent state. He had hoped to find asylum, but this proved vain. After successful negotiations initiated and directed by Samuel ha-lēvī, the Cordovan authorities handed over the rebellious prince, who was incarcerated in a secure fortress.[60]

But Yaddair had numerous adherents who remained faithful to him, and they soon managed to free him. He fled beyond Granada's borders and, undaunted, again began to mobilize an armed force, this time seeking help from the prince of Carmona, Muḥammad b. 'Abdallāh. But this Berber prince felt that the strengthening of the governments of Seville and Granada placed him between the anvil and the hammer. It was clear that the two powerful neighbors of the principality of

Carmona intended expansion at its expense—indeed to swallow it altogether. Yaddair promised the prince that if he would assist in winning Granada he would protect the principality and even enlarge it.

The Berber let himself be persuaded, entered into a pact with Yaddair, and in 1043 they initiated their assault on the kingdom of Granada. But they brought on their own destruction. As usual, they began with isolated raids to test the situation and to see what the reaction would be. Bādīs did not delay; he mobilized his army and dispatched it against Carmona (Samuel ha-lēvī was among the commanders of the expeditionary force). The punitive campaign succeded: The Granadans captured a number of cities, taking booty everywhere. Yaddair was seized and, on Bādīs's orders, he was executed. Simultaneously the forces of Seville also penetrated Carmona, seeing a chance to wreak vengeance upon the Berber prince. He went out to engage them in battle, but was caught in an ambush and slain.[61]

Nevertheless, the war between the kingdom of Granada and the principality of Carmona persisted. Succeeding Muḥammad b. 'Abdallāh, his son Isḥāḳ ruled in Carmona.[62] Its inhabitants and those of the other cities of the principality remained loyal to the dynasty, toward which, in contrast to the other Berbers, they felt sympathetic. Of course the new prince wanted to regain the cities that had been lost in the war with the Ṣinhādja, especially Écija, which was the second most important city of his principality. Isḥāḳ particularly relied on the support of its inhabitants. The Granada garrison was compelled to withdraw from the city; however, in the summer of 1044 an army of Granadans, led by Samuel ha-lēvī, appeared before the gates of Écija and easily triumphed over the forces of Carmona. Écija was finally annexed to the kingdom of Granada.[63]

Samuel put great effort in the preparation of these military campaigns and in implementing them. Like Bādīs, he regarded

Seville as the prime enemy of the kingdom of Granada; in time the struggle with this state and its allies became the keystone of the foreign policy of the Granadan ruler, directed and effectuated by his Jewish vizier. However, the rulers of Granada never lost touch with the political mood of eastern Andalusia. As the rivalry between them and the rulers of Seville increased, they were frequently aware of the need to guard their rear borders.

After Zuhair's downfall the people of Almería invited the king of Valencia to take over. 'Abdal'aziz b. 'Abdarraḥmān did indeed go to Almería but after a time, when he had to return to Valencia, he left his son, 'Ubaidallāh, in charge, with his brother-in-law, Abū 'l-Aḥwaṣ Ma'n, as regent.

But for those Hispano-Moslem principalities of the eleventh century there was no permanence. In the spring of 1042 several governors of districts which had formerly belonged to the kingdom of Almería joined together in revolt. At a specific moment rebellion erupted in the chief cities of provinces distant from each other—indicating a prearranged course of action. The prime mover in this revolt was Abu 'l-Aḥwaṣ Ma'n—the selfsame prince whom 'Abdal 'azīz appointed as his regent in Almería. He drove out 'Ubaidallāh, establishing himself as an independent ruler. Other focal points of the rebellion were the cities of Lorca, located between Almería and Murcia; Jodar, east of Jaén; and Xativa, south of Valencia. Seeking to crush the revolt, 'Abdal 'azīz first attacked Xativa—the revolt in the district nearest the capital of his kingdom was the most dangerous; and indeed, after a hard-fought battle, he succeeded in regaining control. Later, following the example of the Slav princes in eastern Spain, he hired Catalans as mercenaries to launch his campaign against Lorca and Almería. To insure success he asked the king of Denia to join him. Although there was always a certain strain between them, the king of Denia preferred that the entire broad area between

Almería and the environs of Valencia—that is, the region northwest and southwest of his state—be divided between the two rulers than that it fall into one man's hand: Ma'n's. This consideration led him to accede to 'Abdal 'azīz's request and he too engaged in the war.

Ma'n, frightened by the number of troops mobilized against him, hurriedly sent emmissaries to the king of Granada requesting aid and swearing to remain Bādīs's faithful ally. When Bādīs and his viziers discussed the question, they too concluded that it would be better if the eastern coast of the peninsula was divided between several states; they were, of course, also interested in having Ma'n as their ally. To be sure, the army of the king of Valencia and his allies was a powerful one and the road that led to the battle site was difficult, but the welfare of the Ṣinhādja state called for unrestrained effort.

The army was swiftly mobilized and started on its way, led by King Bādīs and Samuel ha-lēvī. This was one of the most arduous military campaigns of his life. The Granadan army had to cross the chain of high mountains east of the capital to reach the city of Guadix. From there columns of soldiers descended to the hill country north of the city in order to bypass the Sierra de Baeza, which reached a height of about 2,300 meters. By forced marches they scaled the mountain passes, and with great difficulty they transported the mules laden with armament, tents, and provisions. By narrow paths where the horses and mules stumbled, and over mountainous elevations covered with thorns and thistles, they advanced as rapidly as possible, led by the Jewish vizier who had advised his king to mount the campaign. Emerging from the city of Baeza on the eastern side, they again climbed into the mountains and finally reached the valley which lay between the Sierra de las Estancias and the Sierra de Maria. There where the valley broadens out lies the ancient city of Vélez Rubio, which was their last stop before descending to the hill country where the battle was waged.

Meanwhile the king of Valencia subdued the revolt in the province of Murcia and reached Lorca, which was at that time a well-populated and strongly fortified city. By the time that Samuel ha-lēvī and the Granadans arrived at Vélez Rubio, the allies were already closing in on Lorca from every side. But suddenly a dispute erupted among them. 'Abdal'azīz, the king of Valencia, wanted to press on beyond Almería without delay, whereas the king of Denia was opposed—he had not bargained for helping 'Abdal'azīz gain control of the entire Almerían kingdom. Indeed, his concern was simply to insure a balance of power with his neighbor; since the king of Valencia had already imposed his mastery over Xativa and the province of Murcia, he had no desire to prolong the war. The troops of Catalans demanded that the king of Valencia pay them their fee and even more than had been agreed upon—his exchequer was bare. Finally, the king of Denia and the Catalans returned to their respective states, leaving 'Abdal'aziz and his forces alone before Lorca. When the Granadan troops appeared the armies of Valencia also pulled back, for they were weary and had no more taste for battle. Thus Bādīs entered the city in triumph. The campaign achieved its goal: Ma'n, the king of Almería, became an ally of the king of Granada.[64]

IV

Thus the early years of Bādīs's reign at Granada, with Samuel ha-levi as his chief vizier, consisted of a succession of governmental crises and military campaigns, which frequently caused Samuel ha-lēvī difficult, anguish-laden moments. None of the dry accounts of the old Spanish chronicles—and nothing that Samuel himself set down in his bulging manuscripts—contain even a faint hint of the emotions, hopes, and disappointments which were his portion. But trials and actions calling for extraordinary daring were the essence of a man's existence in those days. The boundaries of the occult were great and many deeds could be regarded as adventures and journeys into the unknown, which made the desire for experimentation in such matters all the stronger. Because life was short and perilous, people, like shadows cast by fleeting clouds, scurried to its pleasures; those wars and political intrigues were, for them, exhilarating adventures that ran together as a single experience.

For Bādīs and Samuel they were an extended test which the two passed skillfully. The Berber ruler basked in his success; he had subdued his foes within the kingdom and had returned crowned with victory from his wars in the east and west. Samuel ha-lēvī achieved the prominence and security of which he had dreamed as a youth. Not only did Bādīs appreciate and trust him all the more now that his loyalty had been fully demonstrated, but also, because of Samuel's deftness during the crises between Bādīs and the other rulers in southern Spain, the king recognized Samuel's political sagacity. Moreover, various events occurred which redounded to Samuel's benefit. Without implicating himself, he was rid of influential and potentially dangerous enemies.

The first person about whom Samuel had had misgivings to disappear from the political scene was Boluggīn, the brother of Bādīs. Clearly the techniques employed by Samuel in behalf of Bādīs during the struggle over the succession after their father's death had not endeared him to Boluggīn. Since he knew the Berber nature—they could change their minds from morning to morning—Samuel was not at all sure but that one day he might wake to find Boluggīn occupying the throne. However, Boluggīn died shortly after the war with Zuhair. It was rumored in Granada that Bādīs was involved in his brother's death; a persistent report had it that when Boluggīn became ill Bādīs ordered the physician to give him fake medicines.[65]

A year and a half after Aḥmad b. 'Abbās was slain, Samuel was also freed of his associate Ibn Baḳanna, the vizier of the principality of Málaga, who had conspired with and joined Aḥmad b. 'Abbās in various schemes and who had often attacked Samuel's integrity. Samuel lost no opportunity to honor Ibn Baḳanna, but all his efforts were useless. The Moslem vizier persisted, and although he found he could not harm Samuel himself, he maltreated Samuel's friends in Málaga.

In 1039 Ibn Baḳanna participated with the army of Málaga in a war against the kingdom of Seville, and immediately after he returned to Málaga he faced a severe crisis. Prince Idrīs b. 'Alī—who reigned from 1035 in place of his brother Yaḥyā—was still recognized as the caliph in part of Andalusia and in the westernmost region of the African coast beyond the Straits of Gibraltar. Two days after Ibn Baḳanna's return the prince died. At that time the Ḥammudīte principality had two viziers. Ibn Baḳanna, who was a Berber, headed the province of Málaga, whereas Abu 'l-Fauz Nadjā, a Slav, resided in the African coastal city of Ceuta, together with the sons of the previous caliph, Yaḥyā. The intense rivalry and envy between these two viziers ignited with the death of the ruler. Ibn Baḳanna wanted to confer the crown upon his son Yaḥyā, whereas Nadjā preferred Ḥasan b. Yaḥyā, who lived with him in Ceuta. Yaḥyā b. Idrīs was crowned at Málaga, but when Nadjā crossed the Straits of Gibraltar with Ḥasan and an army, Ibn Baḳanna could not muster a defense force. He fled to a fortress near the city until the new rulers persuaded him to return—whereupon they killed him. Thus relieved of a vicious foe, Samuel ha-lēvī rejoiced, expressing his gratitude in a long poem.[66]

But the man who took over the government at Málaga in place of Ibn Baḳanna was no better. He too was a sworn enemy of the rulers of Granada, and Samuel ha-lēvī was uneasy about him.

The Ḥammūdite prince Ḥasan b. Yaḥyā was crowned at Málaga early in 1040, and he occupied the throne for three years. He was backed by the powerful vizier Nadjā, who thoroughly loathed the Berbers—especially Bādīs and his Jewish vizier. A master of intrigue and deceit, he too distressed Samuel. The Ṣinhādja still recognized the Ḥammūdite prince as the caliph, and after the kadi of Seville established the pseudo-Hishām as the "Ruler of All the Faithful," the Granadans even more strongly demonstrated their loyalty to the caliph of the Berbers, who was, for practical purposes, bereft of influence; Nadjā could, therefore, devise his plots in relative freedom. And since it was difficult for Bādīs to reject a request coming from his caliph (particularly when it dealt with a matter of law and religion—such as the imposition of infidels over Moslems), Samuel ha-lēvī's misgivings were not without foundation.

A new crisis now erupted within the principality of Málaga. Ḥasan slew his cousin Yaḥyā b. Idrīs, and to avenge his blood, his wife, Yaḥyā's sister, poisoned him. Nadjā came from Ceuta and persuaded the officers in the army of Málaga to liquidate the entire Ḥammūdite dynasty. To the Berber officers, among whom were some zealous Moslems, this was a profanation of concepts sacred to them since the Ḥammūdites claimed to be descendants of their Prophet; yet they did not have the courage to oppose the vizier. Besides, his promises and presents also had their effect.

After Nadjā won their consent, he attacked Algeciras, where another branch of the Ḥammūdites had ruled since 1035. He intended the total extirpation of their governance. When he became convinced that the Berbers were not wholeheartedly in accord with him, he returned to Málaga in the hope that he could remove them and surround himself with Slavs. But when the Berbers learned that Málaga was to be converted into a Slav state, they murdered Nadjā, cut off his head, carried it to a number of cities, and finally hung it on a gallows in Málaga. Once again Samuel ha-lēvī was rid of a dangerous enemy, and in his flowery language he summoned his friends "to drink from the cup of salvation."[67]

His ruthless foes in the neighboring states having been caught in their own snares, Samuel's position was strong. Nobody in the kingdom of Granada disputed his policy; no Berber and no Jew dared say a word against him. Samuel ha-lēvī consolidated—into his own hand—all contacts with the princes in southern and eastern Spain, held talks with emissaries from other governments, and directed ambassadors going on special missions. He received reports from spies and plotters who came to Granada to receive instructions and remuneration. At the same time he retained control of financial matters, which was his major responsibility. For, in large measure, it was the treasury which supplied the sums required to finance diplomatic and military operations and on which their success depended.

Nor was Samuel blind to the difficult internal problems of the Ṣinhādja. He was particularly attentive to the relations between the Arabic-speaking Andalusian population and the ruling faction of Berber warriors—for there was no one like Samuel ha-lēvī who could prevent this rift from turning into a broad unbridgeable chasm. Anyone who turned to him with a request—whether Berber or Andalusian—found a patient listener, and would depart in a relaxed mood.

With all his duties and burdens, Samuel ha-lēvī also had to participate in the life of the royal court. A chief vizier in a Moslem kingdom was obliged to associate with the princes and chiefs who occupied foremost positions in government, to hold conversations with them, and to join them in drink—when the eye of the *fakīh* was not on them. The Ṣinhādja chiefs were simple Berbers, crude and vulgar. They were far removed from such matters as literature and science, which were subjects of discussion in the courts of the Arab rulers. Like many who are unlearned, they were profoundly discomposed by the intellectuals and the writers, a subconscious envy that at times angered them and converted their aversion into outright hostility. The scholars among the Arabs of Granada, keenly aware of this attitude, were apprehensive of the Ṣinhādja, and many emigrated to states ruled by kings and princes of their own nationality.

But in his position, Samuel had to demonstrate that he was honored to be in the company of the Berber chiefs and that he found talking with them stimulating. To play this game successfully required much energy and not a little strength of spirit. Each day he had to be on guard against the petty but serious intrigues which were common in the court of a Moslem ruler; at the decisive moment Samuel would move with a strong hand to crush the plot without creating a stir. At night he was forced to idle away many hours in the company of the king and his companions, who were repugnant to him, and his situation at these gatherings was at times uncomfortable. More than once a learned writer, one of those who circulated among the capitals of Moslem Spain offering their services, would turn up at the royal court. He would try to make an impression by a display of his extensive knowledge of Arabic literature and by his cogent replies, meanwhile referring to verses in the Koran and citing famous poetry. True, most of the Berber courtiers did not understand a word of what the writer said, but if two or three testified to the king that he possessed exceptional abilities and useful information, that was enough. When these scribes met the Jewish vizier, no matter what they started to discuss, they would bring up religion. Samuel ha-lēvī had to respond, although such discussions in the presence of the Berber chiefs were distasteful to him. But he always won the debate, and the Moslem writers unanimously conceded that there was none to compare with him in defending his religion.[68]

The Berber ruler was not at all interested in such matters; he knew full well that the affairs of government were in good hands. He expressed his appreciation by conferring new titles upon him, such as "head of the guard," which was merely an honorary designation in Moslem Spain.[69]

Samuel ha-lēvī was one of those men who have time for everything. He treasured that warming shelter of the family which strengthens man against the storms of life, and even in the difficult years at the beginning of the reign of King Bādīs, Samuel dedicated much of his time to his household and to his loved ones. After his firstborn, Joseph, there was a second son, Judah; then a daughter was born, and in 1049 his third son, Elyāsāf.[70] In politics Samuel was cool, calculating, and dealt sternly with his opponents; but he was a loving, devoted father to his children. As much involved as he was in the turmoil of political struggles, his strongest emotions were concentrated on his offspring. He applied himself diligently to their education, and in particular to the education of his oldest son, who demonstrated great talents early. When Joseph was but a child, Samuel sought the finest teachers and supervised their work closely.

In 1041 Samuel's brother Isaac died, and his death laid the black pall of grief upon him. Isaac had lived in a city which was one day's journey from Granada; he was respected there by both the Jews and the Moslem nobles for he was not only a learned man, but also one of honorable traits—a generous man whose aid was available to all who sought it.[71] When Isaac died Samuel poured his bitterness into a cycle of laments.[72]

Shortly after he lost his brother, three more relatives died,[73] and when Samuel found himself bereft of the family of his parents, all his love centered on his children.

His eldest son Joseph was especially dear to him. Samuel now began to take a direct part in his education, and when affairs of government sent Samuel far from his family, he would write to Joseph, encouraging him to study diligently. Even in a military encampment he would copy Arabic poems and send them to Joseph, so that he could learn pure Arabic from them.[74] When Joseph grew up, Samuel procured renowned teachers from other cities, and he spared neither trouble nor expense to bring them from far and wide.[75] Because of Joseph's talents and his mature outlook, Samuel treated his son as if he were an adult even when he was still young. When Samuel went to war in eastern Spain in 1042, he sent Joseph a quasi-will containing guides to his conduct which, he counseled, would bring him favor in the eyes of God and man.[76] Two years later, during the war with the principality of Carmona, Joseph came down with smallpox, a deadly illness in those days. Samuel's intimates concealed the matter from him for eight days, until the danger passed. When he did learn of the illness he sent Joseph a letter urging the boy to heed the instructions of the physicians in every respect.[77] The child recovered, but Samuel's daughter became ill and died. Since Samuel was still engaged in a military campaign, he could not himself bury her but instead had to content himself with composing a lament.[78] Medical science was primitive in those times and child mortality was a harsh affliction. Samuel had to drink from this cup of suffering to its very bottom, for his son Judah also died in early childhood.[79]

By then Samuel (or, as the Jews called him, the *nāgīd*) had entered his sixties. The constant pressures and tensions, the many exertions and burdens had physically weakened him and thus lowered his resistance to sickness. When he returned from the war against the prince of Carmona in 1044, he became critically ill. Recovery seemed hopeless. But after three months his condition improved and he gradually recovered.[80] At last the misfortunes of that year ended; Samuel ha-lēvī regained his strength and resumed his activities in the government.

V

As Samuel ha-lēvī reached his prime the glory of the king waned. Bādīs was a strict but fair ruler at the outset of his reign. He later became despotic and his supporters shrank from him with repulsion. At first Bādīs enjoyed the rigors of combat and frequently joined in the wars against his neighbors. Now, as he reached middle age, he shut himself within his palace and relied upon his faithful Jewish vizier. As Bādīs more and more neglected the affairs of government, Samuel's responsibility became a heavy burden. Indeed, even without this complication, the duties with which the chief vizier of the kingdom of Granada was confronted were becoming more difficult annually.

In 1042 'Abbād (surnamed al-Mu'taḍid) became the ruler of Seville after the death of his father, the kadi. 'Abbād was endowed with talent and exceptional perception—a clever and learned man. Driven by a limitless hunger for empire, he was continually plotting the domination of the cities and provinces of Andalusia. Vindictive toward anyone who slighted him, he was unscrupulous in retaliation. He would commit any transgression which furthered his establishment of a mighty kingdom: Seville did grow constantly stronger and 'Abbād's expansionism became the most important factor in the political life of all of southern Spain. The kingdom of Granada was the only state in Andalusia which appeared to him to be strong enough to hinder his plans and to be likely to gather other states about it. Therefore all his energies were directed against Granada.

But between Seville and Granada lay small Berber states which constituted a buffer, and the two powerful kingdoms in western and eastern Andalusia each sought to attract them as their allies—joining either Seville or Granada was likely to tip the balance of power. True, there was a national antagonism between the tribes and dynasties which established those small states in the central region of southern Andalusia and the king of Seville, that of the Berbers and Arabs; however, most of those Berbers came from the Zenāta tribe, who utterly hated the Ṣinhādja. On the other hand, they were worried that their Andalusian subjects would establish ties with the king of Seville. All these Berber tribes were mercenaries or the children of mercenaries who had been brought from North Africa by al-Manṣūr and his sons to serve in his army, later becoming themselves a dominant military class which was maintained by the labors of the native citizenry. These Berbers had no place to which they could return, and clearly they would do anything to retain their dominance. Inasmuch as their subjects hated them, their misgivings of the Arab king of Seville were justified; hence their tendency to keep clear of any entanglement with him.

The largest of these states was the principality of Carmona. It comprised the lowlands south of the Guadalquivir and the hill country behind it, reaching as far as the city of Almodóvar in the east and Ossuna in the south. South of the state of Carmona the members of the Banū Dammar founded a principality whose capital was Morón. It extended over the region of hills and mountains of the Sierra de Morón. This principality, where Muḥammad b. Nūḥ reigned in the 1040s, was weak, and all its neighbors eyed it with avarice. On its southeast, between it and the principality of Málaga, was the state of Ronda, a land of high mountains bisected by the Guadiaro

River. West of the Guadiaro's valley rises the Sierra de Grazalema, and on the east the Sierra de Tolox ascends to a height of nearly 2,000 meters; these chains of mountains make this region a natural fortress. The Berbers of the Banū Yefren tribe who governed this principality were powerful warriors with a reputation for stubbornness—especially their prince, Abū Nūr Hilāl b. Abī Ḳurra.

To the southwest lay the small state of the Berber tribe called Banū Irniyān. This state covered the lowland by the estuary of the Guadalquivir and Guadalete rivers; its chief cities were Arcos and Xeres. The family ruling in this state, the Banū Khizrūn, reigned from the time of the civil wars in the region of Calsena; later they annexed the northernmost districts, including Arcos. The strongest of these Berber princes was undoubtedly Abū Nūr, king of Ronda, a sworn ally of al-Mu'taḍid, king of Seville. However, even the princes of Morón and Arcos acknowledged the pseudo-Hishām as caliph. Only the prince of Carmona, because of his hostility toward the king of Seville, supported the Ḥammūdite caliph at Málaga. But the king of Seville was then preoccupied in the western sector of the peninsula, and without becoming entangled overmuch in the affairs of this region, he fostered good relations with the Berber princes to mask his intentions.

The rulers of Granada—and Samuel ha-lēvī in particular—did not entertain any delusions. They did all they could to influence the Berbers and to bring them into their camps; emissaries were sent to the Berbers and they sent emissaries to Granada. Samuel pulled the strings, of course. To this one a promise that his principality would be enlarged was given, to that one a donation; but the policy of the chiefs of Granada sought mainly to alert those powerful but shortsighted princes to the evil lurking for them in the north, in Seville.

The king of Seville did not sit idly by; he pursued his instigations and enticements, and his labors were not in vain. In the spring of 1045 Samuel ha-lēvī left Granada to link up with a force designed to impose the authority of Bādīs over a rebelling district in the northern sector of the state. Instead of going there by the direct route through the valley of the Guadalbollon River and crossing the mountains north of Granada, he descended into the valley of the Genil River.

Since this was not a military action during a war against another state, Samuel did not view it as perilous and took his son Joseph with him. But he had already sent Joseph back because the boy was homesick, and had reached the western province of the kingdom when he rode directly into an ambush laid for him. Abū Nūr, the ruler of Ronda, had infiltrated Granada with just a few troops after his spies informed him of the route the Jewish vizier was expected to take. Abū Nūr lurked for Samuel where the river valley was especially narrow. He himself, with a detachment of his élite horsemen, stood hidden by tall bushes; behind a hill on the opposite side he placed other troops, among whom were foot soldiers who would attack at the strategic moment. Since Samuel's retinue had not taken the precautions customary in a military venture, there was utter surprise and total confusion when fully armed horsemen suddenly stormed relentlessly down upon the file of Granadans. Samuel and his horse sprang into the river, whose waters were very high in the springtime. His horse swam swiftly and surely to the other bank, but Abū Nūr's horsemen, who wore armor and were laden with heavy shields and lances, did not dare to enter the river. Their swords and lances were useless against Samuel or those of his men who followed his example. The foot soldiers began shooting their bows, but although their arrows hummed around Samuel's head, they miraculously did not touch him, and the attack was foiled.[81]

One would naturally suppose that after this underhanded scheme the relations between the kingdom of Granada and the principality of Ronda would worsen, that Abū Nūr would be more tightly bound to the king of Seville. But the Berber prince anticipated an act of reprisal and because he did not want to rely on the help of al-Mu'taḍid, he reconciled his differences with the king of Granada and made a treaty of peace with him.[82]

After Abū Nūr rejected the king of Seville as his ally, al-Mu'taḍid induced the other Berber rulers to go to war against the kingdom of Granada. Thus began a protracted engagement between the Ṣinhādja and the Berbers of southern Andalusia —prompted only by the crafty Sevillian who intended to drain the resources of Granada and to weaken it by luring his peers into warring for him while he spent nothing.

The war first erupted between the kingdom of Granada and the principalities of Carmona and Morón, which entered into an alliance of amity and defense directed against the king of Granada. When the provocations which were the customary prelude to war began, the rulers at Granada decided not to wait for the spring, the normal season for military campaigning, but instead to begin the battle without delay. In the winter of 1045–46 the army was mobilized, and Samuel went with it on a punitive expedition against the Berber princes. The files of Granadans penetrated to the provinces of Ossuna and Morón, struck the enemy, captured cities, and took much booty.[83]

But the two Berber princes, who acted under instigation from Seville, showed no sign that they would thenceforth live in peace with the kingdom of Granada; instead, they gave rather clear indications that they meant to pursue their action. Because of this the war continued into the spring of 1046. Again Samuel went with the army to raid the enemy's territory. This time too the Granadans were victorious. They destroyed villages, plundered towns, returned laden with spoils.[84] As a result of this war, in which the Granadans were the aggressors, the kingdom of the Ṣinhādja was substantially strengthened.

The army was increased and the area of the state was enlarged. The Ḥammūdite prince of Málaga, Idrīs II (surnamed al-'Ālī), who reigned from the beginning of 1043, was a weak man who was prepared to yield to demands from various sides. He handed his vizier, Mūsā b. 'Affān, over to the Granadans even though he knew they would slay him; he also ceded to them several cities and fortresses in his principality; and he permitted the rulers of Ronda to annex a part of the districts which belonged to Málaga to their principality.

The king of Seville, who followed these events closely—a development which he did not favor—once again directed his energy against the principality of Ronda. After the rulers of Carmona and Morón had absorbed the beatings from the Granadans, al-Mu'taḍid persuaded Abū Nūr to renounce the peace treaty he had made with Bādīs and to launch an armed offense against him. So it was that during the autumn of 1046 the heads of the government of Granada were compelled to send an army to its southwestern border, which, because of the annexation of those Málagan cities, had been moved beyond the city of Antequera. Samuel ha-lēvī also took part in this campaign.[85]

Meanwhile, once again a serious conflict had broken out in the principality of Málaga, and a short time later the neighboring states were drawn into it. A powerful faction which was dissatisfied with the rule of Idrīs revolted against him, naming his nephew, Muḥammad b. Idrīs, as his successor. Idrīs turned to King Bādīs with a request that he help him return to rule. The king of Granada, who during the reign of Idrīs had wielded broad influence in Málaga and hoped one day to convert that principality into a province of his kingdom, was naturally displeased by the removal of the prince who was his cat's-paw. He responded to the prince's plea, not out of concern for his welfare, but from misgivings that the revolt in Málaga would frustrate his own designs.

When it became known in Málaga that Granada was preparing a campaign against the new ruler, the latter sought help from the prince of Ronda, Abū Nūr, who was anxious to keep Málaga from coming under the control of Bādīs. He therefore responded willingly to the appeal for aid, and when Bādīs, together with Idrīs, attacked Málaga in the beginning of the summer of 1047, he failed utterly. This failure jolted Bādīs, for he had hoped to move decisively toward his goal: The annexation of Málaga to his kingdom. Instead of placing the conduct of the campaign in the hands of his vizier, he himself had gone to the battlefield only to have his master plan torn asunder—and all because of the active help of his enemy, Abū Nūr. In total vexation he decided to crush Abū Nūr by attacking his capital, Ronda, that very summer.

After much preparation, a strong Granadan force penetrated the high mountains of Ronda and by exceptional stealth advanced to the capital of the principality. This was a difficult sortie: high mountains and bare, precipitous slopes exposed the martial ranks to savage onslaughts as they advanced into narrow valleys and scaled the lofty crevices—the searing heat was debilitating.

The prince of Ronda called upon the king of Seville, who sent him troops under the command of the eunuch Mukhtār, the commander of his cavalry. The prince of Málaga, grateful to Abū Nūr for his aid against Bādīs and fearful that he might be encircled by the Granadans should they indeed capture Ronda, also went to his assistance.

Ronda itself was a powerful fortress, and before even attempting its capture the Granadans had to subdue the enemy. Since their best troops were cavalry, Abū Nūr and the Sevillian forces preferred battle in the open field rather than a campaign involving siege. For several days early in September 1047 the armies stood facing each other in the Guadiaro valley without armed conflict, but eventually a merciless battle burst like flame; the attacks by the cavalry were made again and yet again, but by evening Abū Nūr and his allies were forced to retreat, locking themselves inside Ronda. The Ṣinhādja pursued. They slew many men and captured several high-ranking officers—Mukhtār himself was caught and killed.

Samuel ha-lēvī, although he was unusually worn by this campaign, nevertheless regarded the victory as an extraordinary success: This time one poem was insufficient to describe the battle. Samuel thus composed two long ones in which he relates the course of the war in detail.[86] However, the Granadans rejected the idea of the capture of Ronda itself, for they could not dare risk a siege which might last into the winter; so they returned to their own land.

The king of Granada intended to exploit this successful campaign to its utmost. Feverish consultations took place in Granada, and Samuel played his usual leading role, though he sought, in his manner, to attribute his advice and suggestions to others. The first problem with which the leaders of Granadan policy struggled was that of the Ḥammūdite caliphs. After what had occurred in the principality of Málaga, the Ṣinhādja were unable to pray on Friday for the peace of the "Ruler of all the Faithful" in Málaga, their normal way of expressing their recognition of the caliph. Yet the election of a new caliph was necessary for them—not only to legitimitize Ṣinhādjan authority in the eyes of the Moslem faithful, but also to draw other princes and to establish an alliance for themselves.

The time was ripe. The Berber princes of southern Andalusia, profoundly impressed with Bādīs's campaign against Ronda, were ready to forsake the king of Seville and to join the king of Granada. Consequently, the rulers at Granada decided to select as caliph the Ḥammūdite prince Muḥammad b. al-Ḳāsim, the ruler of Algeciras. The emissaries went posthaste to the courts of the Berber principalities urging them to join the Granadans; the heads of the states agreed to go themselves to Algeciras to swear allegiance to the new caliph. In the autumn of 1047 there came to this city, which is situated at the southern end of Spain, the king of Granada; Isḥāḳ, the prince of Carmona; Muḥammad b. Nūḥ, the prince of Morón; and 'Abdūn b. Khizrūn, the prince of Arcos; they proclaimed the Ḥammūdite prince to be caliph. The king of Badajoz, who ruled over a broad region in the western part of the Iberian peninsula, and the prince of Huelva also acknowledged their recognition of the new caliph.[87]

This was a salient triumph for the foreign policy of the kingdom of Granada—conducted by Samuel ha-lēvī. His contemporary Arabic writers note that despite being a Jew he wrote the official correspondence in pure Moslem style (even including the blessings accorded to Allah and his Prophet Mohammed in their traditional form); however, they fail to mention how he even chose their caliph—a fact of which they must have been unaware. The recognition of this caliph by the Berbers in Andalusia was nearly total. Abū Nūr, the ruler of Ronda, was alone among the Berber princes in not doing so; the Ḥammūdite, Muḥammad b. Idrīs, ruler of Málaga, lacked power and influence and was of little consequence. The selection of the caliph and the visit of the princes to Algeciras was politically significant. Practically speaking, Samuel succeeded in creating an alliance of kings directed against the Arab kingdom of Seville.

Al-Mu'taḍid, the king of Seville, was fully cognizant of Samuel's primacy in directing the policy of Granada; he therefore exploited Samuel's Jewishness to denigrate him before Arabs and Berbers alike.[88] His court poets worked mightily, composing verse in which they depicted the Ṣinhādja as Moslems outwardly but Jews at heart.[89] Despite his well-planned subterfuges, the king of Seville suffered still another reversal; his faithful ally Abū Nūr, the ruler of Ronda, turned away from him. Abū Nūr annulled his recognition of the pseudo-Hishām and chose as his caliph the Ḥammūdite Idrīs, who had been driven from Málaga.

Success breeds success. Bādīs, the king of Granada, hoped to press his advantage and to bring such defeat to the king of Seville that his expansionist policy would be frustrated for a long time to come. By the spring of 1048, acting in concert with his allies, Bādīs penetrated enemy territory. Bādīs, with the princes of Carmona, Morón, and Arcos, led an invasion of Seville from the west, while the king of Badajoz moved in from the north. The allies destroyed the rich farming districts of the country, concentrating on the region of ash-Sharaf, west of Seville, which was renowned for its olive trees and its horse farms. The Berbers plundered everywhere, killing peasants who refused to reveal where their money and valuables were hidden; they set fire to houses, leveled fruit trees, and burned the standing grain to ashes. The Ṣinhādja in particular vented their hatred against the rulers of Seville. Consumed with rage, they moved from village to village, leaving smoldering forests and rising columns of smoke.

The allies then laid siege to Seville itself. But the siege of the big city, which was protected on one side by the Guadalquivir, failed. And even as success breeds success, so failure leads to failure. When the allies were compelled to suspend the siege, a number of the Berber princes seceded from the alliance.[90] Since they could not overcome the king of Seville—even when they acted collectively under the leadership of Bādīs—they concluded that al-Mu'taḍid was the stronger and destined to win the struggle for superiority in Andalusian politics.

This campaign, on which the rulers of Granada had placed such great hopes, was the turning point in the relations between their kingdom and its neighbors to the west. Up to now Granada had been the aggressor, but after this unsuccessful venture it was forced into a posture of defense. Samuel ha-lēvī, who had been the architect of the alliance of the kings, was taken aback: the structure which he erected had collapsed like a house of cards. Such are the fortunes of politics—there is no surety and what today appears sound and strong may disappear by tomorrow.

However, the determined draftsman of Granada's policy renewed his efforts to achieve his objective: to win allies for the Ṣinhādja kingdom and to prevent its encirclement by the king of Seville.

Meanwhile, Muḥammad b. al-Ḳāsim, the "caliph" of Algeciras, died, whereupon Samuel advised the king to make peace with Muḥammad b. Idrīs, the Ḥammūdite Prince of Málaga, and to recognize him as the caliph. Of course, Bādīs hearkened to Samuel's counsel and did as he proposed. In accordance with the fashion of Moslem Spain's politics, recognition also denoted a political alliance. So when Bādīs dispatched a force to capture a fortress and annex the district to his kingdom in April 1049, the prince of Málaga provided him with supporting troops.

Samuel ha-lēvī, who was in command, conducted operations energetically but cautiously—all signs indicated that the siege would end with the capture of the fortress. But once again the unexpected intervened. At the decisive moment of battle, the Málagan leaders, reversing their political decision, left the command tent. Their desertion was plainly visible to the besieged who stormed forth at once and took Samuel captive. The soldiers who had heard about him, and knew that he was the progenitor of Granada's policy, wanted to kill him forthwith—their wildly jubilant shouting and their very gestures clearly indicated this. Once again Samuel was in gravest danger.

But the enemy officers rebuked their men, for they had another plan. A heated debate ensued among them. Samuel felt each second as it dragged by, his end apt to come the next minute. In torment, he hastily reviewed the course of his life

—its successes and its failures, its joys and sorrows. He prepared to meet his fate and even as he witnessed the wrangling over his life, he made a vow that if he was indeed spared he would perform an extraordinary deed of reverence and piety. His loyal Granadans marshaled their forces and freed him.[91] Samuel escaped death. His hoped-for alliance with Málaga fell apart.

The foreign policy of the kingdom of Granada became progressively worse; however, under the political conditions then prevailing in Andalusia, it was impossible for the rulers of Granada to accept the idea of remaining isolated and inactive in the diplomatic arena for even a little while. The relations between the Hispano-Moslem states were so frequently shifting that there was no room for defeatism. And before long the gate of opportunity opened again. At the start of 1050 it seemed that the grand alliance of the Berber rulers against the kingdom of Seville would be renewed.

Al-Muẓaffar, the king of Badajoz and himself a Berber, made an alliance with Bādīs and the prince of Carmona; the Berber rulers then attacked Seville. But, after some initial successes, Al-Muẓaffar suffered crushing defeats. Meanwhile, Bādīs vacated the western region of Seville. Al-Mu'taḍid succeeded in persuading the prince of Málaga to invade Granada while its army was tied down by war in the west. When Bādīs heard that the troops of Málaga were raiding the villages of Granada, he immediately ordered a retreat. Near the southwestern border of the kingdom of Granada the ranks of the Ṣinhādja encountered the Málagan and, in severe reprisal, slew numerous men, chiefs, and officers. Samuel ha-lēvī, who took part in all these actions, saw the hand of God in the defeat of the army of Málaga—a punishment for their treachery against him in the previous year—and, as was his wont, he expressed his feelings in ornate poetry.[92] Soon the prince of Málaga himself paid dearly for his own treachery.

But these acts of vengeance were small matters, leaving the political situation unchanged. As a result of the failures of Granada's policy, the kingdom of Seville grew considerably stronger. Inasmuch as its enemies exhibited a lack of ability, nearly all the Berber princes of southern Andalusia once more went over to the side of Al-Mu'taḍid. The prince of Morón did this without much hesitation, particularly since the kingdom of Seville had increased in size and become a more palpable threat to his territory. In the latter part of 1051 and during 1052 al-Mu'taḍid had annexed to his kingdom the tiny principalities of southwestern Andalusia, wherein Arabs and *muwalladūn* ruled: first Niebla, then Huelva, Silves, and Santa Maria. The annexation of these principalities enlarged the kingdom of Seville substantially and endowed it with added strength to undertake new activities. Indeed, al-Mu'taḍid was simultaneously occupied in the west and in the regions east of Seville.

His primary goal in the east was the nearby principality of Carmona. As a first step toward its conquest, the king of Seville sought to sow divisiveness and envy among the Berbers ruling Carmona, endeavoring especially to foment strife within the prince's family. A short time later he also launched a military action which would ultimately embroil the Granadans. In the spring of 1052, Sevillian troops as well as troops of Berbers from among Seville's allies penetrated to the district of Ossuna, which belonged then, as it had formerly, to the principality of Carmona and which bordered upon the kingdom of Granada. The invaders laid siege to one of the fortresses in this region and raided the entire vicinity. The prince of Carmona called for help from the king of Granada, who was his ally, and inasmuch as the Ṣinhādja themselves were interested in keeping the army of Seville far from their borders, Bādīs responded to the request. Samuel ha-lēvī, at the head of the army which went out against Seville, depicted the progress of the battle in one of his poems.

As the Granadans drew near, the troops of Seville raised the siege against the fortress and shut themselves into another. This fortress was strong and the Granadans had considerable difficulty in controlling their siege of it; but when the Sevillians would make a sortie, many of them were felled by the Granadans. Thus, after their political failures, the leaders of Granada viewed this campaign as a success.[93]

The heavy aggression of the king of Seville continued without letup, and in that same year, 1052, Samuel was compelled to go to war a second time. But within two weeks the enemy retreated, to Samuel's great joy; there were only a few days until the first of Tishri, and he strongly desired to spend the New Year holiday and Succot with his family.[94] Although the invasions by al-Mu'taḍid's armies did not result in losses of either men or property for the Granadans, Bādīs regarded this as a new challenge by the prince of Málaga. Bādīs swiftly responded. He sent Muḥammad b. Idrīs a gift—a cup of poison—the prince died within three days.

There was no abatement in the political turmoil involving the princes of Moslem Spain during the eleventh century. When the fighting ceased—for a while—in one region, it broke out in another. Throughout all those years in which Samuel was the chief vizier of the kingdom of Granada, there was practically no year in which he did not have to go to war. In the spring of 1053 there was quiet on the western front because the king of Seville was preoccupied with consolidating his authority within the new provinces of his kingdom. But then Bādīs was called upon to give support to his ally in eastern Spain, the king of Almería.

At that time Almería was ruled by Muḥammad b. Ma'n, who succeeded his father in 1051. Because this prince was a young boy, his neighbors attempted to attack Almería and tear from it various regions, large and small; even the governors of the provinces raised the standard of revolt. That year ʿAbdalʿazīz, the king of Valencia, and the king of Toledo joined together and, in collaboration with the governor of the province of Lorca, penetrated the kingdom of Almería. Muhammad b. Maʿn's uncle, who was the most powerful person in the kingdom of Almería, went out at the head of its army to face this array of kings; he also sent a plea for assistance to the king of Granada. Since the preservation of good relations with the neighboring kingdom to the east was still an important principle in the policy of Granada, Bādīs himself led his army; he had with him, as usual, his vizier, Samuel ha-lēvī.

Once again the warriors of the Ṣinhādja army climbed over the mountains, and after a tiring campaign they reached a coastal city which the enemies of Almería were besieging. As always, the king of Valencia had brought with him not only his Slavs but also Catalan mercenaries, whereas the king of Toledo's army was composed almost entirely of Berbers. When the ranks of Granadans suddenly appeared, the enemy retreated and the siege of the city was lifted; but the war itself ended unfavorably. The kingdom of Almería lost most of its provinces.[95]

VI

In 1053 the sixty-year-old Samuel ha-lēvī could survey his life with much pleasure despite his various political failures. He could surely say with justification that all matters in the kingdom of Granada came to pass by his word. One Arabic poet accused the Jews in authority in Granada of not only enriching themselves and flaunting their wealth, but also of taking Moslem wives.[96] But Samuel's power was so great that most of his enemies suppressed and concealed their own inflammatory thoughts—he determined the course of government in every area. Notwithstanding that he was a Jew, the Berbers properly appreciated his worth; their praise and esteem was known everywhere. No other Jew was ever the first minister of the government and commander of the army of a Moslem kingdom.

No doubt he derived intense satisfaction from his high position—which had, after all, been his goal in the faraway days of his youth. In a military campaign in 1046 he passed the very place where the group of refugees with whom he had reached Málaga had tarried. Recognizing the area, he compared his situation at that time with his later greatness and wrote:

Do you recall, O sandy pass,
As with my staff I traversed you, atremble in flight?
While today I pass through you, and behind me
Follow myriads who, like their fathers, obey me.[97]

These verses are not empty boasting; they reflect the individualistic approach that was characteristic of Spaniards of that era. The success of Samuel Ibn Nagrīla was exceptional. Indeed, in those Moslem states the fate of men depended upon the arbitrary will of kings—dignitaries were appointed and removed frequently; but Samuel retained his post for decades. Envy and hatred prevailed among the Berber chiefs and the Andalusians were masters of intrigue; yet, as if he were a superior being, they set no snares against Samuel. Although he was a truly fortunate man, mere good luck did not account for his status.

Samuel ha-lēvī was a total Spaniard—all his emotions and desires were dictated by the spirit of his age. Like all his countrymen, he was vindictive and unforgiving. His desire for vengeance was as strong as any of his contemporaries, and he showed no mercy to his foes. Although he endeavored to conceal his pride, he still enumerated his privileges and attainments daily, even hourly. The Andalusians of Hispano-Christian origin would invent long genealogies for themselves to show the high station of their ancestors—Arab nobility and Moslem heroes—and the Berbers imitated them. Samuel ha-lēvī held that the merit of his forebears, who had sung in the choir of the Temple, exceeded theirs,[98] and, of course, he despised all those officials who daily awaited his downfall and all those chiefs whose hands were outstretched to harm him whenever trouble brewed.

Notwithstanding his loyalty to the king of the Ṣinhādja and his devoted service to him, he never identified with the Berbers and had no desire even to appear as one. He was a proud Jew who saw himself continuing the great tradition of prophets and sages, and although he was involved in politics and warfare, he was a man of profound religious feelings. To this eleventh-century man there was no contradiction between his loyal activities in behalf of the Ṣinhādja and his loyalty to his faith and to his people. Both were completely honest loyalties. Besides being the solution to Jewish life in alien lands which Jews fell back upon in a multinational, multireligious country, it was also the characteristic union of secularism and religion in the Middle Ages.

Like al-Manṣūr, who made a copy of the Koran with his own hands, Samuel had the time to produce copies of all the books of the Bible.[99] The compelling drive behind his climb up the precipitous slope of royal service was his desire for power and fame. However, when Samuel ha-lēvī became the chief vizier of the kingdom of Granada he saw the work of God, who raises up chiefs and princes in behalf of His downtrodden people. Samuel regarded his personal enemies as enemies of the Jews, his victories as those of his people everywhere. He convinced himself that this was fact, that it was not his personal glory for which his soul yearned all his many years. He ordered that his triumphs be announced to the Jewish communities in the East and West and be celebrated as Purimlike days, so they would be remembered throughout all generations. His subjective evaluation of his position may have been unjustified, although it certainly had some valid, objective basis. After being at the helm of Granada's government for many years, his own fate and the fate of the Jewish community in Granada were wedded —his downfall was more than likely to bring catastrophe upon his people.

When Samuel went to war, he was no different from his contemporaries. On the eve of battle he would supplicate the Creator, as was the custom among all Spaniards in that era. At the clash of troops and swords, fear and trembling seized him; and as the Spanish Christians saw Saint James doing battle in their behalf, so Samuel would imagine he beheld angels of the Lord hastening to help him. His faith strengthened his belief in his mission and his certainty of its success.

But the never-ending struggle, the personal exertion, the worries and troubles, and especially the numerous military campaigns took their toll; he aged prematurely and complained of weakness and pain, so that by the time he was fifty-five years old, he felt that he was an old man.[100] And he still had many important projects to accomplish.

VII

Throughout his life Samuel ha-lēvī was a man of the pen, creating works both long and short. His literary creations testify to his exceptional talents no less than does the course of his political life. In the field of literature he towered over the intellectuals of his era who wrote of their meditations. Most of them tested their talents in one or two branches of literature and science, but Samuel was highly accomplished in many widely disparate fields.

He was first a gifted Hebrew poet whose compositions are unmatched in Jewish poesy. Most of the Hebrew poets among the Jews of Spain (at least those whose verse has been preserved) wrote poems in praise of their benefactors, songs of friendship, elegies, and sacred verse especially. Samuel ha-lēvī, who was himself wealthy and prominent, did not create verse on commission but, rather, when moved by his own spirit; he left behind a sort of poetical diary. To be sure, all the types of Hebrew poetry produced by Jewish poets in Spain can be found in Samuel ha-lēvī's collections of verse. He too wrote of being parted from friends, praised the character of his companions, and mocked those who did not sympathize with him. But, in addition, in some of the traditional branches of poetry he is superior to the other Hebrew poets in Spain—both those who preceded and those who followed him. His drinking songs are particularly successful, even though in form and content they are not different from those of other Hebrew poets of that period. Because these poems, mostly short, describe personal experiences, they are brimming with life even while they are set in a fixed mold: a description of trees in a garden, the flowers and carpets where a feast is prepared. Like other men of that epoch who were eager to fully enjoy their brief life-span as it sped by, Samuel indulged in drinking and urged the rest of mankind to do likewise.[101]

Samuel's love poems are also among the most outstanding verse of the Hebrew poets in Spain. These verses constitute a stylized description, a literary sport whose aim is to delight the reader. Even though these descriptions of maidens and handsome youths—who, as it were, shoot their arrows into the heart of the poet—are basically no different from those of the other poets, Samuel excels because of his complete mastery of all devices of the Hebrew-Arabic verse of that age. Since he was the master of form and composed easily in many metric patterns, the verse which Samuel authored is perfect from a variety of aspects.[102]

But there is one verse form in which Samuel ha-lēvī particularly distinguished himself, poems unlike any in the Jewish literature of that age. As a commander frequently going forth to war, he had the opportunity to experiment with descriptions of battle. From his earliest years he had displayed a marked proclivity for epic verse (as demonstrated by his epopee on a voyage by sea in his youth).[103] His long descriptions of armed combat are his most characteristic creations and give him a special place in the history of Jewish literature. It is true that Arabic influence is recognizable in them—in their form, in their imagery and metaphors; but the Jewish spirit also pulsates in them, for he emphasizes in verse his unbreakable ties to the faith of his fathers. This stress on faith is not artificial but, rather, a frank expression by a Jewish warrior confronting death and drawing upon all the inner resources with which he can surmount his terror. Having withstood the test of his fear and having buttressed his determination, he went on to relish the fighting and never tired of expressing his personal reactions.

His poems depict at great length the progress of the battle—the slaughter of the foe, the corpses devoured by beasts of prey, his elation at the misery of the widows and children of fallen soldiers. The poet repeatedly stresses that he has won a victory through the merit of his saintly forbears and that the God of Israel is his deliverer. Nevertheless, one can only wonder at his wholehearted enthusiasm for the wars between the kingdom of Granada and its neighbors and his willing self-sacrifice in his struggle over one or another fortress despite the apparent conflict with his loyalty to the prophecy concerning Israel. His yearnings for the days of old are interwoven like a silken strand throughout his verse. In his heart the poet does, however, deem himself to be the "David of his generation,"[104] a scholar and a warrior fighting in behalf of his people—and describing his battle in the same terms as did the author of the Psalms. But the contrast between the incandescence which is reflected in the description of the wars of the Berbers and Arabs and the intense longing for the redemption of Israel and Zion which bursts forth in his poetry is still amazing to a reader of a later age. In the poet's view, the longings for the return to Zion were sincere, but they were a messianic hope, a vision of the millennium; hence he did not regard the wars of the Sinhādja as being outside his concern.[105] He believed that he was not alien in Spain, and his attitude to the Jewish dream of the future was that of any observant Jew in medieval times. In Samuel the *nāgīd*'s world of thought and feelings there were no contradictions: As a Spaniard of the eleventh century, he believed with a perfect faith that God directs the course of battles and even participates in them, since for people of that age the two worlds—the one which we grasp through our senses and the world beyond the reach of our senses—were one.

What was most conspicuous in the approach to life's problems by those generations was the bleak pessimism which colored their feelings and reactions. Because the range of the unknown was vast and the impotence in the face of natural perils so marked, humans were oppressed by insecurity and fear all their lives. The poetical works of Samuel ha-lēvī vividly reflect these feelings, especially the profoundly moving elegies he composed upon the death of his brother and the verses lamenting the signs of old age.[106] The awe of death expressed in these poems, which is manifested in intensified piety on the one hand, and the advocation of a life of drinking and merriment, of turning night into day, on the other—these two streams of thought derived from the same source: man's helplessness in the Middle Ages. Thus a complete, homogeneous man appears to later generations as a split personality abounding in contradictions.

With the aid of his sons Samuel arranged his poetry in three collections, giving them the names of biblical books which are related to them in content: *Ben T'hillīm* ("Son of Psalms"), *Ben Mishlē* ("Son of Proverbs"), and *Ben Ḳōhelet* ("Son of Ecclesiastes"). The first collection, containing sacred verse, has not been preserved.[107] The two other compilations are collections of epigrams, culled in part from the ancient Jewish and Gentile literature and in part from the writer's own thinking. Aside from the Bible and the *aggada* and *midrashim* (folkloric and homiletic Hebrew literature), the most important sources were the Arabic books for amusement—especially the *Kalīla wa-dimna,* which had been translated from Persian to Arabic in the middle of the eighth century, and the books *'Uyūn al-akhbār* by Ibn Ḳutaiba (died 889) and *Al-'Iḳd al-farīd* by Ibn 'Abd Rabbihi (died 940).[108] The selection of proverbs and aphorisms was, however, not a mere literary exercise but was linked to the various circumstances at different stages of Samuel's life, which explains the frequent contradictions reflected in the many maxims in *Ben Mishlē.*[109] One finds epigrams expressing faith in man alongside warnings not to put one's trust in man, proverbs which teach the virtue of being content with little and sayings extolling wealth, and maxims proclaiming the moral obligation to forgive one's foe as well as sayings abounding in a lust for revenge.[110]

The smaller *Ben Ḳōhelet,* which contains only one-third the content of *Ben Mishlē,* has aphorisms on only a few subjects: the mystery of life, life and death, youth and old age and God's decrees, the insignificance of man, substance and wealth, wisdom and folly, labor and ease.[111] This compilation also demonstrates amply the great literary ability of Samuel ha-lēvī, for whom it was not enough merely to discharge maxims from one vessel into another: He created a new literary product notable for its precision of thought and its brevity.

Aside from being a multitalented poet, Samuel ha-lēvī was also a student of the Hebrew language, and from time to time he wrote treatises on questions of grammar.[112] As he neared old age, he started to prepare a large lexicon, a treasury of the language of the Bible, which he called *Kitāb al-Istiyḥnā* ("The Book of Riches"). This lexicon, written in Arabic, is arranged alphabetically, and each entry is divided into three sections: a list of all the meanings of the root, explanations by grammarians and biblical commentators of words derived from a given root found in Scripture, and a list of grammatical forms deriving from it. Because of the extended quotations from exegetical literature, such as the work of the Saadya Gaon, Samuel's lexicon attained such large dimensions that it is doubtful he succeeded in finishing it. But no matter. Even in this area he deserves to be given merit as a pioneer, for he was one of the first to compile such a lexicon.[113]

Yet more: This statesman-poet-philologist found time to write commentaries on books of the Bible. His commentaries, whether or not he completed them, have been lost, except for quotations in the works of later writers. But from these quotations the principle their author adopted may be plainly discerned: He commented on Scripture verbatim, not turning to homiletic exegesis unless the context made this absolutely necessary.[114]

The versatility and productivity of Samuel ha-lēvī is astonishing. How many men could succeed in such numerous and diversified disciplines? Yet his most amazing achievement surely was the writing of a treatise against the Koran. To be sure, during the Middle Ages there were many Jewish scholars who dared advance arguments against the Islamic faith and even give them circulation by committing them to writing. But these treatises were usually written in Hebrew and rarely found their way into Moslem hands. Moreover, the writers were generally scholars whom the Moslem masses did not know, nor were they prominent in communal life. Not so Samuel ha-lēvī, whose station was anathema to fanatic Moslems.

The content of Samuel's treatise was an affront to Moslems. Most of the writings about Islam by Jewish scholars were comprehensive theological essays or polemics defending Judaism against the arguments of the Moslems, who sought to demonstrate from the Bible that Mohammed was a real prophet, and so on. But the Jews were careful not to denigrate the sacred book of the Moslems. And then along came Samuel to point out the Koran's contradictions and errors. He called attention to Sura 41:8–11, where it is stated that the world was created in eight days, while according to Sura 32:3 it was created in six days. He juxtaposed the statement in Sura 55:39 that on the Day of Judgment no man would be asked to account for his deeds with that in Sura 7:5, which states the very opposite view. It is true that the contradictions Samuel pointed out occurred in Suras written at various times, but he also found discrepancies in verses in the selfsame Sura. In Sura 4:90 it is stated that both the good and the bad stem from God, while in verse 91 the view is expressed that whatever good befalls one comes from God, but evil originates in the person himself.

When this treatise came to the attention of the Moslems it provoked outright anger. The very appointment of an infidel to the office of vizier in a Moslem state constituted a violation of the laws of Islam, which forbade giving a non-Moslem dominance over those who are devotees of the religion of Mohammed. Now this particular Jew exacerbated the fury by profaning their sacred book. The theologians were prompt to react to his treatises with their own polemic works. One of these, by 'Alī Ibn Ḥazm, has been preserved. This great Moslem theologian and author and Samuel ha-lēvī had carried on a debate many years before, in 1013. Since then Ibn Ḥazm had broadened his education and his knowledge of Judaism had deepened, as *Al-Fiṣal li 'l-milal wa'n-niḥal,* the treatise on religions that he wrote at the end of the 1020s, demonstrates. In this sweeping book he sought to demonstrate that the Pentateuch is not a divine book but, rather, one written by ignorant men and replete with errors and actual blasphemy. In his polemical writing against Samuel ha-lēvī, Ibn Ḥazm reiterates what he had stated in his great work; then, after refuting Samuel's arguments, he again points out what he considered to be the contradictions, errors, and censurable parts in the Pentateuch. His argument runs thus: According to the Pentateuch the prophets (as the heroes of the Bible are called by the Moslems) are sinners; for in Genesis 12:13 and 20:2 we are told that Sarah was the sister of Abraham and in Genesis 38 we are told that Judah had carnal relations with his daughter-in-law; Exodus 6:20 states that Amram married his aunt Jochebed, who "bore him Aaron and Moses." According to the laws of the Scriptures it is forbidden to marry two sisters at the same time, yet we find that Jacob married Leah and Rachel; and even if the Jews were to argue that this was permissible at the time, they would be accepting the principle of "abrogation" (the assumption that God alters the laws He gave mankind)—which is one of the chief arguments by the Moslems against the Jews. Ibn Ḥazm lists what he considers to be anthropomorphic expressions found in the Pentateuch, such as, "The Lord is a man of war" (Exodus 15:3), and criticizes Judaism because Genesis 32:31 states that Jacob saw God face to face and Exodus 24:9–10 says that Moses, Aaron, Nadab, and Abihu and seventy elders of Israel saw Him—despite the fact that according to Exodus 33:20 this is impossible.

To be sure, Ibn Ḥazm had already advanced such arguments in full in his great work on religions. But since then the circumstances of his life, his approach to religious problems, and even his temperament had undergone a change. The young intellectual who engaged in amatory pursuits, politics, and literature had become a stern, embittered theologian surveying the failure of his ambitions. He who had dreamed of the revival of the Omayyad caliphate at Cordova could only regard with consternation the appointment of a Jewish vizier and regard this as decisive proof of how much Spain had come under the dominance of the usurping kings. Himself the son of a vizier, Ibn Ḥazm had been reared in affluence but was now impoverished, wandering from place to place, persecuted by the new rulers. At the same time he heard a great deal about the status and wealth of the Jew from Cordova who had become a high dignitary in Granada. So it is not astonishing that he was enraged when he learned about the treatise against the Koran which Samuel ha-lēvī had written.

But apparently there was another reason for his anger against Samuel. According to an Arab writer, in 1038 Ibn Ḥazm served in the army of Zuhair, king of Almería; taken captive by the Granadans, he found himself in mortal danger but was freed by Bādīs.[115] This incident was not forgotten, and in addition to arguments against the Bible, his polemic against Samuel hurls invectives at the king of Granada for appointing a Jew as vizier, like other "provincial kings" who consciously broke Moslem law and gave dominance to Jews so that they could enrich their exchequers. He points to Samuel as one of the traitorous Jews who rose to greatness by this route, becoming so wealthy and so arrogant that they dare to insult even the things sacred to Islam. In this treatise, he castigates Samuel ha-lēvī writing, among other things, that he is an utter fool, vain and mad,[116] although in *al-Fiṣal* he unequivocally states that Samuel is the most learned Jew he has ever met.

Samuel ha-lēvī, poet and philologist, also wrote works dealing with halakha. He was, after all, a distinguished scholar who in his youth had been among the disciples of Rabbi Moses b. Ḥanōkh, the great rabbi of Cordova. On occasion, he would disengage himself from his official work, spend many hours meditating over the ponderous volumes of the Babylonian and Jerusalem talmuds, recording his own strictures and conclusions in halakhic matters. Shortly after his departure from Cordova he wrote a commentary in Arabic on obscure chapters in the Gemara. In his own commentary (its title is unknown) he criticized the commentaries of the *g'ōnīm,* the heads of the Babylonian academies—especially those of the *gaon* Rabbi Hai. Written under the influence of his teacher Rabbi Ḥanōkh, Samuel's commentary was meant to attack the heads of the academies in Babylonia while stressing the greatness of the Spanish scholars.[117]

Many years later Samuel began a large work on the interpretation then in vogue of the laws. Written in rabbinic style, in Hebrew, entitled *Hilkh'ta g'bharātā* ("The Great Law"). Samuel had in mind writing a book that was more complete, precise, and organized than *Halākhōt g'dōlōt,* which many relied upon in his day. His method is to cite a halakha from the Gemara, juxtapose it to its counterpart in the Jerusalem Talmud, weave around it the words of the *g'ōnīm* as found in their responsa and writings, and then discuss them. In writing *Hilkh' ta g'bharāta* he was much influenced by the methodology of *Halākhōt g'dōlōt* and *Sefer ha-m'tībhōt,* which were written two or three generations earlier in Kairawan, and especially by Rabbi Ḥanōkh's method of instruction.[118] But unlike his commentary on the difficult chapters in the Gemara, this book reveals no special tendency to dispute the views of Rabbi Hai; on the contrary, he cites Hai's views copiously and with esteem. Just as circumstances of life altered for Spanish Jews, so did their attitude to the heads of the Babylonian academies; and, no doubt, during the years which passed since Samuel composed that commentary, his attitude also changed. It is clear that he devoted substantial time to the writing of this major work—a sort of compendium of the Talmud—and that his statement in the superscription of a poem written in 1049—that after being delivered from the hands of his enemies he vowed to write the *Hilkh'ta g'bhāratā*—is not precisely so. This may have prompted him to apply himself to this work with special diligence in order to bring it to a conclusion.[119] Old age was coming nearer, evinced by his increasing weakness, the affairs of the kingdom were a heavy burden, and military campaigns closely followed each other—who knew whether he would ever be able to gratify himself with the completed task.

VIII

Although harassed day and night by affairs of the kingdom and thoroughly immersed in literary projects, Samuel followed the custom of the other dignitaries in socializing with his intimates. A vizier in a Moslem kingdom did not live quietly apart from the community, but spent a good deal of time with friends and acquaintances.

Among the parties in the home of Samuel ha-lēvī, one was engraved in the memories of the guests as long as they lived. It took place on one of those long summer days when the heat of the afternoon fades quickly as evening approaches; a refreshing breeze wafted in from the high mountains east of the city. The *nāgīd*'s house sat on a hill above the Jewish neighborhood, and his guests, who lingered on the small balcony in front of the gate to the house, could enjoy the magnificent view of the sweeping valley of the Vega, which extended to the blue hills far off on the horizon. On the left the mountain slopes actually touched the edge of the city, and the outlying gardens clambered up them, their greenery mingling with the woods and underbrush which covered the cliffs. In the twilight hours a quiet hovered over the valley . . . neither voice nor rustle was audible . . . songbirds were at rest . . . hills, valley, and city became one—an all-encompassing oneness. The sun sent the last of its pink rays over the valley, tinting the mountainsides that kind of violet which settles into indigo when light is no more. Tranquillity spread over the world on this typical summer evening in 'Īr Rimmōn (Pomegranate City—Granada's Hebrew name).

The guests entered the house by way of a narrow corridor first opening onto a square court and then leading into a spacious salon, whose floors were covered with thick red carpets from Armenia. Rugs of puce and dark brown hung on the walls, and along their entire length were spread mattresses fashioned as divans covered with cushions of brocade and other precious cloth. The guests were dressed in white silken garments and wore the high, silk gauze hats called *ḳalansuwa.* Some wore cloaks with sleeves and collars trimmed in gold—the raiment of distinction that Moslem kings were wont to give anyone they wished to honor. There were old men as well as young, but the graybeards among them had dyed their hair the color of their younger years. A slave, garbed in wool, busied himself with small chores.

The *nāgīd* himself arrived, his tall figure bent, his white hair turbaned after the fashion of the Berbers. The invited guests arose and nodded to him as he held out his hand in a greeting of peace. He turned to this one and that one, inquiring about his health and about his family. The guests began chatting among themselves, and occasionally the echoes of faraway laughter and joyful cries could be heard. This was the night of Mahradjān, the festival of the longest day, which Christians and Moslems celebrated on June 24. The Granadans lit bonfires in the streets and disported themselves with revelry everywhere, but the Jews observed it rather modestly. The *nāgīd's* guests, about twenty people, were accustomed to the noise and paid no attention to it. They awaited a sign from their host, and when it was given they arose, turning to face the east. A guttural voice called out, "*Bār'khū*—Bless ye the

Lord who is blessed." They were reciting the evening prayer.

When the prayer ended two youths served ewers of wine containing fruit and piled quantities of cakes and sweets on low tables covered with leather cloths. The younger members of the party filled the exquisite glasses with wine and offered them to their elders, while bestowing blessings and good wishes upon each other; the conversation continued in a pleasant and dignified fashion. After a while one of the youths who studied at the talmudic academy recited a Hebrew poem, metered and in rhyme, whose last lines were in the Romance language. Again the chatting guests were offered drinks and fruits.

A man, tall and bearded, wearing a capacious cloak, came into the salon and was seated opposite the *nāgīd.* In flowery Arabic he began to recite a long poem. No one knew who the poet was, but after he left the *nāgīd* revealed that he was Abū Aḥmad ʿAbd alʿazīz Ibn Khīra, surnamed al-Munfatil. A Cordovan, he had corresponded with the *nāgīd* and sent him poetry;[120] the *nāgīd*'s guests marveled and expressed their enjoyment of the poet's composition. Samuel's intimates now surrounded him, and out of the good spirits his wines induced in them, addressed him by the name of Abū Ibrāhīm.

A band of musicians entered, garbed in scarlet and yellow cloaks, men whose long hair was parted in the middle. Sitting on a sort of divan, they opened with a tender and quiet melody, accompanied by their instruments—one plucked with an eagle's feather on a five-stringed, belly-shaped harp, others strummed guitars. Again the youths circulated among the guests serving a dough made of fruit studded with row after row of hazel-nuts and pistachios; the raucous call of a parrot evoked a delighted storm of laughter.

Later the guests went to the courtyard where, in the middle of a small garden, stood a fountain whose waters sprayed down upon the marble floor in a shimmering arc illuminated by candles concealed within.[121] Some reclined on low benches alongside the walls, and others strolled here and there; and now, as the host's eyes drooped, an indication that he was weary, his guests discreetly arose and left amid parting benedictions.

Nearly all those present that evening and at similar gatherings in the *nāgīd*'s house were government officials with responsible positions in the ministries. There were a considerable number of Jews in the service of King Bādīs. Those who held the higher posts were appointed directly by Samuel, and the rest received their positions through his recommendation or were engaged because the directors of bureaus wished to find favor with the Jewish vizier.

Most served in the treasury, particularly those bureaus dealing with tax collections—offices where Jews were in the majority.[122] Some did not work for wages but would lease the right to collect taxes in various districts, as was the practice in Moslem countries. The highest post among the Jewish officials was held by the *nāgīd's* brother-in-law, Abu 'r-Rabī' Ibn al-Maṭūnī. He was appointed overall tax collector and was named the minister of finance after Samuel ha-lēvī became chief vizier.[123] The Berber princes and governors who were in charge of the provinces also engaged numerous Jews, especially to handle the financial affairs of their districts and of their private estates.

Granadan Jews could, without fear, register a complaint with or make a request of the government—they were sure of the desire for justice and the righting of wrongs. Many became wealthy, acquiring land[124] and estates,[125] engaging in their livelihoods undisturbed, enjoying peace and security.

Samuel's greatness and the flourishing comfort of the Granadan Jews became known in lands near and far, bringing Jews from other Moslem states in Spain and from other lands to the Berber kingdom. Individuals and families migrated to

Granada to live under the protection of the *nāgīd;* persons in need sought recommendations to the *nāgīd* from his friends.[126] He responded willingly to such pleas for assistance from fellow Jews who turned to him and generally endeavored to help as much as he could.

The Jews in Spain referred to Samuel ha-lēvī simply by the title "the *nāgīd,*"—there was no need to use his given name. Indeed, he was not only the vizier of King Bādīs and the protector of his own people but also the head, the chief rabbi, of the Jewish community in the kingdom of Granada, a role he filled with an acute sense of responsibility. He did not tolerate quarrels or disputes within the communities, and he silenced conspirators and mischief-makers with great severity.[127] Every important lawsuit was brought before him, and legal questions were also directed to him in writing; drawing upon his vast knowledge, he would respond.[128]

Whenever possible he would also teach the sacred law in the talmudic academy. Those hours—when he was free of the burdens of government and, with his disciples, could plunge deeply into talmudic discussion—were particularly pleasant for him, giving him immense satisfaction.[129] The scholars listened eagerly to his explanations and in time, without a formal appointment, he became Rabbi Ḥanōkh's successor as chief rabbi of Spain.

He not only taught the students but supported them generously so they could continue to devote themselves to their study of the sacred law, the Torah. (Like the tradition in which Samuel ha-lēvī was reared, Arab nobles considered aid to those in want one of the finest of attributes.) The thick volumes of the Talmud were exceedingly costly, and often two or three students—or even more—had to share one book. Samuel paid scribes well to make copies of the holy texts, which he gave to penniless scholars and to talmudic schools. A number of scribes worked for him regularly, and they produced books renowned for their accuracy. Besides his gifts to the students at the schools of Granada, he supported scholars in other countries: Morocco and Tunisia and the Near East—Egypt, Palestine, and Babylonia.[130]

But the relations between Samuel and the scholars were not those of a rich, generous benefactor and impecunious beneficiaries. An outstanding, learned man himself, there were common interests linking them together in their meetings and exchanges of letters: their knowledge of the sacred law, their erudition and fresh interpretations, the books they had already written and those which they were preparing to write. Throughout his life Samuel sent them letters of friendship and poetry expressing his sentiments; he missed no opportunity to extend greetings to them. Anyone who was far away or for some reason had left his circle eventually realized that a successfully written Hebrew poem could make amends and heal the breach.[131] A man named Joseph wrote to Samuel ha-lēvī and his brother Isaac a girdle poem (a medieval Arabic verse form) whose closing lines were in Romance on the occasion of Samuel's offer to erect a synagogue in the city where Joseph served as cantor.[132] At one time the relations between the *nāgīd* and Joseph deteriorated, but later the two became reconciled by sending verse to each other: Samuel sent him a pacifying poem and Joseph responded in kind.[133]

Samuel carried on a lengthy correspondence with the poet Isaac Ibn Khalfōn. Their friendship was a continuation of the friendly relations between their parents, but more than that, it derived from their kinship of soul, for both poets had a strong secular tendency. Ibn Khalfōn sent letters and verse to the *nāgīd* during crises in Samuel's life, to which the *nāgīd* would respond in his best, flowery style. When Samuel was dismissed from his first post and was imprisoned, Isaac Ibn Khalfōn comforted Samuel, writing scornfully of his foes, urging Samuel to avenge himself. Samuel responded in the same scornful tone[134] (as he always did when his enemies obstructed him)[135] by replying that these people were too contemptible to be worthy of his notice. Their friendship faltered when they had a disagreement during a feast and the exchange of letters was discontinued for a time; ultimately, however, Samuel sent the roving poet some verse and asked him to renew their friendship. Isaac answered in a conciliatory vein,[136] and the last line of his poem contains a plea, couched in allusive language, for assistance: The *nāgīd* responded promptly with a generous gift.[137] Undoubtedly he understood the bitterness in the hapless poet's heart and was willing to forgive any slight to his own dignity. Isaac Ibn Khalfōn asked him for aid more than once (the practice of poets at that time who were not at all reluctant to seek support from rich and high-ranking benefactors).[138] The *nāgīd* never hesitated in sending him a substantial sum of money, as well as words of encouragement.[139] In any event, he endeavored to calm the tempestuous spirit of the poet who, suffering the anguish of poverty, spoke caustically of the attitude of people to the poet and his art.[140] When Ibn Khalfōn divorced his wife and had a dispute with members of her family who slandered and attacked him, he considered seeking relief through the Moslem authorities, but Samuel dissuaded him. To keep him in check he adjured the poet to ignore the calumnies and insults leveled against him by the woman's relatives.[141]

Samuel also fostered contacts with Jewish scholars in the Near East, sending them verse and asking about their activities. During the military campaigns he wrote letters and verse while in camp, and on returning to Granada he would turn them over to messengers *(faidj)*.[142] After he reached middle age he treated the Jewish scholars of Babylonia with great respect and turned to them with questions concerning halakha. The discussions between him and these scholars were carried on through the scholars of Kairawan, and they would attach the responses on his questions to those they sent to the heads of the talmudic academies in Tunisia.[143] Samuel ha-lēvī addressed questions to *gaon* Rabbi Hai, whom he particularly admired;[144] he was absorbed by the information he received about the personality, writings, and teachings of this great head of the academy. Great was his joy when a scholar who had studied for a long time at the *gaon*'s school came to Granada from Sicily. This scholar, Maṣliaḥ b. Elijah Ibn Albaẓaḳ, described his esteemed teacher in refreshing detail.[145] Samuel, discerning the quality of Maṣliaḥ and the breadth of his understanding, and finding his word reliable, asked him to write a special biography of the *gaon* and forward it to him in Granada when it was completed; upon his return to Sicily, Rabbi Mas .liaḥ did what the *nāgīd* had requested.[146]

At the end of the tenth century the academy of Sura was once again opened, although it was now in Bagdad. For sixteen years, from 1017 to 1033, this academy was headed by the *gaon* Rabbi Israel, the son of the *gaon* Rabbi Samuel b. Ḥofnī, with whom Samuel ha-lēvī also maintained ties.[147] The *nāgīd* even corresponded with the exilarch in Babylonia, Rabbi Hezekiah, a descendant of the exilarch David b. Zakkai, Saadya Gaon's opponent. In the first half of the eleventh century the office of exilarch was restored to this branch of the family after having been held by the family of Josiah, the brother of David b. Zakkai, whom Saadya had set up in opposition to him.

Hezekiah was a man of learning and distinction, and after the death of Rabbi Hai in 1038, no one more deserving than he could be found as a successor. Thus for many years he combined two positions: exilarch and head of the Academy of Pumbedita. He and Samuel ha-lēvī maintained contact with each other, and among other things Samuel sent him a long poem entitled "Z'mīra" in which he writes of Hezekiah's office with sincere esteem.[148] The head of the Babylonian academy discerned Samuel's extraordinary erudition through their correspondence, and he was fully aware of Samuel's nobility in his continuing effort to broaden the dissemination of Jewish learning—hence they awarded him the title of *rosh ha-sēder* (head of the academy).[149]

Samuel also maintained steady contact with the Jews in Palestine, especially with the academy called Pride of Jacob, annually sending them gifts and offerings for their synagogues.[150] From time to time he would pass along tidings of his successes in battle—in 1046, for example, he sent the academy a long poem about a successful military campaign.[151] When Daniel b. Azariah, a member of the exilarchic family in Babylonia, became head of the academy five years later, Samuel also corresponded with him.[152] Samuel sent him a poem of greeting upon learning of his appointment, and after receiving his reply sent him another long poem.

He also exchanged letters with the heads of Egyptian Jewry. In Fostat, which had the largest community in Egypt, there were two congregations: the Palestinian Jews and the Babylonian Jews. The rabbi of the "Jerusalemites" (the Palestinian congregation), was at that time 'Elī b. 'Amram. In a letter to the *nāgīd* he asked for assistance, writing in grandiloquent, flattering phrases that when the Torah scrolls were taken out of the ark in his synagogue, prayers were offered for the welfare of the *nāgīd* and his children, even as they would mention the exilarch Daniel b. Azariah during the prayer.[153]

Ties were also maintained between the leaders of the Babylonian congregation and Samuel ha-lēvī. The head of the Babylonian congregation in Fostat was Sahlān b. Abraham, who was not only an estimable scholar but also a composer of liturgical poetry. Samuel ha-lēvī respected him highly and sent him some of his poems.[154]

Since Kairawan was relatively near, its Jewish scholars and Samuel ha-lēvī had especially intimate ties. The heads of the talmudic academies there acted as intermediaries between the North African and Spanish communities on the one hand and the academies of Babylonia on the other—just as they had in the past. Moreover, in the first half of the eleventh century brilliant scholars, men of renown throughout the Jewish Diaspora, lived in Kairawan. At the beginning of that century the greatest of that group was Ḥushiēl b. Elḥānān, who had gone to Tunisia from southern Italy on a family matter, but before it was resolved succumbed to the pleas of the Jews of Kairawan to become their rabbi and the head of a talmudic academy there. Rabbi Ḥushiēl was an inspiring teacher and directed the study of the halakhah along new paths. He stressed the importance of the Jerusalem Talmud and prompted his disciples to comprehend the reasons for the halakhah and its bases without turning to the scholars of Babylonia with their questions. For Samuel ha-lēvī, who asked him questions and respected his answers,[155] the death of Rabbi Ḥushiēl was a source of lyrical sorrow. At the news of his death the *nāgid* proclaimed a fast, arranged memorial services in Granada and Lucena, and sent emissaries to Cordova and other cities requesting that those communities do likewise. In a letter of condolence to the rabbi's son, Rabbi Ḥānānēl, Samuel gave an account of the memorial services and in turn asked him for information concerning his father's colleagues and disciples. This letter and a poem in it were written in Aramaic.

Rabbi Ḥānānēl—a son worthy of his father and a man of reputation among the medieval commentators of the *Gemara* —responded with a letter also in Aramaic which included a poem in that language.[156]

Rabbi Ḥushiēl and his son were not the only Jewish scholars in Kairawan with whom Samuel corresponded and developed a close relationship; Rabbi Nissīm b. Jacob was foremost among those with whom he had contact. Rabbi Nissīm, a disciple of Rabbi Ḥushiēl's, had also studied under his son Rabbi

Ḥānānēl; later he himself became head of an academy and an authority on halakha. He wrote a large work called *M'gillat s'tārīm,* a collection of halakhot and traditions from responsa; he also wrote commentaries on tractates of the Gemara and a key to the Talmud. The heads of the Babylonian academies designated him as their representative in Kairawan and in this capacity he transmitted Samuel ha-lēvī's letters and questions to the *gaon* Rabbi Hai. But, on a more personal level, Samuel and Rabbi Nissīm corresponded with one another frequently, exchanging poetry and ideas, each esteeming the judgment of the other;[157] in time a real friendship developed between them —Samuel shared Rabbi Nissīm's joys and grieved at his distress. When his only son died at an early age, Samuel ha-lēvīwrote Rabbi Nissīm a letter of condolence;[158] and since Nissīm was a needy scholar, he sent him money from time to time.[159]

The *nāgid* did not exchange correspondence and verse only with leading scholars, but also with the more ordinary, many of whom turned to him for assistance or a recommendation. For instance, he took the time to give Rabbi Jesse, a Moroccan scholar who was staying in Granada, a letter to Rabbi Nissīm in which Samuel extols his erudition and requests that his friend intercede with the community of Kairawan in Rabbi Jesse's behalf.[160]

IX

Though Samuel was interested in the welfare of Jewish communities in other lands and tried to do good for them, his first concern was for the Jews in the kingdom of Granada, where he had the greatest authority. Under his aegis the Jews in this state became exceptionally powerful, but of course the flourishing of the Jewish communities in Granada was tied to the growth of its economy too. All the Moslem provinces of Spain were richer and more industrialized than they were to be for many generations after they were reconquered by the Christians, and Granada in particular benefited from this substantial economic boom. The growing of sugarcane and cotton, which the Arabs had brought to Spain, was developed, especially in the vicinity of Elvira and Guadix, and gold, silver, copper, iron, and marble were mined near Elvira. The Arabs made improvements in mining methods, introducing clay ducts connected to lead pipes to draw the water out of the mines. Better mining methods led to greater yields, and some of the surplus metals were sold to other countries at great profit. Most metal served as the raw material for various industries in Spain itself where jewelry and a variety of other articles were made.[161] The Jews produced and marketed all these products. Many of them were artisans, and certain occupations were so-called Jewish occupations: dying, tanning, and goldsmithery.[162] The artisans and merchants prospered and many became wealthy. The status of the Jews in this province of southern Spain was never so good and its numbers never so large as in the middle of the eleventh century.

Within the city of Granada there was a large Jewish community numbering more than five thousand,[163] and it continued to grow as the city itself expanded when it became the capital of the kingdom. After the Ṣinhādja made Granada their capital, Elvira—the chief city of the province for many generations—became deserted as its inhabitants moved to the new capital (the movement away from Elvira actually began earlier during the civil wars, when bands of marauding Berbers spread through all of southern Spain and pillaged its cities). The Ṣinhādja who took up residence in Granada were mere warriors whose needs were amply served by the local artisans and merchants who, in turn, earned comfortable livelihoods from their most recent rulers. But in an effort to populate their capital the

Berbers pressured the inhabitants of Elvira to move to Granada, and the city which had heretofore been small now mushroomed.

Before it became the capital of the Ṣinhādja, the city of Granada had almost the same boundaries as the Jewish city north of the Darro River. The neighborhoods north of the river had long been desolate and in ruins. When they established their capital the new rulers settled among the remains of buildings and fortifications of an earlier time, in the area which today surrounds the Church of San Nicolas; this sector, which was encircled by walls, became the al-ḳaṣaba of the kings of the House of Zīrī. Soon new quarters sprang up on the slopes of the hill where the artisans and merchants lived, and these too were enclosed by walls. These fortifications were begun by King Ḥabbūs and completed by his successor, Bādīs. Thus another city was founded north of the Darro, and in time the whole district was called by the same name as the Zīrīte king's fortress: al-ḳaṣaba (or "the old ḳaṣaba,"—the ḳaṣaba of Bādīs).

Al-Ḳaṣaba was not large. A wall that began at a square known today as Plaza Larga surrounded it on the north and ran in a westerly direction, south of Cuesta de la Alhacaba, to the al-Unaidar Gate (now called Puerta Monaita). The city extended westward to a street which is still known as Calle de Zenata because west of the wall was the suburb where the Zenāta (Berber mercenaries) and their families lived. The southern wall went around a mosque that stood where the Church of San José was later erected; from there it turned east as far as the spot where the Convent of the Señora de la Victoria stood in the days of the Christian kings. There the wall turned north once again to the Plaza Larga.

The king's palace stood in the northwest corner of the city, in the vicinity of the Church of San Miguel (El Viejo) and the Convent of Santa Isabel la Real. In the southeast corner was a large quarter, Coracha, so named because of a bulge in the wall;[164] in the center of it stood a mosque on the exact site where, during Christian rule, the Church of San Juán de los Reyes stood. The street bears that name today. Thus the big Elvira Street was outside the walls of al-ḳaṣaba, in an outlying district that is the noisy, business center of modern Granada. Where the cathedral stands the Great Mosque, dedicated in 1055, was built. This area too was surrounded by a wall, even though it was not yet densely settled and contained empty fields. The city's fortifications continued westward from the al-Unaidar Gate to the Gate of Elvira and then southwest to where the Calle de Mesones now begins. Throughout the Middle Ages the western wall of Granada ran the length of this street. Near the point where the wall reached the Darro River stood the gate called Bāb ar-ramla, for which the great square Plaza de Bibarrambla is named.[165] Close to the river (the Jewish quarters spread along the other bank), was Tanner's Gate (Bāb ad-dabbāghīn);[166] a considerable number of Jews were engaged in this occupation and, as usual, they plied their craft outside the city's walls and near the river.

The Jewish city south of the Darro was also enclosed within a wall and fortifications, some older and some built by the Berbers. Its wall wound from the Tanner's Gate south to the Bāb aṭ-ṭawwābīn (Gate of the Brickmakers), today's Campillo Square.[167] Going eastward from there, it girded the district of the Matías Church, reaching the vicinity of the Dominican monastery, Santa Cruz. One of its towers still stands on the Plaza de los Campos. From there the wall continued to the Plaza del Realejo, the site of the Bāb al-fakhkarīn (Potter's Gate), so called because just outside that gate was the Potters' quarter. Then the wall ascended the hill in a northeasterly direction, and where the streets Calle de los Alamillos and Cuesta de Santa Catalina now meet there was a gate called Bāb Maurūr (later called Bāb ash-shams [Gate of the Sun]).[168] The wall reached the summit of the hill upon which the fortress Ḥiṣn Maurūr, later called Torres Bermejas, stood. Since this fortress protected the quarters south of the Darro River, the Berber rulers kept it in good repair.[169] From there the wall, which was topped by round turrets, descended to the as-Sabīka Valley, to the Gate of the Valley (Bāb al-Khandaḳ), and continued from the edge of the Red Hill to the Gate of the Timbrels, which sealed off the Darro Valley.

The Jewish area within the walled city was large compared to Jewish quarters in other Spanish cities. It was not merely a neighborhood, it was a true city. Moreover, notwithstanding the influx of Berbers and Andalusians from various places, the Jews still made up a large proportion of the total inhabitants both south and north of the Darro River, and they occupied a relatively large area.[170] Many new houses were constructed in the Jewish city; floors and wings were added to old houses to accommodate the additional inhabitants. The center of the Jewish city lay within the district bounded by the streets now called Calle de Pavaneras and Calle Rodrigo del Campo, and even the area around the Matías Church was populated by Jews.[171]

After the new sections north of the Darro became the city's center, they also became the focus of economic life. Many Jewish craftsmen even opened shops and stores there, on various streets according to their occupations. At the western end of the northern section of the city, on the other side of the Tanner's Gate, was the Street of Sandalmakers (Zanḳat al-Kharrāzīn)—the majority of whom were Jews.[172] Two bridges linked the new city of the Berbers and the Jewish city. One was at the western end of what is now Plaza Nueva but was then still a valley without streets and squares. This bridge was called Ḳantarat al-ḥadjdjāmīn.[173] In the time of King Bādīs a second bridge was built by the judge ʻAlī b. Muḥammad Ibn Tauba between the first bridge and the Gate of the Timbrels, near the mosque on whose site the Church of San Pedro now stands. It was named for Ibn Tauba: the Bridge of the Kadi.

During this period of the rapid development of Granada, a system was installed to bring water from the rivers into the homes.[175] Although the center of the city shifted to the region north of the Darro—where the king's palace and the seat of government were located—the Jews' cemetery remained far to the north, west of the Gate of Elvira, on the site of the present-day Plaza del Triunfo.[176]

New houses being erected incessantly, entire streets sprouting in places where only some years earlier uncultivated fields existed, annual military campaigns—all this activity meant a thriving economy for Granada, the capital of the Ṣinhādja rulers and their chief army base. Labor and commerce prospered and money was plentiful. But there were some branches of industry for which Granada was especially famous. The silkworm was raised in the area around Granada, and in the city itself the precious raw material was processed and silk textiles of a superior quality were produced. The products of Granada's goldsmiths and silversmiths were also greatly renowned and were exported. The Berber soldiers had a great need for various leather goods: for their armor and helmets, as covers for their shields, and for saddles.

Most of the artisans making these products were Jews who engaged in the same occupations as their forbears. The Jews of Granada also marketed the rich agricultural products of the Vega plain, engaging especially in the export of an exceptionally fine sugar. Some Jewish merchants in Granada came from old families that were well endowed with property and had lived in the city a long time. Among them were the officials and tax farmers who conducted the business of the state, as well as that of Berber chiefs. One was the family of Ibn Ezra, which had been a favorite of the royal court even in

King Ḥabbūs's time, when the head of the family was Jacob Ibn Ezra.[177]

Besides artisans, merchants, royal officials, and tax collectors, the Jewry of the Pomegranate City included physicians[178] and scholars who made practical applications of their knowledge, and intellectuals whose interests lay particularly in literature and poetry. During the time when Samuel ha-lēvī was the chief vizier of the Ṣinhādja kingdom, a self-effacing scholar named David Ibn Ḥadjar was a judge of the Jewish community in Granada. He was thoroughly at ease with the Talmud and in all the branches of Jewish knowledge. He also wrote books; one, *Abridgment of the Laws of Divorce,* written in Arabic, is sometimes cited in collections of responsa of that epoch.[179] He also wrote a book on Hebrew grammar, *The Book of Kings.*[180] The post of judge in a large community like Granada was a difficult one for Rabbi David, and he shrank from it. Like other Spanish Jews at the time, he wanted to go to Palestine and devote his life to study and worship. Samuel ha-lēvī, who knew him well, wrote poetry to him and encouraged him to carry out his heart's desire.[181] Rabbi David was only one of many, for in those days there was a Talmud school in Granada where distinguished scholars taught, and a poet who lived in a remote city addressed a poem to Samuel ha-lēvī requesting him to extend greetings to the head of this school.[182]

But Samuel did not take only scholars under his aegis. Intellectuals interested in literature and verse enjoyed special favor with the *nāgīd,* for who else could understand their feelings so well and appreciate the ability of the young people who composed Hebrew verse, and who else could give them so much encouragement? They wrote verse in honor of the *nāgīd,* and he listened attentively while they in turn delved wholeheartedly into his poetry. A contemporary writer reports that there were three poets in Granada who were especially prominent: Joseph b. Ḳaprīl, who had come to Granada from Cordova,

Abū Ibrāhīm b. Lebh, a scion of an old family in Spain, and Abū Isḥāḳ Ḥadjdjādj.[183]

Besides Granada, the largest Jewish community in the Ṣinhādja kingdom was that of Lucena. As it had been earlier, this city was a city of Jews, where they could live undisturbed in freedom. Therefore it had an attraction for Jews elsewhere, and from time to time even Jews from northern Spain, which was under Christian rule and whose atmosphere was pervaded by religious fanaticism, came to Lucena to live among their own people. A gravestone apparently engraved in the eleventh century bears the name of Rabbi Amicos—a Jew from northern Spain who had migrated to Lucena and died there.[184]

As was the case in many cities during the Middle Ages, some of the city's inhabitants made their living from agriculture. On its outskirts were vineyards belonging to Jews who themselves tended them. The Jews of Lucena also raised sheep and cattle. A manual of deeds written in Lucena in 1021 contains various agreements connected with agricultural work, such as tenancy of vineyards, the lending of the stone for an oil press, the sale of cattle, accepting rams for sire in order to get a half share in the offspring, and the like.[185]

There were also merchants in Lucena who maintained business ties with the large cities of Spain—Granada, Seville, and Toledo—as well as with countries in the Near East. The Jews of Lucena would travel to the Near East (especially Egypt) on business, trade with the local Jews, and establish friendships; and upon returning to Spain they would correspond for many years. One Jew from Lucena who visited the Near East in the second half of the eleventh century was Samuel b. Solomon b. Abraham b. Solomon. In Egypt he became acquainted with M'bhōrakh b. Saadya, a respected physician and a person of influence at the royal court who served for some decades as the *nāgīd* of the Jews of Egypt (1079–1110). Samuel b. Solomon wrote him letters from Lucena.[186]

When Cordova declined as the main focus of the cultural life of Spanish Jewry, Lucena once again rose in importance as a center of Jewish learning. But this community did not fill the role formerly held by Cordova. When Moslem Spain was divided into several states in the eleventh century, a number of centers were established among the communities scattered throughout these states. In the first half of that century Lucena became the center of learning and instruction for the Jews of Andalusia, a town where Jewish studies flourished and scholars lived. One notable Jewish writer of that epoch refers to Lucena as "the city of song [poetry]," and indeed at that time Hebrew poets and philologists, as well as talmudic scholars of renown, lived there.

In the middle of the eleventh century a man named Abū 'r-Rabī' b. Baruch, famous as a Hebrew poet among all the Jewish communities of Andalusia, dwelled in Lucena.[187] He was an admirer of Samuel ha-lēvī and wrote poetry in his honor. In the second half of that century R. Samuel b. Hananiah became known for his noble character and achieved reputation for his knowledge and his writings. He was a pious man who was contented with very little, a talmudic scholar who was well versed in all branches of Jewish literature and in history. He also wrote metered verse and letters which amazed his contemporaries.[188]

The foremost of the scholars of Lucena at that time was R. Isaac b. Judah Ibn Gayyāt. He was a member of an old esteemed family in Lucena, as his Arabic name indicates—which he himself sometimes translated into Hebrew, calling himself Ben Mōshī'a.[189] He was a distinguished scholar familiar with the whole Talmud. But as was the custom of the Jewish scholars in Moslem Spain, he did not limit himself to the study of the halakhah—he had a knowledge of secular culture and perused the treatises of Arabic philosophers. But having grown up among the Jews of Lucena, he had little contact with Moslem scholars and was not as conversant with their literature—his greatest devotion was to Jewish lore. He delved into the commentaries of the *g'ōnīm* and their responsa and into the works of the men who came after them; in this respect there was no one in his generation to compare with him. In his eyes the views of the *g'ōnīm*—even their superstitious beliefs—were preferable to the opinions of the philosophers and intellectuals,[190] and in whatever measure he accepted their doctrines, he was more attracted by the *Sefer ha-y'ṣīra* ("The Book of Creation"), which coordinates them with the sacred Scriptures.

Samuel ha-lēvī encouraged Isaac Ibn Gayyāt, and at intervals he would come to Granada to study with the *nāgīd* himself.[191] Cited as an authority on Oral Law and known as a sharp-witted talmudist by the time he reached maturity, he was chosen as Lucena's rabbi and the head of the yeshiva[192] where he taught for several decades.

Rabbi Isaac Ibn Gayyāt was a prolific writer and poet: in Arabic, he wrote a commentary on the Mishnah and the Gemara entitled *Kitāb as-Sirādj.* This work, which is called in Hebrew *Sefer ha-nēr* ("The Book of the Lamp") or *Sefer ha-m-'ōr* ("The Book of Illumination") was occasionally quoted by the talmudic authorities of his era and of later generations.[193] (His responsa written from the yeshiva were also generally written in Arabic.)[194] But he became famous among scholars for his collection of halakhot, *Halākhōt k'lūlōt,*[195] in which he attempted to explain the halakhic practices then in vogue, not by following punctiliously the order of the Gemara but by citing a halakhah and explaining it in terms of other halakhic references in the Gemara, the Jerusalem Talmud, and geonic opinion. He quotes the responsa and commentaries of the *g'ōnīm* profusely, but is not afraid to differ with their opinions.[196] He also cites extensively the important halakhot and decisions as well as the commentary of Rabbi Ḥānānēl, but he appears to depend especially on the opinions of *gaon* Rabbi Hai: wherever the views of the *gaon* and those of Rabbi Ḥān ānēl conflict he accepts the *gaon*'s opinion.[197] The interweaving of halakhot from the Gemara and geonic responsa, the demonstration of parallels between the Babylonian and Jerusalem talmuds, the examination and criticism of geonic decisions, and the drawing of a conclusion from this discussion —the same method that Samuel ha-lēvī employs in his treatise *Hilkh'ta g'bharātā,* and it appears that Ibn Gayyāt used this treatise as a model for *Halākhōt k'lūlōt.* However, he abridged the geonic responsa and, keeping in mind the practical purpose of his work, did not engage in a great deal of casuistry, simply stated his conclusions without prefatory remarks.[198] His *Halākhōt k'lūlōt* was well received by the early authorities, especially the halakhot relating to the festivals.[199]

Rabbi Isaac Ibn Gayyāt also wrote commentaries on books of the Bible; these, too, were in Arabic.[200] In the commentary on Ecclesiastes (which has been preserved) he explores its grammatical and conceptual aspects, basing his conclusions on proofs culled from philosophic thought.[201] In this work he clarifies each verse from its linguistic aspect, and those Hebrew words which in his view require clarification he explains by using Arabic words which have the same meaning. But primarily his work reveals a psychological bent: His purpose is to explain man's several endopsychic faculties. Like the contemporary intellectuals who adhere to the neo-Platonic school of thought as it was developed by the Arabs, Rabbi Isaac Ibn Gayyāt explains that every human being possesses an animal-like soul which dies with the body and a godly soul which ascends to heaven.[202] This soul emanates from the "intellect" and therefore its "illumination" is weaker than that of the intellect.[203] When he writes of these matters he bases himself upon the "philosophers" but usually does not mention them by name, referring only to *shuyūkh* ("elders" or, as here, "those competent") philologists and commentators;[204] generally he refutes their opinions and is prolix in so doing. At any rate, his commentary was well regarded in the Middle Ages, and writers who had a particular interest in psychology valued his explanations.[205]

Lucena's rabbi was also a talented, skilled poet—he wrote very little secular poetry,[206] but his religious poems alone number four hundred, at least. Ibn Gayyāt wrote hymns for the festivals and for the four Sabbaths preceding Passover, lamentations for the mourning of Tisha' b'Ab, penitential hymns for the month of Elul and a *ma'mad,* (a complete cycle of hymns) for Yom Kippur. All types of hymns are represented in his religious poetry: general liturgical hymns and hymns to introduce special portions of the service; *ḳ'rōbhōt, r'shuyōt, tōkhāhōt, ōfānīm,* and *m'ōrōt.*

Most of his poems are not metered, but he did employ the ornamentations of verse which the Hebrew poets learned from Arabic poetry. For example, Ibn Gayyāt wrote verse in which each stanza begins with the last word of the preceding stanza and others in which each stanza has the same number of words. He especially favored the girdle poems of the Arabs, and he would frequently use half a biblical verse as a refrain. With great skill he wove fragments of scriptural verse into every line—his command of Hebrew was superb and these scriptural phrases blend with his own words in complete harmony to the eye and ear. He employed biblical language, and, like the Spanish poets, insisted on a simplicity and quality which imparts a certain nobility to his verse.

The content typical of poets among the higher strata of Spanish Jewry (or those poets who wrote in their behalf) is also apparent in his religious verse. Whereas the Jewish poets of the Near East introduced into their hymns many allusions to matters found in the Midrash and Gemara, Rabbi Isaac Ibn

Gayyāt speaks in his verse of the marvels of nature, in which the grandeur of the Creator is revealed. In hymns of the Yom Kippur morning service he writes of the creation of the world as portrayed in Genesis, employing phrases culled from it. He refers to the Ten Spheres and describes the angels who stand before the chariot singing in awe and reverence. In hymns for the *Musaf* prayer he points to the human body and the functions of its limbs, which only the Creator could construct and through which His wisdom is revealed.

A number of these hymns reflect views which had been disseminated by "The Epistles of the Pure Brethren" and other philosophical treatises. No doubt simple people did not understand the allusions to the opinions of the philosophers found in these hymns, and a Hispano-Jewish poet of the early thirteenth century made the just observation that "they were far from understanding;"[207] but notables of the Spanish communities who perused Arabic literature thoroughly enjoyed them. To be sure, the religious verse of Ibn Gayyāt, which expressed the dominant attitude in the large communities, contained intimations of a yearning for national redemption, a bitter lament over the length of the exile, and a longing for vengeance against nations which oppress the Jews. His hymns, widely circulated because of his graceful language and the clarity with which he expressed his ideas, were lauded by his contemporaries and succeeding generations.[208] Rabbi Isaac Ibn Gayyāt himself collected his hymns, arranged them according to the order of the service, and added the halakhot pertaining to them; as a result they constituted a *maḥzōr* (both a holy day prayer book and a code of laws governing its use).[209] His liturgical hymns are included in many "rites" of the Jewish communities in East and West, particularly in Tripoli, North Africa.[210]

Rabbi Isaac's hymns, which were typical of a transitional epoch, were well received because they suited the new spirit in Hebrew literature. Although influenced by the hymnologists of the Near East, he did endeavor to break away from them, seeking new paths. Saadya Gaon was already leaning in this direction, but it was especially pronounced among such Spanish poets as Rabbi Isaac Ibn Gayyāt. It is therefore not surprising that his writings and hymns brought great renown—both to himself and to the community of Lucena, which was regarded as the Jerusalem of Andalusia.

The distinguished community of Lucena outshone those of the cities and towns nearby. The chief city of this province (the western province of the kingdom of Granada) was Cabra, northeast of Lucena. This city lies in a valley at the western rim of a chain of mountains in southeastern Spain, on the northern slopes of a sierra named for it, Sierra de Cabra. Agriculture was its chief source of livelihood, especially the marketing of such plantation crops as olives; and it served as a government center and the chief city of a wide area.[211] There had been a Jewish community in the city for a long time, and the Jews of Cabra included the intellectuals and scholars who migrated to the big cities in Spain, serving both Moslem and Christian rulers.[212]

In the northern province of the kingdom of Granada the largest Jewish community was that of Jaén, which had long been the home of one of the important Jewries in the southeast part of the Iberian peninsula. After the Berber victory in the civil war, this province was given to a clan of the Banū Yefren, one of the most powerful of their tribes. The Ḥammūdite caliph al-Ḳāsim (1018–21) appointed as governor of the province 'Abdalmalik, grandson of al-Manṣūr and the king of Valencia's nephew. After being under 'Abdalmalik's control for a number of years Jaén was annexed to the kingdom of Granada.[213] It became the second most important city of the Ṣinhādja kingdom and for a full generation enjoyed tranquillity and security.

As the entire city flourished and grew, so too did the Jewish community. The Jews of Jaén—or Djayyān, as it was called by the Arabs—engaged in all branches of trade; they prospered, and by the middle of the eleventh century it was an affluent community. Tanning, a "Jewish" occupation, was of primary importance in Jaén's economy.[214] In a collection of responsa dating from the end of the eleventh century there is a mention of a Jew from Jaén, a permanent resident of the city unaccustomed to travel, who later "went to eastern Spain, residing there ten years," deserting his wife and then remarrying unbeknownst to her.[215]

As the number of Jews in Jaén grew, the members of its community spread to other cities. A letter written at the beginning of the twelfth century mentions a well-to-do Jewish merchant called Ibn al-Djayyānī, (the son of a Jew from Jaén), who lived in the second half of the eleventh century and went to reside in another city.[216] Some Jews from Jaén also migrated to Palestine. A note found in the Geniza at Fostat, which dates from the eleventh century, to judge from the style of the handwriting, served as an amulet for a Jaénite who migrated to Palestine. To his name—Abraham bar Judah, may he rest in peace—are added the words "a Spaniard from the city of Jaén surnamed aṣ-ṣarrāf." So he was probably a banker.[217] The rabbi of Jaén at the end of this epoch—called simply Rabbi Isaac of Jaén—corresponded with the distinguished Jewish scholars of his generation.[218]

Guadix, then known as Wādī Ash, was the largest city in the eastern part of the kingdom of Granada. Located 53 kilometers northeast of Granada, at the foot of the Sierra Nevada, it was the center of a district rich in rivers and brooks; cotton and various fruits were grown there, and silkworms were raised. The agricultural products were processed within the city proper, and the silk which was manufactured there was particularly famous. Some Jews in Wādī Ash were engaged in the manufacture and merchandising of silk, and some of them were merchants who traded overseas. In the 1040s one of these merchants, Sulaimān b. Saul, was a trader in silk and fine clothes in Sicily and Tunisia.

In the second half of the eleventh century there was a well-organized Jewish community in Wādī Ash, maintaining close ties with the Jewries of Granada and Lucena. Testifying to this are booklets of questions directed from Wādī Ash to a notable rabbi at the end of the eleventh century, portions of which exist in manuscript in fragmented form.[219]

In the region of the eastern border, the chief city was Baza (which the Arabs called Basṭa). This region is mountainous; south of the city the Sierra de Baeza rises to a height of almost 2,300 meters, and the mountains to the north are similarly high. But right around Baza, and particularly to the northeast, there is a valley where there were plantations of fruit trees and where silkworms were raised. In the days of Moslem rule, Baza was renowned for its manufacture of brocade, processed from the local silk. Rugs made within the city and named after it were sold throughout Andalusia; Baza also had a factory which produced woolen textiles.[220] A strong fortress stood in the center of the city, for it had been the capital of the province since the days of the Omayyads,[221] but most of its sections were suburbs not surrounded by walls.[222] During Zuhair's rule it belonged to the kingdom of Almería, but after Bādīs's triumph it was annexed to the kingdom of Granada.[223]

In the time of Samuel ha-lēvī there was a Jewish community in this city. The Jews of Spain, with their special link to the making and merchandising of silk, naturally were to be found in such a silk center as Baza. Since it was not a large community and its members, like the other people in the city, were mostly preoccupied with business affairs, it is not mentioned in literary sources. Yet in this small, out-of-the-way city there remains one vestige of the Jewish quarter, located opposite what is now the Santiago Church (formerly a mosque). It is the ritual bathhouse, a small structure with three rooms for baths. Its design testifies to its having been built in the eleventh century.[224]

X

The unique success of Samuel ha-lēvī contributed in large measure to the growth of the Jewish communities in the kingdom of Granada—and since their security depended upon the fortunes of the vizier, the Jews were somewhat concerned about the future which would follow his demise. And indeed, although his multitudinous labors aged Samuel ha-lēvī prematurely, he retained his post—patiently ironing out difficulties in the highest echelons of government, quashing troublesome intrigues, making peace between quarreling dignitaries, appeasing the dissatisfied.

Withal, his most demanding role was the command of the army: Even in his sixties he was compelled to go to war, leading the armies of the kingdom, despite the debilitating physical effort that entailed—but there was no one else to take this responsibility and to depend on without hesitation or apprehension—so he carried this burden as before. Each spring Samuel prepared for a new military campaign and, in the almost endless warring of eleventh-century Moslem Spain, he sometimes had to prepare for a second campaign in the fall.

When he returned from the 1053 war in eastern Spain, he received appalling news from the western borders of the kingdom of continual troop movements in the Berber provinces. Spies confirmed that the enemies of the Ṣinhādja were preparing for a major action. A general mobilization of the army was organized in Granada, and by summer, Granadan regiments began to cross the border again.

Al-Muʿtaḍid, the king of Seville, had a well thought-out strategy. Instead of sending his best troops against the army of Bādīs, he delegated the task to the Berber states bordering on the kingdom of Granada (as he had done before); but this time he sent them to attack it in separate units and from various sides. The invasion by the army of the principality of Morón across Granada's western border and the penetration by the army of the principality of Ronda into its southwestern districts were designed to weaken the Granadan forces, ensuring success for the Sevillian army. Samuel ha-lēvī was obliged to divide his own troops and to fight on several fronts. When the battle on one front abated somewhat—either because the enemy was exhausted or because forces were being deployed for a new attack—it would break out with greater ferocity on another front. News of raids in unexpected places came in just when there were urgent calls for aid from remote and isolated districts.

The dispersal of the Granadan army emboldened the Berbers to carry on large-scale pitched battles against it, and they severely defeated the Granadans a number of times. The war continued four months, until the coming of winter forced the Berbers to stop their fighting. In a poem written in December of that year, Samuel ha-lēvī admits that he returned from the battlefield weary and broken, whereas the successful Berbers were encouraged.[225]

Samuel became even more depressed because of the ominous report that, shortly after he returned to Granada, the king of Seville had invited all the Berber princes to a meeting in his capital. Why were they going there if not to plot anew? Samuel ha-lēvī was right in his assumption that nothing good could come of the assembly. Encouraged by their success, the Berber princes gathered in Seville to plan a decisive assault on the Ṣinhādja.

Impatient and apprehensive, while he awaited further information, an incredible account reached Samuel. One of those abrupt changes—one of those unforseeable turnabouts—in which history abounds had occurred.

Al-Mu'taḍid invited the princes of Morón, Ronda, and Arcos to honor him with their presence at the circumcision of his sons: He had other intentions. After some polite words upon their arrival, the king had them imprisoned and put in irons —an incarceration that lasted for more than three years.[226]

The report of the imprisonment of the princes circulated with electrifying speed throughout Spain, arousing bewilderment everywhere. For many years past the Berber chiefs in southern Andalusia had been allies of the king of Seville—serving his interests, going to war when he gave the sign, and always at his bidding—now he had summarily thrown them into prison as if they were disreputable and nameless. The trickery of al-Mu'taḍid terrified all the Andalusian princes and their officials, for it demonstrated the full extent of his deceitfulness and his numerous machinations.

But Samuel ha-lēvī received the news with joy. He derided the princes who had been ensnared in the nefarious king's trap, at the same time feeling that al-Mu'taḍid had erred: He now had checked the onslaughts of his former allies and weakened them. The unlikelihood of an attack on Granada in the near future prompted Samuel to write a long poem which he called "Zimra" (Song).[227]

While people were still stunned by the king's action and more and more details became known, information concerning its consequences began to trickle in. Al-Mu'taḍid wanted to exploit the imprisonment of the princes, confident that their removal would throw their governments into confusion and thus vitiate Berber influence. He sent regiments of his army against the principalities of Morón and Arcos, which were neighbors of the kingdom of Seville, in an effort to conquer and annex them speedily. But this hope was not realized.

Al-Mu'taḍid's troops did succeed in taking a few districts and some of the Berbers entered his service, but the dynasty of Ibn Khizrūn in Arcos and the Banū Dammar, rulers of Morón, were not subjugated. In Arcos the place of the imprisoned 'Abdūn was taken by his brother, Muḥammad, who defended himself vigorously against the army of al-Mu'taḍid. In Morón, Muḥammad b. Nūḥ's son, 'Imād ad-daula Manād, who had been designated as successor, acted as ruler.

When word of his father's incarceration reached him, 'Imād ad-daula vigorously defended Morón and its satellite towns against the army of Seville. In an effort to compel the subjects of the Berber prince to submit to him, al-Mu'taḍid sent his forces against Morón again and again, ordering them to demolish the areas belonging to the principality, to destroy the villages, and to set the crops afire. But 'Imād ad-daula held to his position and fought indefatigably against the army of Seville. It was only natural that this ruler, who was engaged in a desperate battle with a more powerful neighbor who sought to absorb his principality, would be ready to accept help from any side and tend to enter into a pact with the king of Granada. The rulers of the small state of Carmona were always enemies of the Arab king of Seville, and when they learned of his action against the three Berber princes, they renewed their treaty with Bādīs.

The armies of Granada and the two Berber principalities fought the army of Seville during the summer of 1054, and as usual Samuel ha-lēvī, who had been the architect of the new alliance, headed the Granadan forces. The campaign was crowned with success, but upon his return to Granada Samuel fell ill. He felt the utter waning of his energies, and a poem he wrote at that time appears to be from the pen of one preparing for death.[228] His illness worsened and as the pains intensified day by day, Samuel ha-lēvī concluded that his end had come. The physicians despaired, giving him only two weeks to live.

But after two months of keen suffering, the crises passed. The aching ceased, but Samuel was so weak he could barely walk, and his emaciated body was almost skeletal. His eventual recovery seemed like a miracle to him, a kindness from God. Samuel's family and friends were overjoyed, and he himself composed two poems expressing his gratitude to the Creator of heaven and earth.[229]

He returned to his office and resumed governmental matters once more, despite the hardship it imposed upon him. King Bādīs concerned himself less and less with affairs of government, pursuing his pleasures and wallowing in inebriety. The assurances given to the rulers of Morón and Carmona and the need to maintain the alliance with them—which was vital to the kingdom of Granada in view of the threat of an attack by Seville—necessitated, in Samuel's opinion, a new campaign against the kingdom of Seville. In the spring of 1055 Samuel again placed himself at the head of an army and went into battle. The Granadans crossed the frontier of the Arab kingdom, penetrated to the region of ash-Sharaf in western Seville, and carried out successful raids there—their sole purpose was to ruin the economy of the foe through destruction in this rich region. To be sure, these raids did not develop into serious battles, but their progress satisfied the allies.[230]

Of course the king of Seville retaliated, mounting a punitive campaign against the Berber states, his neighbors on the east. Again they sent an urgent plea for help, and in the fall Samuel once more led a Granadan army against the forces of Seville. A short time later, in the winter, the Granadans, under Samuel's command, fought in the mountainous region north of Málaga. Some fortresses were besieged and then captured in these actions, and the Granadans took many prisoners. Their triumph in this winter campaign stirred such exaltation in the capital that the returning army was welcomed with shouts of gladness.[231]

This was Samuel ha-lēvī's last military venture. Some months after his return he became fatally ill. His body was too weak to endure the rigors of war and he had no resistance against disease. He died in the spring of 1056, with his two sons and other members of his family at his bedside.[232] In Samuel's last moments he could reflect on a life replete with noble deeds and extraordinary successes such as only a few mortals enjoy.

Though his family was aware of his ebbing strength for some time, his death was still a blow they could scarcely bear. All the Jews of Granada remembered his favors and his efforts to raise them to their present high status—even those who had not benefited directly from the luster of his personality knew that one of those sublime persons, unique in his time, had left their midst. When the Jews of Granada learned that the *nāgīd* would no longer walk among them or gaze upon them with the kindly glance which induced in them a sense of security and joy, the mantle of despair and sorrow enveloped them. No one stayed at home on that very bitter day when they accompanied the body of their beloved Samuel ha-lēvī to its grave. Young and old, men, women, and children, the ailing and the feeble came out to pay their respects. Moslems passing near the western wall of al-Ḳaṣaba could hear the wailing cry from a thousand mouths, a sobbing so heartrending that Arabic historians were still recounting the event generations later. The *nāgīd* was buried in the old cemetery in front of the Elvira Gate; when the funeral was over the Jews of Granada returned to their homes orphaned as though by a father's death.[233]

When the report of the *nāgīd*'s death reached the other Jewish communities in Spain, they too went into heavy mourning, and everywhere they assembled in public lament and the recitation of prayer for the dead. The rabbis eulogized the deceased leader with eloquent orations, and the poets composed elegies. Isaac Ibn Gayyāt, the rabbi of Lucena, wrote a long poem in Aramaic which was recited publicly during the memorial service.[234] Memorial services were also held in the large communities of North Africa and the Near East. The rabbi of the Palestinian congregation in Fostat informed the bereaved family that he had arranged for the recitation of the prayer for the dead in his synagogue;[235] similar condolences were sent to the family from all over the Jewish Diaspora. Truly, in every country people were aware of the loss which Jewry sustained in the death of this radiant man.

XI

During the Middle Ages, in European and Arab countries, a son inherited his father's occupation after first serving an apprenticeship with him. Townspeople whose fathers engaged in a skill learned that same skill and, throughout their lives, made their living from it. Similarly, it was customary to appoint the son of a high official to his father's post if he was suited to it. Such was the practice in Moslem Spain, and when a vizier died his son was given preference in succeeding him. Samuel ha-lēvī had deliberately trained his son Joseph to become a vizier in the kingdom of Granada. Everything that he was taught—a thorough knowledge of Arabic literature and Moslem history, and above all, the art of writing letters and documents in the fashion of Arab scribes—was directed toward that end. Beyond that, Samuel passed on to his son the practical skills needed to serve the princes and persuaded the crown prince, Boluggīn, to engage Joseph as his secretary.[236] In attending to the numerous, ramified interests of the prince, who owned huge estates, Joseph acquired experience in business matters which could not be learned from his tutors.

After Samuel ha-lēvī died, the Berber ruler hesitated in appointing his successor. On the one hand, Bādīs remembered what Samuel had several times told him of his son's capabilities; but he pondered appointing a youth—not yet twenty-one—to the high office in which lay the fate of the kingdom. He sought the counsel of his intimates, his senior Berber dignitaries, and his other advisers. Among the officials was his boyhood friend, 'Alī Ibn al-Ḳarawī, who had become a vizier when Bādīs became ruler; Bādīs followed the loyal Ibn al-Ḳarawī's advice and appointed Joseph as chief vizier despite his youth.[237]

Joseph immediately began to fulfill his duties with devotion and energy; within a short time the king was convinced that he had not made a mistake in his choice. Joseph was quick to learn his job, and events demonstrated that his knowledge and counsel were sound. It was not long before Bādīs relied upon him as he had upon his father; the Berber chiefs were amazed at the extent of the trust the king placed in his young vizier.

The prime requisite of the viziers in the Berber kingdoms of Andalusia was to keep the coffers of the treasury filled by every possible means. The Ṣinhādja kings (like the other Berber rulers) could not ignore the hostility displayed toward them by their subjects who were natives of Spain—rebellions and upheavals could force them back to their African homeland. Hence, for their own security and that of their children, they tried to amass those treasures which they could readily carry with them. Because the young vizier was successful in this fiscal objective, Bādīs was as pleased with him as he had been with his father.[238]

Joseph's foreign policy was equally as successful: The kingdom of Granada achieved the goal that Bādīs had been striving toward for many years. A major factor in the relative security of the kingdom during the first years of Joseph's ministry was the result of the involved relations between the king of Seville and the small Berber states in central and southern Andalusia.

In the spring of 1057 the Ṣinhādja succeeded in enlarging their kingdom considerably by annexing a neighboring state that had become inordinately weak—the Ḥammūdite principality of Málaga was rent by years of internal conflicts and frequent changes of rulers. When Muḥammad b. Idrīs al-Mahdī was poisoned in 1053, his nephew Idrīs b. Yaḥyā succeeded him, but relinquished the throne after occupying it only briefly. The populace then recalled to office Idrīs II (b. Yaḥyā b. ʻAlī) who had been deposed some years previously; Idrīs ruled until his death in 1053. He was succeeded by his young son Muḥammad, surnamed al-Mustaʻlī. The prestige of the Ḥammūdite dynasty was then at its lowest and the military power of the state of Málaga was insignificant. It was clear that the principality soon would be absorbed by its more powerful neighboring states.

The Granadans were naturally apprehensive that the king of Seville (who had already taken Algeciras) would also annex Málaga—especially since the Andalusian inhabitants of Málaga did not hide their inclination toward him. The Granadans feared that he would then encircle their kingdom. The heads of the government of Granada, spearheaded by Joseph, initiated bold action. They distributed gifts among the dignitaries of the Ḥammūdite principality and wrote letters trying to influence them. In November 1056 the heir apparent wrote a letter in his own hand to the judge of Málaga, Abūʻ Abdallāh Ibn al-Ḥasan al-Djudhāmī, who was also a vizier of the Ḥammūdite prince. In it he promised him, to the accompaniment of oaths to the Lord and on the Koran, that if he became the ruler of Málaga the judge would be allowed to retain his position and not pay taxes on his private estates.[239]

Under the command of Boluggīn the army of Granada took up positions over the entire length of the border of the Ḥammūdite principality and entered Málaga without opposition. To symbolize the importance of the occasion King Bādīs himself came to take over the government. The last prince of the Ḥammūdite dynasty left for Almería, and Boluggīn was appointed by his father as regent of the new province within his kingdom.[240]

At the same time, in the spring of 1057, astonishing news spread over Andalusia. The wily king of Seville had freed the Berber princes from prison—but upon their release he had them choked in the bath.

The Berbers in Carmona, Morón, Arcos, Xeres, and the other Andalusian cities were of course outraged when they learned what al-Mu'taḍid had done to the princes. They resolved to continue their stubborn war against the Arabic king—he would have to pay dearly for their lives. The Ṣinhādja in Granada were also shocked, but they were somewhat less surprised. This was added proof that the hostility of the Arab king toward the Berbers was boundless and that they must make war against him to an unequivocal end.

Thus the struggle between the king of Seville and the desperate remnants of the principalities of Morón and Arcos went on. After several years al-Mu'taḍid was still frustrated in his efforts to overpower the Berbers and capture their diminished principalities. From time to time the princes of Morón and Arcos were joined by an expeditionary force from the king of Granada, whose interests dictated that the king of Seville be prevented from annexing those areas to his kingdom.

But the king of Granada had lost heart for fatiguing military ventures and placed his chief vizier in charge of these actions. So, like his father, Samuel, the young Joseph became the commander. A Hebrew poet from Granada composed a poem in honor of Joseph on his return from a war against "the king of the Arabs" in a river region and the conquest of his fortresses.[241] The military successes of the Ṣinhādja, on the one hand, and the ambitions of the king of Seville to expand his territories, on the other, tightened the links between the state of Cordova and the kingdom of Granada, and there is no doubt that Granada's political position strengthened. Stressing this alliance, King Bādīs several times visited Cordova, where splendid receptions were accorded him; Joseph accompanied him on these visits, and he too enjoyed the treatment customary for a high dignitary. Probably life's vagaries were in his thoughts—his father had fled from the city of the caliphs in poverty, and now he himself returned to it as a man of status.[242]

Joseph had inherited from his father not only the office of chief vizier of the kingdom of Granada but also the function of the *nāgīd;* this made him the secular and spiritual leader of the Jewish communities in the Ṣinhādja kingdom. Like his father, he was recognized by the king as the head of the Jewry of Granada, responsible for the taxes imposed upon it. Like his father, he also filled the role of rabbi and teacher. Even in his father's lifetime Joseph began teaching in the local Talmud school,[243] and after Samuel's death he continued whenever his governmental affairs allowed time. Joseph's contemporaries valued his instruction highly and passed along his interpretations of the Torah and the comments emanating from him and his father.[244] A contemporary Jewish writer reported that men came from faraway lands to study with Joseph and that his disciples became the most distinguished rabbis in Spain.[245]

A gifted poet like his father, he composed Hebrew poems on various subjects, religious and secular,[246] and when the occasion called for it he could write verse in Arabic.[247] Like Samuel, he engaged scribes to make copies of Hebrew and Arabic books for him and enlarged the library bequeathed by his father so much that Jews and Moslems praised it. Joseph was a true intellectual and his interest in books, old and new, was not the affectation it often was with other patrons.

Just as his love of culture was handed down from his father, so too was a feeling of solidarity with his Jewish brethren. Throughout his life he sought to aid his people and to elevate their status in every possible way. On an even bigger scale than his father, he appointed Jews to posts in the kingdom and granted them rights which they had never before enjoyed. In those days the Jews of Granada who held offices in the royal service constituted a wealthy and influential stratum of functionaries. The high rank attained by some of the Jews of Granada was well known among the Jewish communities of many lands. A letter sent from Tunisia to Fostat in the 1050s relates, among other things, that "there came to al-Mahdīya our Andalusian companions, who reported that Joseph, the son of the *nāgīd* (may his memory be for a blessing), enjoys peace—may the Lord increase his honor; and all our brethren holding office in the land of Ben Ḥabbūs as well as the entire community enjoy peace."[248]

Joseph extended his aegis to Jewish scholars everywhere, encouraging them to produce literary works and giving them aid.[249] He established contact with the heads of the Talmud schools in North Africa, the Near East, Babylonia, and other countries, as his father had done, and he corresponded with the exilarch in Bagdad. The exilarch, Rabbi Hezekiah, who became the head of the academy after the death of the *gaon* Rabbi Hai, had a long struggle with enemies among the Jews of Babylonia, and indeed a poem sent to him by Samuel ha-lēvī alludes to those "oppressors."[250] During Joseph's term as chief vizier of the kingdom of Granada the power of those enemies increased, and after they became associated with the heads of the Moslem government Rabbi Hezekiah was thrown into prison and severely tortured. Two of his sons fled to faraway Spain to the *nāgīd,* Joseph, who welcomed them with great honor and did all he could for them.[251]

Daniel b. Azariah, the head of the Pride of Jacob academy in Palestine, also dispatched letters to the young *nāgīd* at Granada and was a beneficiary of his aid. Joseph corresponded with 'Elī b. 'Amram, rabbi of the Palestinian congregation at

Fostat.[252] From time to time he sent a gift to this scholar, and 'Elī would gratefully mention his name during a moment in the Sabbath and festival services when the congregation would be standing.[253] When Daniel b. Azariah confirmed Joseph in the title of *nāgīd* (it was the practice of the heads of the academies to confer the honorary title upon wealthy men who had shown them kindness), 'Elī b. 'Amram bestowed his blessing upon him, appending to his letter a poem in his honor and in honor of his brother Elyāsā.[254]

Joseph, the son of Samuel ha-lēvī, inherited much of the prodigious talent and nobility which led him from one success to another. But he was different in temperament from his father—and this proved to be his drawback. A Hebrew writer from Spain who had heard trustworthy accounts of Joseph within his own family and a Moslem writer relying on early sources depict his character in almost identical language. Both report that his most prominent character trait was an exaggerated haughtiness which resulted, in their view, from his being the son of a high dignitary and from being born amid wealth and honor.[255] Whereas his father knew how to win friends, Joseph was one of those gifted men who gain admiration but not affection. Joseph's awareness of his intellectual superiority no doubt intensified his often tactless candor and his tendency to underrate his peers. Truly, Joseph did not fulfill his father's precept: "He that is slow to anger is better than the mighty, and he that ruleth his spirit than he that taketh a city."

But there was another palpable reason for his insolence: Joseph was unhappy at home. Samuel, dedicated to Joseph's welfare and anxious for him to have a worthy wife, arranged to have him marry the daughter of his friend Rabbi Nissīm, head of the renowned Talmud school at Kairawan. This was one of the happiest events of Samuel's life, for Rabbi Nissīm and his son Jacob also came to Granada. How honored he felt to have the great scholar as his guest, what hopes he placed in the nuptials he arranged. Rabbi Nissīm lingered awhile, teaching at the school in Granada as his son-in-law and other able young men eagerly sought his instruction. Thereafter Joseph looked upon Rabbi Nissīm as his teacher, later writing letters to him in the language of a disciple addressing his master.[256]

The marriage, however, was unsuccessful. Though Rabbi Nissīm's daughter was indeed learned and possessed fine qualities, she lost Joseph's favor after the first raptures of the honeymoon evaporated. Now having a taste of the sensuous pleasures, Joseph, an exceptionally handsome person, became obsessed by his passions. Tall, shapely women excited him; his tiny wife—"the midget," as he called her—could not gratify him. He became a bitter and troubled man.[257]

Gradually Joseph's conduct reflected his mood. When he controlled his desires, his resentment exploded in harsh, coarse language directed at innocent people; when he disported himself like the Berber nobles he displeased the Jewish community, which had not witnessed such conduct by his father. But how can one maintain an equanimous stance in public when there is no serenity at home?

Joseph's pride and dissatisfaction impelled him to live like the rich noble who flaunts his wealth and his lofty status—but the splendor merely camouflaged his shaky position at the mercy of a tyrannical ruler and somewhat compensated for his ungratifying home life. Whereas Samuel ha-lēvī had lived among his own people in the Jewish section of Granada, Joseph's residence was on the high hill where the palaces of the Naṣrid kings were later erected, the hill of *al-ḥamrā.* He built a luxurious house, with marble floors, which became notorious throughout the kingdom. His intimates—affluent Jews occupying high posts in the royal service and acting as tax farmers—also moved to this area, building magnificent homes for themselves.[258] Joseph's coterie of influential Granadan Jews conducted itself as if its position was secure.

Moslem Spain was composed of many nationalities. Its citizenry, its army, and its nobles came from diversified origins. In the kingdom of Granada, whose rulers were Berbers of the Ṣinhādja tribe, the inhabitants were mostly Moslem Andalusians with an admixture of Christians; but Berbers of the Zenāta tribe, "Slavs" (soldiers of Christian derivation), and Negroes served in the army. The Spanish Jews—descended from a long line of native-born ancestors—formed a vital element in the cities and outnumbered the ruling Berbers. However, the wealth and power of these infidels were a constant irritant to the Andalusians. The raucous parties held in the palace of Joseph (or, as they called him, Abū Ḥusain)—at which Arab poets sang paeans of immense flattery to him—and the grandiose appearance of wealthy Jews—with youths running before them to clear their paths in the streets—caused numerous discussions among the indignant Moslems. They were revulsed by those Moslem poets who composed hymns in honor of the Jewish vizier; for example, al-Akhfash b. Maimūn Ibn al-Farrā was one sharply condemned by his colleagues.[259] The Moslems grudgingly endured Berber rule but when unbelievers attained dominance, their animosity doubled and redoubled. Moreover, they perceived the open contempt these Jews had for the Moslem faith—time and again their jests were offenses to the sanctity and the honor of the Moslem prophet. Joseph himself scorned much that is written in the Koran.[260] He simply ignored Spanish sensitivity in matters of faith.

Joseph and his intimates not only irked the Moslems; they even embittered their fellow Jews. With Joseph, they made decisions on all problems which affected the Jewish communities of Granada according to their own benefit and not that of the broad masses: Their status in the government abetted their highhanded attitude toward their brethren. The craftsmen and small merchants who constituted the majority of Granadan Jewry openly avowed that Joseph and his group did good in their behalf and did protect them; nevertheless, the imperious grasping of authority within the Jewish community was considered indefensible. It was rumored that Joseph—who mingled with Moslem nobles—did not observe the commandments of the Torah and held all religions in scorn. Humble Jews began to doubt the commitment of the wealthy to traditional Jewish precepts, which were adhered to over the generations.

A contemporary Arabic author, who had creditable knowledge of events in Granada in the days of King Bādīs, writes at length that Joseph dealt kindly with his fellow Jews but at the same time disregarded Jewish law and Jewish scholars. This writer also reports that Joseph's disrespect for the entire Jewish faith galvanized the intense wrath of the Jews.[261] In the manner of medieval authors, he refers to the deeds of one person, but for practical purposes his reference applies to an entire class: Those affluent Jews—the tax farmers of the kingdom of Granada, the purveyors to its armed forces, the administrators of the nobles' estates—kept themselves apart from other Jews. Indeed, proximity to the royal court resulted in class divisions among the Jews. It was firmly established that being in the circle of intimates of royalty, more than anything else, brought one success and wealth.

This breach—which rent the Jewish community of Spain and which was to have fateful consequences for many generations—was only in its germinal stage. All the problems of Granadan Jews were overshadowed by the worsening relations between the Berbers and the Andalusians. It was surely clear to anyone of perception that should Joseph fall, he would drag all his associates with him and overwhelm all Granadan Jewry with disaster.

XII

The flaws in Joseph's character, in part, developed from his exposure to political dangers which required quick, assertive decisions. He had neither the authority nor the respect enjoyed by his father; nor did his foes sit idly by. They were not going to accept insults from such a youngster; whoever suspected an injustice or an affront complained loudly and incited his friends to act against Joseph. Since King Bādīs was now grown old and was practically inactive in the affairs of his kingdom, noblemen—and even noblewomen—began fomenting such chaos and weaving such plots that the royal court almost stifled under their weight.

Bādīs had indeed taken note of his experiences during the last year of his father's rule and the beginning of his own reign. He therefore had arranged for the orderly succession to his throne, which would prevent the eruption of a civil war and which would preserve the kingdom he established with great effort. While only in middle age he had appointed his son Boluggīn as his successor and thereafter gave him the resounding surname "Saif ad-daula" (the royal sword). Boluggīn was neither clever nor energetic. He was indecisive and was easily influenced on all sides. He was a prodigal who was always in need. But he was sociable, and therefore the Berbers and Andalusians liked him. For a long time Joseph succeeded in maintaining a good relationship with Boluggīn. Joseph supplied the crown prince with the large sums of money he needed and thus forced Boluggīn into a sympathetic attitude toward him. The relations between them were sound and, after Boluggīn returned from Málaga (where he was the king's regent), even friendly. Joseph at one point persuaded Bādīs to take the taxes of the Guadix region from the vizier 'Alī Ibn al-Ḳarawī and to give them to him so he could maintain a fund for the king's heir. Boluggīn, in gratitude, assured Joseph that when he became king he would remember this service and raise Joseph yet higher—over all the officeholders in the kingdom.[262] Ibn al-Ḳarawī's family did not forget the matter either. They had just lost a major source of revenue.

Boluggīn, involved anew in financial difficulties, again sought Joseph's service. He complained that Bādīs's wives were pampering his son Tamīm, spending large sums upon him, which he needed for himself and which he felt should go to him. And thus ensued another of those convoluted, sordid intrigues with which the court abounded. The women, for some reason, had once maligned Joseph to Boluggīn. Now, in retaliation, Joseph advised the prince to go to the king with charges against the women. They in turn cleared themselves. The frustrated Boluggīn naturally blamed Joseph for the thwarted action[263] and thereupon his attitude toward his benefactor and counselor changed.

The sons of 'Ali Ibn al-Ḳarawī and of his brother 'Abdallāh could now approach Boluggīn: They became his friends and his constant drinking companions at the frequent banquets where Boluggīn drank himself into torpidity. Their time for revenge had come. They sought to convince the prince to effectuate the dismissal of Joseph; they planned ultimately to prove that it was best to execute him. Boluggīn was incapable of understanding that the intentions of his new friends were not to his benefit but to theirs. This entire family lacked all moral restraints: With no religious conviction, they readily forsook their ancestral faith to become Moslems so that they would attain status and power within the government. This calculated move typified their entire way of life. Such was their duplicity that they brought false tales of the Jewish vizier to Boluggīn, and went to Joseph reporting calumnies which never even occurred to the prince about Joseph.[264] These evil men succeeded. The relations between the prince and the vizier deteriorated further—instead of friendship, suspicion and repulsion prevailed. Boluggīn believed the slander that Joseph had embezzled the monies from the Guadix region and addressed a complaint to his father. But Joseph, armed with documents signed by Boluggīn himself, proved that the prince did receive everything; the Jewish vizier was blameless. Joseph now felt the necessity of revealing the truth to the king: He described Boluggīn's profligacy, the cause of his difficulties. Bādīs chided his son and there can be no doubt that this exacerbated the already keen hostility which Boluggīn felt toward Joseph.[265]

Boluggīn began his plans to slay Joseph, and when the prince drank his fill he talked openly. Servants aplenty reported to Joseph, knowing that they would be rewarded handsomely for this information. The crown prince, far enough into his plot to assign various roles to his subordinates, wavered at the last moment, as was his wont, and again nullified his plan. Capricious as he was, even as he played with schemes to murder him, Boluggīn visited Joseph at home, whiling away the time in friendly gatherings.

Joseph, fully aware of his precarious position, determined to preserve his life by any means. Using whatever sources were available, he promised the prince's servants payment if they reported all Boluggīn's words and actions to him; and in another direction, he gathered his Jewish friends and took counsel with them. After basic and protracted reasoning, they decided to establish ties with Māksen, Bādīs's younger son, so that Boluggīn, the drunkard, could be displaced and his brother enthroned. But Māksen was notorious for his boorish traits, and he had no following among the Ṣinhādja. Doubts and apprehension once again enveloped Joseph and his friends. They were not blind to the seriousness of the situation likely to be created with the death of the king and Boluggīn's ascent to the throne.

While they were weighing the matter, seeking a way out, they were given the solution—sudden and extreme. One day in 1064, Joseph invited the crown prince to his home to enjoy there the liquor forbidden to Moslems. Boluggīn accepted the invitation and, with his entourage, went to Joseph's house, spent some time there, enjoyed the music and imbibed much drink, but upon leaving the house he felt ill, vomited and fell, was brought to his own home, and died there two days later.

When the incident became public, everyone was convinced that the crown prince was poisoned by the Jewish vizier. Indeed it was no secret that Boluggīn and Joseph were scheming against each other; the only question was: Who would be the first to fell his enemy? Many of the Berbers wanted to deal suitably and harshly with Joseph, but the moderate faction won: The king himself would have to determine the punishment. Bādīs was desolated by his son's death, and quite correctly the Berber chiefs presumed that they could rely on his decree. However, Joseph demonstrated to the king—with decisive proofs—that members of Ibn al-Ḳarawī's family and some of his friends had lured Boluggīn into the debauchery that gave them the opportunity to poison him. (Joseph incidentally explained that if he had wanted to slay the crown prince, he would not have done it at a feast in his own house.) Bādīs, convinced, drove several members of the Ibn al-Ḳarawī family from the capital city, confiscating their property; he put some of Boluggīn's friends and servants to death. Others, to save their lives, fled from Granada. To the chagrin of the Berbers and Andalusians, Joseph became more firmly entrenched in his post, his relationship with the king was intact, his great foe was liquidated.[266]

Joseph continued to perform his duties energetically, the income of the royal treasury continued to grow, and all official activities in Granada proceeded in normal fashion. The king devoted himself to his pleasures and left the reins of government in the hands of his vizier. For weeks and months he was absorbed in his pursuits and kept his distance from affairs of the kingdom. But al-Mu'taḍid gave him no rest. A report reached Granada which destroyed the king's serenity and stirred him into action; suddenly Joseph confronted the need to oppose Bādīs.

When eight years previously al-Mu'taḍid had sent the princes of Arcos and Morón to their unenjoyable bath, he had spared the ruler of Ronda because of Abū Nūr's extremely loyal actions through the years. Al-Mu'taḍid therefore liberated Abū Nūr and sent him back to his princedom. Yet Abū Nūr, in a more subtle way, was still imprisoned. The king of Seville was striving toward the liquidation of the Berber states and the annexation of their lands; and if he seemingly showed mercy to his friend, al-Mu'taḍid was actually taking a shrewd step, laying the groundwork to end Abū-Nūr's princedom.

Al-Mu'taḍid gave Abū-Nūr a letter purportedly written by one of his wives wherein she claimed that his son Bādīs, who governed Ronda during his imprisonment, had had improper relations with her. In all truth, that young prince was a violent person lacking a sense of propriety; but that letter was written by the king of Seville solely to create a rift in the Berber dynasty of Ronda. The stratagem was successful. As soon as Abū Nūr returned to Ronda he slew his son—but the grief and the suffering which assailed him when he learned how he was misled by the king of Seville sent him to his grave before the year passed. He was then succeeded by another son, Abū Naṣr.

Al-Mu'taḍid meantime continued to tear district after district away from the Berber states. His agents bribed some

Andalusians among the guards of the fortress where Abū Naṣr was sojourning, and one day in 1065 they attacked him. When he found himself alone and defenseless against a band of armed men, Abū Naṣr jumped from the upper floor of his palace and was killed instantaneously. The plotters easily became masters of the princedom (the Andalusian population took no part in the struggle for dominance) and thus, together with all its provinces, Ronda was annexed to the kingdom of Seville.[267]

Bādīs was appalled by these occurrences. The ease with which al-Mu'taḍid's hirelings dominated Ronda forced him to realize the weakness of the Ṣinhādja rule at Granada and his own precarious condition. It was as if the old king awoke from a deep, protracted sleep. Overwhelmed by terror—by day and by night—he rent his garments in distress, desisted from alcohol, and ceased associating with women (even though he had been unable to live without them until now). At times he sank into depression, sitting for hours withdrawn into himself; at times he was maniacally boisterous. Finally he revealed a plan to his vizier Joseph: To forestall an attack like the one in Ronda and to cow his subjects, he decided to send detachments of soldiers to the Great Mosque on Friday and slaughter the Andalusians worshiping there. The king expected Joseph's agreement. Bādīs needed encouragement. However, Joseph at once told him that he disapproved of the plan, brought Bādīs to realize the danger it held, and urged him to postpone its implementation and to give it more thought.

The king was adamant; the ensuing argument was protracted. Joseph, altogether agitated, dared to raise his voice and to ask: "If the deed is actually performed, does my lord, the king, believe that the Andalusians in the other cities of Granada will agree and remain quiescent in their localities? I fear me that they will rise up as one man and then the few men will have to confront a multitude. I see in my mind's eye dense rows of naked swords drawn against my lord, the king. Like a flood of mighty waters which engulfs all obstacles—so will they come against the Ṣinhādja." But all his words were in vain. The debate ended with Bādīs repeating that he was determined to do as he had planned, and ordering Joseph to keep the matter in total secrecy. The king commanded that the next Friday troops be stationed, their weapons ready and prepared for action.

Joseph, believing that the plot would surely bring chaos and disaster upon the kingdom, resolved to warn the Andalusians surreptiously. It was difficult for him to do this himself: He did not want to be the direct source since Bādīs had imparted the plan to him as a royal secret and, further, the Andalusians would place no credence in him. He therefore sent several women to inform a number of respected natives of the king's plot so that they would avoid going to the Great Mosque on Friday. Of course the news spread—there is no surer method of speedily broadcasting information than that of reporting it as a secret. On Friday only a few ordinary people appeared at the Great Mosque. All the preparations were useless. Bādīs, realizing that the secret had become public, summoned Joseph and accused him of having revealed and undermined the plan. Joseph, afraid to confess, denied the king's charges and argued that the mere act of mobilizing the army had alarmed the public. When he saw that he had not yet stilled the king's wrath, Joseph said: "God was good to my lord, the king, inasmuch as he implanted within him a course of action which would bring fear to them. Truly, he has been saved from their revenge. Let my lord observe closely the state of affairs, weighing and clarifying it carefully, and I am sure he will be convinced of the true value of my advice from the beginning and how correct my opinion is even now." Then one of the senior Berber chiefs arose and, boldly speaking to the king—without having been asked for his opinion—justified Joseph's views.[268] Eventually Bādīs realized that his vizier was, in all truth, right;

but the fact that Joseph had dared to oppose him rankled Bādīs.

A series of incidents now occurred which redounded to the glory of the kingdom of Granada and proved beneficial to the chief vizier. Had these events terminated unsuccessfully for the Ṣinhādja, the blame would have been placed squarely upon Joseph.

Ever since his armies took Algeciras, al-Mu'taḍid wove far-reaching plans for expansion in eastern Andalusia: His immediate goal was the city of Málaga. As was his custom, the king of Seville plotted his action with great diligence. The Andalusians in Málaga hated their Berber rulers with an all-consuming hatred; al-Mu'taḍid could easily attract them and stir them into rebellion. But he waited eleven years until, in his opinion, the proper moment had come. At the outset of 1066, on a date set in advance, the inhabitants of the city rose against the Granadan authorities while columns of the Sevillian army appeared before its gates. The garrison (composed of Negroes) occupying Málaga's fortress held fast and made contact with the king of Granada. While al-Mu'taḍid's troops drank and caroused—without taking any measure for their security—columns of the Granadan army hastened to the aid of the besieged garrison in the ḳaṣaba and slaughtered the surprised army of Seville.

The city reverted to Granadan rule and the crown prince of the kingdom of Seville, who led the expeditionary force, fled in shame, not daring to return to his father until he was forgiven for the defeat.[269] Naturally, the Granadans were elated. Not only was Málaga at that time the city second in size and importance in the Ṣinhādja kingdom—and its only port—but every defeat of the king of Seville was an accomplishment for the rulers of Granada. Joseph, sharing the joy, hoped that the jubilance would cause the episode of Boluggīn's death to be forgotten. But before many days went by, Joseph perceived that the triumph at Málaga had begotten yet a new peril—as serious for him as was Boluggīn's hostility.

Among the officers who participated in the deliverance of Málaga was an-Nāya, a Slav from Seville. He was involved in a conspiracy against al-Mu'taḍid, planned by one of his sons. When the king quashed the cabal and severely punished all connected with it, an-Nāya fled to Granada where he received a post as an officer in the army. He demonstrated courage and unusual dedication in the Málaga campaign; later he was outstanding as an exceptional soldier. He remained in the garrison of Málaga, taking part in forays which were periodically mounted from there to the provinces in southern Andalusia which belonged to the kingdom of Seville; from time to time King Bādīs received reports of an-Nāya's heroism and his talent for leadership. Since the commander of the Málaga region, Muḳātil b. Yaḥyā, called an-Nāya one of the most courageous and loyal officers in the entire army, Bādīs designated him to be his associate in command of the forces of the province. Moreover, an-Nāya became a favorite of the king, who would be a guest at his home whenever he was in Málaga.[270]

An-Nāya was of Christian origin and was permeated with hostility toward the Jews. Craving a position in the highest echelon of government, he never missed an opportunity to slander the Jewish vizier. During one of their drinking bouts, when Bādīs was in a drunken stupor, an-Nāya brought the conversation to the affairs of the kingdom. He pictured Joseph as deceiving him, robbing the Andalusian subjects while goading them on to greater hatred of the Berbers, and, further, as amassing a mint of money by embezzling treasury funds. The Slav officer proposed that he personally would slay the vizier —and the besotted king gave permission to an-Nāya to do as he pleased.

As usual, the king's servants informed Joseph of all that was discussed at those gatherings; of course, they received their reward and were asked to continue bringing information on whatever was said and done within the king's circle. However, the peril of the ambitious Slav officer was too serious for Joseph to be content with information purveyed by servants. Joseph attempted to divide the king and an-Nāya, but his efforts were in vain.

Joseph's quandary deepened for yet other reasons. Earlier, during his controversy with Boluggīn, Joseph had looked to his brother Māksen for support. However, after the sudden death of the crown prince, Māksen expressly accused Joseph of poisoning Boluggīn and, naturally, their friendly association dissolved. Nevertheless, Māksen's mother contacted Joseph's uncle, Abū'r-Rabīʿ Ibn al-Māṭūnī, the minister of finance—whom the king had awarded with the title of "governor" *(ḳā'id);* she asked him for payments from the treasury before they were due, and he acceded in order to please her and her son. To Joseph this was a tactical error: The status of the Jewish officials in the kingdom of Granada depended upon their solidarity against the Berbers and Andalusians; were they to undermine each other, their end would come speedily. Joseph acted with dispatch. After securing the help of a number of Berber nobles from among Māksen's many enemies, Joseph accused the mother to Bādīs—directly—of embezzling monies from the treasury and of promoting intrigues. When the nobles present testified to Bādīs that the charges were true, the king ordered her (and several other women who were her collaborators) to be put to death. Subsequently, Joseph invited his uncle to a feast in his house and slew him with his own hands. But, as if this ostensible act of loyalty to Bādīs were not enough, Joseph sent the king a precious gift in a further demonstration of fealty.[271]

XIII

Thus Joseph once more succeeded in suppressing a budding conspiracy, but by heartrending means . . . and yet, was it not clear that he would soon again be confronted with new and more difficult perils? An-Nāya surely would continue voicing his indictment to Bādīs. Certainly, one day the aged king would heed an-Nāya, and then what would this drunken tyrant do? He might strike at the Jews under his rule, destroying them in vengeance. These were the thoughts which assailed Joseph, and the situation seemed hopeless. The hostility of the Berbers toward him (and all those close to him) was readily evident—and Joseph well knew what thoughts the Andalusians harbored.

He pondered over his affairs day and night, thoughts taking possession and then being rejected. He analyzed the entire complex with his keen mind, endeavoring to find a portent for the future. One thing his deliberations made clear to him—halfway solutions would neither give him ease nor achieve his goal. He concluded that the solution would have to be one that released him from the constant tension of dependency on the kindness of drunken, perverse rulers and the fear of conspiracies devised in the harems of lecherous kings. Once Joseph began searching for such a solution he looked into every possibility; he asked the opinion of friends but concealed his innermost thoughts. Joseph carefully weighed their reactions and gradually a plan took form—it had sweep and imagination but was not at all made of the stuff of dreams.

When Joseph's penetrating gaze swept over the political arena of Moslem Spain and the factors operating within it, he came, time and again, to the conclusion that the strength that could be mustered was limited. What, he asked himself, was the number of men in the Ṣinhādja army? Was it thousands? Did they not have to augment their army with large troops from among the Zenāta—their old, sworn enemies—and also Negroes from the Sudan and Slavs because the Ṣinhādja numbers were indeed small?

What was the military strength of the princedoms of Arcos and Morón? The Berbers ruled those spacious provinces for several decades. A small faction of military men enjoyed the good of the land and benefited from the labor of their Andalusian subjects, who were revolted by the constant warring and who submitted to despised, alien masters.

Those Slavs—formerly captives and slaves and a mixed multitude of eunuchs and mercenaries, reckless and irresponsible men, who hired themselves out to Moslem princes and now had become lords who had carved their own sizable kingdoms in eastern Spain—how many thousands did their combined armies number? In all their wars did they not find it necessary to get help from Catalan mercenaries? Their subjects supported them with taxes and contributions during their wars; their dominance was firm from the mouth of the Ebro to the borders of Granada.

What was the secret of this remarkable phenomenon of the hold of minorities over alien, hostile multitudes? What was the power that sustained these states? There could be no explanation other than the unity prevailing among those groups of Berbers and Slavs—their single goal: to preserve their privileged status.

Was the number of Jews in Granada fewer than that of the Ṣinhādja or the Berbers in the states west of this kingdom? Surely they would number several thousand after they were joined by Jews of North Africa and of the other provinces of Spain—it could not then be difficult to assemble several regiments of true fighters. Were not Lucena's Jews and their brothers in the villages historically skilled in weaponry? Did they not also know how to defend themselves effectively when attacked? And if their numbers were insufficient, they could be augmented by hirelings from among the Slavs and Berbers for whom battle was an occupation—they hired themselves out to any faction which paid generously. These were Joseph's meditations.

Why then be dependent upon the kindness of Bādīs and his companions? Why be as clay in his potterlike hands? Why suffer the daily apprehension of constant intrigues against him? Had not Samuel, his father, trained him to be a ruler over the many and his own master? Until now he had fulfilled what he had been taught:

Let your mouth speak fair words to your foe,
But in your innermost thoughts beware of his deeds;
Store up in your heart the evil he does to you,
And when the time is opportune hasten to slay him.[272]

Had not his father desired that he become a great lord when he wrote: "Wax great and exalted over the greatness of your forebears"?[273] Or when he addressed Joseph with:

Ascend to my office that I may be deemed
As David and you as ḳōhelet.[274]

This, then, was Joseph's destiny. For this he was created and reared—why should his plan fail? Was he any whit less than the crude Berbers and maniacal Slavs?

It was possible to seize control of one of the Spanish provinces and to hold it with the aid of the Granadan Jews and with the help of additional troops—if he could only execute the plan correctly. It was best to proceed cautiously, implementing the scheme step by step. The king of Almería was only the son of a man who was appointed by the king of Valencia as regent and, rebelling against the king, had himself crowned. Obviously, anyone who attained the status of a viceroy had soldiers at his disposal and could hire new soldiers. He therefore must exchange his office of chief vizier of the kingdom of Granada, an office without a grasp upon any province whatsoever, for that of a viceroy in another country.

Joseph's friends had suggested that he flee to a neighboring state, but he rejected the suggestion on the premise that the ruler of the country to which he might go would deliver him to the Ṣinhādja. It certainly was not worthwhile for that ruler to become involved with the kingdom of Granada on Joseph's behalf. Joseph must give him something which would attract and impel him to support the Jew. Joseph considered the king of Almería, al-Mu'taṣim: Surely, the king desired to renew the glory of his kingdom which once was powerful and large. If Joseph proffered help in the conquest of the neighboring kingdom of Granada, there could be no doubt that the king would reward him. As chief vizier, Joseph had the power to extend valuable aid if the king of Almería decided to attack Bādīs. Joseph felt that the king of Almería must therefore lay the groundwork for his conquest of Granada and its annexation. Joseph's stipulation would be that the king transfer himself and his court to Granada and designate Joseph as his viceroy in Almería.

There was no better locale for this plan than Almería. It was a city on the seacoast, a city rich in industry and commerce; its large revenues from the taxes of its citizenry and the customs paid by seafarers supported the royal court and regiments of soldiers. Moreover, Almería had a strategical advantage: Maintaining contact with its ships at sea, Almería could withstand an enemy attack for a longer period than could a landlocked city of equivalent size. This was the identical factor which elated King Bādīs on his conquest of Málaga, and immediately after its capture, he began to convert its ḳaṣaba into a strong fortress; it would serve as a secure refuge for his dynasty. Yet, if the enemy nevertheless were to prevail, how easy it was to escape from such a city and to cross over to the not distant Morocco![275]

XIV

Joseph's plan evolved slowly in his mind, and when it crystallized he did not implement it immediately. After all, this was an act of treason against the king who had expressed utter faith in him and who had placed the government in his hands. It is understandable that Joseph could neither readily violate this trust nor could he easily start on a course laden with personal hazard. Meantime some of his father's friends suggested that Joseph should cultivate Tamīm, Boluggīn's young son, whom Bādīs loved and who was apt to inherit the throne. Tamīm was the darling of the king's harem; Joseph therefore had talks with the women, and together they made plans to liquidate Māksen and to prompt Bādīs into designating Tamīm as heir-apparent.[276] Joseph doubted that this solution would secure his status—Boluggīn's death still cast its long shadow upon him. Yet even as Joseph was plagued by doubts, he performed his functions as he always had. He supervised the activities of the various departments, inspected the accounts the tax collectors brought in, cultivated ties with the Berber states in central Andalusia, received ambassadors from other kingdoms and dispatched his emissaries to them.

Withal, it did not escape Joseph's notice that the king kept his distance from him and, absorbed by his pleasures, inclined toward an increasing belief in the slanders of an-Nāya. And an-Nāya, sure of himself, spoke to the king in any vein he wished—even with Joseph present. Joseph needed no penetrating insight to realize that his standing was now too precarious for him to postpone the grand plan: to establish a princedom in Almería for himself and his people. His friends concurred.

The first step was to open negotiations with the king of Almería. It appeared at the outset that the king did not relish such a daring action. Al-Mu'taṣim Muḥammad was not a fighter and had never shown a lust for conquests. Primarily, however, he was grateful to Bādīs who had led his army in 1053 to defend him against his enemies; since then the Almerían prince sought to please Bādīs in all things. But when Joseph proposed the annexation of all of Granada to Almería, he could not resist the temptation. To be sure, he vacillated so that the negotiations were not lacking in retreats and failures. Progress was slow.

When Joseph held talks with an emissary of al-Mu'taṣim (who had come to see the king of Granada), he betrayed Joseph and revealed the plan. This emissary, an Andalusian whose name was 'Abdal'azīz b. Muḥammad Ibn Arḳam, at first intended reporting to the king but later, not having an opportunity, went to Bādīs's grandson 'Abdallāh. Joseph, of course, could not go to Almería, and since he had to discuss matters directly with those in charge of Almerían policy, he requested al-Mu'taṣim to send once again an emissary to Granada. The emissary would go to Bādīs but would clarify all details of the action with Joseph. The king of Almería sent one of his favorites—a "fraternal nursling" (one who had shared the same wet nurse). But this emissary was unenthusiastic; he emphasized the difficulties and did not minimize the stand of the Ṣinhādja, who were likely to fight desperately.

Joseph assured him that his views were valid and began to remove from the capital those Ṣinhādja chiefs who in his opinion were likely to defeat his plot. The most important of these were Musakkan b. Ḥabbūs al-Maghrālī and Yaḥyā b. Yefren, an esteemed chief of the tribe of Talkāta. The first was appointed governor of Jaén and the second was sent to Almuñecar as its governor. Joseph convinced them that their move was necessary since they could keep these important fortresses in the control of the Ṣinhādja and protected against the Slavs, friends of an-Nāya; this explanation was accepted by the chiefs. Simultaneously, Joseph withheld consignments of food and supplies to the garrisons in the eastern sector of the country until they were abandoned by entire companies. Joseph could now assure al-Mu'taṣim that it would not be difficult for him to conquer the eastern and central provinces of the kingdom of Granada. Al-Mu'taṣim ordered his army to cross the border of Granada, and as Joseph had said, they easily took the eastern regions. All the provinces of Baza and Guadix fell into their hands; but instead of advancing to the Berber capital, the Almerían soldiers were halted in the mountainous region north of the Sierra Nevada. Al-Mu'taṣim wavered.

While Joseph endeavored to induce the reluctant king to complete the action which had begun successfully, he took steps to prevent any reprisals which might be made against him when Almerían regiments appeared in Granada. Some of al-Mu'taṣim's officers had made imprudent remarks in those cities which they had taken, and Joseph knew statements were voiced among the Ṣinhādja that he was an accomplice in the treachery. Justifiably he was apprehensive that, as the army of the king of Almería drew near, the Ṣinhādja would vent their wrath upon him; he therefore prepared for himself and his associates a refuge. It was now several generations since the "red" fortress on the lofty hill south of the Darro River had been destroyed; in it the Arabs, in the days of the Omayyads, entrenched themselves in their battle against the *muwalladūn.* Joseph reconstructed the ruins and built a strong fortress on the western edge of the hill—to this day known as the "Ḳaṣaba" of the Alhambra.[277] Joseph, however, needing safety until the arrival of the Almerían army, moved with his family to the fortified quarter of Berber Granada (where the king's residence was located and which was called al-Ḳaṣaba).[278]

Fortuitously, Joseph was given the opportunity to remove Māksen, Bādīs's younger son, from Granada. Māksen hated Joseph and had sufficient power to concentrate the Berbers around him in a crisis. A Berber officer had addressed a complaint to Bādīs during a survey of the King's forces in preparation for a campaign in the fallen districts. The appointment of Slavs to posts of high command in the army infuriated the Berbers. The officer went on to say that if Bādīs would place Māksen at the head of the army, the Ṣinhādja would go anywhere they were asked. Bādīs was alarmed at this: He feared that the Berbers might reject him because of his inaction and would name his son king. When Joseph saw the misgivings Bādīs had because of Māksen, he exploited the situation and encouraged the king to exile his son from the capital.[279]

But despite Joseph's precautions—and they were many—his position grew more difficult from day to day. The conquest of the eastern provinces by the Almerían army caused obvious dissatisfaction among the Ṣinhādja, who grumbled among themselves about the do-nothing king; they voiced loud objections against the Jewish vizier who was not taking proper action in defense of the kingdom. As is customary in times of failure and defeat, all the complaints against the rulers—real or imaginary—were aired . . . and all the barbs were aimed at Joseph. The accusations relating to political complications accompanied the charges relating to the enrichment of the Jewish vizier and his associates. The Andalusians gleefully joined in the outcry against the Jews—the streets of Granada resounded with their short, derisive songs. This form of propaganda certainly served to undermine the vizier and his coterie, but the one who most roused the populace was an Arabic poet who wrote a long poem against Joseph and the Jews.

The poet, from Elvira, named Ibrāhīm b. Mas'ūd b. Sa'īd at-Tudjībī, was popularly called Abū Isḥāḳ. He had studied Moslem law under the judge of his city, Abū'Abdallāh Muḥammad Ibn Zamanīn, who was a renowned scholar; later he went to Granada, becoming the secretary of the judge Abu' l-Ḥasan 'Alī Ibn Tauba. As did his fellow Moslem theologians, Abū Isḥaḳ too, throughout his lifetime, malevolently viewed the dominance of the Jews in Granada. However, Ibn Tauba was respected in the royal court and a familiar visitor with Bādīs so that while he lived Abū Isḥāḳ was guarded in his utterances; after Ibn Tauba died, which was while Joseph still served as chief vizier, Abū Isḥaḳ no longer restrained himself. Not wishing to act alone against a Moslem theologian, Joseph requested that the king remove him from the capital. Bādīs acceded and drove Abū Isḥāḳ from Granada; he thereupon returned to his native city of Elvira, took up residence at a retreat for ascetics, and occupied himself with study and worship. He composed poetry, infused with the ascetic spirit of withdrawal from mundane pleasures. These poems were popular with the masses who quoted them frequently, particularly during their funerals. However, Abū Isḥāḳ was scarcely the dedicated ascetic his poems seem to prove. He intended deriving pleasure from all that was physically good in this world, to attain wealth and fame, and he regarded the Jewish vizier as the prime cause for the failure of his ambitions.

When Abū Isḥāḳ heard of the ferment at Granada he wrote a "ḳaṣīda" (a satiric poem) against Joseph, which spread quickly and gained a wide circulation. Its success derived both from its form and content. Abū Isḥāḳ's poetry does not employ the esoteric words and ornamental phrases Arabic poets favored, but familiar words, well known to anyone with the merest knowledge of Arabic. The poet does not use veiled allusions but expresses himself clearly. Departing from accepted practice, he touches on his theme at the start of the poem: Your king (he thus addresses the Ṣinhādja) committed an error and a sin when he appointed a vizier who was a Jew instead of a Moslem—something forbidden by Moslem law. One transgression leads to another and a concommitant of having a Jewish viceroy is that the Jews, formerly despised and subjugated, are now masters—the Moslems dependent upon their favors and living in fear of them. Abū Isḥāḳ describes the Jews who benefit from their tax collecting and conspicuously display their wealth: "The ape [Joseph] has paved his house with marble and brought into it running water and his associates batten themselves upon luxuries and wear magnificent clothes; whereas the Moslems eat dry crusts of bread and wear rags." Abū Isḥāḳ, by turns, addresses the king and the Ṣinhādja, warning Bādīs against punishment for his deeds, and depicting the situation for the Ṣinhādja; finally, he calls upon the king to slay the Jewish vizier immediately, to spare none of Joseph's rich associates, and to take for himself the treasures they had garnered.[280]

Abū Isḥāḳ's inflammatory poem was copied by men in every quarter who recited it to anyone unable to read—groups of people assembled, listening attentively to the interpretations of pseudo-intellectuals (those were especially among the Ṣinhādja, who had a scanty knowledge of the nuances of Arabic language). All who grasped the substance of the poem expressed concurrence and added all sorts of their own interpretations. During the last days of December 1066, when the poem of the Elviran Abū Isḥāḳ was circulated in Granada, the atmosphere became charged with explosive elements.

On a Sabbath night, the eve of the ninth of Tēbhet (December 30), Joseph was host—in his temporary home in the ḳaṣaba—to some of his friends, Jews and Moslems, officeholders at the royal court. He sensed that his guests were not their usual selves and that they were uneasy; therefore, he sought to reassure them by allusion and by direct reference to the transformation about to occur with the imminent arrival of the Almerían army. After his guests partook—with their customary relish—of the vintage wines and superb confections, Joseph thought that he had succeeded in calming them. However, one of the Moslems, utterly drunk, suddenly turned to him and asked whether the king was still alive, adding that, according to reports, Joseph had killed him. The guests were astounded and, because of his question, openly rebuked the Moslem. The man, disturbed and confused, ran into the streets screaming that the king had been assassinated by the vizier Abū Ḥusain and that the army of Almería stood at the gates of the city. People were still in the streets at that hour, and on hearing the tumult, many emerged from their homes. Within a short time a large crowd gathered and Granada was abuzz—the demand now came from various sides to slay the Jewish vizier—without delay.

When Joseph learned the extent of the uproar he hastened to the palace, succeeded in reaching Bādīs, and begged him to go to the gate to show himself to the crowds. Although silence prevailed briefly among the people when the king first appeared, the suppressed anger erupted into curses and invectives. Bādīs immediately reentered the palace and Joseph followed. He fled to one of the supply depots adjacent to the kitchens and blackened his face as a camouflage, but the Moslems found and recognized him. They drew Joseph ha-lēvī from his hiding place and killed him.

All the resentment and hatred of the masses were vented that Sabbath morning. That was the day which they awaited. The Berbers who entered the palace during the night were from the most esteemed Berber class, but the mob of Andalusians who assembled the next morning were dissolutes thirsting for blood and loot. Together with Berber soldiers, they dragged Joseph's body—like the carcass of an animal—through the streets of Granada. And then they hung him on a cross fashioned from two boards, near the city gate.

After their venomous assault upon the corpse of the hated vizier, they crossed the Darro and, with terrifying shrieks, broke into the Jewish quarters. The Berbers had their swords, the Andalusians were armed with hammers and axes. A group of young men tried to block the path at the entrances to the Jewish sector, but their desperate opposition intensified the passion of the Moslems. After the mob overpowered the defenders, they broke into the homes and began their massacre. They smashed the wooden doors with their axes and people were dragged, frightened and shivering, to be beheaded by a sword blow. The mob watched with enjoyment. Its triumphant roar mingled with the cries of pleading women and the wailing of children. Here an old man was stabbed, there a woman was hung from a beam; here a rapist violated a woman while his companion ravished her daughter, and when they were sated, they slaughtered both; the beheaded corpses of infants were everywhere. The bodies of men lay with bellies split asunder and weltered in their own blood; close by small girls lay dying, quivering in final, convulsive jerks. Streams of blood flowed into the narrow streets, hollowed by the rains.

Spoils were brought together: rugs and couches covered with precious textiles; heavy iron chests, not yet broken open but whose weight signified the riches within; bundles of garments; heaps of vessels of all sorts. The rioters came and went for hours, having donkeys with them on which to load the valuables, and not ceasing until they divested the houses of every worthwhile thing. Nothing remained in the homes but smashed furniture and corpses smeared with congealed blood.

On that Black Sabbath hundreds of the Jews of Granada were murdered.[281]

3

THE JEWISH COMMUNITIES OF SPAIN IN THE ELEVENTH CENTURY

I

Throughout Andalusia, Jews and Moslems alike were wholly absorbed by the news of the riots in Granada—information reached every city and village within a few days. Among the Jews particularly there was intense concern. Many had relatives in Granada and this one worried about his brother, that one feared for his children. Their apprehensions were verified within two or three weeks when they learned that their kin indeed had perished in the tragedy. In all the cities of Granada, Jews rent their garments and assembled in memorial services. The heads of the community proclaimed a fast day and even those who were not in mourning for relatives donned sackcloth and ashes; everyone gathered in the synagogues to recite psalms and study the Mishnah. Rabbi Isaac Ibn Gayyāt composed an elegy which was recited before a large gathering at Lucena.[1]

All Spanish Jewry felt that its crown and glory had fallen with the destruction of the great and wealthy community in Granada which was their pride. They were crushed when they heard details of that bitter, violent day . . . when they heard how noble men were hanged, the old dishonored. No more did they feel the equal of their non-Jewish neighbors; it was as though they had dreamt an evanescent dream and it was gone. The slaughter in Granada showed them the tenuousness of their position in alien lands. Over the generations they had come to believe that they were as much citizens of Spain as were the Moslems and Christians, the Andalusians and Arabs, the Berbers and Slavs—now it was clear: Spain was a land of exile as were all the other diasporas.

The Jews of Spain were sobered by their disillusionment and they anticipated that trouble would overtake them in other cities as well: the non-Jews would gather, doing as the Moslems of Granada had done. The Jews in the cities of the Ṣinhādja kingdom were especially apprehensive.[2] As long as the *nāgīd* Joseph was the chief vizier of the kingdom, they felt secure. Although they complained about his actions, they found shelter in his protection and did not fear the hatred of the Andalusians or the savagery of the Berbers; now they were like a flock of sheep without a shepherd.

The fears of the Jews of Granada were well founded. After Joseph and his associates, the Jewish dignitaries of Granada, were slain, confusion enveloped the kingdom. Bādīs was consumed with anger at the slaying of his vizier. He refused to believe all he was told about Joseph, and particularly of his plot with the king of Almería. The Berber chiefs despised the old ruler, who was weak and useless; they were clearly free to attack the Jews in any way they chose. Musakkan b. Ḥabbūs al-Maghrālī, the officer who was sent to Jaén by Bādīs on Joseph's advice to become the governor of its province, met Prince Māksen on the way. The Berber officer took the prince (whom Bādīs exiled from the kingdom) with him to Jaén to use him in the implementation of his own plans, at the opportune time. Some days later, when the Berber heard of Joseph's assassination and of Bādīs's utter helplessness, he instantly proclaimed Māksen the independent ruler of Jaén and its province. He then imposed upon the Jews of Jaén the obligation to pay him a large sum of money and succeeded in obtaining it.[3] At that time the community of Lucena also suffered hardships and its rabbi, Isaac Ibn Gayyāt, intended depicting them in a poem, though he did not manage to fulfill his intention.[4]

The respect the Jews of Andalusia had enjoyed with the populace waned; and, in the spirit of Spaniards who are known for their pride, they were strongly affected by the change of attitude. It seemed as if all wayfarers hissed and wagged their heads at them in contempt. Those who yesterday were friends, today were enemies. Moslems who had profited from the beneficence of Samuel the *nāgīd* and his son now vociferously demonstrated their hatred. Only a few kept faith with their former benefactors. One of these, the Arabic poet al-Akhfash b. Maimūn Ibn al-Farrā, went to Almería and glorified the memory of Joseph with verse; and when the Moslems complained, he retorted that loyalty was a supreme law—even permitting the eulogizing of an infidel. The Arabic historian who reports this adds that one of the sons of the Almerían king exonerated the poet.[5] But, indeed, there were only a few of his kind.

Meantime, those who fled and succeeded in hiding during the riots, or who were saved by loyal Moslem friends or by Moslems whom they bribed, began arriving in the communities of Andalusia. Panicked, terrified, in urgent want they came —individuals and families, widowed women with their children and their enfeebled fathers; their tales, terrifying and shocking, shrouded the atmosphere in gloom. The relatives of the refugees, endeavoring to assuage their pain, provided for their immediate needs and for their future. Joseph's wife was rescued and went with her son to Lucena. Rabbi Isaac Ibn Gayyāt, who over many years had enjoyed the support and encouragement of Samuel the *nāgīd* and Joseph, welcomed them with honor and considered it his duty to care for them. Because of his effort, the community of Lucena allotted them funds which sufficed to maintain them with dignity. Rabbi Isaac intended to teach the lad, whose name was Abū Naṣr Azariah, and to make him a rabbi and communal leader—as were his father and grandfather—but he died when he was twenty years old.[6] Among those also rescued from the slaughter was one of the sons of the Babylonian exilarch Hezekiah. The two brothers had migrated to Spain and dwelt in Granada under the aegis of the *nāgīd* Joseph; one was swept away in the catastrophe, and the other eventually found refuge in Saragossa, which had an important Jewish community.[7]

After some days passed and the fury subsided, many of the Jews in Granada came out of hiding. Fugitives who found asylum in towns and villages nearby were encouraged on hearing that the king was condemning the rioters, and returned to their homes. But it was only then that they grasped the immensity of their tragedy: Their heartache was even greater when, after the initial shock, they had to adapt to the new situation. In time, however, the Jews of Granada gradually returned to their daily concerns. Workshops reopened, trading resumed. Houses and courtyards whose owners and occupants were slain during the riots were considered "heirless property" and were confiscated by the Moslem authorities; however, after prolonged efforts the Jews succeeded in redeeming those properties.[8] But the structure of the community was markedly different from what was before the massacre. The influential group of affluent men and high officials disappeared; the artisans and laborers who worked for them lost their livelihoods and struggled to support their dependents. Persons of property were compelled to sell their realty. Such a case is discussed in a judgment rendered by an Andalusian rabbi at the end of the eleventh century. Some Jews of Granada jointly owned a fig-tree orchard and, after the persecutions, the wife of one of the partners and the heirs of others, who were apparently all killed during the riots, sold it. The sale was effected in the absence of two of the partners, and with the ensuing quarrels the case was brought before the rabbi.[9]

The community was bereft of its leaders who were part of the government elite; and they were replaced by others of lesser influence. There is a document from that time in the Cairo Geniza which was given to a Granadan Jew who left for Egypt. According to its text, his father was close to the king—one of those who ate at his table—until the calamity reduced the importance of the Jews of Granada. Among other things, the document relates that he is leaving for the Near East to fulfill a religious duty (apparently relating to a levirate marriage) and the Jews of Egypt are requested to aid him, inasmuch as he himself is shy and will request nothing. This document is signed by three members of the Granadan Jewish lawcourt—Samuel bar Isaac, Isaac bar Joseph, and Samuel bar Judah.[10]

After the riots, the kingdom of Granada was no longer the center of the Jews in southern Spain. The communities in the kingdom of Granada were replaced by those of the kingdom of Seville and, more particularly, by the Jewry of Seville itself. After Cordova's decline Seville developed into the most important city of Andalusia. Seville, the capital of a relatively powerful state, grew wealthy, and as it grew, so did its Jewish community. Seville, in the eleventh century, was an important manufacturing center for cotton textiles.[11] All branches of commerce flourished; collections of Arabic biographies of that epoch contain numerous data about merchants who came to the city from Oriental countries and settled within it—testimony to the trade links with countries on the eastern rim of the Mediterranean Sea, reaching into Persia.[12] Seville's economic rise, in large measure, was linked to the political changes in Andalusia and to its rise as the capital of a kingdom.

The establishment of the kingdom of Seville was primarily the achievement of King al-Mu'taḍid. In the despotic governments of the Middle Ages and especially those of the Moslems, the king's personality was of critical importance: This Arab monarch was a capable ruler with a precise goal—to impose his sovereignty over all of Andalusia. At the outset he enlarged his kingdom in the west. In 1044 he annexed the principality of Mertola, where an Arab prince of the Ibn Ṭaifūr family was in power. In the early 1060s, al-Mu'taḍid established his mastery over the small principalities in the southwest sector of the peninsula and then directed his efforts toward the small Berber states in southern Andalusia. In 1059 he let it be known that Hishām II had died, leaving a will in which he designated himself the ruler over all of Spain. Seven years later al-Mu'ta ḍid succeeded in annexing to his kingdom the remnants of the principalities of Morón and Arcos. 'Imād ad-daula Manād, the prince of Morón, surrendered to al-Mu'taḍid's army and handed the city to him, whereas Muḥammad Ibn Khizrūn, the ruler of Arcos, wanted to give his city to Bādīs, king of Granada, in exchange for a fortress in his kingdom. However, al-Mu'taḍid's troops ambushed Ibn Khizrūn when he departed his city with his possessions, killed him, and slaughtered the troops Bādīs had sent to accompany him; Arcos then fell into the hands of the king of Seville.[13] Thenceforth the domain of al-Mu'taḍid spread over all the regions which today comprise southern Portugal and western and southern Andalusia.

Al-Mu'taḍid's successes were primarily the result of his machinations and his brutal acts. When his son Ismā'īl rebelled against him in 1063, he slew him with his own hands and, to serve as a warning, imposed severe penalties on his associates. He ordered that their limbs be torn from their bodies, sparing neither the women nor their maidservants. Arabic writers relate that he decapitated his slain enemies and planted flowers in their heads. He would place the skulls of his most distinguished foes in a chest with tags bearing their names. Nevertheless, al-Mu'taḍid was convinced that he was a monarch who aspired for the good of his subjects and who dealt considerately with them.

After the expulsion of the Ḥammūdites from Seville, the government proved hostile toward its Jews, who numbered more than five thousand by the middle of the eleventh century.[14] The kadi and his son and heir, al-Mu'taḍid, were haughty Arabs whose avowed goal was to renew the dominance of their race over the Iberian peninsula. They fought most of their wars with the Berbers. The fact that a Jew was the chief vizier in the most powerful Berber kingdom, directing its policy, resulted in their combining Berbers and Jews (whom the dominant Arabs regarded with contempt in any case). Arabic poets composed verses extolling the military ventures of the kadi and his son, al-Mu'taḍid, as holy wars against the Berbers and Jews.[15] Samuel the *nāgīd* depicts the status of the Jews in one of his poems about the wars with the ruler of Seville and alludes to incitements against them:

In this land of wrongdoers
The children of the living God
Are pelted with the barbs of their tongues.

And later on:

And I can recall that which this assembly bears in its heart
Against my lowly maltreated people.[16]

These verses are not poetic hyperbole. Al-Mu'taḍid took such action in order to stress the dominance of the Arabs and Islam. He struck at non-Moslems by renewing old statutes which were imposed on Christians generations before and which they had ceased observing. A contemporary Moslem author relates that al-Mu'taḍid compelled the Christian clergy to become circumcised.[17] But he was not observant of his own faith and made no attempt to conceal this fact. His attitude in general toward religious matters and his position vis-à-vis his non-Moslem subjects was ambivalent—just as his character was made up of strong contradictions.

During the second half of al-Mu'taḍid's reign, political expediency obliged him to impose his yoke not too heavily upon the members of the non-Moslem communities: Christian power in northern Spain had increased. After the kingdoms of León and Castile united, they attacked the scattered and divided Moslems. The Moslem kings and princes took heed and avoided furnishing the Christians with any pretext to harm them, and since they were compelled to treat the Christian Mozarabs properly, they did not oppress the Jews; those Moslem rulers who tended to persecute non-Moslem communities had to exercise restraint. Even those who pretended to be devout named non-Moslems to important positions because they hoped to gain advantage from these appointments. In al-Mu'taḍid's court there was a Christian official who was close to him and was also one of the high officers in the army. This official, Sisenand b. David (surnamed Abū 'Āmir), was a Mozarab from the province of Coimbra; after serving the Arab king of Seville for many years, executing missions for him to Fernando, king of León and Castile, and acting as commander in numerous forays against Christian regions, he went into the service of the Christian king.[18] There were Jews too among those who were close to al-Mu'taḍid. One, Joseph Ibn Migash of Granada, found refuge in Seville when he fled his city early in Bādīs's reign because of his underground activities against the king.[19]

Members of the Jewish community who had no vested interest in the government benefited from the flourishing economy of Seville; most of Seville's Jews were artisans engaged in a variety of occupations. Over many generations a thriving textile industry had developed, producing cotton cloth renowned especially for its beautiful hues; moreover, according to an ancient Arabic writer, only the Jews knew where to locate superior grades of dye. The observations of this writer prove that Jews had a monopoly in the craft of dyeing in Moslem Spain, even as it was a Jewish occupation in other Moslem countries.[20] Jewish butchers had their shops near those of the Moslems, and Arabs were counted among their customers.[21] There was, of course, a strong group of merchants among Seville's Jews who were exporters and importers with commercial ties in the Near East. One of these was Saadya b. Moses who gave Samuel b. Sahl, a Jew from Khorasan, a letter to Solomon b. Judah, the head of the Talmud academy in Jerusalem (he died in 1051).[22]

The Jewish community of Seville was not lacking in intellectuals either. The number of Jewish physicians in Seville was considerable and they were popular among the Moslems. An overly zealous Moslem theologian protests because his coreligionists consulted them, but whereas his language is forceful in other passages in his book on the improvement of society, he observes in this passage only that "it would be desirable" not to allow Jewish (and Christian) physicians to treat sick Moslems.[23] Jewish scholars were in constant touch with Moslem scholars, acquiring from them copies of classical works in the sciences which had been written in Arabic; even this contact evoked the wrath of this devout theologian.[24] Side by side with the Jewish artisans, merchants, and physicians of Seville, there were rabbinic scholars and poets who wrote in Hebrew. Among the poets of that era was Abūn b. Sh'rāra who came from Lucena to settle in Seville. He was a devotee of Samuel the *nāgīd* and composed fervent verse in his honor.[25] Abūn b. Sh'rāra was one of many who went to the burgeoning city, knowing that it would be easier to earn his livelihood there than anywhere else. Thus, within the community of Seville there were elements with varied standards of living: the poor who existed through their daily toils and merchants whose livelihoods were assured. In the winding and narrow streets of the old Jewish quarter, these affluent merchants owned houses which, from their exteriors, seemed like houses of the poor, but inside they were magnificent, their floors paved with marble.

In the days of the Omayyad caliphs the number of Jews in central and southern Andalusia was relatively large. In all its cities and towns, there were Jewish communities—large and small—which without doubt were superior in size and importance to the communities of other regions in the Iberian peninsula. In the eleventh century, however, Andalusia ceased being the exclusive population and cultural center of the Jews of Spain. Many left the places in which their forebears had dwelt for generations. This was a wave of migration which began during the civil wars and the breakup of the caliphate, one which encompassed sizable groups of Andalusian Jews, and one which, even though its pace slackened, continued over a long period, linked as it was to specific economic circumstances in eleventh-century Andalusia. Catastrophe struck the villages. Writing in the 1070s, the geographer al-Bakrī stresses that the majority of the villages in the province of Cordova were emptied of people and agriculture was neglected: The continuous, protracted warring among the successors of the caliphs—the mobilizations and the confiscations (and the accumulated losses from their intemperate ways) had their effect, indeed.[26]

The ruin in other areas of the economy was no less. During the reign of the Omayyad caliphs, Cordova served as a focal point for the economic activity of all the regions south of the Guadalquivir. Artisans and small manufacturers labored primarily for the market of the capital of the caliphs. After its downfall many of the enterprises of central and southern Andalusia were liquidated; those which continued to exist had to seek new markets. The new customers were the officers and civilian staffs of the small royal courts which arose during that period throughout the peninsula. In time, instead of sending their products directly to the courts, the artisans and manufacturers moved to the chief cities of these new states—sometimes by request, sometimes on their own initiative.

With reduced manufacturing in this region, trade—both domestic and foreign—contracted also. Those selfsame factors which troubled its industry led to the decreased volume of trade in Andalusia's products: The wars of the princes in Andalusia were almost all short forays, unimportant encounters compared with the wars of 'Abdarraḥmān III and al-Manṣūr and their massed forces. These Andalusian princes did not require such huge quantities of equipment and supplies.

A third, critical factor in the shrinking Andalusian commerce was a change in the trading methods of the Mediterranean basin. Until the end of the eleventh century, all of southern France was terrorized by Moslem predators from Spain who were entrenched on the seacoast, at Garde Freinet. Many settlements were devastated, others were abandoned by their inhabitants and the trade routes rendered desolate. When the rulers of Provence succeeded in ridding the area of the marauders, the economic life of all the provinces in southern France resumed and a new epoch began. But the French and Italians now replaced the Andalusian traders who once supplied this region with Oriental wares.

The Jews constituted a majority among all those branches of industry which had flourished in Andalusia and provided many with dignified livelihoods. The metalsmiths, the manufacturers of fine textiles, the tanners, the producers of leather goods, the spice merchants, and the slave dealers were largely Jews. In the first half of the eleventh century they supported themselves with difficulty or now had completely lost their businesses. There were artisans engaged in the occupations of their forebears who refused to abandon their craft, uprooted themselves, and wandered to other provinces in Spain.

Andalusia, however, was not emptied of Jews. On the contrary, Jews continued to dwell in the major cities, in the small towns and villages; Andalusia, until the middle of the twelfth century, remained the largest Jewish center in the entire peninsula.

There was a Jewish community located in Ronda. This ancient city, which was called Arunda in the time of the Romans and Visigoths, was regarded, during the days of Moslem rule, as an impregnable fortress; in the age of the caliphs it was the chief city of the province of Tākurunna. Although the number of Jews in Ronda was never large, there were always traces of them in the city chronicles; and, as in all the cities of Moslem Spain, they had their own quarter.[27]

A small Jewish community also existed in the city of Algeciras, during the eleventh century. Then, as now, this port city served as an important transit way station to the continent opposite it; it was closer to Africa than any of the other cities in Andalusia. The city was the capital of a small principality of Ḥammūdites since 1035, but it was conquered in 1055 by troops sent by the king of Seville. The last Ḥammūdite prince, al-Ḳāsim, was forced to surrender.[28]

The active commercial traffic and the close ties with northern Morocco resulted in the growth of a Jewish settlement within the city. A letter from that period, written in polished

Arabic and directed to the Algeciras community, extols the generosity of the Jews, who extended a gracious welcome to those who chanced to go there. This letter[29] was written as a recommendation for a scholar, teacher, or a religious ministrant. A fragment of an exchange of letters (dating from the end of the eleventh or the beginning of the twelfth century) between the cantor of Algeciras and a prominent Hebrew poet has been preserved.[30] Apparently Algeciras had a well-arranged community which included religious functionaries.

From ancient days Jews had settled in the western provinces of Andalusia and in those now included in southern Portugal. The region, luxuriantly fertile, is especially so in the districts west of Seville; also rich in mineral deposits, in that period it attracted and sustained a dense Arab population. The princes who ruled there in the first half of the eleventh century and who arose amid the Arabs were enlightened and wise rulers who did not burden their subjects.

Niebla, on the right bank of the Rio Tinto, twenty-seven kilometers from Huelva, was a major city. Now it is a small town, but in Moslem times it was large and fortified; its commerce blossomed and, in the days of the caliphs, it was the leading city of the region. In 1022 Aḥmad b. Yaḥyā al-Yaḥṣubī established a principality in Niebla which also included the districts of Gibraleón. He and his son and successor, Yaḥyā, are described as rulers who showed consideration for their subjects. But the loyalty of their subjects was futile against the intrigues of al-Muʻtaḍid, who wanted to annex this area. He initiated hostile action and, in 1051, the prince of Niebla was compelled to quit his city and to go to Cordova.[31] Niebla was an amalgam of Arabs, of Spaniards who had become Moslems, of a Christian community with a bishop,[32] and of a Jewish community which had endured over many generations.

There was a close bond between the Jews of Niebla and the Jews of Seville (the distance between the cities was a two-day journey). In a collection of responsa from the close of the eleventh century there is mention of a Jew who went to the "town of Labla"—the Arabic name of Niebla. He married a woman in Seville and wanted to bring her to Niebla; the rabbi handed down a decision that the law permits him to do this and if the woman should refuse she would be held to be a rebellious wife.[33] One of the two churches in Niebla today, the Church of San Martín, is no other than a remodeled synagogue of former times.[34]

The city of Beja, in southern Portugal, suffered acutely during the civil war, its fortress totally destroyed. Subsequently, Beja was annexed to the kingdom of Seville and became the chief city in its western province. The king refortified it, stationed a garrison there, and a period of new immigration began. In the eleventh century Beja, noted for its flourishing industry, became renowned for its linen industry and its tanneries.[35] The small Jewish community developed once again, and lasted until the end of Moslem rule.[36]

The Jewish population in the western part of the Iberian peninsula—called Lusitania by the Romans—was still generally sparse during the eleventh century. In this sector, the number of Jews was far less than in the south, north, and east. The Jewish writers of the Middle Ages left us much information about the communities and the personalities in all the other regions of the peninsula during the tenth and eleventh centuries—but we search their writings in vain for similar information concerning the contemporaneous Jewish settlements of western Spain and Portugal. The names of their writers and scholars are missing. We only read of the decline of the community of Mérida and of the men whose forebears had dwelt there and left. We can come to no other conclusion but that these communities were small and impoverished.[37]

The districts in the center of Portugal were still remote from the great trade routes, comparatively few settled there, but

Jewish communities existed in all the important cities. After the breakup of the caliphate a large kingdom arose in this region, which encompassed the Spanish province of Estremadura and central Portugal to the Duero River in the north; its important cities were Badajoz (the capital), Coimbra, Evora, Santarem, and Lisbon. This kingdom was established soon after the outbreak of civil war when Sābūr, who was appointed governor of the region by al-Manṣūr, became an independent ruler. After Sābūr's death in 1022, a Berber chief who was his vizier seized control. The Berber was 'Abdallāh b. Muḥammad (known as Ibn al-Afṭas); he and his successor al-Muẓaffar were warlords who actively engaged in wars with their Christian and Moslem neighbors; but they were also interested in literature. The son and heir of al-Muẓaffar, 'Umar al-Mutawakkil, was a scholar who composed verse and who befriended other scholars and poets: He encouraged them in their writing and appointed them to positions as viziers.[38] Under the rule of this dynasty, Badajoz (known in Arabic as Baṭalyaus)[39] became a leading capital. Founded by 'Abdarraḥmān b. Marwān on the left bank of the Guadiana (Wādī Yāna) in the ninth century, in 1032, the city was encircled by a wall of hewn stone, and on its high section in the north a fortress was erected. As a consequence of Mérida's decline, the city grew and continued to develop. Gradually suburbs were built before its gates, especially on its eastern side, at the site now known as Campo de San Roque.

The Jews settled in Badajoz when it became the capital of a large kingdom—the artisans who worked for the army and the merchants who supplied the royal court earned ample livings. In the eleventh century, there were merchants among the Jews of Badajoz who engaged in international trade, traveled to other lands and sojourned abroad for a considerable time. One, Ismā'īl b. Isḥāḳ, dwelt for several years in the city of Tyre in Syria; but he also traveled from there to Tripolitania

MOSLEM LISBON

1. Castello del Moro
2. Castello de São Jorje
3. Mosque
4. Misericordia Church

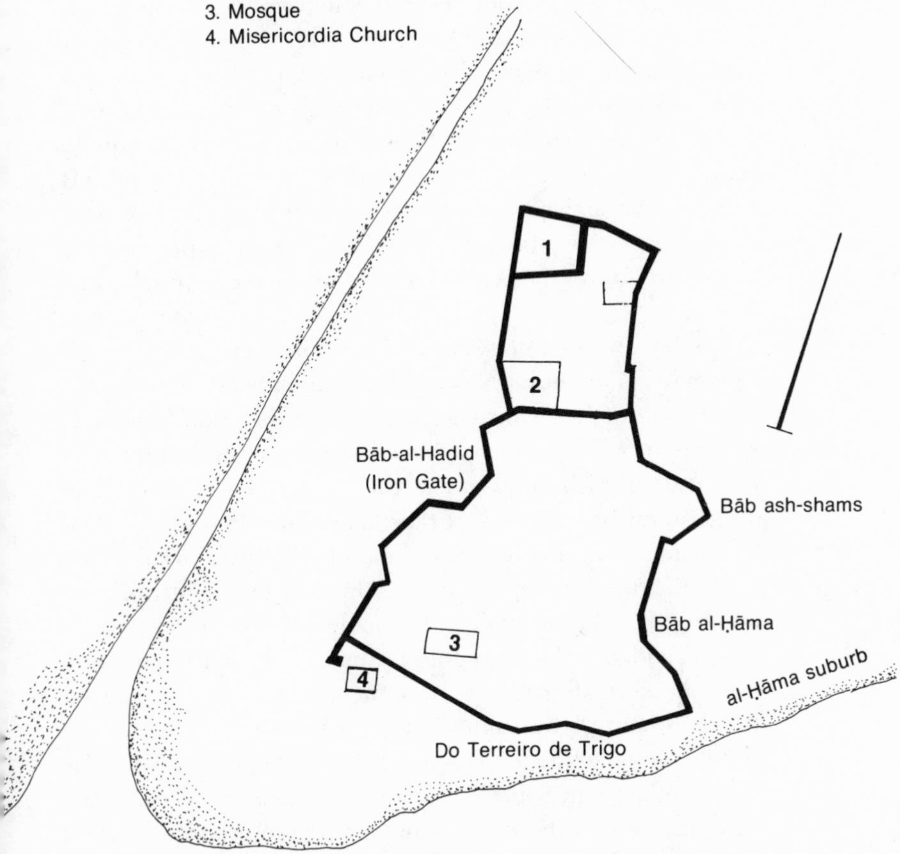

and Egypt. Letters which he sent to friends in Aleppo, Tyre, and Jerusalem were found in the Cairo Geniza. In them he urges his friends to provide him with news of his family in Spain, particularly directing them to Jews of Toledo who travel to the Near East (no doubt the members of this community, which was relatively near his native city, maintained contact with Badajoz).[40] There were men among the Jews of Badajoz who were knowledgeable in the secular branches of learning and some were intimates of the king. Arabic writers quote verses composed by al-Mutawakkil while he waited for his brother who arrived on Saturday instead of Friday. In these verses he glorifies the Sabbath, stating that, in expressing his delight, he strengthens the claims of the spokesmen for Judaism.[41]

The Jewish community in the city of Santarem, in the central region of contemporary Portugal, was already established during the era of Moslem rule—long before the end of the eleventh century.[42] Santarem, which lies some seventy kilometers northeast of Lisbon, from earliest times was the chief city in a region outstanding for extraordinarily fertile soil. The Arabic writers who mention Santarem heap praises upon it and opine that nowhere in the world is there as abundantly blessed an area. In addition there were mines in the city's environs which yielded amber and gold for export abroad.[43] Santarem was indeed an affluent city. Atop the high hill near the city, on the right bank of the Tagus River, the Arabs erected a fortress, but the city itself extended along the banks of the river. The Jewish quarter in Santarem was in the oldest part of the city near the structure which, now a museum, was formerly a mosque and later the Church of San João de Alparão. (According to an ancient tradition, in Roman times this was a government building from which the commands of the emperors were issued publicly.) The Jews' Street itself was the same street on which the Church of San Ildefonso was later erected.

FIRST JEWISH QUARTER OF LISBON

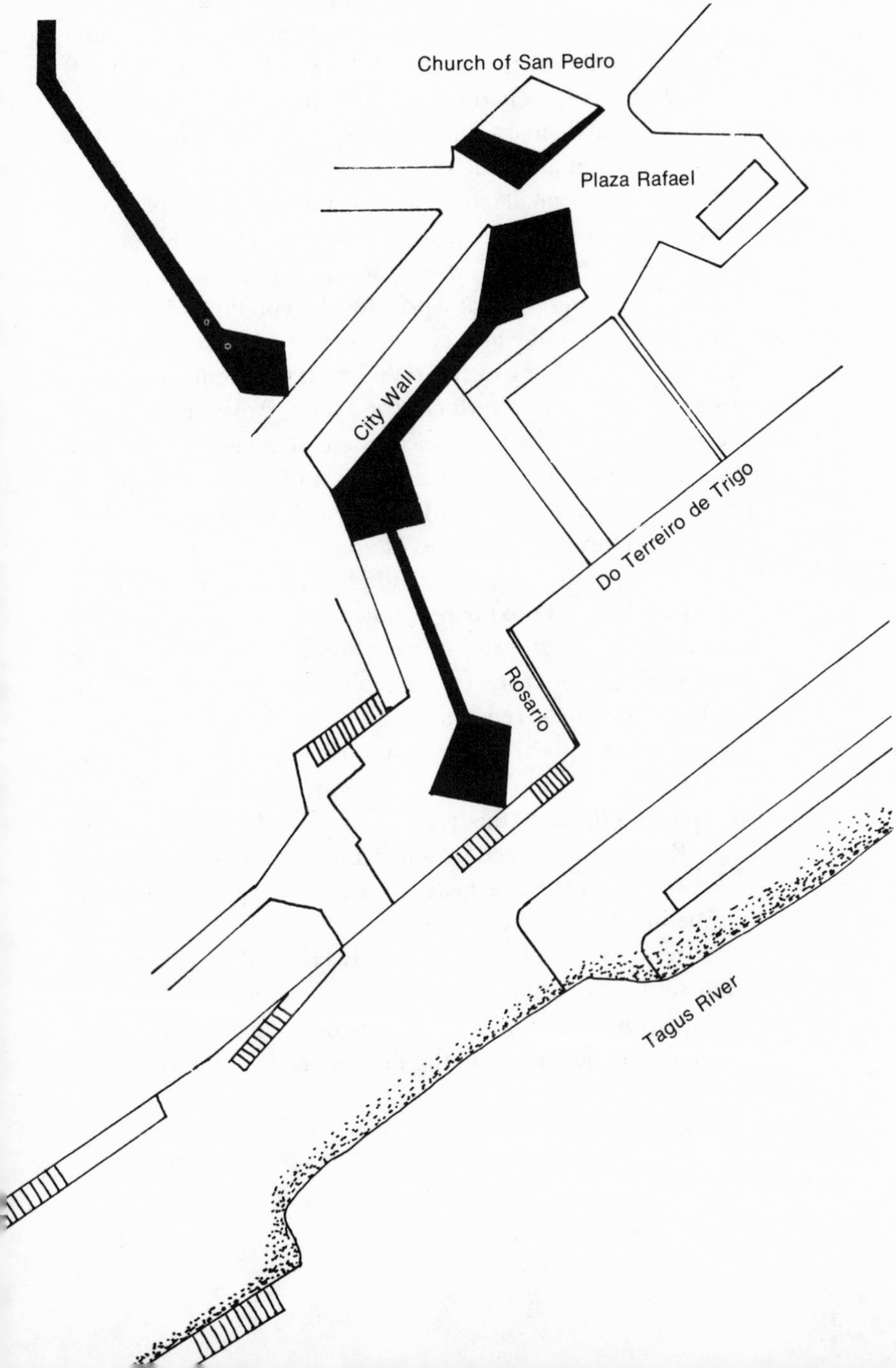

This church was demolished in the seventeenth century, when the entire street was destroyed in an earthquake and later turned into an area of gardens. The street began near the houses of the family of the Conde de Oviedos, and its other end was located near the houses of the Knights of Saint John.[44]

Although the Jews had settled early in Santarem, establishing the site of their dwellings in the center of the city, they settled in Lisbon at a much later time. In the days of Moslem rule Lisbonwas a small city, not the capital of a large province. However, Lisbon was far from a deserted village: Except for a few years in the 1040s, when it was in the hands of the king of Seville, Lisbon served as a port for the kingdom of Badajoz, with a lively economy and cultural life of its own. The city—surrounded by a wall which the Visigoths had built—extended only along the hill upon which stood the fortress and along its southern slope. In the east the city's wall descended to the gate Bāb ash-shams (later known as Porta do Sol), turned west to the al-Ḥamā Gate (later called Porta d'Alfama), on to the Chafariz del Rey and to the site where the Misericordia Church was built later, and again ascended north to the Iron Gate. Atop the hill stood the fortress now known as the Castello de São Jorje; and on the site of the church called Sé stood the chief mosque.[45] Suburbs sprang up to the east and west: The suburb of al-Ḥamā, renowned for its hot springs, stretched southeast; new quarters were established too in what is now the business center of modern Lisbon (popularly called the lower city). Formerly this area, a cove of the estuary of the Tagus River, was covered by water; but even though a channel bisected it from the northeast to the southwest,[46] it was dry long before Moslem rule ended.

The Jews came to Lisbon relatively late and they were unable to settle inside the walled city. At first they established a small quarter to the south of the city on a small street linking the arch of the Rosario and the Plaza Rafael. This street, even

JEWISH QUARTER OF BAIXA
(lower city, New Lisbon)

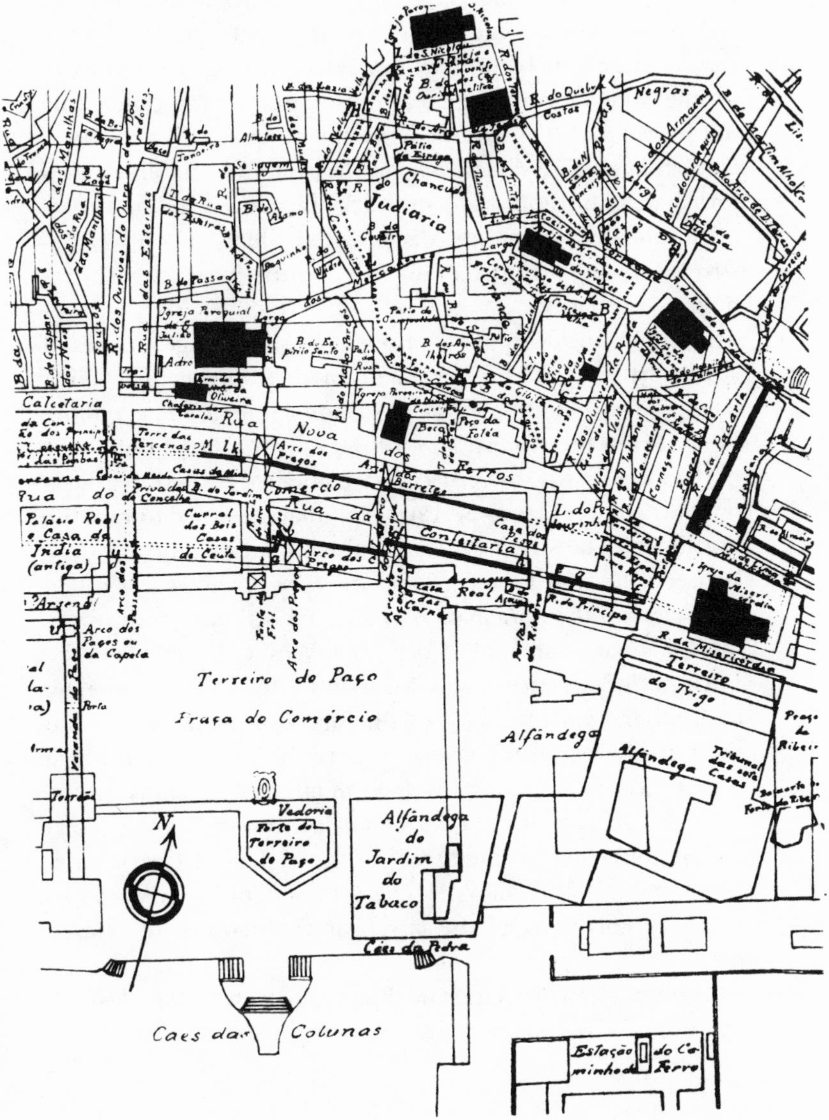

today called Judiaria, was actually located by the city wall, but since the waters of the Tagus at that time covered the site of Do Terreiro do Trigo Street, the community had to establish a new quarter as it outgrew the old one. As usual, the Jews chose a site at the edge of the settled area. In the west of the city, in the heart of present-day Baixa, a neighborhood was formed which for many generations thereafter was called "the old Jewish quarter" or "the large Jewish quarter," because at a much later period it was again necessary to establish a new Jewish neighborhood: The network of narrow, winding streets of the old Jewish quarter disappeared when Lisbon was destroyed by an earthquake in 1755 and the lower city was rebuilt.

In numerous documents of the later Middle Ages names of streets of this quarter are mentioned, testifying in explicit language to the occupations of Lisbon's Jews in those remote times: From the eastern gate of the neighborhood the Street of the Locksmiths (in Christian documents referred to as Rua das Ferrarias Velhas or Ferraria da Judiaria) turned toward the northwest. The street which was the boundary on this side—between the Jewish quarter and the area outside—was called the Street of the Shoemakers (Zapataria—a major industry in Moslem Spain—and later Correaria). West of the Street of the Locksmiths ran two streets from south to north, paralleling each other, which were called the Street of the Dyeworks and the Little Street of the Dyers, a hint of the occupation which was so prevalent among the Jews in all Moslem lands. In the southern section of the quarter was a street called the Street of the Merchants or the Street of the Sellers of Coats (Gibitaria), namely, the tailors.[47] The cemetery of the Jews of Lisbon was northwest of the city near the Plaza of the Intendante.[48]

The large Jewish center in the second half of the eleventh century was still in the south—in Andalusia—in those provinces where Seville was the focal point of all political and economic life.

Among the states neighboring the kingdom of Seville, the principality of Carmona was one of the most powerful; and in it existed a Jewish settlement which had struck deep roots in this region. In their accounts the Arabic chroniclers expatiate upon all those wars in which Muḥammad b. ʿAbdallāh, prince of Carmona, was involved. At times he would be the ally of the kadi, the ruler of Seville, and at times he would oppose him; once he was deprived of his authority and expelled from Carmona by Yaḥyā b. ʿAlī, the Ḥammūdite, but he succeeded in returning in 1035. Arabic writers depict him as forceful and cruel; but they unanimously acknowledge that his attitude to his subjects, Berbers and Andalusians, was fair and that he won their sympathy. He and his forebears were rulers of Carmona from the days of al-Manṣūr, and when the Berbers spared the city during the civil war, many Cordovans escaped to Carmona and its suburbs. After Muḥammad b. ʿAbdallāh was slain in 1043, his son Isḥāḳ, who was like him in character and followed in his ways, reigned in his place. Carmona flourished and its inhabitants prospered in his time. The third of the independent princes of Carmona was ʿAzīz b. Isḥāḳ. During his reign the pressure of the king of Seville upon the Berber principality increased. Almost unceasingly al-Muʿtaḍid's columns raided the borders of Carmona, and ultimately ʿAzīz saw no possibility of continuing the struggle with the overpowering state of Seville. ʿAzīz, too proud to submit, proposed to the king of Toledo that he give him one of the cities in his kingdom in exchange for Carmona, which was near Seville. That king agreed, giving him the city of Almodóvar, which had once belonged to the principality of Carmona. Al-Muʿtaḍid, however, aware of the ambition of the king of Toledo to conquer Cordova, persuaded him to relinquish Carmona. In exchange, al-Muʿtaḍid promised to aid him in conquering the city of the caliphs. Thus was Carmona annexed in 1067 to the kingdom of Seville. 'Azīz, unable to withstand Seville's forces even at Almodóvar, was captured and died in Seville.[49]

Carmona, thirty kilometers northeast of Seville on a hill overlooking the Guadalquivir, is one of the oldest cities in Spain. The remnants of its ancient wall, demolished turrets, and mighty fortresses recall the remote times when Iberians, Phoenicians, Romans, and Moslems ruled the city, each adding to its fortifications, layer upon layer. The highest point in Carmona is at its eastern edge, and there, near the gate called Puerta de Marchena, stood the city's fortress. (When the Moslems ruled, it was the governor's residence and later, after the disintegration of the caliphate, it was the prince's palace.) The Cordova Gate was in the northwest corner of the city, and close by another fortress was erected; a subterranean passageway connected the two fortresses. At the low, southern edge of Carmona, where it lay more exposed to attack, were the Seville Gate and its powerful fortress. The main street,—or, as the Romans called it, Cardo Maximus—bisected the city from this gate to the Gate of Cordova, and situated at its center stood the chief mosque (formerly a Visigothic church), until the Christians returned and conquered it, erecting there the church Iglesia Prioral de Santa Maria.[50] The city's environs were densely populated, the countryside was enriched with streams and wells, the plantations yielded bumper crops.

The Jewish community of Carmona existed for hundreds of years, and the city's name became a common surname among Spanish Jews who migrated to Turkey.[51] However, it was never a large community; even in good times it never numbered more than two hundred.[52] In the eleventh century, when Carmona was the capital of the Berber principality of the Banū Birzāl, the Jewish settlement flourished; its members engaged in trade and maintained close ties with the Jews of Seville. At the end of that century a question was brought before a rabbi concerning "Reuben of Carmona, who had lent money to Levi and received as a pledge his courtyard and when the time for its redemption arrived and he went to Seville to present the promissory note to Levi for payment, Levi had nothing to offer him and obligated himself to raise the money for him by selling the courtyard. And since Reuben could not tarry there, he permitted Simeon to collect the money for him."[53]

As in all the cities of Spain, the Jews of Carmona had their own quarter. It was near the city's southern wall. At this point the wall ran from the right (north) to the street called Barbacanas Altas. The wall was semicircular at the end of this street, and there, at the edge of the curve, was a gate; from there the wall continued west, the length of the southern side of the street which is today named San Teodomir. The Jewish neighborhood included San Teodomir, and the streets now known as Jose Arpa, the western part of Postigo Street, and the street which winds and descends from the south to the north —Juderia. In the later period of the Middle Ages, there was a gate (Arquilío) in the square which lies between the Postigo and the upper end of Juderia; in the middle of Postigo Street there was yet another gate. During the days of Moslem rule, when the Jewish neighborhood extended to the wall, this area was its central focus.[54]

During the rule of the Omayyad caliphs, in the eleventh century, Cordova was the most important Jewish community throughout Spain. Although it did not have the largest population, it did have officials who were in permanent contact with the royal house and who defended Jewish interests, and it did have the finest of the scholars who revitalized Jewish culture and who served as the teachers of gifted young men. But in the 1020s a radical change occurred in the status of the community, even as the status of the entire city was altered.

The inhabitants of the ancient capital of the Omayyads

longed for a stable government and feared the rule of the aristocracy more than the despotism of the kings.[55] Time after time, repeated efforts to reestablish the caliphate ended in failure, and a kind of republican government eventually was formed with Abū 'l-Ḥasan Ibn Djahwar at the head.

But even as the Arabic historians extol the wisdom of Ibn Djahwar and the constitution which was the product of his spirit, their accounts demonstrate to what degree the status of the city had declined when compared to the Omayyad epoch. The arrogant vizier of Almería, Aḥmad Ibn 'Abbās, remarked that he could find only "an ignoramus or a pauper" among the Cordovans; and it is stated in one of the works of an Arabic historian that after the liquidation of the Omayyad rule the people of Cordova became boors in an alarming measure.[56]

The shrunken Jewish community became impoverished and its cultural level declined. Craftsmen had difficulty earning their livings, and many of Cordova's Jews, who once were affluent merchants, now were destitute. The Jews of Cordova, once active in the manufacture of silk and the marketing of its products, suffered especially from the decline of the city's economy. Many of the common people lacked the skills for earning a livelihood. Even the leaders of Andalusian Jewry spoke derisively of the paupers of Cordova. Rabbi Isaac Ibn Gayyāt speaks, in one of his Aramaic poems, of Moses b. al-Ḳurṭubī, who requested assistance because he was poverty-stricken and did not have fine clothes.[57] This man was the son of a Jew who fled Cordova as did a host of others at that time. Men named al-Ḳurṭubī are mentioned in various documents which were written in Spanish provinces quite remote from Andalusia after the disintegration of the Omayyad caliphate. Even the families of religious ministrants wandered to distant places.[58] A member of one of these families was Mūsā al-sōfēr b. Mar Yōsēf (on whom be peace), b. al-Ḳurṭubī, who wrote a treatise in Arabic on the "Obligation to put on phylacteries and how to make them."[59]

The Jewish quarter in the northern sector of Cordova was liquidated during the civil war and the Berber conquest. The number of Jews in the city had dwindled, and thus no one considered restoring it again; the neighborhood in the southwest part of the inner city was more than adequate for the reduced community, now no more than one thousand residents.[60]

The intellectuals—the scholars and writers—left the wretched city to seek supporters and patrons in the flourishing cities of the "provincial rulers." One of the most important scholars in Cordova in the beginning of the eleventh century was Rabbi Joseph b. Samuel. He was a member of a family which included some who had held office and were community leaders, and he himself became a judge. When the distress in the city increased he left, migrated to another place, and there too was accorded honor and numbered among the heads of the Jewish community. Samuel the *Nāgīd,* who was acquainted with Joseph b. Samuel in his youth, corresponded with him, addressing him in verse form.[61]

In those years a Moslem master craftsman whose name was Muḥammad Ibn aṣ-Ṣūffār dwelt in the city, and he was one of the first in Europe to construct astrolabes. He maintained contacts with Jews who were interested in astronomy, and after he migrated to Toledo, he made an astrolabe in 1029 which apparently was first sold to the Jews of Toledo who eventually passed it on to the Jews in Cordova. This is attested by names engraved in Hebrew letters on the two tablets which are consonant with the geographic latitude of these two cities.[62]

Nevertheless, even in those difficult years after the Berber conquest of Cordova and the frequent changes of rulers, there were scholars who engaged in research and who remained in the Cordovan community. The second quarter of the eleventh century was a low period in the fortunes of the community; in the last half of that century during the rule of Ibn Djahwar and his son, the community experienced a resurgence. The economic condition of Cordovan Jewry improved somewhat; once again there were men of wealth among them, and there were people to sustain the religious functionaries and scholars. There were also intellectuals in the community of Cordova during that period who left the products of their spirit as a legacy.

The greatest of this group was Rabbi Isaac b. Baruch Ibn al-Bālia. His full name was Isaac b. Baruch b. Jacob b. Baruch, and his family, which came originally from Mérida, was one of the most esteemed in the community of Cordova.[63] Isaac b. Baruch was born in 1035, and there in his native city he first pursued the traditional studies—Bible, Mishnah, and Gemara. In those days a Jewish scholar arrived in Cordova from France; he was named for a city in the southwest of his native land—Perigors.[64] Isaac Ibn al-Bālia showed him kindness, providing for his needs; and in return Perigors consented to give him special lessons. Later the young Isaac went to Lucena and studied with Rabbi Isaac Ibn Gayyāt, who was then the greatest of the rabbis of Andalusia. When Samuel ha-lēvī heard of the talented youth he assisted him by sending him gifts and books and encouraging him to continue his studies. Along with the other Jews of Cordova, the Ibn al-Bālia family had become impoverished, and the *nāgīd's* aid was essential for Isaac. The *nāgīd* Joseph also showed him kindness and aided him generously.[65] The youth studied the exact sciences, which the Arabs—and the Jews who dwelt among them—called by an all-inclusive name: "the learned disciplines of the ancients" (meaning the Greek disciplines, because they were based on investigation, in contrast to the science of Islam, which was based on tradition). Manuscripts of those Greek classical texts, in Hebrew translation, were abundantly available in Cordova, and

Isaac Ibn al-Bālia indeed did acquire considerable knowledge in mathematics and astronomy. He frequently visited the *nāgīd* Joseph in Granada, tarrying with him for a while and then returning to Cordova. At that time he wrote a treatise on the Jewish calendar in which he dealt with principles set down in the tractate *Rosh Hashana,* engaging in a dispute with other writers—such as the *gaon* Rabbi Saadya and Ḥa b. Mar Ḥassān—who dealt with these questions before him.[66] This treatise, which he dedicated to the *nāgīd* Joseph, is regarded as an important work, and Jewish scholars of later generations cited his words and discussed them with deliberate care.[67] Rabbi Isaac Ibn al-Bālia also wrote a commentary on the difficult passages of the Gemara; he entitled it *Ḳuppat Rōkh'līm* ("The Peddler's Box"), but he did not succeed in completing this treatise. After the fashion of the intellectuals in Moslem Spain, he wrote poems at times which were considered excellent by his contemporaries.[68] He was in Granada during the riots in 1066 and, after being saved by what was held to be a miracle, returned to Cordova.[69]

In that same generation, in the second half of the century, there also dwelt in Cordova Joseph b. Meïr Ibn Mahādjir, who was one of the notables of the community. He too was the scion of a respected family which also had a Romance name—Shartamicas; it was one of the senior families in Andalusia and close to the Moslem rulers. Joseph himself was an intellectual who wrote liturgical poetry[70] and held an esteemed position in the Jewish community; because of his distinguished lineage, he was surnamed nāsī (exilarch).[71] Ōhēb ha-nāsī b. Mē'īr ha-nāsī Ibn Shartamicas, another member of this family, also composed liturgical poetry.[72]

II

In the middle of the eleventh century, all the regions of the *Meseta* were under the rule of the Dhu-Nūn dynasty—Berbers who dwelt in Spain since the Moslem conquest. They governed the districts northeast of Toledo (the region of Shanṭabarīya, named for the city of Santaver which was later abandoned); now a large area in central Spain, bisected by the Tagus and Guadiana rivers, belonged to their kingdom; Toledo was now their capital city. For a long time they were stubborn rebels, but as Caliph 'Abdarraḥmān III gained power, they gave their loyalty to the government at Cordova. However, they did not achieve importance until the last days of Omayyad rule; in fact their status was rather modest[73] and their moment arrived only when the caliphate disintegrated.

In the 1020s—when chaos prevailed in Moslem Spain—the populace of Toledo also rebelled, forcing the city to become an independent republic. The inhabitants chose governors from among themselves, but, typically, they were dissatisfied with their rulers and within a short time they deposed them. At first they appointed 'Abdarraḥmān b. Mateo, and after him his son 'Abdalmalik, as governor until he was dismissed and Ya'īsh b. Muḥammad Ibn Ya'īsh al-Asadī became the governor of the city; the people of Toledo complained and deposed him too.[74] After more experiments with a republican form of government, and after despairing of their elected leaders[75]—there was no end to factional strife—some of the city's notables invited the princes of the Dhu-Nūn family to reign over them. Thus, it was late in the 1030s when Ismā'īl b. 'Abdarraḥmān came to Toledo.[76]

Ismā'īl, who was surnamed aẓ-Ẓāfir, succeeded in bringing order to the city and within a few years also succeeded in imposing his authority over all the provinces of which Toledo was the hub. Embraced within this broad area were the province of Cuenca in the east and the region of the Jarama River in the north (the mountains of the Sierra de Guadarrama and the Sierra de Gredos in the northwest formed a natural boundary between the Moslem territory and that of the Christians). As in the days of the caliphs, the southern slopes of the mountain chains were in Moslem hands, whereas the sparsely populated provinces of Segovia and Avila, north of the mountains, were within the boundaries of Christian dominance.

When Ismā'īl died in 1043,[77] he was succeeded by his son Yaḥyā, who was surnamed al-Ma'mūn. He was one of the Moslem kings who won great renown in his generation: his wars were numerous and his court splendid. Soon after he mounted the throne, al-Ma'mūn was attacked by the Arab ruler of Saragossa and for three years a brutal war, in which the subjects of al-Ma'mūn suffered acutely, waged relentlessly. As was customary at that time, each Moslem king entered into an alliance with Christian rulers: al-Ma'mūn became an ally of the king of Navarre and the king of Saragossa made a pact with the Castilians. A brother of al-Ma'mūn and one of his nephews joined the enemy and guided the battle, so that the enemy soldiers wrought havoc in the northern and western districts of the kingdom. When this war ended in 1047, another flared between al-Ma'mūn and the king of Badajoz.[78] Meantime the Christian kingdoms in the north united and threatened the dominions of the Dhu-Nūn. In the beginning of the 1070s, the king of Castile and León effected a penetration of the dominions of al-Ma'mūn, and he was compelled to agree to pay a yearly tribute. Notwithstanding these failures, al-Ma'mūn persisted in aspiring toward conquest and indeed, in 1065, he succeeded in imposing his dominance over the city of Valencia and its environs.

Al-Ma'mūn was archetypical of the Hispano-Moslem ruler in his era. On the one hand he was a warrior, involved in disputes with his neighbors; on the other hand, he was an intellectual,

9
7
8
5
6
Tagus River

JEWISH QUARTER OF TOLEDO

1. Calle del Angel
2. Calle San Tomé
3. Calle de San Clemente
4. Calle Colegio de Doncellas
5. Calle Brio Nuova
6. El Tránsito (Synagogue of Samuel Ha-lēvī Abulafia)
7. Church of San Juan de los Reyes
8. Church of Santa Maria la Blanca
9. Gate of the Jews
10. Plaza de Valdecaleros
11. Great Mosque

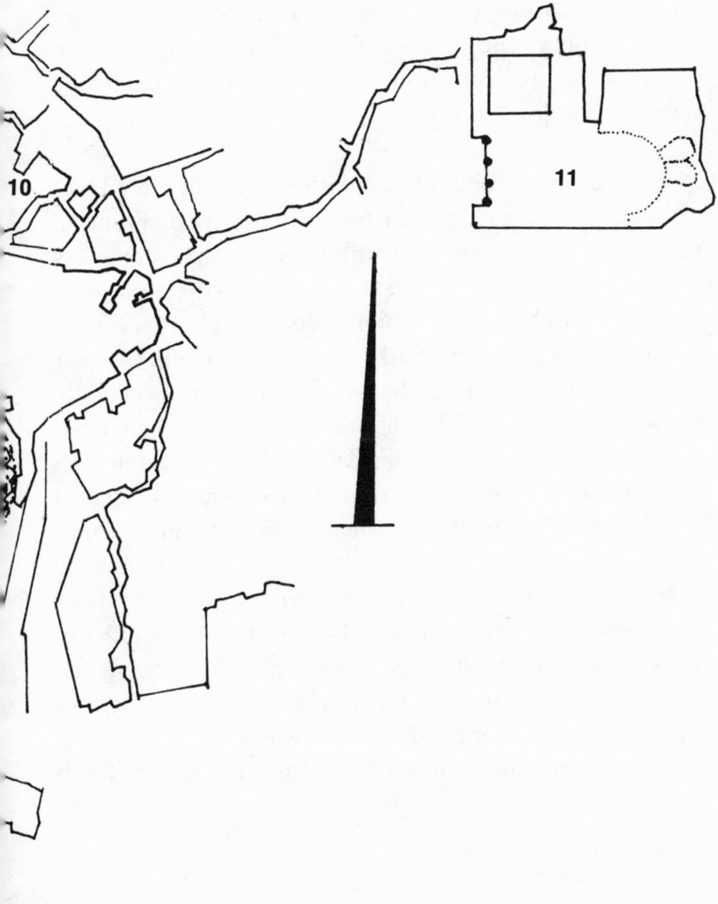

deriving pleasure from the company of poets and writers. He himself composed poems, and as Arabic writers of that period did, he also produced an anthology of stories. His fêtes were legendary in Spain and in North Africa; his palace and its extraordinary pool were equally famed. (The pool, an engineering marvel, had an island in its middle and on this island was a glass pavillion which was cooled by streams of water flowing from the dome.) However, the outlay for his wars, the tribute he had to pay to the king of Castile and León, and the sum which his royal court consumed all required huge funds —an onerous burden for his subjects and a massive weight for the subordinates who were appointed to obtain them. Al-Ma'mūn's fiscal policy, one that was followed by the majority of the provincial kings, had important consequences regarding the status of the Jews in his kingdom.

In those days, when Toledo became the capital of a big kingdom, the settlement of Jews in the city increased. From all parts of Spain they came, and within that large community there were various groups, distinguished by their place of origin, who maintained their unique identity. There were the Jews from Cordova who had fled their city during the civil war and after its conquest by the Berbers. Writing in the middle of the twelfth century, a Jewish author notes that "their descendants can be discerned to this day."[79] Similarly, from such cities of Christian Spain as Barcelona, Jews who engaged in trade came to and ultimately settled within Toledo.[80] Entire groups of Jews from distant lands were found within that big city. The same writer, who himself dwelt in Toledo, relates that he saw there scholarly descendants of the Khazars,[81] refugees who fled when their kingdom was destroyed in the seventh decade of the tenth century. There also were Karaites among Toledo's Jews; indeed, the city was a center in Spain for the sect (Ibn Hazm testifies to the existence of Karaites in

Toledo in the middle of the eleventh century).[82] In the eleventh century the Jewish population of Toledo was approximately four thousand.[83]

The social stratification of the Jews of Toledo was also strikingly diversified. There was practically no occupation that they did not pursue. The majority of the members of the community were such artisans as tailors, feltmakers, masons, smiths, dyers, butchers,[84] and there were many, of course, engaged in all branches of commerce (greengrocers, flour dealers, etc.).[85] Some of the city's Jews who made their living from agriculture owned vineyards in nearby villages; some of those who cultivated the land themselves[86] traveled from their homes in the town to the outlying districts—a common practice in Spain to this day. The Jews were deemed good farmers by the Christians, and Catholic priests turned to them to cultivate their fields.[87] However, the farmers comprised a small group compared to the number of craftsmen and traders in the sizable Jewish community of Toledo.

Above the multitude of the middle class existed a group of men who had become wealthy through such successful businesses as wholesaling: Jews from Toledo went abroad to the Near East where they engaged in commerce on a grand scale, exporting Spanish goods and importing Oriental wares. These affluent, cultured Jews maintained houses within the city and extensive property on its outskirts.[88] They had ties with their rulers, becoming agents and administrators in the government. They obtained the office of tax farming, managed the royal estates and, in time, became the valued advisors in political affairs who carried out various missions in behalf of their sovereigns. The needs of the Moslem rulers in Spain were relatively greater in this epoch than they were formerly: As usual, their constant wars, their prodigal ways, and the tributes they paid to the Christian kings resulted in frequent financial stress, so that they required businessmen—skillful and energetic—to conduct their affairs. However, the status of those Jews given this assignment was not like that of their contemporaries, the Jewish bankers who were agents and aides of the Christian rulers of central Europe. It is true that the Moslem rulers in Spain chose them because of their talents; but they also regarded these Jews as representatives of a powerful faction within their domains.

The number of Jews in the cities was considerable in relation to the entire population; and, as a group, they enjoyed even greater significance inasmuch as their fellow inhabitants were not of one faith or of one nationality. From the viewpoint of the Moslem kings, the Jewish community was of much importance in those weak and embroiled states whose subjects were divided among themselves. In the eleventh century, Jews had not yet lost their ability to fight a war and troops could be mobilized among them for guard duty, for garrison service, and for the battle. However, the chief motive which led rulers to establish ties with Jews was their business talent. When they made Jewish businessmen into government officials, the Moslems hoped they would have access to the large sums of money available to these Jews and their brethren. The funds could be in the form of loans or the taxes which the Jewish officials would collect from the members of their own community and the balance of the population. These officials were able and resourceful; the Moslem rulers were not disappointed. Thus, in the eleventh century the rise of Jewish nobles and dignitaries began in the states of Moslem Spain, and the kingdom of Toledo was typical of those principalities.

The rulers of Toledo were Berbers, a large part of the population in the capital was Christian or Moslem of Spanish extraction; the population in the hamlets and villages was as varied. But the division on national lines was not the only one. The devout among the Moslems complained against al-Ma'mūn, who spent his days warring with other Moslem rulers instead of mustering strength to defend his subjects from Christian raids. A Moslem king such as he was prepared to favor any powerful group of his subjects; although they were not of his faith, they were likely to offer him important aid. In this fashion, affluent Jews began appearing among those close to the king and as various officials in the court.

The family of Ibn Shōshān[89] was foremost among those Jews in Toledo who received appointments as officers and dignitaries. When Samuel ha-lēvī once received a letter from a man, he replied with a poem wherein he referred to the man, calling him "the noble Shōshān."[90] Another Hebrew poet composed a poem in honor of Saadya Ibn Shōshān, "the faithful dignitary," stating, among other things:

The rulers of Sheba will bow down to you,
Your excellence towers above that of kings.[91]

These two men of the Ibn Shōshān family[92] were the first in a long line of tax farmers for Toledo's kings. Leaders of their community, they and the other wealthy families of the Jewish community were residents of the upper quarter, in the northeast part of the Jewish sector, near the mosque which, after the Christian reconquest, became the Church of San Román.[93] Documents of that period mention several times the square known as the Square of Abū Sulaimān David Ibn Shōshān, which was near the Street of the Barcelonan.[94]

The Ibn Naḥmias family held important positions within the Jewish community for many generations,[95] and many of its members were distinguished scholars. One, Abū Isḥāḳ Ibn Naḥmias, purchased half a vineyard in 1083 from a Moslem woman in the outlying village of Chalencas; the purchase price of three hundred mithkāl indicates the broad acreage of the vineyard.[96] The family was also known as Naamias: a document from Toledo, dated 1112, mentions Joseph b. Naamias, the son-in-law of Joshua b. Isaac Zaidōn, in connection with a matter dealing with the funds of an orphaned girl, the daughter of Joseph bar Moses b. Ḳapsūt.[97] To be sure, this family was not closely associated with the government, but the inscription on a gravestone of one of its descendants states that he was of "the stock of the pious and the seed of the exalted princes and chieftains; and his ancestors stemmed from the earliest generation of exiles, the aristocracy of the children of Israel."[98]

Two members of the distinguished Ibn Falcón family—Jacob and Joseph—are mentioned in a document from the middle of the eleventh century.[99] For generation during the era of Christian rule, descendants of this family were rabbis and associates of the rabbinical court in Toledo, as well as tax farmers for the kings of Castile; and after the expulsion of the Jews from Spain, among those who still bore the name Falcón were a renowned cabbalist in Safed in the sixteenth century and a judge in Constantinople in the eighteenth century.[100]

Contrasted to those men of wealth who were rooted in the soil of Spain, those men of property who sought to increase it in every way possible, there was also a considerable number in the large Jewish community of Toledo who regarded Spain as a diaspora, like the other countries, and yearned to be restored to the land of Palestine. Rabbi Solomon b. Judah, the head of the talmudic academy, Pride of Jacob, in Jerusalem, who died in 1051, confirms in a letter to Sahlān b. Abraham in Fostat that he received ten gold pieces for the poor of that city, willed by Abraham b. Nāḥūm of Toledo.[101] Others, however, found it insufficient merely to send contributions; they were impelled to migrate to Palestine. Among those migrants in the fifth decade of the eleventh century were a man and his sons from one of the respected families of Toledo—the family of Ibn Israel (or Israēlī).[102] The man's name was Saul and that of one of his sons, Simeon. A letter which Simeon sent to his sister, Ballūṭa, in Toledo in 1053, is a detailed account of the hardships suffered by the immigrants. When their father reached Jerusalem he became blind, paralyzed, and eventually insane; however, the son maintained his position of esteem even among the Jews of Jerusalem. Two of the Spanish migrants, Mūsā b. Hānī and Joseph b. Ḥayyīm, died, and one, Bōnīl Ibn Dabbūḳa, disappeared. Two Jews of Toledo, who migrated separately, were taken captive on the way, brought to Byzantium, freed after many troubles, and reached Ramla. One was Ibrāhīm b. al-Hārūnī, and the other was Ibrāhīm Ibn Padāndj, a member of an old Toledo family.[103] Ibn Padāndj inclined toward Karaism as did many of Toledo's Jews, and at first he intended to remain in Ramla to join the sect there. However, a complex series of events precipitated by an attempt to enforce Karaite marriage laws prevented the realization of his plans. With the encouragement and aid of Simeon b. Saul, Ibn Padāndj left Ramla with his family for Jersualem, where he joined the Karaite sect to which his brother Jacob belonged. Although Ibn Padāndj stayed within this community two years, he eventually withdrew—the marriage law again proving an obstruction. Simeon b. Saul, once more intervening on behalf of his fellow townsman, persuaded the orthodox Jews in Jerusalem to accept him as a resident within their quarter,[104] and at this point Ibrāhīm Ibn Padāndj renounced Karaism altogether.

In Toledo, there were Jewish scholars who totally devoted themselves to studying both the written and oral law of Judaism, and in the fashion of the learned Jews of Spain, they pursued the study of the Hebrew language; there were also students of the exact sciences, mathematics, and astronomy. In the Hispano-Moslem kingdoms of the eleventh century an atmosphere conducive to investigative study prevailed: The rulers were not devout and the majority made no special effort to appear as such—no one disturbed these students of the sciences in their examination of the recondite and their examination of the mysteries of the skies. At a time when the countries of Christian Europe were still engulfed by ignorance, eminent scholars dwelt in the Moslem cities of Spain. They drew all the knowledge of past generations from the translations of Greek writings and the works of Arabs in the Near East and added to it from their own resources.

Just as the rulers set no restraints upon them and even encouraged them, the scholars themselves did not set obstacles in the path of their non-Moslem colleagues; men of various faiths combined to carry on their studies in fellowship. In the sixth and seventh decades of the eleventh century a Moslem scholar in Toledo gathered around him an active circle of Moslem and Jewish astronomers. His name was Abu'l-Ḳāsim Ṣā'id b. Aḥmad Ibn Ṣā'id. (He was a judge in Toledo, and he died in 1070 at the age of forty-one.) Although Ibn Ṣā'id was a Moslem theologian, he was free of prejudice against members of other faiths: In his treatise on the history of the scholars he devoted a chapter to the Jewish scholars, stating, among other things, that he found the correct rules governing the appearance of the new moon and the sun's circuits (which are based on intercalation in a cycle of nineteen years) in calculations of the Hebrew calendar.[105]

A major role in the activity of the astronomers was played by Abū Isḥāḳ Ibrāhīm b. Yaḥyā, who was also known as az-Zarḳāla or az-Zarḳāl. Initially he was the master craftsman who provided the instruments that the scholars in Toledo needed for their observations. Somewhat later he delved into scientific literature, invented new instruments, and ultimately, after the death of Ibn Ṣā'id, became the leader of the circle, the teacher and master of the scholars. The result of their work, which demonstrated a marked advance over the studies of the astronomers in the Near East, was the composition of *The Toledan Tables,* a work which was also known by his name and which was translated into Latin as early as the middle of the twelfth century (in Toledo) by the renowned translator Gerard of Cremona.[106] Az-Zarḳāl, who dwelt in Toledo for some years after Ibn Ṣā'id's death and later moved to Cordova, collaborated with Jews in other localities; one, a Jewish astronomer in Sicily, turned his findings over to him.[107]

There were also small, historically insignificant Jewish communities in the other cities, towns, and villages of the Tagus basin during the eleventh century. Generally the Jews in these lesser settlements of central Spain were engaged in agriculture, which in that era was a major livelihood for Andalusians;[108] some Jews who owned farms lived in villages and others dwelt in settlements surrounded by walls, but they followed the common practice of traveling to their outlying fields. One of these communities was in the town of Escalona, northwest of Toledo, on a bank of the Alberche River: It is deserted now—its houses and its ancient monasteries are in ruins and the walls which encompassed it are demolished—but under Moslem rule Escalona was a flourishing city and one which, because of its proximity to the border, was fully fortified. Its Jewish settlement remained after the city came under Christian dominance in 1083.[109]

Situated on a wide plateau, not far from the place where the Alberche River empties into the Tagus, is the old city Talavera de la Reina. In the days of Moslem rule Talavera was the chief city of a sizable area and, as in our own time, a focal point for its economic life. But in that period Talavera was paramount as a fortress. The Moslems guarded the fortifications zealously. More than once the city served as the goal of military expeditions by the troops of the kingdom of León and was even conquered by them three times in the first half of the tenth century. In the eleventh century, Talavera was still prominent, noteworthy for its strong fortifications and its outstanding citadel (one of the most important in all of Spain).

Centuries have passed since then. Once a border fortress, Talavera is now located in the heart of Spain, but lofty arches, remnants of powerful turrets, and walls on which abut the city's houses, still remind passersby of the stubborn battles which raged in former times on the banks of the Tagus.

As its populations grew over the generations, Talavera was encompassed by a second and then a third wall. The first wall, which stood in its place from earlier days, ran from the fortress in the southern sector of the city, at the site of the gardens of the one-time Augustinian monastery on the bank of the Tagus, extending the length of the streets presently called Calle Sevilla, del Cuerno, and Carnecerias, reaching the plaza now called del Generalísimo, formerly de la Constitución, where one of the town gates, later called Puerta de San Pedro, was located. From this gate which was south of the plaza (on Calle del Arco de San Pedro), the wall veered west the length of Calle Corredera del Cristo and thence to the southwest along the streets del Charcón and Entre Torres to the riverbank, where the southern wall was erected. In the western wall, at the point where the Calle San Clemente reaches the southern end of Calle del Charcón, is the Mérida Gate, and in the southern wall, opposite the old bridge, is the Gate of the River; in the course of time, smaller apertures were opened in the wall. The city's center was located in the area encircled by this wall and here, where economic activity was concentrated, dwelt the distinguished families. In the sixteenth century the plaza near the Pedro Gate was still called Plaza del Comercio and the Carnecerias Street was known long ago as de las Zapaterias. After the town expanded during Moslem rule, a second wall was erected to protect the suburbs. Ultimately a third wall was built, branching out from the second wall in the north near the Gate de las Alcantarillas, running the lengths of the Streets of San Jimenez, Cañada de la Sierra, and Paseo Padre

JEWISH QUARTER OF TALAVERA DE LA REINA

1. Calle Padre Juan de Mariana
2. San Miguel
3. Second Wall
4. Calle del Charcón
5. First Wall
6. Calle de San Clemente
7. Mérida Gate
8. Calle Entre Torres
9. Calle de los Templarios
10. Callejón de los Judios
11. Calle de San Estéban
12. Third Wall
13. Calle de Olivares

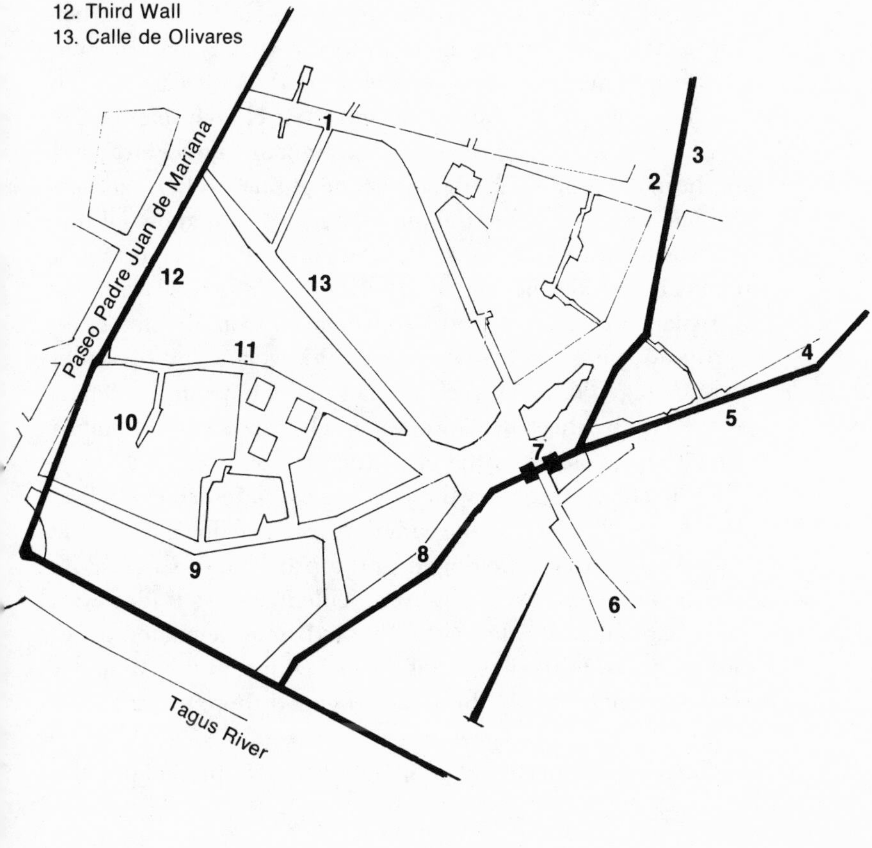

Juan de Mariana, until it reached the river. De Cuartos, the gate of this wall, still stands.[110]

A Jewish community existed in Talavera for hundreds of years, maintaining close bonds with the Jews of Toledo.[111] The community, numbering more than four hundred, was relatively large;[112] Ibn Ḥazm reports that Karaites also lived there.[113] The Jewish quarter is still known in Talavera. It was located in the western end of the city, between the second and third walls: It extended the length of the Paseo Padre Juan de Mariana, on the two sides of the western part of the de los Templarios Street—where the Callejón de los Judios is a reminder of the early Jewish community—and north to the other side of the Calle de San Estéban to the vicinity of the Calle Olivares;[114] near the Jewish neighborhood on the east was the neighborhood of the Mozarabs and their church, named for San Estéban.[115] Thus, in contrast to most of the central and southern cities of Spain, the Jewish neighborhood in Talavera was outside the *madīna*, the inner city. (It is not known if this site was fixed upon because the Jews arrived in Talavera at a relatively late period, or because they collaborated with the Christians in the north and were removed from the inner city by the Moslem rulers.) The Jews, however, many of whom were engaged in metalworking, had their shops in the center of the city by the San Pedro Gate. The Jewish community's cemetery was north of the city near the abattoir.[116]

In the eleventh century there were several Jewish communities in the districts of the kingdom of Toledo, east of the capital. One, Uclés, belonged to the province of Cuenca; its Jewish settlement was long-lived. Toledo's Jews traded with the inhabitants of Uclés, visited it, and some remained to reside within it. In the middle of the eleventh century a member of the Toledan family Ibn Israel engaged there in trade and ultimately settled in Uclés.[117]

The magnificent capital of Spain, with a two-million population, was a small town in those remote days. Madrid, which the Arabs called Madjrīṭ, was a border town that developed near a fortress. This fortress, called al-Mudaina (citadel), was located where the king's palace now stands and in the area to the south, whereas the city (al-madīna) lay to the east and southeast. In the east it extended to the place northwest of the Plaza Mayor where the Gate Bāb Wādī'l-ḥadjāra was located, and thence the wall went toward the south to a gate called, at a much later period, Puerta de Moros. From this gate the wall turned northwest, once again linking up with the citadel.[118]

In the eleventh century Jews were already living in Madrid, but their number was small. In the letter Simeon b. Saul wrote to his sister in 1053, he informed her that Mūsā of Madrid (al-Majrīṭī) and his sister had died. The Jewish merchant of Badajoz, Ismā'īl b. Isḥāḳ, in one of his letters from Syria, also mentions Jews of Madrid. From his words it is apparent that, as among the Jews of Toledo, there were merchants in the Madrid community who visited Egypt in connection with their trade.[119]

Jews also dwelt during this period in the small city of Alcalá de Henares, which lies thirty-four kilometers northeast of Madrid, on a bank of the Henares River along the former main road from Saragossa to Toledo. Alcalá was an important city; in Roman days (when it was called Complutum), and even in Visigothic times, it was a bishop's seat; then, however, the city was located southwest of contemporary Alcalá, opposite the mouth of the Camarmilla, a tributary of the Henares.[120] The Arabs erected a fortress on a lofty hill located east of the city on the left bank of the river, naming it Ḳal'at 'Abdassalām or simply al-Ḳal'a. It was a small, strategically important fortress which commanded the route of invaders into northern, Christian Spain.[121] Ancient Complutum, deserted by its inhabitants, became a ruin, but east of the city, near the grave of two Christian martyrs, a new settlement bearing its ancient name arose. Thus for hundreds of years two settlements existed, the one opposite the other—the settlement near the grave consisted almost entirely of Mozarabs.[122] Jews were living in the city when, through the initiative of Bernardo, the archbishop of Toledo, the city was taken by the Christians in 1118. His successor, Raimundo, fixed the privileges of the inhabitants, establishing equality between Jews and Christians.[123] After the town reverted to Christian dominance, the settlement in the fortress on the left bank of the river decreased; the number of inhabitants in the settlement near the church in which the saints were buried steadily increased. The Jewish quarter in Christian Alcalá was in the oldest part of the city, on the Calle Mayor which turns eastward from the Plaza de la Picota, near the church, and which served as a graveyard at that time.[124]

The most important town in the northern regions of the kingdom of Toledo was Guadalajara. The Arabs also called it Madīnat al-Faradj after a Berber family, but Jewish sources always referred to the city as Wādī a'l-ḥidjāra, as did the Arabs who gave it the name of the Henares River which flowed nearby. In the days of the Dhu-Nūn kings it was a flourishing city: It served as a market for the agricultural products of all the northern regions in the kingdom, and especially for the saffron crop which they exported to all the other provinces of Spain.

The Jewish community in Guadalajara was small but ancient.[125] Writing in the first half of the seventeenth century, the town historians reported that when it was conquered in 1081 the Castilian commander Alvar Fañez found Jews there and let them remain.[126] An allusion to the Jewish community in Guadalajara is found in a collection of poems by a contemporary Hebrew poet. He extols a Jewish officer who went to Guadalajara shortly after the conquest to defend the Jews when fanatic Christians attacked them.[127]

The Jewish quarter was within the city, in its northern sector, and to this day the name of a street reminds us of its location. Eastward it extended to the place now called Plaza del Marques de Villar Ejor and encompassed the streets on both sides of the thoroughfare now named Calle del Doctor Benito Hernando. In the west the quarter did not go beyond Herranz Street. For a long time the main synagogue stood on a small street which connects Del Injeniero Marino Street with Calle Benito Hernando (formerly called Calle del Museo and before that Caldederos, the Street of the Kettlemakers). The street still bears the name Street of the Synagogue. The region outside the western gate of the city, in which were located the potters' market (Alfarería) and a Moslem palace (Alcazar), was surrounded by an earthen wall encompassing the area of the Ortiz de Sarate hospital and the area on the other side of the Street of the Railroad; the Jewish cemetery was west of this street.[128]

On the left bank of the Henares, eighty-five kilometers northeast of Guadalajara, lies the city of Sigüenza. It was an influential city in ancient times, but it was impoverished under Moslem rule. However, Jews dwelt in Sigüenza even during its decline. They are mentioned in a royal document of Alfonso VII, written immediately after the final conquest of the city in 1124.[129] The Jewish quarter, which is known from documents of the later Middle Ages, was at the southwestern end of the city on the street still known as Street of the Synagogue. The quarter was then outside the city, but in a document dating from 1415 it is called "the new Jewish neighborhood," whence it is inferred that the neighborhood was formerly within the city.[130]

Soria, in the upper valley of the Duero River, was among those cities in the center of the Iberian peninsula which were under Moslem rule in the eleventh century and later belonged to the kingdom of Castile. Although Soria is located beyond the large range of mountains, the Sierra

Guadarrama and the Sierra de Muedo, it was in the hands of the Toledan kings of the Dhu-Nūn dynasty.[131] During the tenth and eleventh centuries Soria was taken by the Castilians a number of times, but was repeatedly reconquered by the Moslems. Inasmuch as Soria was located on the banks of the Duero at the site of a principal bridge, a new settlement emerged after all the devastation wrought upon its inhabitants by relentless foes: Caravans of merchants crossing the river at this point and garrisons of the Moslem rulers provided livelihoods for merchants and craftsmen.[132] Nevertheless, by the end of the eleventh century, Soria's population was meager. The few quarters within it were alongside the main street leading to the bridge over the Duero, in the vicinity of the Church of San Pedro; south of this church there is a towering, old fortress which served as a refuge for the small settlement during the frequent raids of Christian soldiers.

Jews were already in the city in those days. A manuscript of the Bible which was completed in 1104 was written in Soria for a Jew called Samuel bar Jacob Sarūdjiēl, who was close to the ruling authorities and who also held an office (the noble dignitary).[133] The Jewish quarter was near the fortress in the center of the city; proximity to the fortress gave the Jews a sense of security. The business center of the settlement was west of the Church of San Pedro; later, a church called Santa Maria del Ecoge (the market) was built there. Calle de Comedias, in the heart of Soria, is proof that the Jewish neighborhood remained in the city's center throughout the Middle Ages: This street was formerly called de la Juderia.[134]

However, in that era, Jews dwelt not only in Soria, where they found security in the shadow of the fortress and the garrison, but also in open and semi-open settlements in the disputed border zone. To this day one of the settlements in the Soria region on the right bank of the Rituerto River is called

JEWISH QUARTER OF GUADALAJARA

1. Plaza del Marques de Villai Ejor
2. Calle del Injeneiria Merino
3. Calle del Herrahz
4. Calle del Doctor Benito Hernando
5. Costa de San Miguel
6. Plaza Santa Maria
7. Calle de Doctor Ramon Cajal
8. Calle de la Mina
9. Calle de la Ronda

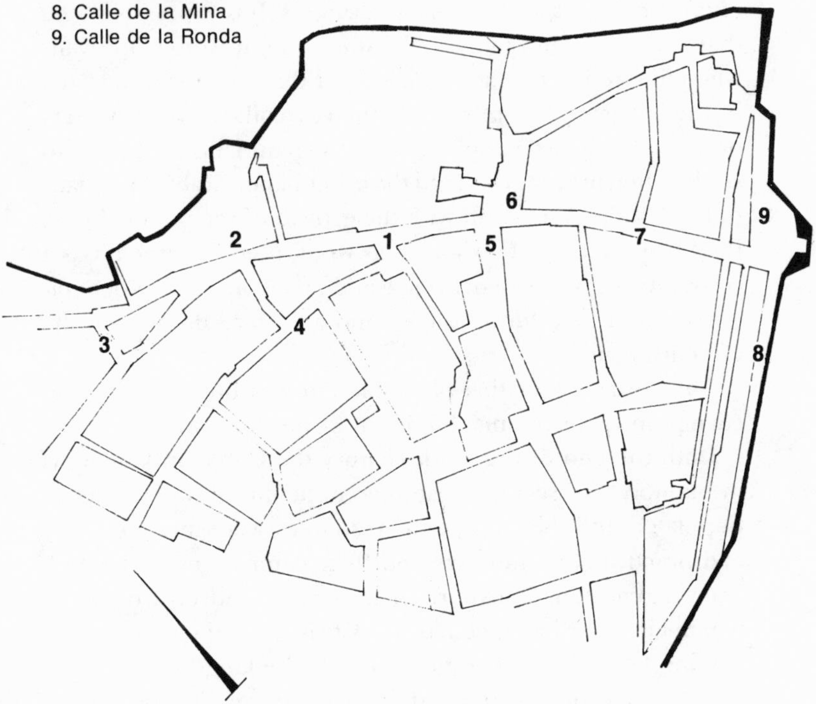

Aliud; and this is, of course, al-Yahūd, the name of the Jews in Arabic.[135]

III

Writers of the Middle Ages mention a number of Jewish scholars, thinkers, and poets who dwelt in Saragossa during the eleventh century, but there is almost no reference to this community in the era of the Omayyad caliphs. It is expressly stated that some were not natives of Saragossa but were Cordovans who migrated to northern Spain after that city was devastated by the Berbers. Only rarely, and then casually, do those writers note that ordinary people from among Andalusia's Jews also settled then in Saragossa. On the other hand, Arabic historians of the Middle Ages dealt with the growth of the population in the Ebro Valley, but, as was their wont, they explained it as a consequence of the beneficence and grace of the king of Saragossa who ruled during the second and third decades of the eleventh century.

The truth is that this phenomenon was linked to a great change in the economic life of all of northern Spain.

Until the end of the tenth century the Christian kingdoms in the northern sector of the Iberian peninsula were sparsely populated and their economic resources were meager. They had practically no industry and their commerce was limited. They had nothing to export; their imports, entirely from Moslem Spain, were brought in by the Christian and Jewish traders coming from there. The ties between the kingdoms of León and Navarre on the one side and Christian Europe on the other side of the Pyrenees were insignificant. The poor kingdoms of northern Spain did not mint coins and the coins in circulation were mainly those of the caliphs in Cordova.

With the fall of the caliphate and the disintegration of Moslem Spain, the Christian kingdoms of northern Spain became stronger from both the politico-military aspect and the economic. With the cessation of the frequent, devastating invasions which the Moslem armies wreaked upon wide regions over many generations, their population increased, grew affluent, and alongside the rural, agricultural settlements, cities developed which absorbed the surplus of people. But this bestirring also resulted from the renewal of contact with the trans-Pyrenean countries. In the eleventh century, Christian northern Spain exported such products as the Spanish copper mentioned in a French chronicle which relates an incident that occurred in 1026.[136]

However, the new economic boom was connected initially with the increased movement of pilgrims to Compostela from the beginning of the eleventh century: They came from beyond the Pyrenees from Provence and all the other regions of southern France to prostrate themselves at the grave wherein, according to Christian belief, the Apostle James was buried. The custom of visiting this shrine was actually reinstituted at a relatively late period. The belief that James's bones were brought to Spain and that his grave was located at Compostela was not widespread in Spain before the end of the first third of the ninth century;[137] the sacred grave was first mentioned in a literary work in 885. Although pilgrimages from all the regions in Christian Spain and from France began in the tenth century, the number of pilgrims was small because Moslem forays rendered the highway perilous. In the eleventh century the pilgrimage movement reached sizable dimensions, embracing members of various classes and nationalities. Pilgrims came from France and Flanders, from Germany and distant Austria.[138] The movement grew stronger constantly. A later Arabic writer, no doubt basing himself on an ancient source, likens the shrine of Santiago de Compostela to the Kaaba[139] and a Christian source reports that when the mission of a Moslem ruler reached the road of the pilgrims—in the first half of the twelfth century—it could not pass through because of the dense crowds.[140]

The Christian rulers of Spain properly evaluated the importance of the pilgrimages both in establishing political and cultural relations with France—which was stronger and more developed than Spain—and in the economic development of their kingdoms. Sancho al Mayor (1004–1035) who established a united and strong Christian kingdom, was the first to lighten the long journey to Santiago de Compostela and the kings who succeeded him—members of his dynasty—did as he. They granted the pilgrims juridical protection (a matter of high priority in those days when personal security was virtually nonexistent). The pilgrims received the right to move freely on all the roads in the Christian kingdoms of Spain and were exempt from payment of road tolls. A pilgrim was given legal relief if he wanted to sell something but could not find the guarantors required by medieval law; the Spanish authorities also ordered that pilgrims should not be required to pay prices higher than those charged the country's inhabitants.[141]

Establishing hostels, however, was the foremost concern of these Christian rulers. Such accommodations were erected at Arconada (near Fromista), at Nájera, and at Irache (near Estella) by the middle of the eleventh century. In the second half of the century, action to improve the roads, build bridges, and to establish hostels was taken not only by the kings, but also by the hermitic ascetics (because of his deeds, one was called Santo Domingo de la Calzada, Santo Domingo of the Highway, and the city west of Nájera is so named in his honor).[142] But those who were most active in promoting an increase in the pilgrimages were the large monastic orders of Cluny and the Augustinians;[143] and orders especially devoted to this purpose were also founded.

The number of travelers from France and other countries to Santiago grew from year to year during the last third of the eleventh century, and some demonstrated the wish to remain in Spain. The Christian rulers of northern Spain, who were interested in establishing and developing cities, encouraged them, giving them writs of privilege on condition that they settle within their kingdoms. Thus, in the cities throughout the length of the highway leading to Santiago de Compostela, settlements of Frenchmen were founded; almost all were merchants and craftsmen who came chiefly from southern France. The main road which passed through Estella, Logroño, Nájera, Belorado, Burgos, Sahagún, León, and Astorga became a major commercial artery. In Burgos this road met a more northerly one which emerged from Bayonne in southern France and traversed Toulouse, Miranda de Ebro, and Briviesca; on this road too there was considerable movement of pilgrims and traders.

The trading ties of Christian northern Spain with the Moslem south were maintained, however. A Christian treatise (ca. 1140) on the shrine of Compostela states that there is an abundance of Moslem wares in Galicia.[144] An edifying story in a French monk's letter (written in the first half of the twelfth century) illuminates the solid commercial relationship between Moslem Spain and the Christian regions in the north of the peninsula. The monk relates that he went to Saragossa and wanted to visit the monastery near Valencia in which Saint Vincent is buried. In those days the direct route from Saragossa to Valencia was considered extremely dangerous because of the hostility between the Moslems and the Christians, and two monks from Valencia, who happened to be in Saragossa, advised him that it would be better to go to distant Santiago. There he could join merchants traveling to Valencia since their welfare was guaranteed by the Moslem authorities.[145]

The great change in the economic life of northern Spain was expressed in various ways. One was the change in the monetary system. During the eleventh century the Christian governments of northern Spain began to mint coins—obvious evidence that the odd assortment of coins formerly used no longer sufficed for the increased volume of trade and consequent broadened circulation of money . . . direct results of tributes which the Christian kings of Spain exacted from the Moslem rulers. During two generations an unending stream of gold coins flowed from the courts of the Moslem kings to Christian northern Spain. These formerly poor kingdoms became rich. Not only the Christian kings, but also their nobles and clergy, grew wealthy. Their demand for merchandise and their ability to pay high prices now constituted an attracting force to merchants and artisans from other regions of the peninsula and beyond it.

The stream of migrant craftsmen and merchants swept along with it members of other strata. Among the emigrants who left riven and devastated Andalusia to settle in the cities on the banks of the Ebro were scholars, notable physicians, and scientists who raised the cultural level of the region which the Arabs called the upper frontier.[146] The circumstances attendant upon life in these provinces were not unfamiliar to them—the language was their own, and they did not face the difficulties of adapting to another environment.

As a result of the economic arousal, inhabitants of other provinces in the Iberian peninsula moved to the new cities on the road to Santiago—a good number of Jews among them. At first, some came merely to trade in these towns and stayed to dwell in them, but some came with the sole intention of settlement.[147] Even cities within the Moslem sphere which were close to the new trade artery benefited from the economic boom in the Christian area. There were strong commercial ties between the Moslem region and that of the Christians in northern Spain; and, on their part, the merchants and pilgrims who came from France and the Lowlands, from Germany and Italy, formed a demand for Moslem products. Many Moslems and Jews, whose livelihoods in Andalusia and the other regions of Moslem Spain were straitened, came to settle in the Moslem towns lying in the basin of the Ebro River. Large suburbs sprouted before the gates of Saragossa and beyond the Ebro in those days.[148]

These same Moslem towns also maintained regular commercial ties with the now affluent Barcelona (the many Jews who dwelt in Barcelona and the other towns of the principality made trade easier for the Jewish merchants of Andalusia). The rulers of the principality of Barcelona and the other principalities in Catalonia endeavored to sustain free trade and to guarantee the welfare of merchants coming to them from Moslem states; the Jewish merchants especially benefited from the regulations and agreements which were made among the rulers of these states. The regulations of these princes—and particularly the custumal of the principality of Barcelona, the Ustages of 1064—refer to this subject in plain language.[149]

The most important factor, however, in the growth of the Moslem districts of the Ebro region, and especially in that of the Jewish settlement, was no doubt the flourishing of the towns on the road leading to Santiago. For this reason, the more daring and those having initiative among the migrants from the south wended their way beyond the Ebro, crossed the borders of Moslem Spain, and settled in the Christian kingdoms in the northern part of the peninsula. Individuals and families came to the cities on the entire length of the road to Santiago and settled within them.

Despite the marked religious spirit prevailing in Christian Spain, the inhabitants of these kingdoms adopted a relatively tolerant attitude toward the immigrants. The Council of the Clergy in the district of Oviedo, which assembled at Coyanza in 1050, prohibited Christians from occupying houses in which Jews dwelt[150] (apparently joint occupancy by Jews and Christians in the middle of the eleventh century was common), yet those very hostels in which the devout pilgrims lodged en route to the grave of the apostle at Compostela were also available to Jews. A Latin poem (composed at the beginning of the thirteenth century) concerning the large hostel at Roncesvalles lists all of its merits and states that "its portals are open to everyone, not only to Catholics, but also to heathens, Jews, heretics, and idlers."[151]

In the economic development of Christian northern Spain much importance lay in the establishment of Jaca, which was for a long time a small, rural settlement. In 1063 Sancho Ramirez made it the capital of his new kingdom of Aragon and, to attract settlers to his city, he bestowed special privileges upon the Frenchmen. The town burgeoned. Situated at the foot of the Pyrenees, on an important road junction, its geographical location was very convenient. Two roads meet at Jaca: the road of the pilgrims who crossed the Pyrenees at the Somport Pass intending to reach Santiago by fording the Ebro near Logroño, and the road leading from Saragossa to Bearn in southern France. The number of Frenchmen who settled in Jaca was considerable; Jews likewise soon came to settle in the city (in a deed of gift dated 1068, wherein a Christian named Iñigo Aznares grants the main church of Jaca various gifts, he also mentions his dealings with Jews).[152] The king of Aragon did not encourage Jews to settle in Jaca. He was in fact interested in Christian settlers from the other side of the Pyrenees; therefore, at this early period, fewer privileges were given to the Jews in the Fuero than to the Christians.[153]

Estella, lying midway between Pamplona and Logroño, also became a primary trading city at the end of the eleventh century. Founded in 1090, the town was to be a settlement of

Frenchmen, but Jews also promptly settled Estella, as affirmed by a document issued in 1093 in which King Sancho Ramirez awards the church of the town a tithe of their taxes.[154] Indeed, Jaca and Estella were relatively important cities (Jaca was for a time the capital of Aragon), but in that era Jews even resided in such villages on the road to Santiago as Ruesta, on the left bank of the Aragon River, between Jaca and Sangüesa.[155]

Jews also lived in the small towns and villages which were not on the road to Santiago but in its environs. A Jewish community existed at the end of the eleventh century in Monclús, a town on the right bank of the Esera River, in the province of Sobrarbe—and a few of the Jews of the city were wealthy, possessing much property.[156] Jews were already settled in some of the towns of Old Castile—through which the road to Santiago ran—at the start of the eleventh century. When the road became an important trade artery at the end of that century, Jews began to appear in the documents of other towns as well. The Jews of Miranda de Ebro were first mentioned in a document of 1099, wherein the king of Castile designates the privileges of the inhabitants of the city.[157] Jews also dwelt at that time in the district of Carrion de los Condes, which lies midway between Burgos and León.[158]

The settlement of Jews from Andalusia and other parts of Moslem Spain in towns along the route to Santiago de Compostela and within its vicinity is attested primarily in the data —especially in the Arabic names of the Jews—in documents such as bills of sale and gifts which are preserved in the archives of monasteries and churches. A document from 1052, containing a long list of vineyards and fields which the king of Navarre gave the newly erected cathedral in Nájera, mentions as owners of property upon which these vineyards and fields abut the Jews Yuces (should read Yucef, which is really Yūsuf), Sulaimān, Ḥasan, and Mūsā the Ḥazzan (cantor).[159] All these Jews no doubt were recent immigrants since it was their custom to adapt the common names of their country. The name of another Jew also mentioned in this document is given as Forrizuel—which is a corruption of Forūziel—a family name among Andalusian Jews, as in Cabra, southeast of Cordova.[160] In a general way, this document notes expressly that the owner of a certain property is a Jew, but this was not done in other documents and because of the corrupt spelling of the names it is often difficult to tell whether Jews are indicated.[161] Family names which clearly point to their forebears' origin in the Moslem south also appear in the documents of later-generation Jews in the former Moslem cities near the road to Santiago. One Joshua Ibn Shaprūṭ is a witness in a document written in 1190 at Huesca, near Jaca.[162] A deed written in that same city in 1207 testifies to the transfer of a garden which had belonged to Joseph b. Joseph Ibn Shaprūṭ and which had previously been mortgaged.[163] In a document written by Jews at Huesca in 1305 the family name Ibn al-Ḳurṭubī appears.[164] Jews came to the Ebro region not only from Andalusia but also from districts in central Spain—a document from the mid-twelfth century mentions one Joseph of Toledo as an inhabitant of Tudela.[165] Some of the immigrants to whom the authors of these documents traced their descent no doubt came to northern Spain in the middle of the twelfth century, but others came on the wave of immigration in the middle and in the second half of the eleventh century.

Almost all the Jewish quarters in the towns of Andalusia and in the central region of the Iberian peninsula were located within the *madīna*. But Jewish communities existed in many of these towns before the Moslem conquest and, because of their loyalty to the Moslem rule, either were centralized within them by the Arabs after the conquest or were permitted to settle within the *madīna* at a later period (especially was this the case in towns such as Saragossa and Calatayud in which Jews had dwelt from the days of the Omayyad caliphs). In the towns of Old Castile, in which Jews had settled at the start of the eleventh century, the quarters were also mainly inside the inner city (the Jews in Nájera struck roots during the first half of the eleventh century). In the days of Sancho el Mayor (1004–1035), Jews were given important juridical privileges, and various locations in the city were named for them.[166] Their quarter was at the southern end of the city in the district of the Church of San Miguel.[167] In the town of Belorado, too, the Jewish neighborhood was inside the city, on the Calle de los Castrillos and Calle de San Martín which is now Raimundo de Miguel.[168] In Burgos, the capital of Old Castile, where Jews were living by the first third of the eleventh century, the quarter was situated on the southeastern slope of the fortress near the street now named Fernán González.[169] Also in Vitoria, on the road linking Burgos with Bayonne, the Jewish neighborhood lay within the city,[170] and this was also true of Miranda de Ebro.[171] In the tenth and eleventh centuries the Moslems and Castilians divided between them the small town of Agreda, which lies in the upper valley of the Queiles River. The Moslems controlled the southern bank, whereas the northern bank was held by the Christians. The Jewish quarter was on the southern bank near the river, but within the walls erected in the days of ʻAbdarraḥmān III.[172]

This was not so, however, in the majority of the cities in northern Spain which extended the length of the road to Santiago and its environs. When large groups of Jews from southern Spain arrived at these cities, they often found no place within the city and therefore were compelled to settle outside. Until 1063 Jaca consisted of two adjoining quarters—the monastery of San Pedro and the nearby structures in the northwest, and the palace of the king of Aragon together with the neighborhood in the southeast. The town which arose under the initiative of King Sancho Ramirez was built between these two quarters, encompassed by a wall and fortifications; the Jewish quarter was outside the city, on its southern edge. Thereafter, in 1135, a wall was also built around this area, El Castellar, and was included within the city.[173] Also at Logroño, the city where the road to Santiago crossed the Ebro River, the Jewish neighborhood was outside the city's wall—between the gate called Puerta de la Cadena and the San Gil district, and the river.[174]

And the same occurred within the Moslem cities near the road to Santiago. Throughout all the generations that a community existed, the Jewish neighborhood in Huesca was outside the wall which surrounded the inner city on the southwestern side. In the days of the caliphs and the princes who replaced them, Tudela and its district were a sort of protrusion of the Moslem region into the provinces held by the Christians and, therefore, among Moslem cities, it was one of the towns nearest the road to Santiago. Its Jewish quarter was, to be sure, within the city which was encircled by a wall, but in its lowest part, situated at the very end. Also in Tarazona, near Tudela, the Jewish neighborhood was outside the inner Moslem city.

So, too, in the towns of this region which were a considerable distance from the road to Santiago, the Jewish quarters were located outside the inner city. The Jews benefited directly from the prosperity linked with the flow of pilgrims, and no doubt they settled in these towns at a relatively late date, or they may have come to them in consequence of the great migration to the environs of the road to Santiago. Such a town was Lérida, in which the Jewish neighborhood was outside the old, western wall.[175]

Not every Jewish quarter outside the inner city was established in the eleventh century. In many towns of the Ebro region Jews already were living for some time in neighborhoods which were a form of suburb, even though they were protected by walls. However, the area lying between the inner and outer walls of the city was only settled in part, and the migrants had no difficulty in settling and building new houses there.

The immigrants from the Moslem south who came to settle in the Christian kingdoms and principalities of northern Spain faced several obstacles. Predominant was their lack of security. In those days members of every class and faith suffered uncertainty, but Jews were particularly vulnerable—without civil rights in their new places of settlement. Members of another religion and speaking the language of the Moslems, they were uneasy among the Christians. The Jews met open hostility at times—zealous Christians regarded it permissible to attack them—especially since they had recently arrived from the land of the enemy.

It is characteristic that among the not too voluminous data concerning the appearance of the Jews in northern Spain in the middle and latter half of the eleventh century, there are items which testify to severe assaults inflicted upon them by Christians in various districts. In 1047 a trial was held in León in connection with attacks upon Jews who dealt in the business of silk, wool, and linen textiles.[176] In that year a powerful Christian knight slew two Jews on a mountain near Albelda, south of Logrõno, in Old Castile. When the inhabitants of Albelda petitioned Alfonso VI (ca. 1082) to affirm their right not to pay ransom for murdered persons whose bodies were found within the borders of their town, they referred to this incident since they then were not obligated to pay a fine.[177] A letter sent from the community of Nájera to other Jewish communities in the region illuminates the episode. This letter, concerning an act of violence and murder—and which may even be linked with the murder in 1047—reports how a Jew was slain and his possessions spoliated, and how the murderers intended burning his wife alive. The Jews of Nájera relate that they succeeded in redeeming the widow and her daughters with a payment of twenty-five pieces of gold and apparently with the intercession of some priests. As was customary in such incidents, they turned to the nearby Jewish communities with a request that they participate in the payment of the redemption money.[178]

In the kingdom of Aragon, too, the Jews had little security. In 1084, when King Sancho Ramirez awarded the rights of ownership of the fortress of Garissa, in the province of Huesca, to the one who had built it, he mentioned among the borders of the land belonging to the fortress "that hilltop on which the Jew was slain."[179]

Economic advantages outweighed dangers: The Jews in Moslem Spain continued to knock at the gates of Christian towns. As in all migratory movements, this one too encompassed members of various classes. A document written in 1056 at Nájera mentions García Sanger, the fisherman "who was a Jew" (but became a Christian).[180] However, most of the immigrants were artisans and merchants who succeeded in their new environments and, despite all their difficulties, achieved affluence. In the Latin documents of that epoch, the majority of the references to Jews cite their landed property, fields, and especially their vineyards. To be sure, not all the vineyards that belonged to them were cultivated by them. The Jewish settlers in northern Spain also acquired the vineyards to make their savings secure, as was done by Christian merchants; moreover, the need to provide the Jewish communities with wine from grapes grown and harvested by Jews was, beyond doubt, a factor in their acquisition of vineyards. In any event, the property of the Jews in various sections of northern Spain was quite extensive by the end of the eleventh century. In 1097 Domingo Laínez and his wife gave a gift of eight lots of land which they had bought from the Jews of Villa Nueva de Pancorbo to the monastery of San Millán de la Cogolla.[181] As the name New Village indicates, this was a settlement of immigrants.[182]

In the town of Monclús, in the kingdom of Aragon, the Jews acquired considerable property at the end of the eleventh century. In the archives of the cathedral of Roda are deeds of sale in connection with the sale of land implemented by Jews in a later generation. As their names indicate, the owners of the lands were new settlers; some of the names are Hebrew and some Latin, but most of them are Arabic. In 1130 a Jew named Vita (Ḥayyīm), a nephew of Savasorda (ṣāḥib ash-shurṭa, one holding office with a Moslem ruler), sold a vineyard located in Monclús to the Church of San Vicente in Roda. Khalaf 'Abdallāh was the guarantor; Joseph b. Amargaso and Ferro (Barzilai), Vita's brother, were witnesses. That same year an adjoining vineyard in Monclús was sold to the Church of San Vicente by the Jew Ferro (no doubt, the aforementioned) together with his nephews Jacob b. Yuçef, Jacob, Judah, and Joseph b. Samuel; the guarantors included Moses b. Amargoso and Khalaf Almazak, and the witnesses were Yuçef b. Amargaso and Yuçef the baker. The vineyard sold by Vita abutted upon the vineyard of Khalaf and the land of Samuel, the brother of Ferro. Ferro's vineyard was near that of Khalaf Ginto. These documents therefore demonstrate that the four brothers Samuel, Yuçef, Ferro, and Vita were men of extensive property.[183] In the same year, Khalaf Mascarel sold the church a vineyard in Monclús. The vineyard abutted that of the church and of another belonging to the seller; in 1133 he sold the church yet another vineyard. Ferro Avincollo was the guarantor, and Khalaf Aaron was the witness.[184]

The documents preserved in the archives of the churches and monasteries indicate not only how extensive were the properties that the Jewish immigrants had amassed, but also that these immigrant-settlers were not distributed evenly throughout the various districts along the road to Compostela, or, as it was called in those days, the French Highway (El camino francés). To be sure, at the end of the eleventh century there were Sahagún Jews (and Moslems) who settled there,[185] but generally the immigrants settled in the Christian cities and towns along the eastern part of the pilgrims' highway and in the Moslem cities in its vicinity. Whereas the pilgrims' road westward from Burgos underwent no change over a long period, the roads by which the pilgrims from France reached Spain varied from time to time, or more precisely, the importance of the various roads changed. In the eleventh century, special importance attached to the Somport Pass from which the pilgrims would descend to Canfranc and to Jaca and beyond into the Aragón Valley to Puente la Reina. On the other hand, until the middle of the twelfth century, few came by way of the Ibañeta Pass in order to reach Pamplona and continue thence to Puente la Reina.[186] Because of the preference of the Somport-Canfranc road, the Christian and Moslem settlements in its vicinity flourished—and in remote cities, like Monclús, or in Moslem cities, like Huesca, which were on the verge of ruination, Jewish communities prospered.

The rate of immigration from the Moslem south to the Ebro Valley varied in different periods. Those Jews from Andalusia and the other regions of Spain who settled in the suburbs of the cities of Aragon did not come there at one time, but rather over a long span. The migration to those districts on the banks of the Ebro which were under Moslem dominance was especially strong in the first years after the fall of the caliphate and in the last third of the eleventh century. Those medieval Arabic tales which explain the migration as the result of the action of outstanding rulers are not altogether mistaken. In the 1020s, a Moslem kingdom was established in the Ebro Valley whose rulers were competent and provided their subjects with the necessary security for the orderly progress of the economy.

By the time the dominion of al-Manṣūr's sons collapsed and civil war erupted, several generations of the Arab family of the Banū Tudjīb had ruled the provinces on the banks of the Ebro (which the Moslems called the Upper Frontier). They held sway over what is now Aragon until 1039, when they were succeeded by another Arab family, the Banū Hūd. Mundhir II, the third ruler of this dynasty, was murdered in that year by 'Abdallāh b. Ḥakam,[187] who was compelled to flee to Rueda, on the Jalón River (a fortress then called Rūṭat al-yahūd because it was once inhabited by Jews).[188] Both the founder of the new dynasty, Sulaimān Ibn Hūd (until 1046) and his successor, Aḥmad, were vigorous rulers. Aḥmad succeeded in once more uniting all the provinces over which Sulaimān had ruled.[189]

In the days of Aḥmad, Saragossa was one of the wealthy towns of Spain. A contemporary Arabic historian said, though exaggerating, that the town resembled Cordova when it was at the height of its splendor.[190] As a Moslem metropolis near the frontier, it served as a meeting point for merchants from both sides, and in a general way the geographic proximity to the lands of the Christians was readily noticeable. That blend of Oriental-Moslem culture with that of Christian Spain, which was characteristic of all of Moslem Spain, was especially prominent in Saragossa. The narrow streets and the fronts of the houses, without windows but with balconies enclosed by intertwining iron network, had a pronounced Oriental character. Yet the wide gates, adorned with panels of black marble, testified to a cultural heritage from the West.

The crowds of people moving about in the streets, which were paved and sloped to a depression in the middle, were a multitude of various nationalities. As was customary in Moslem countries, the retail sellers bawled the prices of their wares, which had been delivered to them by the wholesale merchants; vendors of cooked foods walked about with steaming pots on their heads. Eye doctors sat on the street corners smearing kohl on the eyes of men and women; magicians squatted nearby surrounded by idlers and curiosity-seekers. In front of the dim niches which served as their shops, leather-workers displayed their wares—saddles, harnesses, belts, cases for personal papers, and pieces of leather dyed in variegated hues for bookbinding; in front of the shoemakers' shops—and hung over the entrances—were row upon row of shoes and sandals of red or blue leather and boots of all kinds. But the densest traffic was in front of the shops in which silk textiles were sold. Here the merchants carefully weighed each coin given in payment for the expensive merchandise. Here moved groups of merchants coming from Navarre, Castile, and France, wearing tight-fitting coats buttoned up to the chest and wide breeches reaching down to their knees. Companies of helmeted Christian knights, whose swords dangled against their thighs, the elite horsemen of the Saragossan forces, abounded in the streets and occasioned no surprise as the Moslem theologians, in their broad white coats, chanced upon them.

The Jewish settlement in Saragossa existed uninterruptedly for many generations and, with approximately twelve hundred residents, was relatively large for a Jewish community in those days.[191] The majority of Saragossa's Jews earned a living from various branches of industry. Fur-processing, the production of linen textiles, as well as the clothes made from them, were among the specially flourishing industries in Saragossa. That Jews in good numbers engaged in both is demonstrated by the street names in the old Jewish quarter and by documents of a much later period. Jews were involved in the manufacture of leather goods and metalworking.[192] Aside from the artisans, merchants constituted the strongest element among Saragossa's Jews. They engaged in retail trade within the city and maintained commercial ties with the Christian states in northern Spain, with the principality of Barcelona, and with the southern provinces of France.

Within this large community there also was a significant body of intellectuals whose scholarship supported them amply. One was the physician Ménaḥēm Ibn al-Fawwāl (the bean merchant), who lived during the first half of the eleventh century. Besides being a practicing physician with a fine reputation among Jews and Moslems alike, he was also well-informed in the field of philosophy. He wrote a treatise, in the form of questions and answers, on the rules of logic and on the basis of natural science, naming it *Kanz al-muḳill* ("The Storehouse of the Poor").[193] The book is permeated with the scientific views which were current among the Arab intellectuals, for the learned men among Saragossa's Jews generally took an active part in the Arabic cultural life of the city and thus contributed significantly to the synthesis of the various intellectual elements which produced the later Spanish civilization.

Some, among the men of property, the affluent merchants, and the intellectuals amid Saragossa's Jewry, even found means of becoming intimates at the royal court of the Tudjībids, serving as their counselors, and numbering among the officers of their government. These rulers had no prejudices against their non-Moslem subjects. Just as they entered into friendly relations with the Christian kings, so they respected intellectuals of other faiths and appointed them to authoritative positions. The rulers of the Banū Hūd dynasty followed their example. These Moslem monarchs believed that there could be no greater distinction than that of bringing rare talents to their court—renowned writers and creative thinkers—whether devout Moslems or heretics or members of other faiths. Aḥmad, philosophically inclined himself, surrounded himself with dignitaries and intellectuals of diverse nationalities and faiths. His chief vizier, who bore the resounding title of Dhu 'l-wizāratain (the Holder of Two Vizierships) was, for a long time, a poet of Christian origin who kept his Christian surname—Ibn Gundisalvo.[194] When the liberality of the king of Saragossa became known among the church circles beyond the Pyrenees, they toyed with the idea of persuading the Moslem ruler to convert to their faith. In consequence, at the end of the 1020s they twice sent missions consisting of clergy to Saragossa, seeking to convince the king that Christianity was indeed the true faith.[195]

Although the kings of the Tudjībid and Banū Hūd dynasties were tolerant toward Christians and Jews, they nevertheless distrusted their Mozarab subjects and at times, because of the action of the Christian rulers with whom they maintained contacts, retaliated against them. The selfsame Aḥmad, a philosopher surrounded by a coterie of scholars and poets, perpetrated the massacre of his Christian subjects in 1065 because his realm was invaded by Christian forces.[196]

From this aspect the position of the Jews in the royal court of Saragossa was far more satisfactory. They were less suspect of siding with the Christian rulers, and they did not have to atone for misdeeds of rulers of their own faith. Jews entered and left the court, moving freely within it. In those days the type of Jewish dignitaries, learned and imbued with pride, became a crystallized entity in Saragossa and the other capitals of Moslem Spain such as were known particularly in the period of Christian dominance in the later Middle Ages. The spirit of tolerance which prevailed in the royal courts of the provincial kings of Moslem Spain in the eleventh century enabled those Jews to attain eminence. They were like their Moslem and Christian counterparts. They too assumed authority and exercised dominion over their coreligionists to a degree which made them hateful to their common brethren. This development was especially conspicuous in Saragossa, whose distinguishing feature, among the Moslem capitals, was that members of the different faiths lived together in compatibility.

In the 1040s, one of the intellectuals of the community served as a counselor to King Mundhir II and held a high office in his government. His name was Abū Isḥāḳ Y'ḳūtiēl b. Isaac and his family's name was Ibn Ḥassān. He was a member of an esteemed family, his father being a man of means and a patron of young scholars.[197] Y'ḳūtiēl was a student of the texts of Jewish law and of secular learning and was also a man of worldly affairs. The last king of the Tudjībid dynasty valued his counsel and designated him one of his officers. Y'ḳūtiēl used his influence to protect his people: He subsidized talented young scholars—poets and authors; and, as was the wont among many of the wealthy Jews of Spain, he made contributions to talmudic academies and Jewish scholars in Palestine and Babylonia. However, again as was the wont of people like him, he did not limit his contacts with the Oriental Talmud schools to the sending of money, but also exchanged opinions with them about problems of Jewish law.[198] The poets who looked forward to his gifts composed poems in his praise, extolling his noble traits of rectitude and liberality. Y'ḳūtiēl came to a bitter and swift end: In 1039 he was slain together with other officers who were intimates of Mundhir, the last of the Tudjībid kings.[199]

During that epoch, the Jews of Saragossa were distinguished by their intensive cultural life. The Talmud school was never devoid of scholars and writers working diligently in the production of books. Among Saragossa's Jews were representatives of differing concepts, scholars, poets and writers, theologians steeped in Jewish lore, philosophers and scientists.

One of the prominent intellectuals was Abū 'Amr Joseph Ibn Ḥasdai. He was the scion of a distinguished Jewish family of Cordova and in his youth was among the companions of Samuel ha-lēvī. Despite the catastrophe, he remained in the town of the caliphs for a long while. However, he eventually took the wanderer's staff and migrated to Saragossa. After Joseph Ibn Ḥasdai became known publicly and won renown for his outstanding Arabic style, the king of Saragossa (of the Tudjībid dynasty) appointed him secretary at the royal court. Notwithstanding his interest in Arabic literature, he did not neglect the cultural heritage of his ancestors. Together with other Jewish intellectuals of his time, he occupied himself with Hebrew philology, biblical exegesis, and composed poetry. Although he did not write much verse, he acquired fame as a gifted poet because of one poem. Two of his relatives had migrated to one of the cities in the kingdom of Granada, but even there they had no luck. Joseph Ibn Ḥasdai therefore addressed a long poem to Samuel ha-lēvī thanking him for the aid he had already extended to his relatives and requesting that he continue to assist them. Samuel responded in his best flowery style, promising to fulfill his request. Joseph Ibn Ḥasdai entitled his own poem, written in 1046, *Ha-Shīra ha-y'tōma* ("The Orphaned or Unusual Verse"), that is, a pearl without compare. It is indeed different from most poetical creations of that epoch. It has none of the hyperbole so conspicuous in the Hebrew poetry written on the pattern of the laudatory verse of the Arabic poets. Ibn Ḥasdai's contemporaries and later generations extolled it in the highest, admiring his mastery of the Hebrew language and his artistry as a writer of verse.[200]

The sizable circle of talmudic scholars who devoted all their time to the study of the Gemara and the geonic responsa encompassed men of amazing knowledge and profundity. One such scholar who dwelt in Saragossa was Rabbi David b. Sadya, an author and a judge in the local community. Among other works, he wrote a comprehensive halakhic treatise in which he analyzed the strictures against the *Halākhōt g'dōlōt.* This treatise was written partly in Arabic and partly in the language of the Gemara. Another work, on the laws pertaining to oaths in talmudic jurisprudence, written in Arabic, was *Kitāb al-Aimān* (in Hebrew, *Mishp'ṭē sh'bhū'ōt,* "Laws Pertaining to Oaths").[201] Among Saragossa's Jews at that time there was no lack of those who were sympathetic toward Karaism or who altogether embraced the doctrine of the Karaites. The bill of sale of a certain shop, written in Saragossa shortly after its conquest by the Christians at the beginning of the twelfth century, notes that the shop was located opposite Zalema Alcarao.[202]

In those days—when a man was not persecuted for his views—there arose among the Jews of Saragossa an intellectual, Moses b. Samuel ha-Kōhēn Ibn Djiḳaṭilya, who expressed his audacious opinions on religious matters. He was a native of Cordova who had migrated, as did many others, to Saragossa.[203] However, he was not of the first émigrés who left the city when it was taken by the Berbers; rather, he was of that generation which grew up after the great change occurred in Moslem Spain; he wrote his treatises in the third quarter of the eleventh century.[204] His prodigious talents, his extensive knowledge of Hebrew and Arabic literature, and his command of both languages made a strong impression, especially since he was also a brilliant speaker. His preaching amazed his audience, and as was the way of contemporary scholars, he could compose poetry extemporaneously. But he was excitable, incapable of self-control, and at times his abnormal behavior provoked opposition to him.[205] He therefore eventually left Saragossa for southern France, where he met the wealthy and highly esteemed Solomon the *nāsī* (president or exilarch). For Isaac, the *nāsī*'s son, he translated—from Arabic to Hebrew—Ḥayyūdj's treatises on gemmate verbs and verbs having weak letters and included his own notes and comments.[206] Moses Ibn Djiḳaṭilya thus became the first translator to transmit the creations of Judaeo-Arabic culture to the Hebrew language.

He also wrote a treatise on Hebrew linguistics in Arabic, *Kitab at-tadhkir wa't-ta'nīs,* which means "A Book on the Masculine and Feminine." It is a lexicon arranged alphabetically, not according to roots but rather according to words. The author enumerates biblical words which are masculine though their plural form is feminine, or feminine though their plural form is masculine; also words which have no singular form and other similar irregularities. In the Middle Ages this work was regarded by Hebrew philologists as an exemplary study and brought its author great renown.[207] Like most grammarians of those days, Moses Ibn Djiḳaṭilya was involved in biblical exegesis[208] and wrote commentaries as an addendum to the commentaries of Saadya Gaon. But his contemporaries and the following generation also praised him as a great poet. He composed sacred as well as secular poetry which was written in meter and distinguished for its purity of language. Among other subjects, he wrote poems in praise of the *nāgīd* Samuel and his son Joseph, and on occasion composed poems in Arabic.[209]

Nevertheless, the uniqueness of Moses Ibn Djiḳaṭilya is displayed as a biblical exegete. He wrote commentaries in Arabic on the Pentateuch, Isaiah, the twelve minor prophets, Job, and Daniel. Except for some fragments and quotations in the works of later writers, his commentaries are lost,[210] but the little that has been preserved suffices to show that he was an exegete of independent thought who approached the study of Scriptures in a scientific spirit and with a critical attitude which was at variance with—and even opposed to—the approach of most of his contemporaries. He was a faithful disciple of Ḥayyūdj, whose method guided him in his philological commentary; for by his discovery of the rule of triliteral roots, Ḥayyūdj led the study of the Bible along new lines and laid for it a sound foundation. Inasmuch as Ibn Djiḳaṭilya was a grammarian, his interpretations revolved around philology; they generally were brief and at times hard to understand.

But the conspicuous aspect in his exegesis is his endeavor to interpret the books of the prophets against their historical background. Contrary to accepted opinion, he argued that the oracles of some of the prophets were not directed toward the Messianic Era but to the beginning of the era of the Second Temple. Thus Micah 4:11 refers to Zerubabel, and Zechariah 9:9 to Nehemiah. He makes a nice differentiation between the two sections of Isaiah's prophecies, but does not assign them to two persons. The first section of these prophecies he regards as being directed to the era of Hezekiah, whereas the second refers to the Second Temple. To be sure, there were biblical commentators preceding Moses Ibn Djiḳaṭilya who expressed similar opinions, but for him it became a principle to which he held with great consistency. It must be noted that designating the prophecies as references to the Second Temple was a view characteristic of the Karaite exegetes[211] (and there were many in Saragossa). Moses Ibn Djiḳaṭilya was a commentator with a distinct rational tendency. He did not negate the miracles, but he did endeavor to explain the tales concerning miracles so that they would not contradict the laws of nature. Thus in his explanation of Joshua 10:12–13, he states that the sun and the moon did not cease moving, but the light of the sun lingered longer than the customary time.[212] In comparison with the accepted view of his age, his opinions on the authorship of the Book of Psalms were revolutionary. In those days the entire Book of Psalms was ascribed to King David, and when Moses Ibn Djiḳaṭilya proffered the view that some of the psalms were composed during the Babylonian Exile—for example, Psalms 42 and 77—his statements were regarded by everyone as rank heresy. Moses Ibn Djiḳaṭilya did not flinch from quoting the biblical commentaries written by church scholars in his exegesis. It is true that even before his time, the *g'ōnīm* Samuel b. Ḥofni and Rabh Hai availed themselves of the commentaries of the Christians. However, they had before them the *Peshita,* written in language close to that of the Gemara, whereas Moses Ibn Djiḳaṭilya read the translations of the Bible and the commentaries written in Latin. At times he cited their statements to dispute them, but he did not always contradict them.[213]

Many of his contemporaries, on hearing his observations or reading his works, were shocked, but he in fact represented the scientific approach of a substantial segment of Spanish Jewry, that approach which is prominent in the various branches of their literary achievements. This is after all a common phenomenon. The minority represents the spirit of originality of a societal or national group, that spirit which is the trend of its history and its accomplishments, whereas the majority combats it out of a passive devotion to tradition. Sometimes the conservatives are ultimately compelled to join those pioneers who are the vanguard of society; but at times the conflict between the daring and active minority—progressive and innovative—and the static majority is protracted over many generations without coming to a resolution. Such was the situation among the Jews of Spain in the eleventh century. Moses Ibn Djiḳaṭilya was one of the trailblazers of that cultural achievement which is the historical contribution of Spanish Jewry to the culture of the Jewish people and to all of humanity. He was the true representative of that sociocultural milieu which crystallized at the royal court of Saragossa, in the Jewish circles which had entrée to it and in the courts of the other provincial kings in eleventh-century Moslem Spain—that tolerant Spain which was open to the influences of alien cultures.

The community of Saragossa was the center of the Jewish settlements in the cities of the provinces north and south of the

Ebro River as well as in the hamlets and villages. Strong links joined together the Jews of the provincial towns with those of Saragossa. Especially, there were family ties existing between them. Among the Jews of Aragon there were large, ramified families whose members dwelt in various cities and hamlets. Many of the Jews in the towns and villages, and even in those settlements which were considered medium-size cities, earned their living from agriculture. They owned land which they tilled with their own hands; they also leased fields and vineyards to cultivate from the Moslems and Christians. It naturally followed from this that entire communities gathered into the small villages.

One of those rural communities existed in Alagón, northwest of Saragossa. The Jews of Alagón had an organized community, and various documents preserved from that era are edifying in this respect. Alagón was captured in 1119 by Alfonso the Battler, king of Aragon, and some twenty years later Christians began to buy land from the Jews. The names of the Jews mentioned in the deeds of sale both as sellers and witnesses are, for the greatest part, Arabic—proof that the Jewish settlement was an old one. In 1136 a man named Iñigo Galinez bought a field in Alagón from the Jew Yaḥyā, and among the witnesses were the Jews Ishmael and Isḥāḳ.[214] In that same year Iñigo bought an orchard of fig trees from the physician Ibn Banist; Judah Ibn Corna was the guarantor and Eliezer Ibn Laṭīf and Saul, the rabbi of Alagón's Jews, were the witnesses;[215] five years later this Christian bought another orchard from the same physician. The deed of sale mentions as guarantor Yaḥyā Ibn Paḳūda, the brother-in-law of Jacob who was the *leztero* of Alagón (i.e., the collector of taxes imposed on trade), and as witnesses the aforementioned Ishmael, here referred to also as *leztero,* and Isḥāḳ, who is called *ḥazzān* (cantor) and is described as the brother of Jacob.[216]

In the southern districts of the country, where the Tudjībids first ruled, and after them the Banū Hūd, there were two important cities, and flourishing communities existed in both.

The chief city of these provinces was Calatayud. The heads of the government dwelt in this city; when Sulaimān Ibn Hūd divided his kingdom and appointed his son Muḥammad as governor of this province, the city became the capital of an independent principality. But after some years passed, the kingdom of Saragossa became reunited, and Calatayud was once again the chief city of its southern province. The city was the focal point of the economic life of the region and had a mint which produced silver and gold coins. Educational activities in Calatayud were extensive (Arabic historians have transmitted to us the names of several of its inhabitants who were renowned scholars). The Jewish settlement in Calatayud, which had its beginning in the days of the Omayyad caliphs, continued throughout this entire era and struck deeper and deeper roots into its economic life. In the middle of the eleventh century it numbered some eight hundred.[217] A Jew who lived in Calatayud is mentioned in one of the poems of Samuel ha-lēvī; the *nāgīd* sent regards to the man whose name was M'bhōrākh and who lived in the Fortified City, which is a poetic term for Calatayud.[218]

Daroca, thirty-five kilometers southeast of Calatayud, is now a small town with approximately four thousand inhabitants. But under Moslem rule it was a prospering city which Arabic geographers of the Middle Ages described as large and well-populated.[219] Daroca was a major city in a rich agricultural region for which it served as a marketing center. It was built upon a mountain which rose from the narrow, deep valley of a tributary of the Jiloca River and on its slope. This mountain, which is northwest of the valley and is named for the hermitage San Cristóbal, was protected by a fortress near its peak and was surrounded by a strong wall. The city's main thoroughfare, Calle Mayor, in the midst of the valley, was not yet included within it. When the city grew, suburbs which ascended the mountain slopes were annexed. A Jewish community existed in Daroca for several generations, though it never became large; when the town was taken by the Christians, its Jews received the same rights as its Christians.[220] The Jewish neighborhood was on the slope of the San Jorge mountain, on the other side of the valley, to the east, and there, near this quarter, their cemetery was located.[221]

The city of Tudela (which the Arabs called Tutīla), in the Ebro Basin, was already well-established, affluent, and highly cultured during the Moslem period. As in our own time, so too in that day, it prospered from fertile surroundings watered by tributaries flowing down to the Ebro from mountain ranges in the north and in the south. Moreover, the city was an important port to which ships could sail on the Ebro.[222] Goods from northern Spain—such as pelts—were exported from Tudela to Oriental countries.[223]

The site upon which the city was built seemed to be designed by nature to serve as the fortress it became, for it was protected on the one side by the Ebro and by its tributary, Queiles, on the other. During several generations of rule by the Crescent over the Iberian peninsula, Tudela was the most northerly city in the Ebro Valley held by the Moslems and its district was a protrusion into Christian Spain. In the eleventh century Tudela was a northward defense point over the Ebro Valley against Navarre and westward against the Castilians who had already penetrated the districts south of the city. Tudela was a major city of the upper frontier, and from the time that an independent kingdom was established there (the capital being Saragossa), Tudela was the leading city of its western province. The first king of Saragossa, Mundhir I, designated as governor of Tudela, Sulaimān Ibn Hūd who was also the governor of Lérida.[224] After Sulaimān himself became king of Saragossa and fixed the order of succession, he appointed his son Mundhir ruler of Tudela. Thus, at the end of the 1050s, Tudela became, for a short time, an independent principality, and there the son of Sulaimān Ibn Hūd, aẓ-Ẓāfir, minted coins which, in the manner of sovereign kings, bore his name.[225] But Tudela was not only a rich city and a center of government, it was also a focal point for an intense cultural life: In the middle of the tenth century the town was inhabited by Moslem scholars to whom disciples swarmed from other cities in the Ebro region.[226]

Ancient Tudela, built at the foot of the fortress, included the streets San Miguel, San Nicolas, Pedro Ortiz, and nearby side-streets. At a much later period of Moslem rule, when the city's population increased as a result of its economic growth, the area encompassed by a wall was expanded, including within it the region between the Mardancho Brook and the Queiles River in the south. However, as this area was not fully settled in its early years, it had ample space for the erection of the chief mosque (the cathedral now stands in its place).[227] The eastern wall of the city had, from old, run in proximity to the Ebro, the southern wall along the left bank of the Queiles; the western segment turned from the end of Yanguas y Miranda Street northward and, as it continued from the east of the Paseo de Villa Nueva, reached Mediavilla Street.

Tudela's population continued to grow rapidly, and in proportion to its small area, its density was large. The houses were high in the old section of the city, and several families dwelt in every house.[228] In the low-lying quarters the streets were level, without ups and downs; but at the city's hub they climbed the slope of the hill, so that wayfarers going to and fro among the high houses had difficulty, even as nowadays walking among those narrow, old streets—enveloped with the glory of antiquity—is still difficult.

The Moslem residents of Tudela dwelt in the northern section of the city, in the district of San Miguel Street, in the neighborhood currently called San Nicolas, in the vicinity of the Great Mosque, in the San Jorge quarter, in the market area, and in the blocks near San Julián Street. The Mozarabs' houses were in the eastern section of the city, near the Church of Santa Magdalena, which served the Christians during the period of Moslem rule. Thus their neighborhood was inside the walls which encompassed the old city before it was widened by Moslem rulers.[229]

The Jewish neighborhood was in an area which was annexed to the city through expansion to the south. Whether they were latecomers to Tudela, or their numbers increased by immigrants coming from other Spanish provinces, there was no room for them in the old city on the slope of the hill. Later they were compelled to move their dwellings. In the last years of Moslem rule the Jews dwelt in the southeast section of the city, in the area which is encompassed by the streets now called Del Portal, Cortez, and Verjas as well as south and east from this area. One of the gates of the city, the Saragossa Gate, was located on the south side of Verjas Street.[230] These streets constituted a closed square, which in those days was convenient both for defense and for the fostering of the self-contained community life of its inhabitants. On the northwestern side the Jewish neighborhood extended to the chief mosque, and to the wall of the city on the east and south.[231] The Jewish neighborhood was relatively large and the Tudela community did, indeed, number about one thousand.[232]

As in the other cities of Spain, so too there were in Tudela numerous Jews engaged in agriculture.[233] The social structure of the community was diversified. Along with simple peasants were men of distinguished lineage, and wealthy propertied people. In the first document preserved from the period after the city's conquest by the Christians in which Jews are mentioned, we find surnames and names such as Savasorda, i.e., one who in Arabic bore the title sāhib ash-shurṭa, and Ibn al-Ḥassān, i.e., a member of the family of Y'ḳutiēl.[234]

In the city of Tarazona, south of Tudela, in the latter generations of Moslem rule, there was a Jewish community. Tarazona, an ancient city, is mentioned in sources from Roman and Visigothic times; in the first days of Moslem rule it was the seat of the provincial governor.[235] However, at a later period, Tudela became the government seat as well as the focal point of the district's economic life because of its more central geographic location. The decline of Tarazona began from then on, lasting several generations. In the eleventh century the city, which was surrounded by a wall, extended along the left bank of the Queiles River on the selfsame high hill upon which climb, to this day, old and picturesque streets and upon which stand the houses of nobles—houses which are partly in ruins and yet preserve the heritage of those myriad generations of Romans and Visigoths, Moslems and Jews who found their happiness and their sorrow in them. In the latter days of Moslem rule the Jewish community of Tarazona was small;[236] the number of Jewish families then resident in the city did not reach twenty.[237] The Jews dwelt in that neighborhood which was later known as Juderia Vieja (the old Jewish neighborhood) and today is still called Juderia. This quarter was outside the wall surrounding the inner city, where the Moslems lived. To be sure, the Mozarabs were also kept out of the inner city by the Moslems, and dwelt outside the wall, across the river.[238] The Jews's houses were near the eastern wall, below the palace of the governor (*sudda* in Arabic), where now stands the bishop's palace.[239] The city's wall ran in an east-to-west line, south of the street currently named Del Conde, on whose eastern end was the gate of the city; thence it turned south encompassing the governor's palace. The Jews dwelt in the area between the streets called Del Conde and the wall near the palace and on the slope beneath it, at the site where, at present, the streets called Juderia and Rua Alta ascend the hill. The street now called Juderia, which emerges from the street named De los Aires, is extremely narrow and to this day, at its very end, it measures only two footsteps.

Huesca was the chief city, for many generations, of the districts on the barren and spacious plateau north of Saragossa —and it had an important Jewish community.

At various times during Moslem rule this ancient city was the capital of a small principality. Even after the disintegration of the Spanish caliphate, the governor of Huesca (the Tudjībid Abū Yaḥyā Muḥammad Ibn Sumādiḥ) became an independent ruler. However, he was unable to defend himself against the king of Saragossa and had to abandon his city; the district of Huesca was now a province of the kingdom of Saragossa. After the death of Sulaimān—the first of the Banū Hūd dynasty— and the division of his kingdom, Huesca once again became the capital of an independent principality (ruled by Lope, one of the sons of Sulaimān Ibn Hūd). However, after some years passed, the various provinces of the kingdom of Saragossa were reunited and Huesca was the provincial city it was earlier. Throughout the entire period of Moslem rule, with its many vicissitudes, Huesca was a border city, in danger of incursions by Christian princes in the north; when the kings of Aragon and Navarre grew stronger in the second half of the eleventh century, the plight of the city intensified. The kings of Aragon had good reasons for wanting to take the city: they considered it suitable for a capital, and it was an important way-station on the road to Saragossa. Sancho Ramirez (king of Aragon, 1063–1094), tore district upon district from the province of Huesca, building within its vicinity fortresses which commanded its approaches and its communication lines so that it became a city virtually under constant siege.

Under these circumstances the governors of Huesca concentrated on strengthening its fortifications, building, in turn, a powerful fortress. Huesca was surrounded by a stone wall, fifteen meters high and with many turrets, especially near the gates. There was also a large area outside this wall which was surrounded from the west and south by a weaker, earthen wall.[240] The stone wall extended the length of the streets today called Coso Alto, Coso Bajo, and Ronda de Monte Aragón, whereas the outer wall ran from the Gate of Miguel in the north to Del Angel fountain in the west and thence to the Navarre Square in the south. The inner city was built on a hill, and at the crest, on the site where the cathedral now stands, was the chief mosque; the palace of the governor was north of it, on the site where the palace of the king of Aragon later was built and which now is the location of the school, The Institute. The area between the stone and earthen walls was not fully settled, and in the eleventh century even the inner city was not densely populated: In the last third of the century the number of residents in Huesca amounted, at most, to four thousand.[241] The narrow and winding streets near the mosque did not teem with people in that generation and were as quiet and somnolent as they are today—rapt in contemplation of faraway times which had gone, never to return.

Most of Huesca's inhabitants were Muwalladūn, but there were also among them Arabs who traced their lineage to the Tudjībid tribe and to inhabitants of Medina in the early days of Islam.[242] (Well-to-do Moslems, whose livelihoods came from their rural properties, left the exposed city earlier.) These two groups, who constituted the vast majority of the city's residents, dwelt in its north and center. Near the Church of San Pedro, in the southern section of the inner city, dwelt the Mozarab community.[243] The Jewish neighborhood was outside the inner city, which was surrounded by the stone wall. It was situated between this wall and the earthen one on the southwest. To this day the quarter between Coso Alto Street and the public garden south of San Jorge Street is known as

Barrio Nuevo, the name given to the quarters of the Jews after their expulsion from Spain. The Jewish neighborhood in this location is mentioned in the document of 1110 relating to the establishment of the Church of San Miguel shortly after the Christians conquered the city.[244] The main street of the neighborhood is currently called San Jorge, and its eastern end was near the wall of the inner city, opposite the site on which the Plaza Lizana ascends toward the cathedral. In that era one of the gates of the city, the Ramian Gate, was located there. The western end of the street was near a well, then called the Well of the Jewish quarter and at a later time the Well of the Angel; one of the gates of the earthen wall was near this well. The Jewish neighborhood thus extended to the district where are now the streets Calle Amistad, Travesia de Jardines, Loreto, and Cardedera. In the center of the quarter was a small square, and to the southwest beyond it was a mosque in a structure which formerly served as a church named for San Cyprián and which later, in the days of Christian dominance, reverted to being a Christian house of worship. On this side of the quarter, in the field of Canastello, was the Jewish cemetery; it is mentioned in a document dated 1156.[245] Moslems lived near the mosque, but the area north of the Jewish neighborhood was uninhabited.[246] In this neighborhood Huesca's Jews dwelt until the end of the Middle Ages. A document from the period of Christian rule speaks of the obligation imposed on them to repair the fortifications near their quarter, from the Gate of San Miguel (the northern gate of the city) to the Ramian Gate.[247]

While the Moslem population within the city struggled for existence, the Jewish community multiplied and numbered about two hundred fifty.[248] Therefore Jews are mentioned in the relatively numerous documents which have been preserved from the first days after the city's conquest by the Christians. Along with other inhabitants of Huesca, they are mentioned in a document written four years after it fell into Christian hands. In 1100 a Christian named Fortuño Sanchez wanted to go to Palestine with his wife and he endeavored to sell property to finance his trip, but he did not get a price equal to its value—as he puts it—either from relatives and friends or from Christians and Jews.[249] King Ramiro II, who sought to attract Christians to the city, established in the charter of the inhabitants of Huesca the regulations governing property which Frenchmen would acquire from Moslems and Jews.[250] The Jews did indeed own much realty. In 1114 the monks who were housed in the Church of San Pedro bartered a vineyard belonging to them for one of Caraboçola, a Huescan Jew whose vineyard was in Ḥārat al-Ḳūmis, northwest of the city, near the Jewish neighborhood. The guarantors for the Jew were Zechariah Ibn Ḥamr, the metalsmith, and Abraham, from the village of Ruesta; as witnesses, the Jews Vita Ibengullinellas and Ysmahel Elpellenki were signatories to the deed.[251] Abraham of Ruesta was an old-time resident in Huesca; he farmed and owned land; his relatives also owned land.[252]

For many generations agriculture remained the key means of livelihood for the Jews of Huesca. In the later Middle Ages a king of Aragon stresses in one of his letters that fields and vineyards are a chief source of the wealth of Huesca's Jews.[253] Even in Huesca's environs the Jews owned landed property to the end of the era of Moslem rule. In 1098, two years after he conquered Huesca, Pedro the king of Aragon transferred to the bishop of Huesca the ownership of the village of Septimo and its church, which was the property of the Jew Savasorda, "it being unseemly for a Jew to hold proprietary rights over a church."[254] This, then, was a wealthy Jew, close to the authorities and bearing a title of distinction. However, the majority of Huesca's Jews were simple craftsmen, such as Zechariah Ibn Ḥamr, the metalsmith. Metalsmithing throughout the existence of the community was one of its major occupations; the metalsmiths among Huesca's Jews are mentioned in some documents from the Christian epoch in which reference is also made to a street named for them.[255] As usual, numerous Jews of Huesca engaged in trade, especially in silk textiles. Their factories and shops were in the Jewish quarter, and one of its streets was named, for a long time, for the silk merchants.[256]

The status of the intellectuals, whose craft lay in their scholarship, was as difficult in Huesca as it was in all the frontier cities where there were no princes to sustain them. As did the Moslem intellectuals who moved to the capital cities where they found nobles and patrons who assisted and employed them, so too many Jewish scholars went to the big cities because, in their own small communities, only a mere few could understand or assist them, and even libraries were rarely available. Nevertheless there were men of culture in the provincial towns. An Arabic source writes of a learned, wealthy Jew who lived during the last generation of Moslem rule in Huesca and associated with Moslem poets and writers. His name was Bassām b. Simeon; an Arabic writer, a scion of the Omayyad dynasty, wrote him a letter in which he mentions his lovely soirées and the discussions on literary matters which went on between them.[257] The most prominent of the learned Jews who lived in that age in Huesca was a man of great talent but who abandoned his faith and his people after the town was conquered by the Christians. He was born in 1062, and when he was a Jew, his name was Moses. He acquired a thorough knowledge in Jewish lore, became an expert in Karaitic doctrine,[258] read widely in all the branches of Arabic literature, and was interested in Arabic *belles lettres*. However, he devoted himself primarily to the exact sciences, becoming an expert in astronomy, geography, and medicine. As was the case with many intellectuals within the Jewish communities of Spain, he doubted the truth of the traditional Jewish faith and in 1106 converted to Christianity. Since Moses had attained wide fame, the king of Aragon, who then dwelt in Huesca, consented to be the sponsor at his baptism; the apostate accordingly took the king's name, thus becoming Pedro Alfonso.[259] Later Christian writers report that he also became the physician of the Christian king.[260]

After his conversion, Pedro Alfonso wrote a polemic in Latin against Judaism; it took the form of a debate between the two souls which struggled within him, Moses the Jew, and Pedro the Christian. After the fashion of Christian polemicists, he endeavored in this dialogue to demonstrate through the Bible the tenets of Christianity, particularly the belief in the Trinity and the concept of Jesus as both god and man; of course, Pedro Alfonso professed that numerous prophecies in Scripture predict the advent of Jesus. In a chapter devoted to a polemic against Islam, he calls upon the hollow legends of the origin of the Moslem faith which were widespread among Christians during the Middle Ages, displaying the extraordinary knowledge of this subject which he had acquired in his youth. This book, written in Latin, served the Christian theologians of succeeding generations as an unfailing source for their arguments against Judaism.[261] Pedro Alfonso also published a collection of tales and fables culled from Arabic literature, *Disciplina Clericalis,* which was a thorough success. His Latin translation of ancient Near Eastern secular legends (such as those about unfaithful wives and the like) particularly stressed the moralistic aspect; for this, his work was popular among Christians in western Europe and preachers made use of it for generations. The collection was translated into many languages and exercised an influence on the great writers of the Occident until modern times.[262]

A few years after his conversion, the apostate left Spain and went to England, where he stayed several years. According to a note in a manuscript of a collection of his tales, he served there as the personal physician to King Henry I.[263] We know from manuscripts of treatises that he taught astronomy in England. In a treatise dealing with calculations relating to eclipses of the sun and moon which Walcher (abbot of Malvern) wrote in 1120, he refers to instruction he received from his teacher, Pedro Alfonso. In his book Walcher made use of the Arabic system which divided the heavenly sphere into 360 degrees. More generally, his writings demonstrate the admiration of the Christian savants for the concepts of Arabic science which they learned from the Jewish apostate from Huesca; they also show how these Christians learned to use the instruments—such as the astrolabe and the quadrant—of the Arab scientists. In 1115 Pedro Alfonso wrote a treatise on astronomy (only the introduction and the first chapters have been located), and in the introduction he speaks of the superiority of empirical science—which he taught in Christian Europe—stressing that there is no contradiction between it and the Christian religion. From his words it is evident that he studied Latin translations of Arabic books of science which others, such as Constantinus Africanus, produced.[264] Pedro Alfonso wrote this treatise when he was back on the Continent. He returned to his country and in 1121 was one of the witnesses who signed a bill of sale of property in the vicinity of Saragossa.[265] But for several more years he continued to spread Arabic science among the Christians; in 1126 the famous English scholar Adelard of Bath translated the Tables of Muḥammad b. Mūsā al-Khwārizmī as adapted by Maslama al-Maudjrīṭī and with the aid of the writings of Pedro Alfonso.[266] Aside from his work as a physician and astronomer, Pedro Alfonso also engaged in the field of geographical research, developing such concepts of his own as the notion that man can also live in the equatorial zone.[267]

This intellectual from a small city in Aragon, a pioneer of science and a convert to Christianity, is mentioned in various sources; but the names of the Jewish scholars who remained loyal to their ancestral faith and kept the flame of Jewish learning glowing among Huesca's Jews in those parlous times have disappeared into historical oblivion.

The Jewish community of Huesca was the largest in the districts of Aragon north of the Ebro; there were some that were old and well-established among the others.

In the eleventh century the small town of Barbastro, on the Vero River fifty kilometers east of Huesca, was one of the important links in that chain of fortified border cities which protected the Moslem area north of the Ebro. To be sure, the city was not actually on the frontier: Moslem rule in the middle of the eleventh century extended in the north to the cities of Graus and El Grado in the Cinca Valley, to Naval northwest of it, to Alquézar in the Vero Valley, and to Labata west of the Alcanadre River. However, Barbastro was the main city in this region. The historians of those times therefore mention it in connection with the wars between the Moslems and the Christians who sought to conquer the Ebro region and to drive out the Moslems. In the chronicles of that epoch Barbastro is depicted as a big town with a large population.[268] During the last third of the eleventh century, the city and its environs suffered from the forays of the Christians; many of its impoverished inhabitants moved to more secure locations. Nevertheless, a small Jewish settlement existed in the town even in this difficult period, and documents from the period subsequent to its conquest by the Christians mention some of Barbastro's Jews. The first document after the conquest of the town by the king of Aragon is dated 1113. It is a bill of sale wherein one of the parties is a Jew named Moses, while Joseph and Isaac b. Yom-Ṭōbh are signatories as witnesses.[269]

According to an old tradition, the Jewish quarter was in the vicinity of the chief mosque and the *sudda*, where the bishop's palace was later built. This tradition locates the synagogue at the Plaza del Palacio in the house bearing the number 6.[270] During that period the square, the site in the middle of the main street which ascends from the east to the west and is now called Calle del Fornoz, was the city's center.[271] A document from 1192 cites a shop—belonging to the Jews Ibraut Salomon and Yub Yuçef—situated in the Calle Mayor, the street which is now called Arjensola and emerges from the Plaza del Palacio.[272]

In that era Jews also lived in Monzón, south of Barbastro. Monzón was the chief city of a district noted for its fertile soil. The town was built on the slopes of a steep mountain on the left bank of the Cinca River, which the Arabs called Nahr az-zaitūn; atop the mountain was the fortress. A Jew named Yaḥyā b. David of Monzón held an important position in the twelfth century in the government of Alfonso II, king of Aragon.[273]

The district of the town of Monzón and the districts to the north belonged to the principality of Lérida. From the end of the ninth century this city, which was on the frontier between Aragon and Catalonia, was the seat of either a Moslem prince or a provincial governor; in the days of the Tudjībid rule at Saragossa, Sulaimān Ibn Hūd was the governor and the entire kingdom of Saragossa was in the hands of one family. After the death of Sulaimān in 1046, when the kingdom was divided among his sons, his firstborn, al-Muẓaffar Yūsuf, became the independent prince of Lérida. As were the majority of Moslem kings in Spain in that period, he was both an intellectual and a warrior. On the one hand, he played the host at his court to writers and scholars. On the other hand, he spent his days at war with his brother Aḥmad, now the ambitious king of Saragossa, who attempted to gain control of all the provinces of Aragon their father had ruled.[274]

There was an old Jewish community in Lérida. The ancient city was not only a center of government but also the focus for the economic life of a spacious region on the left bank of the Ebro River. In that period flax was raised on the fertile plain where the city is located, and the export of the textiles made from it was a chief source of income for the town and its vicinity;[275] silk manufacture was also a flourishing industry in Lérida.[276] The merchants of Lérida who exported its products traded primarily with the districts along the seacoast. Thus, from an economic aspect the region of Lérida belonged to the sphere of Christian Catalonia.

The Jews of Lérida and of its environs maintained their strong ties of trade and family with the Jews of Barcelona. The Jewish community of Lérida was small, numbering about thirty families,[277] but its vocational makeup was highly diversified. Most of Lérida's Jews were artisans: tanners (as is demonstrated by various documents),[278] harnessmakers, and cobblers.[279] Among Lérida's Jews there were also, of course, merchants—even rich ones—for the city was an important trading station throughout the Middle Ages; the Jewish community also had its share of those engaged in agriculture.[280]

Ancient Lérida was built in the eastern section of the city at the foot of the high hill upon which the old cathedral was later erected. During Moslem rule the prince's palace stood upon the hill and near it the chief mosque.[281] In those days the inner city, surrounded by a wall, extended between this hill and the Segre River, while a large suburb sprang up in the east. The Madīna's border extended, on the east, to the vicinity of the street called Nolius and cut across the Calle Mayor (in the Middle Ages it was Carrera Mayor) near the Gate of Arlius. In the south the gate traversed the length of the river and near the great bridge was the Gate of the Bridge (Bāb al-ḳanṭara). The wall continued the length of Relotegors Street, bisected the Calle Mayor in a northerly direction near the gate which was later known as the Portal del Sarains and from there ascended in a straight line to the main gate of the fortress

(Puerta Mayor de la Zuda). Beyond this wall, however, was yet another which encircled an additional area west of the city. This wall, which was connected with the north wall of the fortress, extended, in the west, up to the Portal de Boteros (the entry for the quarter of Montagut); from there it extended to the southeast until it terminated in the Puerta de la Cadena and, even further south, the Puerta Rodona. Thence it again veered west descending to the main street of the city which it reached near the head of Romeu Street, presently called Caballeros. From there it again turned east, running from the Cuesta de Jan to the wall of the inner city.[282]

The southern end of the area between the inner wall and the outer wall west of the city and the "projection" constituted the Jewish quarter and was therefore called by the old name Cuiraça, which in western Arabic signifies a projection from a wall, especially a projection to the other side of a river which makes it possible to supply water to the city.[283] In the east the Jewish quarter extended to the wall built by the Romans (its remnants are beyond the block of houses now on the site of the old seminary); the entire plot on which the seminary once stood was included within the Jewish neighborhood. There was a gate in the north (on the street now called Bors which runs from east to west) through which one passed from the Jewish quarter to the quarters north of it. This was the main gate of the Jewish neighborhood and later it was called Portal de la Cuiraça. To the west the quarter comprised Plaza de la Compañia, the Calle de la Compañia, and San Cristóbal (the street once called Calle Real). On San Cristóbal, which was the main street of the Jewish quarter and which crosses Calle Mayor, there was an additional gate near its narrow end; and near this was the Jewish slaughterhouse.[284] Documents after the Christian conquest of Lérida also mention names of streets in the Jewish quarter. South of the former seminary there was the street called Calle dels Pergaminers;[285] south of it was one called Calle de las Especies (the equivalent of the Arabic name al-'Aṭṭārīn); and west of this was the street named Calle de la Juderia. The Cuesta de Jan was outside the Jewish quarter and above it was its third gate, called Portal de la Juheria.[286] The Jewish cemetery was northwest of the city, across the Calle Balmes, in the vicinity of the street of the city of Fraga.[287]

In the eleventh century there was a Jewish settlement in the small town of Balaguer. Northeast of Lérida in the valley of the Segre, Balaguer was, for a time, a Moslem border city. It remained in their hands until the beginning of the twelfth century, but some twenty-five or thirty years before its conquest by the Christians, the count of Urgel had seized control of part of it.[288] Jews were in Balaguer at that time and they had considerable property. One with wide holdings in the town was Yūsuf Cavaler ("the knight"); in a document dated 1092, a tower, a courtyard, and a garden which formerly belonged to him are noted.[289] The family of Yūsuf Cavaler also held property in Barcelona—attested to by several documents from the end of the eleventh century and the beginning of the twelfth.[290] The Jewish quarter in Balaguer was inside the city, in its northern section. According to a local tradition, the synagogue was near the site where the Church of San Salvador stood later (in those days a mosque stood there).[291] However, it is known that one of the two gates in the northern part of the city was then called the Jews' Gate, although it was later called the Gate del Torrent.[292] The Jews constituted a deeply rooted element in Balaguer. When the town was ultimately conquered by the Christians in 1106, and they established the provisions of their government, the conquerors mention Jews in one of their documents along with the Christians.[293]

IV

Valencia was long the metropolis of eastern Spain. This large town is situated in the center of a lowland of extraordinary fertility. Its greening plains are a garden of gigantic dimensions—fields and vineyards, replete with all manner of good fruits, stretch from the seacoast to the blue mountains on the horizon, and water-filled canals, crisscrossing them in every direction, irrigate each field. The Arabs perfected the network of canals, developed the cultivation of silkworm, which was already widespread in some districts, and introduced the cultivation of rice, which became an important crop. Many of the canals fork out from the Turia River, which the Arabs called al-Wādi al-abyaḍ; by its right bank, near the point where its waters pour into the sea, the town of Valencia is situated.

Because of the wealth of the city and its environs, some of the princes, on the disintegration of the Omayyad state, warred eagerly and long among themselves for dominion over Valencia. Sometimes Slavic nobles who had established principalities north and south of the city (the princes of Tortosa and Denia for example) held sway in Valencia—and sometimes Slavs from the city seized control. In 1021 the Slavs in Valencia invited ʻAbdalʻazīz, the grandson of al-Manṣūr (he was a mere lad of fifteen at the time) to be their king. He naturally responded willingly to the invitation, came to Valencia, and did indeed occupy the throne for forty years. ʻAbdalʻaziz, who was given the same surname as that of his grandfather, al-Manṣūr, attempted to widen his dominions, but he never achieved outstanding success. After becoming the king of Almería, for a time he lost control of this town and its provinces,[294] so that only Jativa and Murcia remained to him. After his death in 1061, he was succeeded by his son ʻAbdalmalik al-Muẓaffar, who was not at all like him. In contrast to his father, ʻAbdalmalik neglected the government and lived for his own pleasure. The results were swift. First the province of Murcia broke away from the kingdom of Valencia, becoming an independent principality. In 1065 Fernando, king of Castile and León, mounted a sizable campaign in eastern Spain against Valencia; however, after vanquishing 'Abdalmalik's army, he was compelled to retreat when he was beset by severe illness.[295] Al-Ma'mūn, king of Toledo and 'Abdalmalik's father-in-law, came to his aid; but when the king saw how utterly powerless and helpless 'Abdalmalik was, he dismissed him. Al-Ma'mūn was assisted by his vizier, Abū Bakr Ibn Rūbash (known by the name of Ibn 'Abdalazīz), whom he appointed governor of Valencia. The vizier proved worthy of his office: He endeavored to inaugurate order and to eliminate injustice, and in consequence, he won the affection of the people.

However, as much as the Arabic chroniclers laud this one and denigrate that one in reporting the changes of rulers, it is apparent that they were quite similar in many respects. Most of these rulers were spendthrifts in their mode of living and relied—the Slav princes in particular—upon Christian mercenary troops to whom they paid substantial amounts of money. The majority of them maintained magnificent courts and erected handsome structures which consumed vast sums. The peasants of the regions carried the burden of heavy taxes which the princes imposed. Nevertheless, the cities—and Valencia especially—flourished. A contemporary, Ibn Ḥayyān, relates that the number of inhabitants of Valencia grew and that in his time its walls were repaired and the city's fortifications strengthened.[296] The non-Moslem communities in Valencia benefited fully from this boom; the attitude of the rulers toward them was one of consideration, and some of their members were numbered among the nobles and officials.[297]

To this day, the huge gate called Puerta Serranos is the symbol of Valencia—to all who come to the city it is a reminder of its remote past when Arabs and Castilians, Slavs and Catalans fought over it. Under the Moslem rule this gate was called Bāb al-ḳanṭara (the Gate of the Bridge) and was the principal gate near the river. The city's wall extended from it toward the southwest to the gate called Bāb al-Ḥanash (later known as the Puerta Culera or Valldigna) and thence to the marketplace. From there it turned by way of the street now called Calle San Fernando to the street named Vicente; at the corner of these streets was the gate Bāb Boatella. But San Vicente Street, which today is the main artery of the big city—and in those days was named for an aristocratic Arab family, Banū Wādjib — was outside the city wall. From the east the wall ran to Plaza Del Caudillo; there, west of the plaza where the municipality is located now, cemeteries were to be found. From the plaza the wall turned east by way of Barcas and Pintor Sorolla streets, and before it reached a site which now contains the large Glorietta Square, it again turned north, reaching the riverbank near the Church of the Temple and continuing along it to the Gate of the Bridge. The area of the city which the wall encompassed was not large, but the suburbs were. A short distance from the Boatella Gate there was a suburb bearing this name which contained several quarters; the suburb Ruṣāfa was southeast of the city; in the north, across the river, there also were various quarters.

Whereas the Moslems removed the Christians from the inner city—forcing them to dwell in the suburbs—the Jewish quarter was in the heart of the city, in the vicinity of the Calle de la Paz, which was not yet then in existence. Relative to the size of the entire city, the Jewish quarter was one of considerable dimensions. Its main thoroughfare was the Calle del Mar, which is very old. The city's eastern wall, partly on the site where the university's eastern wall is now, bisected the Calle del Mar in a northerly direction. There, north of the street, where the gate of the Church of Santo Tomas is located, was a city gate called Bāb ash-sharī'a (public worship was conducted on a plaza which extended before it, and in accordance with the linguistic usage of the Arabs of Spain, it was thus called ash-sharī'a).[298] In this district the Jewish quarter included the block of houses north of the Calle del Mar; its boundary was the street which for several hundred years has been named for the Cofradia de la Seo. Near the Calle de las Avellanas the boundary of the quarter again turned south to the western end of Del Mar Street. A plaza was located there which later, in the days of Christian dominance, was called Plaza de la Figuera; nearby was a gate of the quarter. This plaza has almost disappeared because a monastery named for Santa Tecla was erected there, and the site is indeed currently called Plaza de Santa Tecla. In the last days of Moslem rule a public bath was located near the plaza and was named for its owner, 'Abdalmalik.[299] The boundary of the Jewish quarter ran south by way of the street now called Ave Maria and again turned east for the length of a small street named by the Jews Ḳahal (Community) Street or, as Christians pronounced it, Calle del Cal or—in a corrupt form—Calle del Gallo. This street is now included in the large thoroughfare De la Paz. From there the border ran southeasterly to a spacious plaza which the Colegio del Patriarca now covers. This plaza (the Christians called it Plaza de los Cabrerots—literally, goatherds), served as a marketplace and a gate of the quarter was located therein. Thence the boundary line again continued northeastward, reaching the city wall not far from Del Mar Street.[300] The great synagogue was on Del Mar Street, and another synagogue was located between this street and the site of the Colegio del Patriarca. This synagogue was later converted into the Chapel of the New Cross and to this very day a small street exists there which bears this name (Capella de la Cruz Nuova).[301] Near the Plaza de la Figuera, on the southeast, there were shops of silk textiles and of jewelry; near the

JEWISH QUARTER OF VALENCIA

---

ooo Borders of the Jewish Quarter as fixed at the time of the conquest of the city by the Christians

1. Calle del Mar
2. Cofradia de la Seo
3. Calle Ave Maria
4. Calle del Gallo
5. Plaza de las Avellanas
6. Calle de las Avellanas
7. Bāb ash-sharī 'a
8. Plaza de la Cruz Nuova
9. City Wall
10. Colegio del Patriarca

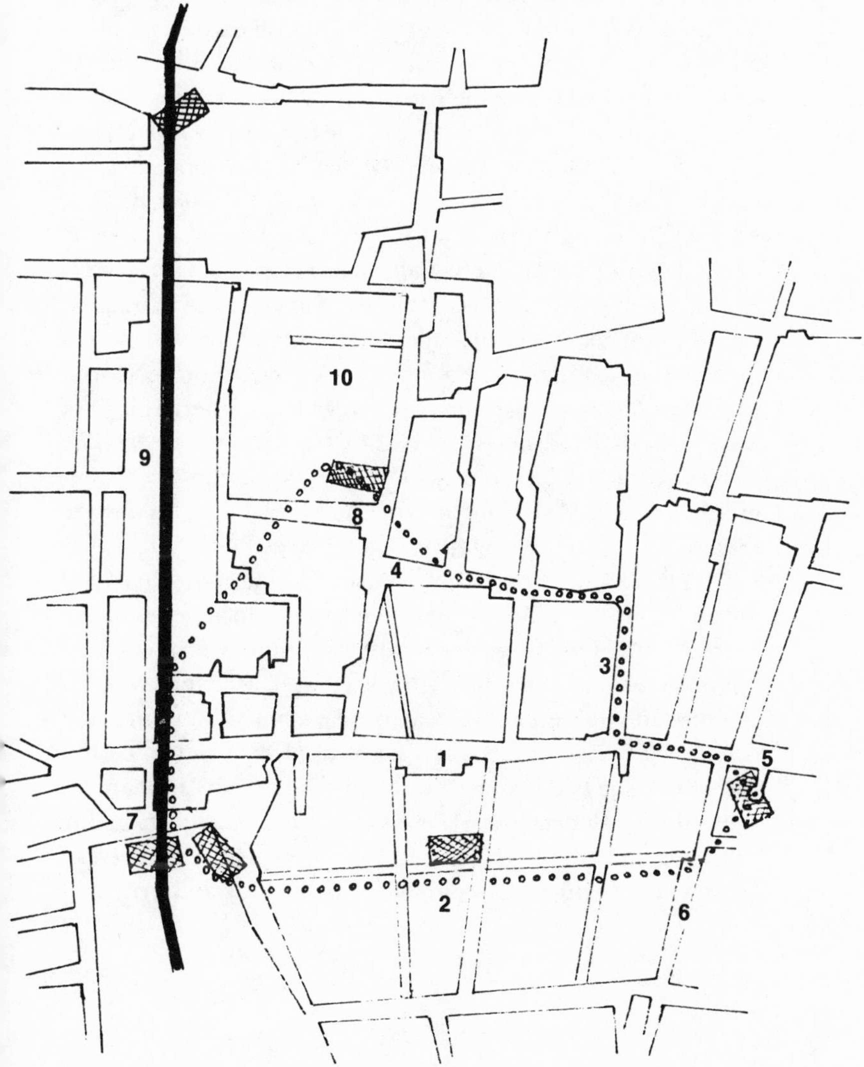

other end of the quarter, outside the gate called Bāb ash-sharī'a, was the Jews' cemetery, in the vicinity of the place where the Chapter House of the Knights of Saint John was later erected.[302]

The names of the streets in the Jewish quarter which appear on the old maps of Valencia indicate the occupations of many of its inhabitants. Indeed, the western part of Cofradia de la Seo Street formerly bore the name Zapateria, the Street of the Shoemakers,[303] and the street south of the Plaza de los Cabrerots was called Argenteria, the Street of the Silversmiths. These were crafts in which many Jews engaged over many generations. To this day, people of the region know that those whose family name is Zabater (which means shoemaker in Catalan and in the dialect of Valencia), or Ferrer (blacksmith), or Mania (locksmith) are of Jewish origin. However, only a part of the Jewish population of Valencia were craftsmen. Several took active roles in the city's big business—in the marketing of the products of the rich agricultural region and in the export of the manufactured goods of Valencia; they dealt with Jewish merchants who came to the town from other regions of Spain and they journeyed abroad by land and by sea.[304] The some one thousand members of the Jewish community[305] generally were merchants and artisans, and few among them were rabbinic scholars and intellectuals. Hence their names were forgotten and only by chance those of some individuals are preserved in the yellowed pages of an old document. In the Cairo Geniza a marriage certificate was found which was written in Valencia in the middle or second half of the eleventh century and designated for a woman named Pīṭbōnia, the daughter of Isaac; it was a replacement of the original certificate which she had lost; her husband's name was Abraham.[306]

North of Valencia, the Slavs established a small principality whose capital city was Tortosa. The principality dissolved in 1060 when its ruler was compelled to yield his authority and to hand the city and its province to Aḥmad, king of Saragossa.[307]

Although the principality of Tortosa was weak and the rule of its princes unstable, the city itself flourished. Tortosa, most often at peace with its Christian neighbors to the north, maintained a good commercial union with nearby Barcelona; its people naturally traded with the regions in the Ebro Basin and with Valencia and its satellite towns in the south. There were relatively large communities of Christians[308] and of Jews in Tortosa, and it was easy for them to visit and to trade with the cities of Christian Catalonia; Jewish merchants from Barcelona, of course, visited Tortosa. Evidence of these commercial links is found in an Arabic treatise from the eleventh century which reflects the corrupted tradition of a historical incident. An Arabic geographer from southern Spain relates that the prince of Barcelona, on his way to Rome, arrived in Narbonne in 1054, fell in love with his host's wife, and imposed the task of kidnapping her upon a group of Jews. According to the Arabic tale, the Jews organized their venture in collaboration with the Moslem king of Tortosa (that is, they used his ships), but their enterprise failed. The attachment of the prince of Barcelona for a noblewoman in southern France in 1053 is verified from Christian sources, and the account in the Arabic source proves that Jewish merchants came and went at the Tortosan port, trading with southern France.[309] Numerous Jews of Tortosa also engaged in agriculture, which is verified in several documents.[310] At that time, and throughout its existence, there were in the Jewish community of Tortosa writers whose works have endured. In the first half of the eleventh century, the Hebrew poet Levi b. Isaac Ibn Mar Saul lived in Tortosa. He was the son of the poet and philologist Isaac Ibn Mar Saul of Lucena,[311] but during his youth he lived in Cordova, leaving the city after it was destroyed in the civil war. He wrote liturgical poems, penitential hymns,[312] and, as did many of his contemporaries, he heaped praises upon Samuel ha-lēvī and his son Joseph in his other verse.

In the eleventh century the Jewish community of Tortosa contained approximately thirty families;[313] its neighborhood was, as in the past, in the northeast section of the city.[314] As in the other towns on the eastern coast of Spain, the Jewish quarter was within the city, surrounded by a wall. The main streets of this neighborhood were the one running from north to south between Sol and Jaime Tio streets and which—in memory of its earlier residents—was called Calle de Jerusalém; the one paralleling it on the east, which is called Calle de Remolins; and Travesía Jerusalém, which connects them.[315] Between this neighborhood and the other quarters of the city was an inner wall which had a gate, the Gate of the Market.[316] The main synagogue—which served successively as a hospital, a barracks for cavalry, and a prison from the end of the seventeenth century on—was at the northern end of Calle Mayor de Remolins[317] near one of the gates in the city's wall. It was thus located at a point farthest from the Moslems, just as were synagogues in other towns.

The ancient community of Tarragona existed throughout this entire era. In the eleventh century Tarragona belonged to the principality of Tortosa, and when Tortosa was annexed to the kingdom of the Banū Hūd—the kings of Saragossa—it too fell to them. Nevertheless, whether the rulers of this province were Slav princes or Arabs, its security against Christian attacks was tenuous: The inhabitants of Tarragona and the nearby settlements could anticipate almost daily forays by the Christians. By the middle of the eleventh century, the Catalans dominated the districts west of Tarragona to the Ebro.[318] When the power of the Catalans increased still more in the second half of that century, the majority of the houses remained empty and from time to time were used as quarters for

MOSLEM TORTOSA

1. Calle Mayor de Remolins
2. Calle Jaime Tio
3. Calle de Jerusalém
4. Calle de Travesía Jerusalém
5. Calle de Sol
6. Calle de Villanova
7. Present-day Market, Site of Gate of the Market

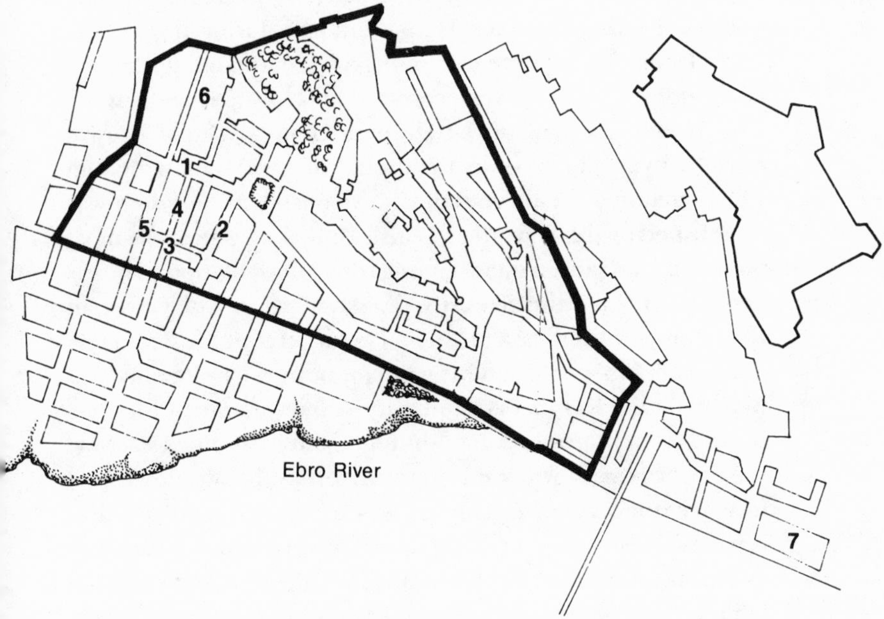

their own bands which raided the Christian districts. (A contemporary Arabic geographer vividly describes the wretched plight of the city.)[319] However, the Jewish community of Tarragona did not come to an end; as in other frontier cities, here too the Jews held fast and a small community remained within the city until the final days of Moslem rule.[320]

In those days, however, Denia, at the southeast edge of the Gulf of Valencia, was a far more important community than those in the north. An ancient city, flourishing in the days of the Greeks and Romans, it is named for the temple of the goddess Diana—Dianium. In that era and during the Middle Ages, Denia was a prime maritime base, commanding the sealanes along Spain's eastern coast and up to the islands in the east. In the first half of the eleventh century, Denia—now a quiet, provincial city—was the capital of a maritime kingdom which included the three Balearic Islands. This kingdom was established by the Slav Abu'l-Djaish Mudjāhid, one of the most powerful and able rulers among the kings of Spain in his generation. Like the majority of Slavs, he was of Christian origin but educated as a Moslem. He pored over Moslem literature from his youth, and his contemporaries extolled his skill in reading the Koran, his familiarity with its commentaries, his overall knowledge of Arabic—but Mudjāhid was first a warrior; the perfect knight who desired to perform valorous deeds and to make conquests. Initially he was the governor of the Balearic Islands, and when civil war erupted he seized control of Denia and its region. On becoming an independent prince, he built a strong fleet which enabled him to control the western parts of the Mediterranean, and his many piratical ventures made the name Mudjāhid feared in the lands of both the Moslems and of the Christians.

In the days of Mudjāhid and his son, Denia was a well-populated, affluent city. Today the city extends along the southeastern slope of a hill opposite Mount Mongo in the south. But in Moslem times the fortress was located there while the city was situated upon the seacoast, protected by the lofty mountain.[321] The eastern wall, extending into the sea, defended its harbor. Arabic writers of the Middle Ages tell of the traffic abounding in the harbor, of the numerous ships constantly sailing in and out, and of Denia's shipyard, where vessels were built and repaired. In those days, Denia was an important commercial depot, a major junction in lines of communication for the Mediterranean Sea, and a departure point for ships bound for the Orient.

A sizable Jewish settlement existed in Denia in the beginning of the eleventh century and like the members of large Jewish communities elsewhere, the Jews of Denia also were scattered throughout the city and its region. The poet Isaac Ibn Khalfón created a poem in honor of "Rabbi Isaac Ibn al-Dānī." This man, according to the poet, was a man of learning and was obviously the son of a Jew of Denia.[322] A twelfth-century document found in the Cairo Geniza cites the transfer of property from Ṣadaḳa b. David to Joseph b. Isaac b. al-Dānī al-Fāsī, on whom be peace.[323] From this it can be inferred that the aforementioned Joseph's grandfather dwelt in Denia in the eleventh century. Many of Denia's Jews, taking advantage of their city, engaged in big business, traveling throughout eastern Spain by sea or land. In particular, the Jews of Denia exported Spain's silk textiles to lands beyond the sea, to Tunisia and to Egypt.[324] At the end of the eleventh century a famous rabbi in Spain was asked about the protracted absence of a Jew of Denia. Since that man was going on a journey to a distant land, he transferred the ownership of his house to his mother in a Moslem court. The mother lived in the house with a woman relative for several years. Ten years after she died the matter was brought before the rabbi by her son, who demanded that the relative return the property to him—no information had been received from his father, and thus it could be assumed that he had died in a remote country.[325] This Jew of Denia therefore started on his travels—undoubtedly for trade—about (and perhaps before) 1070.

The commercial ties between the Jews of Denia and the cities of Tunisia were especially strong. In 1083 a Jewish merchant from Denia brought before the communal court a complaint against a fellow townsman, a Jewish merchant named Abū-'l-Ḥasan Ḳāsim: In the documents of this complaint there is reference to a journey made some years before, to the city of al-Mahdīya, by Isaac b. Abraham and Mufarridj, a subordinate of Abū-'l-Ḥasan Ḳāsim. Traveling in a ship belonging to the prince of Denia, these merchants exported goods from Denia to Tunisia and, with the money they received in payment, purchased merchandise there which they brought back to Spain.[326]

In that generation one of the esteemed families of Denia was that of Ibn Alkhatūsh. The members of this family, too, engaged in trade, sailing to Near Eastern countries. In a letter from Nathan b. Nahrai to Nahrai b. Nissīm (an important merchant in Fostat in the second half of the eleventh century) there is the account of a ship which came from Denia to Alexandria with a large quantity of silk and other wares; further on in the letter it is stated that six more ships are due to arrive from Spain. The letter writer relates that some Jewish merchants arrived in that ship and among them were Mukhtār of Aleppo, Ibn ash-Sharābī, "and the son of Ben Lakhtūdj."[327] This family married into distinguished families—their sons wed girls from good families and their daughters were given in marriage to scholars. Samuel Ibn Alkhatūsh, who lived in the last third of the eleventh century, married the sister of N'thānēl ha-lēvī, a prestigious scholar in Egypt.[328] Of course, the marital ties resulted from their numerous journeys across the sea and their close trade relations.

There were also intellectuals and renowned rabbinic scholars in the community of Denia. One of these was a physician, a native of Toledo who became the court physician to Mudjāhid and his son, 'Alī Iḳbāl ad-daula. This physician, Isaac Ibn Yashūsh, was called Abū Ibrāhīm Isḥāḳ Ibn Ḳisṭār[329] by the Arabs. He was a good physician, knowledgeable in such branches of learning as logic and philosophy, and was quite at home with Jewish literature. As other Jewish intellectuals who were rooted in the culture of Moslem Spain, he had a special interest in the Hebrew language and wrote a book in Arabic on the conjugation of verbs—*At-Taṣārīf* (in Hebrew, *Sēfer ha-ṣērūfīm*).[330] He also wrote a commentary on the Bible (titling it after his name, *Ha-Yiṣḥāḳī*) in which he undertook analysis of the traditional text of the Bible with the scalpel of scientific criticism—just as scholars are doing now. He attempted to identify personalities mentioned in various passages of the Bible. Among other things, he expressed the opinion that the account of the kings of Edom in Genesis 36 was written in the time of King Jehoshaphat and later included in the Pentateuch. Particularly bold was his assumption that many words in the traditional text of Scripture should be changed because they were introduced into verses where they do not belong. Naturally, this line of thought angered the traditionalists. His commentaries no doubt reflected the views of many contemporary intellectuals whose attitude to Scripture was established not only by traditional belief but also by the critical approach which they applied to their general studies. Naturally, the traditionalists vigorously opposed this criticism and emphatically condemned the *Sēfer ha-Yiṣḥāḳī.*[331] Ibn Yashūsh, in his old age, returned to his native city, Toledo, dying there in 1056. One of the Moslem writers who associated with him after his return to Toledo extolled him and lauded his noble qualities.[332]

In the middle and to the end of the eleventh century, rabbis in Denia, distinguished for their knowledge of the Gemara, served as teachers and judges. Some of the members of the *bet din* (court) of that time are known from the documents written in connection with the complaint of the aforementioned merchant in 1083. One document bears the signature of three "receivers of testimony"—Jacob ha-Kūhēn b. Isaac, Samuel bar Jacob, and Joseph bar Abraham, and a second deed, those of Joseph bar Abraham and Isaac bar Ḥiyya.[333]

Aside from the judges, there were scholars in Denia who were renowned abroad. A contemporary of Isaac Ibn Yashūsh, the Babylonian rabbi Samuel b. Joseph had lived in Bagdad where he rose to the rank of *resh kalla* at the academy. Because he was involved in a conflict there, he left his native land and, on reaching Spain, settled in Denia. Samuel b. Joseph corresponded with Samuel ha-lēvī, and the *nāgīd,* in a poem he sent to him, maintains that if he had remained in Babylonia, he would have been appointed head of the academy in place of the now-deceased *gaon* Rabbi Hai.[334] During the next generation, Rabbi Isaac b. Moses Ibn Sukkarī was the rabbi of Denia.[335] It seems that the rabbis of Denia either did not write books or that their works are lost; however, we do have some of the writings of Isaac b. Reuben, the esteemed rabbi of Denia at the close of the 1200s. He was born in 1043 in Barcelona, and in his youth he came to Denia where he married into the distinguished Alkhatūsh family. When his extensive knowledge of the Gemara and the geonic writings became known, he was appointed rabbi and judge of Denia. Mortified, Isaac b. Moses Ibn Sukkarī, who held this office until then, left Spain, and returning to Babylonia, he became head of the academy of *gaon* Rabbi Hai.[336] Rabbi Isaac b. Reuben, who was called Al-Bargelōnī, remained in Denia until his death. He was famous as a scholar and teacher.[337] He wrote commentaries on the tractate *'Ērūbhīn* and some chapters of the tractate *K'tūbhōt.*[338] He translated *gaon* Rabbi Hai's book on the laws of buying and selling from Arabic to Hebrew.[339] Isaac b. Reuben also set his hand to composing religious verse. His contemporaries considered his *Azhārōt* quite successful; he ingeniously wove strands of biblical verse into them and thus they were included in the holiday prayerbooks of many communities in the Maghrib to be read on Pentecost.[340] Although this was his most famous poetic work, he composed other, also beautiful, hymns.[341]

The burgeoning of the Jewish community in Denia resulted primarily from the city's conversion to the status of capital of the maritime kingdom of Mudjāhid and of his tolerant attitude toward the non-Moslem communities. But other cities on the eastern coast of Spain, which did not occupy as significant a role in the political history of the peninsula, also contained important Jewish communities at that time. In the eleventh century one of the largest and wealthiest in all of Spain was the city of Almería, situated at the southeastern edge of the peninsula.

During the first generation of the "provincial kings," Almería was the capital of a large kingdom. The Slavs Khairān (1012–1028) and Zuhair (1028–1038) held sway over all the eastern coast of Spain up to the vicinity of Valencia, and extensive stretches of mountainlands west of the coast. However, the area under the rule of Ma'n, the first of the Almerían kings of the Tudjībid dynasty (1041–1051), did not extend beyond the city of Lorca; moreover, in the days of his son and successor, Muḥammad al-Mu'taṣim (1051–1091), the kingdom of Almería was reduced even more. Al-Mu'taṣim was still a youth when he mounted the throne—the neighboring states and the provincial rulers seized this opportunity to tear region upon region away from the kingdom of Almería and to rid themselves of his dominance. Lorca, too, became independent and ever since then Almería remained a small principality, only covering the vicinity of the capital.

Notwithstanding all this, Almería flourished at that time,

and as a consequence of the development of its industry and commerce, the city did become prosperous. Because of its scanty rainfall, the area is not at all fertile; Almería's affluence is largely due to its excellent harbor, which shelters ships from the winds of the east and the west. During the latter half of the tenth century, Almería became the main base of the Omayyad navy and the primary harbor of all Spain; most of the ships from North Africa and the Near East anchored there and many of Almería's inhabitants grew wealthy from the great volume of trade. After the disintegration of the Spanish caliphate and the decline of Cordova, immigrants from the former capital of the caliphs (as well as from other cities) settled in Almería, which promised unemployed craftsmen and industrialists the security of a capital city in a powerful kingdom. Almería developed into an industrial city: Medieval Arabic writers describe thousands of shops in which costly silk textiles and wares of iron, copper, and glass were manufactured.[342]

Once a suburb of the city of Badjāna, near a watchtower (in Arabic, *mariya*), Almería extended over an area between the hill of the fortress in the north and the seacoast in the south. This was the *madīna* which the caliph ʻAbdarraḥmān III had surrounded with walls. The eastern wall extended from the eastern edge of the hill parallel to what is currently De la Reina Street and the western wall went the length of the Rambla de la Chanca.[343] With the influx of refugees and Almería's economic growth, new neighborhoods quickly developed outside the madīna walls—especially east of the city—and the Slavic rulers built a new wall which encompassed a wide area. In the north this new Almería, east of the old city, reached the heights of Mount Lāham (now called Cerro de San Cristóbal). From there the new wall extended to the gate called Puerta Purchena, then known as Bāb Badjāna; from there it turned, by way of the Rambla del Obispo Orbera, to the sea. Altogether, the suburb which was then surrounded by walls and called al-Muṣallā was two and one-half times as large as the old city.[344] The rulers of Almería—Slav and Arab—built edifices for themselves which glorified their own splendor, but they also erected public buildings. Khairān, Almería's first king, built the fortress named for him—Ḳal'at Khairān (it is still the city's most conspicuous structure). Al-Mu'taṣim, in addition to his other buildings, constructed a magnificent palace, called as-Ṣumādiḥīya; he also carried out construction of water installations by which the water from outlying wells was brought into the city.

The population of Almería steadily increased and in the second half of the eleventh century it numbered approximately thirty thousand.[345] This was large in comparison with the population of other Spanish cities; however, contrasted to the overcrowding prevalent in the other cities of Spain, Almería was distinguished by the breadth of its streets and its many plazas and gardens. The rippling sea on one side and the mighty fortress on the other, the outspread gardens of the whitewashed houses glistening in their whiteness and the tall date palms among them—unlike ever blue skies—gave the city that charm which is unique to the cities of southern Spain and which characterizes Almería to this day.

This beautiful, wealthy city also had a large Jewish quarter which was west of the inner city. No doubt named al-Ḥauḍ (the Basin) because of a large reservoir nearby,[346] it extended over the area between the western wall of the *madīna*, near the Rambla de la Chanca, and the steep slopes of the mountain which the Moslems called Djabal al-kunaisa. The neighborhood, surrounded by turreted walls, did not quite reach the seacoast to the south; there was a cemetery in the area between its southern wall and the coast. The bed of the Rambla de la Chanca was inside the quarter at its southern end, and on the site at which it entered, two square towers, twenty meters apart, still stand. Near the southern edge of the wall, separating the *madīna* from the Jewish neighborhood, issued a large street, the main street of Almería, which divided the inner city and the eastern quarters in the suburb of al-Muṣallā.[347] The Jewish neighborhood was large in relation to the entire city and in relation to Jewish quarters in other cities of Spain. Within it were bazaars, inns, and bathhouses,[348] and near it was the harbor's main pier. This was, therefore, a commercial, much trafficked quarter. However, since the center of trade was within the inner city, near the mosque, and there were also marketplaces in the suburb of al-Muṣallā, Almería's Jews also had shops in other quarters of the town.

Among Almería's some two thousand Jews,[349] there was a stratum of merchants engaged in international commerce. Almería was at the edge of the great trade route of the ancient world which encompassed three continents: the trade route with India and the Far East. The maritime link between southern Spain and Alexandria was well established—its main port was the port of Almería; from Egypt and Syria to the port of Almería came the expensive merchandise of India and the Far East, which was eagerly sought after in European countries.

In common with the other Moslem princes in Spain in that epoch, the rulers of Almería befriended the members of the Jewish merchant class who had business ties with distant lands, and appointed some of them to offices of distinction. In the second half of the eleventh century a Jew was a "vizier" of the prince of Almería (he held office in one of the high posts in his service). An Arabic historian reports that the theologian 'Abdallāh b. Sahl b. Yūsuf, who died in 1087, killed this Jew because, in his view, he had slighted the memory of their prophet.[350] As in other Jewish communities in Moslem Spain, there were also intellectuals whose learning was their craft. One of the Almerían intellectuals in the first half of the eleventh century was Ismā'īl b. Yūnus, who was surnamed al-A'war because he was blind in one eye. He was a physician and was distinguished for his diagnosis of a patient's condition based on external signs. The renowned Moslem writer Ibn Ḥazm, who came to Almería in 1013 and dwelt in the city for a number of years, recounts that he associated with the Jewish physician who was an expert in the "knowledge of physiognomy" ('ilm al-firāsa)—that is, he could tell the character of a person by the nature of his facial lines. According to Ibn Ḥazm, he would sit with the physician in his "shop" and hold long discussions with him.[351] The Jewish physicians did indeed have offices in marketplaces which were in other quarters. A letter sent in the beginning of the eleventh century by the learned merchant Khalfōn b. N'thānēl ha-lēvī to a Jewish physician in Almería bore the address "Al-ḥakīm bi-sūḳ al-Mariya" (the physician in the marketplace of Almería).[352] Like other Hispano-Jewish intellectuals of his time, Ismā'īl b. Yūnus was influenced by liberal religious views. In his important work on various religions and sects, Ibn Ḥazm devotes a chapter to skeptics and in this context also mentions the physician Ismā-'īl b. Yūnus. He states that the prevailing view among the skeptics is that it is impossible to demonstrate that any one religion is the true religion . . . it is impossible to find convincing arguments which do not contain some element of doubt. Among these skeptics, remarks the Moslem writer, there are various groups. One professes utter skepticism: neither maintains a belief in God nor negates it, neither believes in prophecy nor disavows it. Members of this group assert that they are convinced that truth exists in one of the religions but that this truth does not evidence itself in any religion or system of faith in a clear, conspicuous, and convincing manner. Another group professes the same skeptical viewpoint—except it at least does maintain a belief in God. As representative of the first group, Ibn Ḥazm mentions the Jewish physician from Almería, Ismā'īl b. Yūnus. He reports that the pronouncements Ismā'īl voiced in dispute and his energetic defense of the principles of skepticism left no doubt about his views, although he never explicitly declared what his attitude was toward the traditional religions.[353] The Moslem writer did not know the number of intellectuals among the Hispano-Jewish communities who sided with these views in varying degrees, views which prepared the ground for apostasy and active betrayal of their people.

ABBREVIATIONS

BAC Boletin de la Academia de Ciencias, Bellas Letras y Nobles Artes de Córdoba

BAH Boletin de la Academia de la historia (Madrid)

BJPES Bulletin of the Jewish Palestine Exploration Society

CB Catalogus librorum Hebraeorum in Bibliotheca Bodleiana . . . digessit M. Steinschneider

CHE Cuadernos de historia de España

EEMCA Estudios de edad media de la Corona de Aragón

HB Hebraeische Bibliographie

HUCA Hebrew Union College Annual

JQR Jewish Quarterly Review

MAH Memorias de la Academia de historia

MGWJ Monatsschrift für Geschichte und Wissenschaft des Judentums

PAAJR Proceedings of the American Academy for Jewish Research

RABM Revista de archivos, bibliotecas y museos (Madrid)

REJ Revue des Études Juives

ZDMG Zeitschrift der Deutschen morgenländischen Gesellschaft

SOURCES

In addition to those given in volume 1

1. IN HEBREW

Abraham b. Nathan ha-Yarḥī. *Ha-Manhīg.* Berlin, 1855 *(Ha-Manhīg).*

Alfasi, Isaac R. *Sefer sh'elōt u-t'shūbhōt.* Leghorn, 1781 (Responsa Alfasi); *Sefer sh'elōt u-t'shūbhōt ha-Rīf.* Bilgoraj, 1935 (Responsa Alfasi, ed. Bilgoraj).

Āsher b. Y'hiel. *Sh'elōt t'shūbhōt l'ha-rābh rabbenu Āsher.* Vilna, 1885 (Responsa Rabbenu Āsher).

Ashtor, Eliyahu. "Documentos españoles de la geniza, serie primera," *Sefarad* 24:41–80 (Documentos).

Brody, H., and Albrecht, K. *Sha'ar ha-shīr, Die neuhebräische Dichterschule der spanisch-arabischen Epoche, ausgewäwahlte Texte.* Leipzig, 1905 *(Sha'ar ha-shīr).*

Ibn Danān, Saadya b. Maimon. "Ma'mar 'al sēder ha-dōrōt." In Z.R. Edelmann, *Ḥemdath g'nūza.* Königsberg, 1865, notes 25–31 (Saadya b. Danān).

Ibn 'Ezrā, Moses. *Shīrē ha-ḥōl,* ed. H. Brody, vols. 1 and 2. Berlin–Jerusalem, 1935–1942 *(Diwān Moses Ibn Ēzra).*

Ibn Gabirol, Solomon. *Shīrē Sh'lōmō b. Judah Ibn Gabirol,* ed. H.N. Bialik–Y.H. Rawnitsky, 1–7, Berlin-Tel Aviv, 1924–1932 *(Diwan Ibn Gabirol).*

Ibn Migash, Joseph b. Meīr. *T'shūbhōt Rabbenu Joseph ha-levi Ibn Migash.* Warsaw, 1870 (Responsa Ibn Migash).

Isaac b. Sheshet. *Sh'elōt u-t'shūbhōt Bar Sheshet.* Vilna, 1879 (Responsa Isaac b. Sheshet).

Judah b. Barzilai al-Barceloni. *Sefer ha-'ittīm* . . . Cracow, 1903 *(Sefer ha-'ittīm).*

Millás Vallicrosa, J.M. *La poesía sagrada hebraico-española.* 2d ed. Madrid, 1948 (Millás, Poesía sagrada).

Sachs, M. *Die religiöse Poesie der Juden in Spanien.* Berlin, 1901 (Sachs).

Samuel ha-Nagid. *Diwan Samuel ha-nāgīd.* Ed. D.S. Sassoon. Oxford, 1934 *(Diwan Samuel); Diwan Samuel ha-nāgīd,* ed. D. Jarden. Jerusalem, 1966 *(Diwan Samuel ha-nāgīd,* ed. Jarden n. p. 31).

Solomon b. Adret. *Sefer sh'elōt u-t'shūbhōt,* vols. 1 and 3. B'nei B'rak: 1958–1959 vol. 4. Jerusalem, 1960 (Responsa Ibn Adret).

Yōm Ṭōbh b. Abraham al-Ishbīlī. *Sh'elōt u-t'shūbhōt* . . . , ed. J. Kāfah. Jerusalem, 1959 (Responsa Yōm Ṭōbh al-Ishbīlī).

2. *IN ARABIC*

Anonymous author of a history of Moslem Spain in the eleventh century, parts of which are printed as appendix to the third part of Ibn 'Idhārī, *Kitāb al-Bayān al-mughrib,* pp. 287–316 (Anonymous).

'Abdallāh b. Bollugīn. *Mudhakkarāt al-amīr 'Abdallāh ākhir mulūk Banī Zīrī bi-Gharnāta al-musammāt bi-Kitāb at-tibyān,* edited by E. Lévi-Provençal. Cairo, 1955 (Memoirs of 'Abdallāh).

Dozy, R. *Scriptorum Arabum loci de Abbadidis nunc primim editi,* T. 1–3. Lugduni Batavorum, 1846–1863 *(Abbad).*

Ibn 'Abdūn. Le Traité d'Ibn'Abdūn publié . . . by E. Lévi-Provençal *JA* 224:177–299 (Ibn'Abdūn). French translation by E. Lévi-Provençal: Séville musulmane au début du XXIe siècle, Paris, 1947 (Séville musulmane).

Ibn Bashkuwāl. *Kitāb as-Ṣila,* vols. 1 and 2. Cairo, 1955. (Ibn Bashkuw āl).

Ibn Bassām. *Adh-Dhakhīra fī maḥāsin ahl al-djazīra,* part 1, vols. 1 and 2. Cairo, 1939–1942; part 2, MS. Oxford, Marsh 447, MS. Paris Suppl. 2450; part 3, MS. Paris Suppl. 2451; part 4. Vol. 1. Cairo, 1945. *(Dhakhīra).*

Ibn Ḥazm. *Kitāb al-Fiṣal fi'l-milal wa 'l-ahwā wa 'n-niḥal,* vols. 1–5. 1317–1321 (Ibn Ḥazm, *Al-Fiṣal;* Spanish translation: Asín Palacios).

______. *Abenḥazam de Cordoba y su história critica de las ideas religiosas,* vols. 1–4. Madrid, 1927–1932. (Asín).

———. *Ṭauḳ al-ḥamāma fi 'l-ulfa wa 'l-ulláf, Le Collier du pigeon* . . . , translated by L. Bercher. Algiers, 1948 (*Ṭauḳ al-ḥamāma*).

Ibn 'Idhārī. *Kitāb al-Bayān al-mughrib,* vol. 3, edited by E. Lévi-Provençal. Paris, 1930 (Ibn 'Idhārī).

Ibn Khaḳān. *Kitāb Maṭmaḥ al-anfus.* Cairo, 1325 (*Maṭmaḥ al-anfus*).

Ibn al-Khaṭīb. *Al-Iḥāṭa fī akhbār Gharnāṭa,* vol. 1. Cairo, 1955 (*al-Iḥāṭa*).

Ibn Ṣā'id. *Kitāb Ṭabaḳāt al-umam.* Edited by Cheikho. Beirut, 1912 (Ibn Ṣā'id).

———. *Kitāb A'māl al-a'lām.* Edited by E. Lévi-Provençal. Rabat, 1934 (*A'māl al-a'lām*).

Lévi-Provençal, E. *Trois traités hispaniques de hisba* (Texte arabe). Cairo, 1955 (*Trois traités*).

Al-Ḥumaidī. *Djadhwat al-muḳtabis fī dhikr wulāt al-Andalus.* Cairo, 1952 (al-Ḥumaidī).

Al-Marrākushī, 'Abdalwāḥid. *Al-Mu'djib fī talkhīṣ akhbār al-Maghrib.* Cairo, 1324 (al-Marrākushī).

As-Saḳaṭī, Muhammad. *Un manuel hispanique de hisba* . . . publié . . . by G.S. Colin and E. Lévi-Provençal. Paris, 1931 (as-Saḳaṭī).

3. OTHER

González Palencia, A. *Los mozárabes de Toledo en los siglos XII y XIII,* Volumen preliminar, 1–3. Madrid, 1926–1930 (González Palencia).

Menéndez Pidal, R. *La España del Cid,* 5th ed., vols. 1 and 2. Madrid, 1956 (Menéndez Pidal).

Lacarra, J.M. "Documentos para el estudio de la reconquista y repoblación del Valle del Ebro," *Estudios de Edad Media de la Corona de Aragón,* Sección de Zaragoza 2, pp. 469–574; 3, pp. 499–727; 5, pp. 511–668 (Lacarra).

Neuman, A.A. *The Jews in Spain:* Their Social, Political and Cultural Life During the Middle Ages, vols. 1 and 2. Philadelphia, 1948 (Neuman).

Ribera y Tarragó, J. *Disertaciónes y opúsculos,* vols. 1 and 2. Madrid, 1928 (Ribera: Disertaciónes).

NOTES

See Sources for full references

CHAPTER ONE

1. Ibn Hazm, *Al-Fisal,* 5, p. 4; *Sefer ha-rikmah,* p. 227; and cf. Bacher, Leben p. 3. From the two texts it appears that what is meant is immigrants who settled in Spain at the beginning of the eleventh century.
2. T.-S. 13 J 20[17] and regarding a family of a Jew from ar-Raḥba in Kairawan, see C.U.L., Or. 1080 J154 (from the year 1035).
3. Ibn 'Idhārī, p. 77; an-Nuwairī, p. 77. Some say this was the body of a Christian; see the first-mentioned source and also Ibn al-Athīr, 7, p. 500. According to Ibn Ḥazm, *Al-Fiṣal,* 1, p. 59, the body was buried in the mountains of Cordova but this was unusual; cf. Lévi-Provençal, 2, p. 306.
4. According to various history books, this function was filled by Jewish merchants from Moslem Spain who were accustomed to visiting the Christian principalities in the north of the peninsula. This account has no documentary basis, however, and is the product of the imagination of Romey, who tells of Jewish merchants from Toledo who performed this mission; see Ch. Romey, *Histoire d'Espagne* (Paris, 1858), 5:23. Other scholars copied his work and even added their own material, such as suggesting that the merchants were from Cordova or Tarragona. See A. de Bofarull y Brocá, *Historia critica de Cataluña* 2 (Barcelona, 1876), p. 274; *Amador de los Rios,* 1:208. On the other hand, doubt was cast upon this account by V. Balaguer, *Historia de Cataluña* 2 (Madrid, 1885–87), p. 56; S. Sanpere y Miquel, *El año de los catalanes: Revista de ciencias historicas* 4 (1886), p. 40.

   Count Armengol, who began his reign in 992, was the fourth of the counts of Urgel and is called Armengol I.
5. Ibn 'Idhārī, p. 98.
6. T.-S. 12. 218. The sender was a permanent resident of Fostat. See S. Assaf, "Mikhtābhīm mi-Ḳnirūān u-mi-e Alexandria l'-Ibn 'Aukal," *Tarbīṣ* 20:177–78. For the purpose of fixing the time in which he lived, it is worth mentioning that he received letters in 1006 and 1007; see Abram-

son, *Ba-merkāzīm* u-ba-t'fūsōt bi-t'Ḳūfat ha-g'ōnim, pp. 61–62. In the collection of Geniza documents at Cambridge there is a fragment of a letter to him containing the date *Dhu 'l-ḥidjdja* 398, i.e., August 1008. The letter bears the classification number Or. 1080 J 154. On the correspondance of Ibn 'Aukal, see S.D. Goitein in *Tarbīṣ* 36 (1967):ff.; 37 (1968):98ff., 158ff.

7. *Diwan Ibn Gabirol,* part 1, no. 63; and see also lines 25–34. In the opinion of the editors (see the notes and explanations, p. 106) the poem was written in honor of Samuel the *Nāgīd*, but this explanation does not fit the subject matter of the poem; it was composed in honor of a Jew who served one of the princes in the Ebro region or in eastern Spain. From the phrasing in the passage relating to the ties of this Jew with the rulers —it mentions first the princes of "Edom" and following them, "Ḳedar" —it cannot be deduced that he was in the service of a Christian prince, since the poet mentions "Edom" before "Ḳedar" in other poems also, even though he means primarily the area of Arab dominance in Spain. See part 1, no. 109, lines 15–16.
8. Schirmann, pp. 216–17 and see there p. 217, line 17.
9. *Diwan Ibn Gabirol,* part 1, no. 117, lines 14, 24–25; ibid., part 7, no. 6, line 7, and with regard to the author of the elegy, cf. the editors' interpretations, p. 19.
10. Abraham b. Dā'ūd, p. 71.
11. Carmoly, in *Isr. Annalen,* 1840, p. 25b, observed that in his copy of *Sēfer ha-yōḥasēn,* where the author quotes the words of Abraham b. Dā'ūd concerning the events in Cordova, there is a marginal note written by hand near the words "and there are those who fled to Toledo: R. Isaac b. Khalfōn and R. Judah b. Ḥanīdjā" (this, and not Ḥanīna, is correct). Cf. M. Wilensky, *Tarbīṣ* 4:103, who places his trust in this list.
12. *Sēfer ha-riḳma,* p. 319.
13. *Diwan Samuel ha-nāgīd,* no. 14, 1:12. Also cf. Derenbourg, *Opuscules,* p. 3.
14. Abraham bar Samuel al-Andalusī is mentioned in a document from Fostat from the year 1028 (T.-S. 13 J 5'), Moses bar Isaac the S'fārādī in a document from the year 1037, also from Fostat. See Assaf, "Sh'ṭārōt sūrīyīm minha-me'a ha-aḥat 'esre, Ereṣ Yisrāēl, 1:142; see also Ismā'īl b. Abraham al-Andalusī in a fragmented letter (T.-S. 16.27) and Abū'l-Ḥusain Ibn al-Andalusī in a document (T.-S. 10 J 26[6]) which dates from the second half of the eleventh century; see Mann, *Jews,* 2, p. 56. Bodl. 2876[44] is a letter from R. Solomon b. Judah, the head of the talmudic academy in Palestine in the first half of the eleventh century to Abraham ha-Kōhēn b. Mar Rab Ḥaggai in Fostat in connection with the will of Abraham b. Meir al-Andalusi. In this letter the head of the academy inquires whether the deceased did indeed bequeath a part of his property to Ibn Nathan al-Andalusī. The beginning of the letter was published by Mann, *Jews,* II, p. 115. Jews from Spain are mentioned in lists of allocations of alms: Misc. 8[25], T.-S. 20. 13, T.-S. J 1[4], T.-S. K 15[14], [15], [39], [50], [93], [96], [102]. Most of these lists are, to be sure, from the second half of the eleventh century, but it should be remembered that similar

lists from the first half are virtually not preserved. See further S.D. Goiten, Letters of medieval Jewish traders (Princeton University Press 1973), pp. 110, 111, 112, 139.

15. Baer, I, p. 43.
16. L. Serrano, *Cartulario del infantado de Covarrubias*, por L. Serrano (Valladolid, 1907), p. 45; J. Pérez de Urbel, *Sancho el Mayor* (Madrid, 1950), p. 188.
17. See L. Serrano, *Cartulario de San Millán* (Madrid, 1930), nos. 96, 97; and see p. xxxix and cf. L. Serrano, *El obispado de Burgos y Castilla primitiva* 1 (Madrid, 1935), p. 222. Both villages were southwest of Santo Domingo de la Calzada.
18. Baer, *Urkunden* 2, no. 5.
19. Ibid., no. 11. In documents from this region there are names which perhaps are those of Jews without this being indicated, e.g., in a deed of gifts from the year 1007 there is a Zib Vita, from the village of Oca, and this may be Z'ebh b. Ḥayim; see *Cartulario de San Millán*, no. 73.
20. According to a passage in a chronicle written around 1110 and copied in other chronicles, Sancho el Mayor changed the route of the pilgrims who journeyed to Santiago de Compostela from Álava and Asturias to a more southerly line and thenceforth they passed by way of Nájera and Briviesca; see *Historia Silense*, ed. Santos, pp. 63–64. (As Cirot demonstrated, this passage relates to Sancho el Mayor and not to his grandfather, Sancho Abarca, who reigned at the beginning of the tenth century; see G. Cirot, "Per devia Alavae, *BAH* 36:88–93.)
21. See the document published by F. Fita in *BAH* 26:241.
22. See ibid., p. 250.
23. L. Huidobro–F. Cantera, "Juderīas burgalesas," *Sefarad* 13:36.
24. A document of the monastery San Juan de la Peña; see J. M. Lacarra, "Desarollo urbano de Jaca en la edad media," in *Estudaos de edad media de la Corona de Aragon* 4:140. In documents from this district, too, there are names which perhaps are those of Jews of that epoch. In a bill of sale of property in the village of Aragon in 1036, one *Çia Vita* is mentioned as a guarantor and this may have been a Jew whose name was Isaiah Ḥayim (or b. Ḥayim; see E. Ibarra, *Docementos correspondientes al reinado de Ramiro I* (Saragossa, 1904), no. 10. It is true that A. Ubieto Arteta believes that the date of the document is incorrect, but he does not deny that it is original; see A. Ubieto Arteta, "Estudios en torno a la división del reino por Sancho el Mayor de Navarra," *Principe de Viana*, no. 78–79, pp. 48, 54.
25. I. Loeb, "Actes de vente hébreux," *REJ* 4:229.
26. See J. Rodriguez, "Judería de León," *Archivos Leoneses* 2, no. 2, pp. 57, 58–60, 62, 63, 72 (in the last-mentioned document, which was written in 1049, it is not stated that he was then still alive). On Jewish landowners in León see also A. Viñayo Gonzalez, San Martin de León y su apologetica antijudaica (Madrid-Barcelona 1948), p. 65—a document referring to the vineyard of a Jew—dated 1015. See also Muñoz Romero, Colección de fueros I (Madrid 1847), p. 67—the decree of a council in Leon in 1020 concerning the witnesses be required for sale of land—there should be two Christians and two Jews.

27. Ibid., p. 64.
28. Ibid., pp. 65, 66–67 (in this document the seller of the land is called "Juan whose second name is Sulaimān").
29. Loeb, "Actes de vente hébreux," *REJ* 4:226ff. The explanation that the name Eshkafat derives from *escapat* (escaped; see ibid., p. 76) is not acceptable, at least in this case. But it is possible that at a later period those who spoke Romance languages translated the name, which they did not understand, as *mālīṭ* (a refugee, like *pālīṭ*); see ibid. Perhaps it is the name mentioned in documents from the years 1028 and 1032 which are cited above.
30. See Cantera-Millás, no. 3, where all the studies dealing with this inscription are cited. In the opinion of Cantera-Millás, instead of Ḥiyyā one may also read Ḥayyīm or Ḥasan, whereas according to Fita and Loeb the reading should be Yaḥyā. The suggestions for the identification of the father of the deceased which Fita proposed in his articles are more than dubious; see *BAH* 2:206; 4:70.
31. See Cantera's article in *Sefarad* 3:334, 357–58.
32. Cantera, "Epigrafía hebraica en el museo arqueológico de Madrid," *Sefarad* 2:108; cf. there p. 390.
33. See my article "Mispār ha-y'hūdīm bī-S'fārād ha-muslimīt," *Zion* 28:56.
34. This date, given by Abraham Ibn Dā'ūd (see *The Jews of Moslem Spain,* vol. 1, ch. 9, note 30) provokes some doubt because of its proximity to 1013, the year in which Berbers captured the city of Cordova and carried out a slaughter, and because of his account of the circumstances of the rabbi's death, which contains folkloristic elements. But the event is quite close to Ibn Dā'ūd's generation and therefore there is no basis for an a priori invalidation of his account; and see, moreover, the reason offered by Harkavy, p. 43, for maintaining the date in Ibn Dā'ūd's account, in which he states that the exodus of many Jews from Cordova occurred after the death of the rabbi.
35. *Sha'rē t'shūbha* (Leipzig, 5618), no. 99.
36. Al-Barcelōnī, *Sēfer la-'ittīm,* p. 267; *Sha'arē simḥa,* part 1, p. 60, and see there Yiṣḥāk Y'ranen, note 142; *Ha-Manhīg,* f. 64a.
37. See Bacher, *Leben,* p. 86. See also S. Assaf, "Li-ṣ'mīḥat ha-mer-kazim ha-yisrāēliyīm bi-t'ḳūfat ha-g'ōnīm," *Ha-Shilōaḥ* 35:508.
38. *HU,* p. 910.
39. *Diwan Samuel ha-nāgīd,* no. 11, lines 53, 56-57. *Diwan Ibn Gabirol,* part 1, no. 37, lines 21–26. The other *ḳīnōt* (elegies), op. cit. nos. 36, 38, 113.
40. Mann believes that one of the letters he published was perhaps sent to Spain; see *Texts,* 1, p. 149.
41. *Diwan Samuel ha-nāgīd,* nos. 10, 147; *Diwan Ibn Gabirol,* part 1, no. 23, lines 163–76; no. 117, lines 91–94 (where the scholars of Babylonia are signified; like the scholars of the Sanhedrin, they sat in a semicircle).

CHAPTER TWO

1. Ibn 'Idhārī, p. 102.
2. The description of the city by al-Ḥimyarī, pp. IV–V, who relies on al-Bakrī, an author of the eleventh century, is authentic, but should be

given critical acceptance. Certainly it should be relied upon regarding the number of gates (i.e., that there were five gates), although it is possible that additional, smaller doorways were opened, as was customary in the Middle Ages. However, the Arabic author does not fix the location of the gates. Guillen Robles indicates on the city map four gates in the western section; see F. Guillen Robles, *Malaga musulmana* (Malaga, 1880), p. 470. It must, indeed, be assumed that there was another gate besides the Bāb al-baḥr, because the port was there and because the rulers, no doubt, preferred not to open gates on the fortress side. Torres Balbás identifies the second gate with the Puerta de Espartaría which is mentioned in Christian sources of a later epoch; see *Al-Andalus* 10:81. This conjecture is reasonable. As for the Puerto del Rio, al-Ḥimyarī states that it was in the eastern section of the city, but this is surely incorrect. As for the Puerta de Bāb al-khaukha in the north, it is best identified with the Puerta de Antequera, because the road to the city led from there and there was a bridge in its vicinity. Regarding the additional gate which Guillen Robles assigns to the northern section of the city, the Puerta de Buena Ventura, it is doubtful whether it was yet in existence in the eleventh century, and perhaps a pass was opened up there.

3. Guillen Robles places the Jewish quarter outside the city wall, north of the Granada Gate (on the map only; there is no word of this in the text of his book). Apparently he arrived at this view, because the "Catholic kings" designated a residential area there for the Jews. However, in the *Repartimiento* it is stated that the Christian conquerors gave the Jews an unpopulated area—"*despoblado.*" Therefore one should not deduce from this that Málagan Jews dwelt there earlier.

   In order to fix the location of the Jewish neighborhood in Málaga, one should rely upon these data: (a) In an edict by the Catholic Sovereigns in 1490 the Jews are ordered to settle outside the city in the vicinity of the Granada Gate; See *Repartimiento,* 1, f. 127v, a manuscript shown to me by Dr. Bejarano, the learned archivist of the city who is preparing its publication (there a suburb near the Granada Gate is discussed). On the basis of this document alone, it is reasonable to assume, that from an early time, Jews dwelt in the section of the city that was between the walls near the Granada Gate. (b) In a document dating from the years after the conquest of Málaga by the Christians, the street now called Santiago was called Barrio Nuevo; see Garcia de Lena, *Conversaciones históricas malagueñas* (Málaga, 1789–1793), 3:171. This is indeed the name given to the Jewish quarter in all Spanish cities after the expulsion. Yet on the other hand this street was located near the Granada Gate. (c) The information about the Jewish cemetery (see the next note) fits all these considerations and data: It was the practice in all the Jewish communities in Spain to establish cemeteries outside the city in an area near their quarter so that no incidents—such as attacks by the Moslem rabble—could arise during a funeral.
4. Alonso de Palencia, *Guerra de Granada,* trans. Paz y Melía V), p. 302.
5. See my article "Mispār ha-y'hūdīm bi-S'fārād ha-muslimīt," *Zion* 28:53.

6. Ibn Ḥauḳal, p. 110, still mentions Archidona as the chief city of the province. Cf. Dozy, *Recherches,* 1, p. 320.
7. This was in the year 405 of the *hidjra* (July 2, 1014–June 20, 1015). See Ibn 'Idhārī, p. 116, and Ibn al-Athīr, 9, p. 189, where the manifold preparations for the campaign against Cordova are reported. 'Alī must thus have crossed the Straits of Gibraltar in the autumn of 1014 or the spring of 1015. From this the date in which the refugees went to Málaga can also be concluded. It can be assumed that they went there before the city came under the control of this prince, which meant Berber rule.
8. A. Prieto y Vives, *Los royes do taifas* (Madrid, 1926), p. 26.
9. Ribera, *Historia de la música arabe medieval y su influencia en la española* 1 (Madrid, 1927), pp. 199ff.
10. In Arabic letters the name is written ابن نغرالة and sometimes ابن النغرالة ; cf. below, note 116. It was pronounced Nagrīla since in Granada the long *a* (aleph) was pronounced as a long *i;* see A. Steiger, *Contribución a la fonética del hispano-arabe* (Madrid, 1932), pp. 318ff. Colin explained the name as a diminutive of *nadjra,* a species of crow *(corneille),* and this explanation seemed acceptable to Lévi-Provençal; see *Al-Andalus* 3:244. But this word is written نجرة . However, M. Stern interpreted it as "the son of the swarthy woman," i.e., one of the mothers in this family was given this name and it persisted in the family, just as other family names became widespread, e.g., Ibn Djiḳaṭilla, "the son of the tiny woman"; see *Al-Andalus* 13:330ff.; this explanation is no doubt preferable. The family name Nagrīla appears in a document of 1160 as that of a Christian in Toledo: Domingo Nagrīla. As for his blindness, see the Arabic poem quoted by H. Pérès, *La noésic andalouse en arabe classique au XI sic'clo* (Paris, 1937), p. 271.
11. In a poem which he wrote shortly after leaving Cordova (as is stated in the superscription and is in the *Diwan,* no. 14) he speaks of his numerous wanderings; and this observation does not fit the journey from Cordova to Málaga, for the distance between them is not so great. On the other hand, we do know about a meeting he had, shortly after his departure from Cordova, with a writer who dwelt in Almería, and see below.
12. For the name of his father, see no. 25:14, 74:9. Concerning his social status, see the observations of R. Ḥananēl: (that he was the son of a prominent man) in *ha-Karmel* 8:246 and also the statement of the poet in *Dhakhīra* 1, 2; p. 265, and in S. M. Stern, "L'tō'dōt R. Sh'mūēl ha-nāgīd," *Zion* 15:142, line 31. It is quite clear that one should not exaggerate the value of such florid rhetoric as appears in the letters and the laudatory poems, and insofar as the words of the Arabic poet are concerned, they may relate to his extraction from the tribe of Levi; see Stern, op. cit., p. 140, note 23. On the other hand, no one would write in grandiloquent terms about the father of a noted person if it were known that he was from an undistinguished family—this would constitute a mockery. As for his father's economic status, it should be noted that he is not depicted as a wealthy man in any source, but neither should it be inferred that he was miserably poor, as does Harkavy, p. 5, and see below.

13. Abraham b. Dā'ūd, p. 53; *Shīrat Yisrāel,* p. 65 (A. Halkin in his new edition and translation of the book (Jerusalem, 1975) has in the translation (p. 61) "born in Marida," but the Arabic *al-ḳidma* (or al-ḳudma) means "of old", referring to the origin of the family); the superscription to a poem, no. 140, states: "A weakening of the body because of old age beset him during the war, which took place during the summer of 4814 [1054]." The same poem is in Ben Ḳōhelet, no. 138; there he himself says that he is beyond the sixty-first year of his life; see line 3.
14. The name is mentioned in his poems, *Diwan* nos. 40:2, 47:4 and in a superscription to no. 33. Regarding his being the firstborn, see nos. 37:12, 38:1, 40:1, 8, 49:5.
15. No. 37:32.
16. No. 91:17ff.
17. Abraham b. Dā'ūd, p. 53, Yōsēf b. Ṣaddīḳ in Neubauer, *Med. Jew. Chr.,* 1, p. 92. Saadya b. Danān, p. 29a; *Sha'arē simḥa,* part 1, p. 29 and cf. Harkavy, p. 43.
18. See Solomon Ibn Parḥōn, preface to *Maḥberet he-'ārūkh* (Pressburg, 5604), p. xxii; and cf. Judah Ibn Tibbōn, preface to *Sefer ha-riḳma,* p. 3. Ḥayyūdj died around 1006 or 1007; see note 42 to chapter 4.
19. *Diwan* no. 8. There is no proof that this happened while he was in Cordova; the superscription merely states that the incident occurred "in his youth." It should also be remembered that Málaga was a port city and that the wealthy did not often sail abroad. On the other hand, he was already mature and independent when he was in Málaga, whereas superscription of this poem implies that he made this journey when he was young and not independent.

    The account by Abraham b. Dā'ūd that in Cordova he was "a merchant who earned a living with difficulty" is incorrect, as is demonstrated by his poems; see below. Apparently the writer wanted to emphasize, by means of this account, that he achieved greatness by his own effort.
20. No. 17. In the opinion of S. Sachs, the person who is meant is Isaac b. Baruch Ibn Albalia; see *Israelitische Letterbode,* 3, p. 19. However, this is a poem from the days of his youth and he depicts R. Isaac as a judge occupying the bench (see line 10) and Isaac Ibn Albalia indeed belongs to a younger generation than Samuel. David Ṣemaḥ explained that the person meant was the brother of Samuel; see his article, "Leḳeṭ bi-s'deh ha-shīra ha-'ībhrīt bi-S'fārād," *Tarbīṣ* 26:461. But his proof is unconvincing since Samuel gives other people the appelation of "brother" (see no. 72:30), and such is the custom of the Arabs to this very day.
21. No. 9. Ṣemaḥ believes that this poem was written to the *nāgīd*'s son; see his article in *Tarbīṣ* 27:96–97. However, Sassoon, in an introduction to the *Diwan,* p. xx, and Haberman, part 2, p. 152, identify this man with R. Joseph b. Samuel, and it would seem that they are correct.
22. Ibn Ḥayyān in *Al-Iḥāṭa,* p. 446.
23. To be sure, the statement of Saadya b. Danān, p. 29a, that he composed a poem of seven stanzas and that each stanza was written in another language is hyperbole because the man for whom this poem was designated would not have understood much of it. However, in the manner

of all the Spanish intellectuals, he no doubt did compose a poem in Arabic from time to time.

24. No. 2.
25. No. 15:5ff.
26. No. 21:10ff. In another poem too, no. 14, he expresses thanks to a friend who did not disappoint him at that time.
27. No. 21:2.
28. No. 15:10–19, 21:3–6.
29. *Ben Mishle*, nos. 622, 859, 880, 995, ed. Abramson, no. 117.
30. Ibid., ed. Abramson, no. 116; no. 979; cf. Abramson, no. 1052. In addition, see Abramson in his introduction, pp. 25–26.
31. Ibn Ḥazm, *Al-Fiṣal*, 1, p. 152, states that their debate occurred in 404 of the *hidjra*, which began on July 13, 1013. On the other hand, he states in one of his works that he left Cordova on the first day of that year; see *Ṭauḳ al-ḥamāma*, p. 288. No doubt, he remembered this date well, and he did indeed sojourn then in Balāṭ Mughīth, a neighborhood in the western zone of the city (see above, p. 286), from which the residents were expelled after the Berber conquest; see *Al-Marrākushī*, p. 26. Thus it appears that Samuel chanced to come to Almería, where Ibn Ḥazm was then settled; Ibn Ḥazm was in Málaga at some time, but it is not clear when; see Asín 1, p. 42.
32. *Al-Fiṣal*, 2, p. 108.
33. Op. cit., 1, p. 135.
34. In the passage dealing with the break in the rule of the House of David before Nebuchadnezzar as printed (see the following note), an error occurred: in the printed text it is stated that this break came after احرب بابن برام (in the ms., British Museum, Or. 842, f. 27a احريا من حورام and therefore Asín explained it ("emended it") to be Zechariah ben Jeroboam, apparently because according to 2 Kings 16:8, Zechariah ben Jeroboam reigned in Samaria for six months. But in ms. Leiden, Warner 480, f. 260, it is written clearly وبعد اخريا بن بورام and it should be اخزيا بن يورام ; and see 2 Kings 11:3.
35. Op. cit., 152–53; cf. Goldziher, "Proben muhammedanischer Polemik gegen den Talmud," in Kobak's *Jeschurun* 8:76–77, and also *REJ* 8:125.
36. There is no need to invalidate the account of Abraham b. Dā'ūd, pp. 53ff. He was, after all, the grandson of Isaac Ibn Albalia, who was close to Samuel Ibn Nagrīla, and no doubt he had heard the story in his family circle. Samuel ha-lērī himself stresses a number of times, in his poems and epigrams, the importance of letter-writing talent as a factor for success in life. See *Ben Mishle*, nos. 893, 894, 1123. The fact that it is related that al-Manṣūr also attained greatness in this fashion does not contradict the account, but shows that composing letters was a way to become accepted into the service of the nobles and rulers. (It is true that modern Arabic writers and scholars have also invalidated this account, inasmuch as al-Manṣūr advanced from rank to rank until he became the secretary of the caliph's mother. However, the account does not state that he became her secretary at once; rather, it is said that he rose from one level to the next.)

37. See Schirmann, *Zion* 1:266. In Moslem Spain نظر is called a district, see Dozy, *Supplément*, 2, p. 686, and there is thus no reason for the emendation *aḳṭār* which Ṣemaḥ proposes in *Tarbīṣ* 24:462. The superscription should therefore be translated "the districts over which he was appointed." To be sure, the original source does not state what his function was, but from the Arabic authors who speak of his functions, we learn that he was first engaged in the collection of taxes; see below.
38. No. 82 and see the explanations of Ṣemaḥ in *Tarbīṣ* 26:463–64; according to them the entire episode occurred in the principality of Málaga and it was R. Judah who introduced Samuel to the collection of taxes. Against these interpretations it must be noted that in the opening of the poem Samuel expressly speaks of the "parting," and indeed it was he who departed from his place, whereas R. Judah still occupied the judge's bench, as it is stated in line 9: "And if you would hear that which is honest, come with me to the court of R. Judah"; that is, at that time he had not yet received the royal appointment to the post which involved traveling outside his city. This explanation is in line with Abraham b. Dā'ūd's account of his connection with Ibn al-'Arīf; see also the following note.
39. No. 70. The date is given in the superscription whose Arabic text is in Schirmann (see note 37), but *ighrāmihi* should be translated "a penalty was imposed upon him." According to one version, Abraham b. Dā'ūd says that Samuel was appointed to office in 1018, but according to another version "he was in the king's palace" in 1020. If indeed this incorrect version was in the original manuscript of the *Sefer ha-ḳabbāla* the author remembered the date of Samuel's dismissal. At any rate, it is known that by that time he was already in Granada. As for the slaying of R. Judah and his sister's son, it is clear that it was not by chance that this deed occurred at the time of the incarceration of Samuel ha-lēvī.
40. Nos. 71–72. When he left prison he also composed a poem in which he expressed his joy; see *Diwan*, ed. Haberman, part 3, no. 23. Both from the words of his friend, the poet, and from his own words, it seems that the enemies who rose against him were Jews, since the friend who writes to him is acquainted with them; see no. 72:11.
41. No. 55, and see the explanation by Ṣemaḥ in *Tarbīṣ* 27:94–95.
42. This date is mentioned twice by Abraham b. Dā'ūd. It corresponds with what R. Moses Ibn Ezra reports in *Sefer Shīrat Yisrāel*, p. 68,—that he and his son filled a role "over a period of thirty-five years"; if we emend thirty-five to thirty-eight years, according to a reasonable suggestion by Simḥōnī in *Ha-t'ḳūfa* 10:171. According to this emendation, the difference given by Abraham b. Dā'ūd and the one given by R. Moses Ibn Ezra is not much more than one year, for according to Abraham b. Dā'ūd the activities of Samuel and his son add up to thirty-nine years and some months. The new edition of *Shirat Yisrāel* by A. Halkin (1975) p. 66 has, however thirty-five or thirty-four years; but this version can be considered as an additional proof that Moses Ibn Ezra had no exact knowledge of the chronology of the career of Samuel the Nāgīd.
43. See memoirs of 'Abdallāh, p. 30, line 7.

44. The the departure of Zāwī, according to Ibn 'Idhārī, p. 128, and *Al-Iḥāṭa,* p. 525; and see Lévi-Provençal, 3, p. 331.
45. *Dhakhīra,* 1, 2, pp. 139–40.
46. Ibn 'Idhārī, p. 264.
47. Ibid., p. 191; *Primera Crónica general,* cap. 779.
48. Memoirs of 'Abdallāh, pp. 30-31. The accounts of the royal author and of Abraham b. Dā'ūd complement and confirm each other. From 'Abdallāh's account we learn that Samuel reached the top rank of authority after the death of the vizier who had been his superior. Of course, we must not believe the Moslem author who states that Samuel denigrated the young vizier before the king, because this was altogether contrary to his character as described in all sources, including the Arabic. Abraham b. Dā'ūd, too, reports that Samuel attained his high position through the death of the vizier whom he had served as an official. It is true that in 'Abdallāh's account the vizier is called Abu 'l-'Abbās and in the *Sefer ha-ḳabbāla,* Abu'l-Ḳāsim Ibn al-'Arīf, but both names refer to the same person. This vizier, whose name was Abu 'l-'Abbās Ibn al-'Arīf, is mentioned in Ibn Bassām, 1, p. 340, where the letter which the theologian Abū'Umar Aḥmad b. 'Īsā wrote to him is cited. The letter cited there, p. 341, was written by the same person in 1025; the suitability of the time can be inferred. It can therefore be assumed that either Abraham b. Dā'ūd erred in calling the vizier Abu 'l-Ḥāsim or that he had two names, as was customary.
49. Ibn 'Idhārī, p. 264; *Dhakhīra,* 1, 2, p. 269. In these sources it is explicitly stated that he had become a vizier in the days of Ḥabbūs.
50. *Diwan Samuel ha-nāgīd,* no. 10, 17–24.
51. The accepted date—1038—is incorrect. In this matter Dozy, 3, p. 24, depends upon Ibn al-Athīr, 9, p. 201. This oriental historian tells of the aforementioned campaign of the king of Seville against Zuhair, which took place, according to him, in 429 of the *hidjra* (October 14, 1037–October 2, 1038), and he asserts that thereafter Ḥabbūs returned to Málaga, where he died in the month of Ramadān. This passage was corrupted by copyists and should read 427 instead of 429, for it is well known that the words سبع تسع were easily substituted by the copyists. Dozy himself has already demonstrated in another connection (in his volume 3, p. 19) and for other reasons that it should read 427. This conclusion can be reached also from the wording of the entire passage. From its ending, where the Arabic historian gives the date for another incident as "the end of 429," it is clear that the joint campaign occurred in an earlier year. To be sure, this date is also to be found in Ibn Khaldūn, 4, p. 160, but he no doubt copied from Ibn al-Athīr. This campaign therefore occurred, according to Ibn al-Athīr, in 1036; and as for the death of Ḥabbūs, Ibn 'Idhārī, p. 191, and Lisān ad-dīn, *Al-Iḥāṭa,* p. 485, expressly state that he died in 428 of the *hidjra* (October 25, 1036–October 13, 1037). It should also be noted that the passage in Ibn al-Athīr's history does not occur with like wording in every manuscript; see *Abbad.,* 2, p. 34. At any rate, the testimony of Ibn 'Idhārī and Lisān ad-dīn in the matter of the year in which Ḥabbūs died is to be preferred,

and it can be assumed that Ibn al-Athīr (or the source he had before him) was only certain about the month. Even without the date, the passage in Ibn al-Athīr's book is incorrect and is refuted by the words of the other chroniclers. According to Ibn al-Athīr, the war occurred in the same year in which Ḥabbūs died and *thereafter* the king of Granada went to Málaga; but the other sources tell that Ḥabbūs went to Málaga to take the oath of allegiance to Idrīs al-Mu'ayyad *before* he penetrated the kingdom of Seville at the head of his army; see *A'mal al-a'lām* p. 163. Ibn 'Idhārī, p. 191, states that that war occurred in 1036, and from another passage in his book, p. 144, we deduce that Ḥabbūs's visit to Málaga was shortly after Idrīs came there and he was crowned at the beginning of 1036 or at the end of 1035; cf. Seco de Lucena, *Los Hammudies* (Málaga, 1955), p. 31.

52. Abraham b. Dā'ūd, p. 55; Ibn 'Idhārī, p. 264.
53. Memoirs of 'Abdallāh, p. 36; and see Lévi-Provençal, *Al-Andalus* 3:285, who asserts that this family was of Jewish origin; but in Ibn Bassām's passage which he cites (Oxford MS. 2, p. 144b is what it should be, not p. 173b) one of the Ibn al-Ḳarawī brothers is called al-Alslāmī ("one who became a Moslem"), and later verses by his secretary are quoted in which he alludes quite clearly to his Christian origin, e.g., when he counsels him to seek for an explanation for the importance of wine in the New Testament. Pérès translates these verses, pp. 271 and 465, yet notwithstanding all this, he too states there that the Ibn al-Ḳarawī were of Jewish origin.
54. *Diwan Samuel ha-nāgīd,* no. 10:25–39.
55. Ibid., no. 10. The Arabic sources are Ibn Ḥayyān in *Dhakhīra,* 1, 2, p. 166; Ibn 'Idhārī, pp. 166–67 (Anonymous, p. 293; Memoirs of 'Abdallāh, pp. 34–35. Cf. P. Frankl, "Eine Hymne Samuel Hanagids," *MGWJ* 24:179–89, 219–28; Harkavy, pp. 15–22; Schirmann, "Milḥamōt Sh'muōl ha-nāgīd," *Zion* I:270–71, and also his article, "Le Diwan de Semū'el Hannāgīd comme source pour l'histoire espagnole," *Hespéris* 35 (1948): 68–69.
56. Memoirs of 'Abdallāh, pp. 31–33. As is his wont, in his account of the event the royal author does not give a date, and in his work it precedes the episode concerning Zuhair; but he has no regard for chronological sequence. However, there is evidence for the assumption that Yaddair's flight occurred after the victory over Zuhair. (a) If Zuhair had still been alive, Yaddair's faction would have contacted this powerful neighbor, and after the failure of the revolt the conspirators would have fled to him. (b) Had the episode of Yaddair's conspiracy occurred before the war with Zuhair, Boluggīn, the king's brother, who was in contact with Yaddair, would not have been placed at the head of the army. (c) Apparently the death of Boluggīn was connected with the disclosure of the conspiracy; see below. From the account of Lisān ad-dīn, it appears that the episode of Yaddair's conspiracy occurred before the summer of 1039; see *Al-Iḥāṭa,* pp. 463–64. Regarding the flight of the Jews, mentioned above, Abraham b. Dā'ūd relates it after mentioning the death of Boluggīn and not after the coronation of Bādīs, and there is no doubt

that they left Granada with Yaddair's supporters, who had also gone to Seville.

57. Memoirs of 'Abdallāh, pp. 33–34.
58. *Diwan Samuel ha-nāgīd,* no. 29, and see also no. 27; see ed. Jarden, p. 15. Abū Manād—it should read so—in the superscription of this poem is not the Granadan vizier, as was the opinion of Harkavy, p. 23, Schirmann in his article in *Hespéris,* p. 187, and Jarden, ibid., but Bādīs himself, inasmuch as he was given this appellation; see *Dhakhīra,* 1, 2, p. 173, line 4); Ibn 'Idhārī, pp. 201–2; Ibn al-Athīr, 9, p. 201. As for the date of the battle, the Arabic sources state only that it occurred at the start of 431 A.H., which began on September 23, 1039. Its exact time, however, can be fixed from the poems of Samuel. In the superscription to no. 29 the date is given as the night of Monday, the day before Succot; however, in the year 4800 the day before Succot fell on Friday, October 4, 1039, and in all truth the superscription to poem no. 27 states that the armies encountered each other on Thursday, the thirteenth of Tishrī. But in poem no. 29, line 101, it is also asserted that the battle occurred on Thursday, i.e., the thirteenth of Tishrī. Apparently the person who assembled the *Diwan* was misled by the poet's statement that his fate was decided on the second day of the week (Monday). The description of the war by the Arabic writers and the one found in the *nāgīd*'s poems match for, by his own statement, the battle did not develop until the Granadans had retreated. As for the date, see below, note 66.
59. In the language of the *nāgīd,* no. 59, 24: the Zemarite troops Genesis 10:18).
60. In addition, see no. 104, and for a clarification of the date see the plausible comment of Schirmann, *Milḥāmōt,* p. 273; and see ed. Jarden, p. 35.
61. No. 79. The date is given in the superscription: the summer of 4803 (i.e., 1043); but in the Arabic sources it is 434 A.H. (August 21, 1042–August 9, 1043); see Anonymous, p. 312, and Ibn Khaldūn in *Abbad.,* 2, pp. 209, 216. The translation of the title in ed. Jarden, p. 44, is erroneous.
62. Some of the Arabic historians replace this prince by his son and heir, 'Azīz, but Ibn Ḥayyān, a contemporary, mentions Isḥāḳ b. Muḥammad as Carmona's ruler in 435 A.H. and in 439 A.H.; see Ibn 'Idhārī, pp. 219, 229, and he is also mentioned as prince of Carmona in 442 A.H.; see there p. 235, and see *A'māl al-a'lām,* p. 273, and Prieto y Vives, pp. 22–23.
63. Nos. 86, 88. Schirmann, *Milḥāmōt,* p. 280, cites these poems in connection with the war between the king of Seville and his enemies, which is described by Dozy, 3, pp. 50ff. But this war occurred in 1050–1051; see *Abbad.,* 1, pp. 247–48, and especially p. 248, line 3 from the bottom, where Ibn Ḥayyān states that the ruler of Seville did not discontinue the war in the winter, as was customary, but continued to invade the territory of the enemy; see also Ibn 'Idhārī, pp. 209–11, 234–35. Whence the discrepancy in the *nāgīd*'s words and the description of the war, which Schirmann perceived; see loc. cit. The superscriptions do not refer expressly to the conquest of Écija (the poems per se are devoted to other

matters); the interpretation of the "victory" or the "triumph" can be determined from the fact that no. 79 speaks of the conquest of cities in the principality of Carmona. On the other hand, Écija is mentioned in the account of Ibn Ḥayyān (concerning an episode which occurred in 439 A.H. [1047–1048]) as a city under the authority of Bādīs; see Ibn 'Idhārī, p. 230. It is true that Anonymous, p. 312, states that the dominance of 'Azīz b. Muḥammad b. 'Abdallāh was recognized by the same districts which had recognized his father. Aside from the fact that it substitutes 'Azīz for Isḥāḳ, this passage is too general and cannot be taken to mean that 'Azīz succeeded in maintaining his hold over the entire principality.

64. Superscription of nos. 76, 77; see also Ibn 'Idhārī, pp. 167, 191–92, 193; Anonymous, pp. 293–94, 302; Memoirs of 'Abdallāh, pp. 44–45.
65. Memoirs of 'Abdallāh, p. 35; Abraham b. Dā'ūd, loc. cit.
66. No. 32. In the Arabic sources there are two versions regarding Ibn Baḳanna's end. According to Anonymous, p. 289, Ḥasan besieged Málaga; after a severe siege, Yaḥyā submitted; Ibn Baḳanna remained in the post of vizier, but after two and a half years passed, in June 1042, he was slain. Ibn 'Idhārī, p. 217, reports that he was slain at the end of 1042 or the beginning of 1043, after the death of Ḥasan, but there is no doubt that he (i.e., his source) substitutes him for the representative of Nadjā; see below. But according to al-Ḥumaidī, p. 31, there was no siege whatsoever and Ibn Baḳanna, who was persuaded to return to the city, was promptly slain. The superscription on poem no. 32 verifies the second version, inasmuch as it fixes the date of 1040 for the death of Ibn Baḳanna. Codera, "Estudio crítico sobre la historia y monedas de los Hammudies de Málaga y Algeciras," *Museo Español de antiguedados* (1877):450, and Dozy, 3, pp. 36–37, accepted this version.
67. No. 78, and cf. Schirmann, *Milḥāmōt,* p. 278; see also al-Marrākushī, p. 43, Anonymous, pp. 290–91, Ibn 'Idhārī, pp. 216–17. Anonymous states that after the murder of the vizier who was Nadjā's deputy in Málaga, another Ḥammūdite prince was enthroned there on the sixth of the month of Djumādā I or of Djumādā II, 434 (December 22, 1042 or January 21, 1043), but earlier he states that Ḥasan died in Djumādā I, 434 (December 17, 1042–January 15, 1043); therefore the date given by Ibn Bassām for the slaying of Nadjā—February 5, 1043—is to be preferred; see Dozy, 3, p. 37. The Arabic superscription of no. 78 states that this was at the beginning of 4803 (i.e., in the autumn of 1042), whereas the Hebrew says that it was at the beginning of the summer 4803, and this no doubt, is more likely.
68. Ibn Ṣā'id, p. 90.
69. See Stern in *Zion* 15:141.
70. See Sassoon in the introduction to the *Diwan,* pp. xiv–xv.
71. Nos. 34:6, 43:1, 6, 46:1; the poem which, as mentioned above, Stern published, lines 14, 15, 17.
72. Nos. 33–51.
73. No. 37:44.
74. No. 63:96.
75. Ibn Ḥayyān in *Al-Iḥāṭa,* p. 447.

76. No. 76 and see also *Ben Ḳōhelet,* no. 403, and cf. *Ben T'hillīm,* no. 139.
77. No. 86 and see there lines 25, 29, 30.
78. No. 87.
79. See Sassoon, op. cit., p. xvi.
80. No. 88.
81. Nos. 90, 91, and cf. Schirmann, *Milḥāmōt,* pp. 357–58. It is hard to explain the superscriptions of these poems unless we depend upon this explanation. If the *nāgīd* chose the direct route, Abū Nūr would have to penetrate the central district of the kingdom of Granada and, since the Granadans would know this, there could be no ambush.
82. There is an allusion to this in no. 103:9.
83. Nos. 93, 94, and especially 9:31–36; cf. Schirmann, *Milḥāmōt,* p. 358. There is no doubt that the reading should be Ushūna (Ossuna) wa-Maurūr and not Ushūna wa-al-Mudawwar; Almodóvar was a city in another region altogether, i.e., on the banks of the Guadalquivir.
84. Nos. 96, 97. While it is true that there is no allusion to the foe, either in the poems or in the superscriptions, from the frequency of the campaigns it can be concluded that the reference is to a long war which was directed against the same enemy.
85. No. 101.
86. Nos. 103, 105. In the Arabic sources there is no reference to a campaign against Ronda, but they do contain information about a campaign by Bādīs against Málaga which was unsuccessful and about which there is no information in the *nāgīd*'s poems. We are told by Ibn al-Ḳaṭṭān about this campaign against Málaga; see in Ibn 'Idhārī, p. 217.
87. Ibn Ḥayyān in Ibn 'Idhārī, pp. 229–30, and *A'māl al-a'lām,* pp. 165–66. He fixes the date as 439 (which begins on June 28, 1047); and see below, note 90.
88. No. 106:26.
89. Al-Marrākushī, p. 71.
90. No. 106; Ibn Ḥayyān in Ibn 'Idhārī, p. 231, *A'māl al-a'lām,* p. 166.

    In his poem the *nāgīd* refers to the events of the autumn of 1047 and the spring of 1048. First he alludes to Abū Nūr, who violated a peace treaty (line 23): "The foes scorned the covenant between us and them and dealt treacherously"; and it is clear that there was no peace pact between Seville and Bādīs. Further on, he expresses his joy that the new pact with the other Berbers remained in effect (line 24): "We entered into a covenant, but maintained the covenant." After depicting the destruction of the district of ash-Sharaf (lines 30–33), he goes on to describe the siege in lines 35–38.
91. No. 107, and see Schirmann, *Milḥāmōt,* pp. 360–61. Regarding the date in the superscription concerning the recognition by Bādīs of the caliph of Málaga, against whom he had previously fought, see Ibn Khaldūn, 4, p. 155.
92. No. 109; and see Schirmann, Milḥāmōt, pp. 361–62; Ibn Ḥayyān in *Abbad.,* 1, pp. 247–48, and Ibn 'Idhārī, pp. 209–10, and especially p. 211, lines 2–3.
93. No. 110. The progress of events is not clear from the text of the poem. According to the interpretation given to the *nāgīd*'s words by Schirmann,

Milḥāmōt, pp. 262–63, the forces of Seville had already taken the fortress of Ossuna except for one tower, and when the Granadans arrived they entrenched themselves within the fortress; however in his article in *Hespéris,* p. 178, Schirmann explains that when the Granadans came up, the army of Seville lifted the siege of Ossuna and retreated to a strong fortress, where it came under siege. But see line 15, which begins the historical account: "For a company encamped against a castle and captured it"; and later line 23: "We assembled at the coming of the report and sped to the castle on the mountain to save those beleaguered in it." It is apparent that what is referred to here is not a tower inside the city, but a fortress outside the city. Line 24 goes on to say: "Then they entered into the fastnesses and their choicest fortresses, closing the gates." Here, then, the reference is to the enemy's fortress but not to Ossuna, which was one of Granada's allies.

94. No. 111.
95. No. 136. In the superscription, the city which came under siege is called "Ali Asana," and Schirmann therefore was uncertain whether it should be called Alyusāna (Lucena) or Almeriá, see *Milḥāmōt,* pp. 364–65, and *Hespéris,* pp. 179–80. However, it is not only unlikely that the ruler of Valencia would come to besiege Lucena, which was far from his kingdom, but the text of the poem, line 29, states that the tumult of the army on the battlefield was like "thunder and the sea at the seashore," and hence a city in the coastal region of eastern Spain is meant. If the reference were to a siege of Almería—as is indicated in ed. Jarden, p. 109 —the Arabic historians would undoubtedly have mentioned the matter, for Almería was a large and important city; but one searches their writings vainly for information about a siege of Almería. On the other hand, Arabic history books deal with the conquest of the northern districts of the kingdom of Almería by the neighboring kings; see Ibn al-Athīr, 9, p. 206; Ibn Bassām in *A'māl al-a'lām,* p. 220; and see Dozy, *Recherches,* 1, p. 242.

    Ibn 'Idhārī, pp. 174–75, reports on the war between the rulers of Almería and the Berber king of Toledo, which erupted at the time under discussion and in which Bādīs participated, and he also states that this war ended with the defeat of the kingdom of Almería; and Ibn Khaldūn, 4, pp. 160, 162, tells about the intervention by Bādīs in behalf of the kingdom of Almería.
96. See *Dhakhīra,* 2, MS. Oxford f. 144b, and cf. Pérès, p. 271.
97. No. 93.
98. Nos. 69:15–16; 98:37–41, 112:1.
99. No. 26 and see Gan ha-meshālīm-weha-ḥīdōt, *Diwān Don Todros ha-lēvī Abu 'l-'afiya* (ed. Yellin), no. 691, and see explanations and notes, pp. 118–19.
100. No. 106.
101. No. 171.
102. See Schirmann, "Sh'muēl ha-nāgīd k' m'shōrer," *K'nēset* 2 (5697):395, 400–1.
103. No. 8.
104. No. 59:38; 97:43.

105. If I understand him correctly, Y. Baer also expresses a similar view in this matter; see his article "Ha-Maṣabh ha-pulīṭī shel y'hūdē S'fārād," *Zion* 1:21–22.
106. On the other hand, I. Levin offers this explanation: an ethical plenitude in life fortifies one against the fear of death, an ethical existence permeated by fulfilled destinies can even slay death itself. Apparently the *nāgīd* did not have any apprehensions on this score, for in his social-feudal milieu these were apparently lacking for him; see "Sh'muēl ha-nāgīd," *Orlōgīn* 9 (1953):251. And on p. 252 he goes on to say that here we have a conspicuous instance of the triumph of life over religion, the triumph of true experience over an unstable environment, the triumph of art over a religion of rote.
107. This is the conjecture of Schirmann, 1, p. 76, whereas Sassoon is of the opinion that the first collection of verse in manuscript, which he published and which contains the poetical diary, is *Ben T'hillīm;* see his introduction, pp. xxxiv–xxxv. But some of his religious poems *(piy-yūṭīm* have been preserved, e.g., the *s'līḥa* (penitential prayer) "Asher na ṭah sh'ḥāḳīm," which was published in the *Diwan of Ibn Gabirol,* part 6, no. 89; cf. Harkavy, *Ḥadāshīm gam Y'shānīm,* no. 10, p. 25; Schirmann, 1, pp. 143–45; *Shīrīm ḥadāshīm min ha-g'nīta* pp. 161–62; Jarden, *Tarbīṣ* 31: 105; *Sinai* 56:318–19; and see *HUCA* 16:100.
108. Ratzaby, " 'Ben Mishlē' u 'Ben Ḳōhelet,' " *Tarbīṣ* 25:301–22.
109. I. Levin commented justifiably about this in his article: "Leḥēḳer "*Ben Mishlē* shel R. Sh'muēl ha-nāgīd," *Tarbīṣ* 29:156.
110. See S. Abramson in the preface to the edition of *Ben Mishlē* (Tel Aviv, 1948), pp. 15–16.
111. See S. Abramson in the preface to the edition of *Ben Ḳōhelet* (Tel Aviv, 1953), pp. 23–24.
112. According to R. Abraham Ibn Ezra's statement in his work *Y'sōd mōrā,* he wrote twenty-two books dealing with philology; but see Derenbourg, *Opuscules,* p. xxxv, who holds that the polemic writings against another grammarian are under discussion. However, Poznanski made convincing arguments for his assumption that what is being discussed is a lexicon containing twenty-two parts for the twenty-two letters of the alphabet; see his article "Les Ouvrages linguistiques de Samuel Hannaguid," *REJ* 57:254–55.
113. Excerpts of the lexicon were published from the Firkovitch manuscript by Kokowzow, pp. 205–24, and see the Russian segment of his book, pp. 87–88.
114. See Derenbourg, *Opuscules,* pp. xxvi–xxvii, and see Kokowzow, pp. 180–81 and especially 192.
115. *Dhakhīra,* 1, 2, p. 170.
116. The treatise was published in part (with a Spanish adaptation) by E. García Gomez, "Polémica religiosa entre Ibn Ḥazm e Ibn al-Nagrīla," *Al-Andalus* 4:1–28; and later in its entirety by Iḥsān 'Abbās, *Ar-Radd 'alā Ibn an-Naghrīla al-yahūdī wa-rasā 'il ukhrā* (Cairo, 1960), pp. 45–81. Giving due heed to what is reported in the Arabic sources about the cleverness of Samuel ha-lēvī, the editor, after some deliberation, reaches

the conclusion that it was not Samuel, but his son Joseph who wrote the polemic in which he showed the contradictions in the Koran; see his introduction, pp. 17–18. This opinion does indeed have merit, but the comment in the treatise of Ibn Ḥazm in the text published by 'Abbās, p. 47—"as we knew him from long ago"—refutes it. On p. 11 of the introduction the author mentions that Samuel ha-lēvī wrote a treatise on mathematics which is called *As-Sadjīḥ fī 'ulūm al-awā'il ar-riyāḍīya* (The Paved Road to Mathematical Studies), but does not indicate any source.

117. See Margaliyoth, *Hilkhōt ha-nāgīd,* pp. 26–27; and see ibid., pp. 31–32 regarding the time of its writing and pp. 191–217 for fragments of the treatise which have been preserved.
118. See ibid., pp. 21–22.
119. *Diwan,* no. 107, and Margaliyoth, op. cit., p. 23; pp. 68–69 give Margaliyoth's persuasive arguments that the work *M'bhō la-talmūd,* which is ascribed to Samuel ha-lēvī, was not written by him but by Samuel b. Ḥananiah ha-māgīd of Cairo. Like the halakhist and community leader of those days, he did not overlook the liturgy and he composed a list of the *hafṭārōt.* See *Sefer ha-eshkōl,* part 1, p. 67b. (ed. Albeck, 1 p. 180). According to the introduction to a manuscript of *The Book of Yōsīphōn,* he also made an abstract of this book; see Carmoly, *Isr. Annalen,* 1, p. 149. This is dubious, however, and perhaps what was meant was a manuscript in his extensive library.
120. *Dhakhīra,* 1, 2, p. 259., the poem, p. 268, and cf. Stern, op. cit., pp. 138–39.
121. See *Diwan,* ed. Haberman, part 3, pp. 41–42.
122. Memoirs, of 'Abdallāh, p. 32, and cf. Ibn 'Idhārī, p. 264.
123. Ibid., pp. 48, 130.
124. *P'ēr ha-dōr,* nos. 174, 175.
125. Ibid., no. 175.
126. See Schirmann, pp. 171–72.
127. See Stern, op. cit., p. 142, line 27.
128. *P'ēr ha-dōr,* no. 185, and see Harkavy in *M'asef Nidaḥīm* 1:225–26; Ōhel David, p. 727.
129. Abraham b. Dā'ūd, p. 56.
130. Ibid.
131. See the *muwashshaḥ* which Stern published, op. cit., p. 144, lines 3–4: "Who wrote by my hand a bill of divorcement and sent, as one does a dove, to offer incense on the altar," and line 9: "Aforetime, my friend, I was cut off from the palace." Because the writer of the poem was removed from the *nāgīd*'s circle, he writes (lines 10–11): "Therefore I said to him who possessed the true faith, at the Pomegranate City I chose to ring the bell," i.e., he sought to be accepted once again in Granada.
132. Stern published the poem, op. cit., pp. 141–42.
133. No. 30 and Joseph's reply: "He in whose heart is the religion of God and His Torah" is in Reifmann in *Ōṣar ṭōbh* 1881–1882, pp. 54–55, and according to Brody's surmise, p. 54. From the two poems it can be concluded that their authors lived in different cities; see the *nāgīd*'s poem, line 28, "And we made of our letters two live birds," and Joseph's poem, line 30: "In his might, he maintains a road to me, written in a

letter." The *nagīd*'s poem (line 17) gives the name of its recipient, Joseph, and (line 18) alludes to his occupation: "His mouth fashions balsam." It is not to be assumed that this Joseph is Joseph Ibn Ḳaprīl, as Stern conjectures, op. cit., p. 143, since this Joseph did not dwell in Granada.

134. Nos. 70–72. The poem: "Your friendship is poured into my heart" (no. 72) is, to judge from its contents and superscription, the *nāgīd's* reply to the verses of encouragement of Isaac Ibn Khalfōn after his dismissal, and it is not clear why A. Mirsky separates his poem and the aforementioned poems of Ibn Khalfōn; see his introduction to the *Diwan of Ibn Khalfōn,* pp. 14–15.
135. No. 78:28–34.
136. Nos. 64, 65.
137. No. 66. The poem published by Scheiber, Isaac Ibn Khalfōn's panegyric poem addressed to Samuel, *Acta Orientalia* (Academiae Scient. Hung.) 10:91ff., is not Ibn Khalfōn's, nor is it a panegyric for the glorification of Samuel ha-lēvī; see Schirmann, *Kirjath Sepher* 36:385; moreover, in line 7 the poet designates the man whom he addresses as the son of a *nāgīd!* It is hard to assume that Ibn Khalfōn wrote poems in connection with the marriage of his son, Joseph; cf. Schirmann, *Tarbīṣ* 7:295, regarding the time in which the poet lived.
138. See also the aforementioned poem by Ibn Khalfōn, no. 68:11.
139. No. 69.
140. No. 67.
141. Nos. 18–20 and see there, no. 18, line 2, the words of Ibn Khalfōn: "If Israel offers no help, it may perhaps come from an alien nation"; no. 20, line 10: "Forsake slander . . . turn aside from purveying treachery"; and cf. Schirmann in *Tarbīṣ* 7:300, and Haberman in his interpretations of the *Diwan,* part 2, p. 154.
142. Superscription to no. 143.
143. Harkavy, *T'shūbhōt ha-g'ōnīm,* nos. 127–29.
144. See no. 107, 44–45 and see S. A. Wertheimer, *Sefer Ḳōhelet Sh'lōmō* (Jerusalem, 1899), p. 71, and see Saadia b. Danān, 29b.
145. Harkavy, *Ḥadāshīm gam y'shānīm* in the supplement to the Hebrew ed. of graetz (S. P. Rabinowitz), 4, p. 5.
146. See in Neubauer, "Notice sur la lexicographie hēbraïque," *JA* (1862) 2:215; *Shīrat Yisrāel,* p. 104; Zunz, "Mitteilungen aus hebräischen Handschriften," *ZfHB* 19, p. 51, and the same passage complete in B. M. Lewin, "The Fourth Fragment from the Letter of Maṣliaḥ to R. Samuel ha-nāgīd," *Ginzē Ḳedem* 3:67–68; see also Assaf in *Kirjath Sepher* 2:184, 300, and see also R. M. Steinschneider, *Ar. Lit.,* p. 132. It is true that the sources do not state that the judge from Sicily tarried in Granada, but if it were not so, the *nāgīd* could have addressed himself to the men of the academy itself.
147. No. 56 and see Sassoon in the introduction, p. xxiii, and see in the body of the poem, line 6, where there is an allusion to the *gaon's* name.
148. No. 143. According to a letter published by Kamenetzky in his article "Deux lettres de l'époque des derniers exilarques," *REJ* 55:51–53, he was already the exilarch in 1021. According to Epstein the date should

read 1061 or 1071 (see *D'bhīr,* 1, p. 156), but his letters from the year 1036 have been found (see Assaf, *Tarbīṣ* 11:152–53) and from the year 1040 (see Mann, *Texts,* 1, pp. 180–81), and he is mentioned as the exilarch in 1045 (see Sēder ʿŌlām Zuṭa in Neubauer, *Med. Jew. Chr.,* 1, p. 178. There one reads 4807 of the Creation, the year 975 after the destruction of the Temple, the year 1356 of the Seleucid Era on the fifteenth of Elul, and inasmuch as the dates from the destruction of the Temple and the Seleucid Era concur, the date from the time of the Creation should be amended. Therefore one cannot be certain about the identity of the man to whom the poem was sent.

149. See Mann, *Texts,* 1, p. 386. It can be assumed that they also approved his title of *nāgīd;* see below, note 254.
150. Abraham b. Dā'ūd, p. 73.
151. No. 97.
152. The first poem, D. Yellin, "Shīrīm ḥadāshīm li-Sh'muēl ha-nāgīd," *Ha-T'ḳūfa* 26/27:606, and a more amended edition, D. Jarden, "Shīr t'hilla l'Rav Sh'muēl ha-nāgīd," *Studies in Bibliography and Booklore* (Cincinnati, 1962), 6:48ff.
153. Mann, *Texts,* 1, p. 386.
154. No. 95. His name is in line 11.
155. No. 1. Reifmann published a similar poem in *Ōṣār ṭōbh,* 1881–1882, p. 56. Regarding the origin of R. Ḥushiēl, cf. Menahem ha-Me'īrī, vol. 1; R. Solomon ha-Mē'īrī's account in *Bēt ha-b'ḥīra,* according to which R. Ḥushiēl was of Spanish origin, is refuted by G. D. Cohen, *PAAJR* 19: 130–31.
156. The letters were published by Firkovitch in *Ha-Karmel* 8 (1870):245–46; and see David Kaufmann, "Das Trostschreiben Samuel Hanagids an Chananel," *Magaz f.d. Wiss d. Jud.* 5:68–75 and the text in *Ōṣār ṭōbh,* 1879, pp. 64–68.
157. No. 52.
158. No. 6.
159. Abraham b. Dā'ūd, p. 73.
160. No. 71:7–9.
161. Dubler, pp. 13ff., 20, 58ff.
162. Ibid., p. 138.
163. See my article in *Zion* 28:51–52.
164. See R. Ricard, "Couraça et coracha," *Al-Andalus* 19:149ff., and especially p. 158.
165. The opinion that even in the time of the kings of the House of Zīrī this area was surrounded by a wall was expressed by Torres Balbás in his article in *Al-Andalus* 5:166. There are many proofs for this. First, one assumes that the Berber kings connected their city with the Jewish city by means of walls, for were it not so they would be laying their city, which was cut in two, open to attacks from all sides. The fact that the Great Mosque was built in this section of the city also supports this opinion. According to Lévi-Provençal, Bāb ar-ramla is already mentioned in the days of the Almoravids; see "Notes de toponomastique hispano-magribine," *Annales de l'Institute Oriental de l'Université d Alger* 2:221. But from what ʿAbdallāh states (see below) about the ratio of Moslems to Jews in

the city it can be concluded that this region was not heavily populated.

166. L. Seco de Lucena, "Las puertas de la cerca de Granada en el siglo XIV," *Al-Andalus* 7:450–51.
167. Ibid.
168. This gate is mentioned in connection with events in the 1140s; see Ibn al-Abbār in Dozy, *Notice sur quelques manuscrits arabes,* p. 209 and cf. Codera, *Decadencia y desaparición de los Almoravides en España* (Saragossa, 1899), p. 299. Concerning the wall of Jewish Granada, see Francisco Bermudez de Pedraza, *Antiguedad y excelencias de Granada* (Madrid, 1608), f., 8b; José y Manuel Oliver Hurtado, *Granada y sus monumentos árabes* (Malaga, 1875), pp. 204–5.
169. Torres Balbás, *Al-Andalus* 5:166.
170. According to the memoirs of 'Abdallāh, p. 32, the Jews were in the majority, but the prince undoubtedly exaggerates. He was hostile to the Jews and was attempting to show the influence they acquired in the days of Samuel ha-lēvī. According to accounts by Torres Balbás, the inhabitants totaled 26,000; see his article "Extensión y demografía de las ciudades hispanomusulmanas," *Studia Islamica* 3:56, but there is practically no doubt that a segment of its area was partly inhabited.
171. Luys de Marmol Carvajal, *Historia del rebelión y castigo de los moriscos del reyno de Granada* (Málaga, 1600), f. 4b; Simone de Argote, *Nuevos paseos . . . por Granada* (Granada, 1807), 1, p. 98. According to these writers, the Jews did not inhabit the most westerly (i.e., the lowest) section of the city, which is south of the Darro River, but they apparently give data on the settlement of the city at the end of the fifteenth century.

    Even centuries after the expulsion of the Jews the local tradition also places their quarter in the high eastern sector of the city south of the Darro River, in the vicinity of the Church of San Cecilio; e.g., see F. Valladar, *Guía de Granada* (Granada, 1906), p. 472; and these neighborhoods did indeed remain outside the city's wall, built and strengthened by the kings of the House of Zīrī. From this it should be concluded that this tradition belongs to the later Middle Ages or to the early epoch preceding the rule of the Berbers (during which, for security, the Jews dwelt near the fortress on the hill), since it is quite likely that after the erection of the new fortifications the Jews abandoned the outside quarters (those in the vicinity of the church) and moved inside the walls. But even if we assume that in the eleventh century the Jews numbered more than they did at the end of the Moslem rule, there is no proof that Jews lived in the western end of the city, south of the Darro. It is almost certain that in southern Granada there also were sites between the walls within which were no houses.
172. L. Egúilaz, "Arqueología granadina," *La Alhambra* 7 (1904):379.
173. M. Gómez Moreno, *Guía de Granada* (Granada, 1891), pp. 200–1.
174. See Lévi-Provençal, *Hespéris* 10:120; and cf. Torres Balbás, "La supuesta puerta de los panderos y los puentes de la Granada musulmana," *Al-Andalus* 14:419ff.
175. Al-Makkarī, 2, p. 147.
176. Dozy, introduction to Ibn 'Idhārī, p. 91 (102).
177. Abraham b. Dā'ūd, p. 71.

178. See Memoirs of 'Abdallāh, p. 51, and also the *Diwan Samuel ha-nāgīd,* no. 32, in the superscription concerning the physician Abū Madyan, who was undoubtedly a Jew.
179. *Sha'arē Ṣedeḳ,* part #2, no. 22; Harkavy, *T'shūbhōt ha-g'ōnīm,* no. 161, and cf. p. 391.
180. The beginning of Abraham Ibn 'Ezrā's *Sefer ha-moznayim* and his place in the sequence of authors mentioned, testifies as to his time; and cf. M. Steinschneider, *Ar. Lit.,* p. 143.
181. No. 53 and see line 16; from this line it also appears that he was personally acquainted with Rabbi David and it is therefore unlikely that the poem was written in honor of R. David b. R. Saadya in Saragossa (see about him p. 251, this volume). Further on (line 18) he says: "Why should you dwell at the end of the earth?"—an allusion to Spain.
182. See in *ha-Shīra ha-y'tōma,* Schirmann, 1, p. 175, line 47.
183. *Shīrat Yisrāel,* p. 69.
184. See F. Cantera, "Lapida hebraica epistógrafa de Lucena," *Sefarad* 19:137ff., particularly p. 142.
185. S. Assaf, "M'ḳōrōt l'ḳōrōt ha-y'hūdim bi-S'pārād," *Zion* 6:33–34.
186. T.-S. 12.341; see Mann, *Jews,* 2, p. 253; Assaf, op. cit., p. 37.
187. *Shīrat Yisrāel,* p. 69.
188. *Shīrat Yisrāel,* p. 72. The author does not state that he is from Lucena, but reports that he was a friend of the rabbi of the city at that time (see below), whence it follows that at least for a certain period he sojourned in that city.
189. Ibid., p. 105, and this points to it being pronounced Gayyāt, as Goitein says in *Tarbīṣ* 24:468.
190. *Sha'rē simḥa,* part 1, p. 15.
191. See ibid., p. 29.
192. Abraham b. Dā'ūd, p. 60. According to R. Samuel Algazi, in his book *Tōl'dōt Adam* (see *CB,* pp. 1110–11), he was born in 1038; however, Abraham b. Dā'ūd's account saying that "the two *négīdīm,* R. Samuel and his son R. Joseph, honored and respected him," etc., does not confirm this but indicates an earlier date of birth.
193. See Bamberger in the introduction to *Sha'arē simḥa,* p. 4; Horodetzky in the *Encyclopedia Judaica* 7, col. 42; Assaf in *Tarbīṣ* 3:213–14, 339.
194. *Ḥuṭ ha-m'shulash,* col. 3, no. 32; *Sha'rē t'shūbha* (Leipzig, 1858), no. 93; H. M. Horowitz, *Tōratan shel rīshōnīm* (Frankfort on the Main, 1882) part 2, pp. 27–28; Wertheimer, *Ginzē Yerushalayim* (Jerusalem, 1902), 2, p. 2b–7a (according to him and also *Sha'arē t'shūbha,* no. 202—it should be thus and not 201—is a response to R. Isaac Gayyāt, but this is not so; see *Sha'arē simḥa,* part 1, p. 59. One should also question what he says about a quotation in the collection *T'shūbhōt ha-Rambam* [Leipzig, 1859], no. 201).
195. See in the list published by Adler-Broydé, "An ancient Bookseller's catalogue," *JQR* 13:53 and cf. ibid., p. 58 (Poznanski's doubts, ibid., p. 325., are unnecessary).
196. See what he wrote contra R. Sh'rīra Gaon, *Sha'arē simḥa* part 1, p. 114, and contra R. Amram Gaon, op. cit., p. 59, and see op. cit., in "Yisḥāḳ y'ranēn," note 132.

197. See H. S. Taubes, *Likkūṭē R. Yisḥāk b. Y'hūda Ibn Gayyāt* (Zurich, 1952), pp. 17, 19, 26, 35, 39, 59, and particularly p. 31, and see, too, "Hilkhōt P'sāḥīm" in *Sha'arē simḥa,* part 2, p. 83 and further J. Derenbourg, "Die Schriften des Isaak ben Juda Giath," *Wiss. Zeitschr. f. Jüd. Theol.* 5 (1844): 398.
198. See Margaliyoth in the introduction to *Hilkhōt ha-nāgīd,* pp. 37–40.
199. See David de Estella in Neubauer, *Med. Jew. Chr.,* p. 230. *Hilkhōt Pesaḥ* was published a second time with a commentary by D. B. Zomber (Berlin, 1864).
200. His commentaries are cited in the book *Mikhlōl yōfī* by R. Solomon b. Melekh. See on B'rēshīt 49:11, Isaiah 16:8.
201. The translation (without the commentary) of Ibn Gayyāt was published by Jacobus Loevy, *Libri Kohelet versio Arabica* (Leyden, 1884). The translation and commentary were printed by Rabbi J. D. Ḳāfaḥ in his *Ḥāmēsh m'gīllōth* (Jerusalem, 1962), pp. 155ff. as a work by Saadya Gaon. Ḳāfaḥ did not know that Loevy had published the translation.
202. MS. Bodl., Neubauer 2333[2], f. 75a, and see also f. 93b, 1:6 of *An-nafs ash-shahwānīya al-mughtadnīya.*
203. F. 139a, lines 13–14.
204. *Ash-shuyūkh,* ff. 56b, line 5, 60b, line 8, 62b, line 7, 64b, line 8 from the bottom, 67a, line 9 from the bottom, 72a, line 11, 74b, last line, 75b, line 7 from the bottom, 83b, line 1, 86a, line 9, 87a, line 7 from the bottom, etc.
205. In the inventory of a private library from the Geniza there appears among the rest: *Djuz' fīhi sharḥ Ḳōheleth bi-ma'nā* by Isaac b. Gayyāt, MS. Bodl. Heb. d. 76f. 53.
206. A poem in the bridegroom's honor in *Sha'ar ha-shīr,* p. 16.
207. Taḥk'mōnī, p. 39
208. *Shīrat Yisrāel,* p. 72
209. See *Sh'ēlōt u-t'shūbhōt R. Solomon b. Adret,* part 1, no. 538; *Tashbēṣ,* part 1, no. 92.
210. A list of his liturgical poems is in Zunz, *Ritus* 2:109ff.; Derenbourg, op. cit., pp. 401–2; Haberman, *Mizrākh u-ma'rābh* 3 (1929): 352–53; and cf. S. H. Kook, ibid., pp. 456–57. Some of his poems were published by S. Sachs, pp. 11–17; Wertheimer, *Ginzē Yerushalayim, 2* f. 20a f.; Dukes, *Litbl. d. Or.,* 5, col. 345–47; *Sha'ar ha-shīr,* pp. 16–21; Brody, *Mibhḥar ha-shīr,* pp. 114–20; J. Marcus, *American Jewish Yearbook,* 1931, pp. 220–26; S. Bernstein, *Ḥōrebh* 2 (1936):256–57 (most dubious is the identification of the author of the poem which he published there, pp. 253–54); *Tarbīṣ* 10:9; *Tarbīṣ* 11:295–325; *HUCA* (Hebrew section) 16:107–29, *Talpioth* 5 (1952):493–532; J. Mendelsohn, *Ḥōrebh* 9:50; J. Ratzaby, *Sinai* 14 (1944):134–204, *Sinai* 28 (1951):175 (doubtful), 56 (1965):21–51; Schirmann, 1, pp. 301–26; A. M. Haberman, *Ha-Areṣ, Nīsān* 14, 1961; D. Jarden, *Hadoar* 40 (1961):351–52, 671.
211. *A'māl al-a'lām,* pp. 25, 263.
212. Abraham b. Dā'ūd, p. 69. The version al-Ḳabrī is found in ed. Mantua, 1514.
213. Ibn 'Idhārī, pp. 113, 133, 264; *Al-Iḥāṭa,* p. 440; *A'māl al-a'lām,* p. 139; the passage in Ibn al-Athīr, 9, p. 191, concerning the yielding of Jaén to

Zuhair, on which Priety Vives relies (p. 25), is entirely corrupt. At that time the eunuch Khairān, who is mentioned in that passage, reigned in Almería, and instead of Zuhair it should read Muḥammad b. 'Abdalmalik al-'Āmirī. This prince was a son of al-Ḳāsim's wife, and she, no doubt, prompted her husband to appoint her son as governor of Jaén; it is also reported by Arabic historians that she gave her son the financial support needed to mobilize an army. There are two traditions about the duration of Muḥammad b. 'Abdalmalik's rule over Jaén: the tradition in Ibn 'Idhārī that he remained the governor of the province until his death; and a tradition that in 1021 he also became the governor of Murcia and Orihuela, but was driven from there in 1021 by Khairān and went elsewhere in Andalusia; see *A'māl al-a'lām,* pp. 223–24. This implies that Khairān then seized control of Jaén and ruled there to his death. But this is unreasonable because Ḥabbūs, who annexed the region of Jaén to his kingdom at the outset of his rule, was an ally of Zuhair, who would surely not acquiesce in the seizure of an important province in his kingdom or associate with the king who seized it.

214. See J. Martinez de Mazas, *Retrato natural de la ciudad y termino de Jaén* (Jaén, 1794), pp. 143–44, 284–85.
215. Responsa Alfasi, no. 120.
216. S. D. Goitein, "Autografim mi-yādō shel R. Y'hūda ha-lēvī," *Tarbīṣ* 25: 405.
217. J. Elyash, "Y'dī'ōt 'al Ereṣ Yisraēl mē-ha-mē'a ha-aḥat 'esrē, *S'fūnōt* 2 (1958):24; Documentos, no. 3.
218. See *P'ēr ha-dōr,* no. 173ff. (to 182?), and see Derenbourg, op. cit., p. 397, and Moses Steinschneider, *Ar. Lit.*, p. 137.
219. T.-S. 20.122, 20.4, cf. 20.9 (from the year 1047); Responsa Alfasia, *Sh-'ēlōt u-t'shūbhōt,* R. Isaac Alfāsī, MS. Bodl. 2658, f. 72b, no. 28; see in Cowley's catalog, and this responsum is among the published ones, no. 224, except that there the superscription preceding it was omitted.
220. *Ar-Rauḍ al-mi'ṭār,* pp. ٤٤ / ٤٥ Dubler, p. 67, and see pp. 61, 64.
221. Una crónica anónima de 'Abd al-Raḥmān III al-Nāṣir, p. 84.
222. Dozy, *Recherches,* 1, p. 354.
223. See Ibn 'Idhārī, p. 127 (even Guadix, west of it, belongs to the kingdom of Almería); *A'māl al-a'lām,* p. 264.
224. See M. Gomez Moreno, "Baño de la judería de Baza," *Al-Andalus* 12: 151–55; *Ars Hispanica,* vol. 3: M. Gomez Moreno, *El arte español hasta los Almohades, arte mozárabe* (Madrid, 1951), p. 265. For the Santiago Church, see Luis Magaña Visbal, *Baza histórica* (Baza, 1927), p. 319.
225. No. 137.
226. The date of the "invitation" is in Anonymous, p. 295: the month of Radjab 445 A. H. (October-November 1053) and in another passage, p. 313, he states that one of the princes was set free in 449 A. H., (i.e., 1057); Ibn 'Idhārī, p. 271, asserts that the three princes were in prison for "a long time." Dozy, 3, pp. 57–58, was not acquainted with these sources.
227. No. 138.
228. No. 140 only has the superscription. The poem itself is in *Ben Ḳohelet,* no. 138. Cf. Ibn 'Idhārī, p. 272, and Anonymous, p. 296; and see also

the superscription to no. 138, which states that "the agreement was nullified" between the Berber princes and al-Muʿtaḍid.

229. Nos. 141 and 142 and see, in particular, 141:9, 142:26, 30, 32, 34.
230. No. 143.
231. Nos. 144–45. In the opinion of Schirmann, *Milḥāmōt,* p. 371, the campaign in the region north of Málaga was linked with a war against this principality, but this is dubious. From what is reported in the Arabic sources, it appears that Bādīs was not hostile to the ruler of Málaga of that period: Idrīs (II) b. Yaḥyā (surnamed al-ʿĀlī), and his successor; see above, pp. 103 and 105. Perhaps the reference is to those rebeling against the government.
232. Concerning the date of his death, we have two authentic items of information. One is in *Shīrat Yisrāel,* p. 67: that he died when he was sixty-three years old which was in 1055/1056. The second item of information is in Ibn Ṣāʿid, p. 90: 448 of the Hegira, which began on March 21, 1056 and ended on March 9, 1057. Supporting information consists in the statement by his son Elyāsāf in the introduction to *Ben Mishlē,* which his father had ordered him to copy when he was six and a half years old; he testifies there that he himself was born on 23 Marḥeshvan, 4806. From this it can be seen that Samuel ha-lēvī was still alive in the spring of 1052. The superscription over the poem—no. 145—proves that in the winter of 1055/1056 he was still alive. It is therefore necessary to amend Abraham b. Dāʾūd's date, 4815; it should be 4816. For the incorrect dates of the Arabic writers, see Graetz, 6, note 3 (pp. 347–48); and against the view of Sassoon that Samuel ha-lēvī did not die before 1057/1058, see Schirmann, op. cit., pp. 372–73.
233. *Al-Iḥāṭa,* pp. 447, 448.
234. Published by Reifmann in *Ōṣār ṭōbh,* 1882/1883, p. 75. He also wrote a Hebrew elegy—"Heylili Tora"—the beginning of which was published by Margaliyoth in the introduction to the *Hilkhōt ha-nāgīd,* p. 67.
235. See *HUCA* 3:287.
236. *Al-Iḥāṭa,* p. 447.
237. Memoirs of ʿAbdallāh, pp. 37–38. Concerning Joseph's age, see what he himself says about the date of his birth, in Sassoon, p. 1, namely, that he was born on Tuesday, Tishrī 11, 4796, which is the same as 11 Dhu 'l-Ḳaʿda, 426. The Hebrew date corresponds to September 16, 1035, which was a Tuesday, but there is an error of one day in the Moslem date, since it parallels September 17, 1035; it should, no doubt, be amended to 10 Dhu 'l-Ḳaʿda.
238. Memoirs of ʿAbdallāh, p. 38; *al-Iḥāṭa,* op. cit.; Fatḥ b. Khāḳān, "Ḳalāʾid al-ʿiḳyān," in *Abbad.,* 1, p. 51.
239. *Al-Iḥāṭa,* pp. 441–42.
240. Concerning the end of Ḥammūdite rule in Málaga and its annexation to the kingdom of Granada there is varied information in some of the works of the Arabic historians. According to al-Marrākushī, p. 48—and cf. Ibn al-Athīr, 9, p. 108—no prince was crowned in place of Idrīs II. But in this respect his account is not to be relied upon, since here al-Ḥumaid ī's tradition comes to a halt; see in his work, p. 34. This tradition knows nothing about the unsuccessful attempt of Idrīs b. Yaḥyā (b. Idrīs), which

preceded the renewal of his rule. About this Idrīs and about al-Musta'lī, see Ibn 'Idhārī, pp. 218, 266; Ibn Khaldūn, 4, p. 155; al-Maḳḳarī, 1, p. 284, and in the work of these historians can be found the date of the annexation of Málaga to the kingdom of Granada: 449 A. H. (March 10, 1057–February 27, 1058).

241. Published by H. Schirmann in the daily, *Ha-Āreṣ,* the sixteenth of Tishrī, 5700 (1940). It is certain that the king of Seville is meant, and this also corresponds with the verse concerning the war in the land of the rivers, for the central region of the kingdom of Seville spread out around the estuary of the Guadalquivir, where there are many rivers and riverbeds. Also the assertion by R. Moses Ibn Ezra about Joseph—that he wrote poems in which "he lauded heroism in war"—points to his military experience; see *Shīrat Yisrāel,* p. 68.
242. *Dhakhīra,* 1, 2, p. 270. It is true that the Arabic writer interchanges Joseph with his father even in the same passage, but in light of what is told about him there, there is no doubt that the reference here is to Joseph; the proof is that in Samuel's poems there is no mention of a visit to Cordova, a matter he surely would have noted.
243. See a poem in honor of Samuel and his son Joseph published by Stern in *Zion* 15:144, lines 13–16. It is clear that Samuel was still alive at that time; the poet would have mentioned otherwise.
244. See Moses Steinschneider in *He-Ḥālūṣ* 2:61, and cf. R. Abraham Ibn Ezra on Numbers 22:7 and see Herzog in *MGWJ 77:137–38.*
245. Abraham b. Dā'ūd, p. 57.
246. See *Shīrat Yisrāel,* loc. cit. A. M. Haberman published three hymns which in his opinion are those of Joseph, but there is no evidence for this; see *Ōṣār Y'hūdē S'fārād* 4:44–45.
247. *Dhakhīra,* 1, 2, p. 270.
248. See in Mann, *Texts,* 1, p. 247.
249. *Shīrat Yisrāel,* loc. cit.
250. See note 143 above.
251. Abraham b. Dā'ūd, pp. 44ff. Epstein casts doubt on this passage; see his notes to the article by Tykoczinski in *D'bhīr* 1:156. At most he inclines to deduce from it that one son of the *nāsī* reached Granada; see ibid. It is true that redactors have dealt with the passage, but there is no reason to negate the information in its essence, inasmuch as that line which speaks of the coming of two sons of the exilarch appears in every manuscript.
252. See the letter in Mann, *HUCA,* 3:pp. 286–87.
253. See in his letter to Joseph, published by Mann, *Jews,* 2, p. 221–22.
254. See in Mann, in *HUCA,* loc. cit. and cf. Goitein in *Zion* 27:23.
255. Abraham b. Dā'ūd, loc. cit.; *Al-Iḥāṭa,* p. 447.
256. Saadya b. Danān, f. 29b, and see the letter published by Reifmann in *Ōṣār Ṭōbh,* 1881/1882, pp. 45–46, and also see the *Diwan of Ibn Gabirol,* part 1, no. 32, line 28, concerning the tarrying of his son Jacob in Granada.
257. See Abraham b. Dā'ūd, p. 57, and Saadya b. Danān, loc. cit.
258. See Memoirs of 'Abdallāh, p. 130, where reference is made to his uncle's house which was located there; it is reasonable to believe that not only

he came there, especially as Joseph's foes always spoke about his palace, see op. cit., p. 47, where one of Joseph's enemies tells the king that he built himself a palace more beautiful than his, and see below.

259. Al-Makkarī, 2, p. 263. It is not stated there that Joseph is the one meant, but the "Jewish vizier of Granada." However, since the poet later went to Almería and composed poetry in honor of one of the sons of the king who ruled from 1051, and it is clearly stated there that he was loyal to the Jewish vizier after his death, it is reasonable to assume that Joseph is meant, and cf. Munk, *Notice,* pp. 104ff.

Many important scholars assert that Joseph was outstanding because of his unpretentious mode of living as compared with that of the Berber nobles. These scholars were apparently misled by Dozy who had read in the biography of Joseph by Lisān ad-dīn that he was handsome and eminently ascetic (حاد الزهد), see his introduction to Ibn 'Idhārī, p. 90. The correct version is: that he was a man of keen perception (حاد الذهن), see Ibn 'Idhārī, p. 264 and also *Al-Iḥāṭa,* p. 447. Had the Arabic writer depicted Joseph as an ascetic, he promptly and obviously would be contradicting himself.

260. Ibn Sā'īd, *Al-Mughrib fī ḥula al-Maghrib* (Cairo, 1953–1955), 2, p. 114 (where the son is replaced by the father.), and see Dozy, *Recherches, 1,* appendix xxvi. If we believe that the polemic work against which Ibn Ḥazm issued a rejoinder was written by Samuel, then the distinction must be drawn between theological arguments and what Moslems deemed contempt. According to Ibn Sā'īd, Joseph asserted that he would write a new Koran in the form of cinctured verses to be played and sung in public. Considering other statements about Joseph in various sources, there is no basis for disqualifying Ibn Sā'īd's account.

261. *Dhakhīra,* 1, 2, pp. 269–70. The Arabic writer depends on a Cordovan vizier who was well acquainted with the rulers of Granada through his close contact with them. Ibn Bassām's assertion that Joseph wrote a book against Ibn Ḥazm is apparently an error (the polemic of his father Samuel is replaced by the action of his son; and see note above).

262. Memoirs of 'Abdallāh, pp. 38–39.

263. Op. cit., p. 41.

264. Op. cit., pp. 39–40.

265. Op. cit., pp. 41–42.

266. Op. cit., p. 40; Ibn 'Idhārī, p. 265; the passage is cited by Lisān ad-dīn, *Al-Iḥātā,* p. 442, and Dozy copied it from there in the introduction to *Al-Bayān,* pp. 83–84. The date in Ibn 'Idhārī is 458 which began on December 25, 1063 (although in an earlier passage, p. 261, he says that Boluggīn died in 457 (1065) which is no doubt an error, see below). According to this writer, the prince died immediately after the party, but preference should be given to the account of his son 'Abdallāh who states that he died two days later.

267. Anonymous, pp. 313–14; Ibn Khaldūn in *Abbad.,* 2, pp. 209–10; the revolt in Ronda was already described by Dozy in the introduction to *Al-Bayān,* pp. 92ff., in a manner similar to the story, as told above; he correctly conjectures the date of Boluggīn's death.

268. The first source of this account is Ibn Ḥayyān, a contemporary; see *Al-I*

ḥāṭa, pp. 444ff., and see there p. 445 that the vizier who opposed the king was Joseph b. Ismā'īl. In the text which Dozy had before him, the word "ibn" was omitted and he therefore decided to erase one of the two names, erasing that of Joseph. In this manner, and based on other considerations as well, he reached the conclusion that the reference was to Samuel. Aside from the mention of Joseph's name, the description of Bādīs's plan in reaction to the removal of the Berber prince in Ronda, leaves no doubt who is being referred to—Samuel or his son.

269. The Arabic sources are not unified on the date of the conquest of Málaga by the army of Seville. It is certain that it occurred after the death of Ismā'īl, the son of al-Mu'Taḍid, in 1063, because an officer, who by then had fled Seville, filled an important role in the war of Málaga, see below. This is a *terminus a quo.*

Ibn 'Idhārī, p. 273, assigns Ibn Bassām's account of the conquest of Málaga (without mentioning his name, but see *Abbad.,* 1, p. 301) to the year 459 of the *hidjra* (December 3, 1065/November 21, 1066), whereas al-Bakrī—who asserts that he was an eyewitness to these events—gives the date as 459 of the *hidjra* (beginning November 22, 1066). However, to make these data concur with Prince 'Abdallāh's account of the actions of the officer an-Nāya against Joseph, we must give preference to Ibn Bassām and assume that the incursion into Málaga by the Sevillian army occurred at the beginning of 1066.

270. Fatḥ b. Khāḳān in *Abbad.,* 1, p. 52, where it is stated that an-Nāya already was the commander of the army of Granada which freed Málaga. Even more creditable, however, is the account of 'Abdallāh, pp. 46ff., from which it emerges that an-Nāya had not yet attained this status at that time.

271. Memories of 'Abdallāh, pp. 48–49; *Al-Iḥāṭa,* p. 448.

272. *Ben Ḳōhelet,* no. 403:26–27.

273. *Diwan,* no. 76, 16.

274. No. 94:20.

275. Memoirs of 'Abdallāh, pp. 50–51; *Dhakhīra,* 1, 2, pp. 270–71; Ibn 'Idhārī, p. 226. One should not attribute great importance to the report of Ibn Bassām, since his inclination to exaggerate is clearly visible in this passage. According to him, Joseph received great sums from the king of Almería and had the intention of crowning him king instead of Bādīs. Even according to 'Abdallāh, Joseph's plan was to hand the kingdom of Granada over to the king of Almería to guarantee his own position; Ibn Īdhārī states explicitly that his plan was to become governor of Almería and to establish a Jewish state. See Lévi-Provençal in *Encyclopedia of Islam* 4:1231; *Pérès,* p. 270.

276. Memoirs of 'Abdallāh, p. 49

277. Memoirs of 'Abdallāh, p. 54. Based on this information and a poem by Solomon Ibn Gabirol describing the palace of a wealthy man, the art historian, Bargebuhr, argued that Joseph designed the main buildings of the Alhambra and was even able to erect them together with their embellishments, see F. Bargebuhr, "The Alhambra Palace of the Eleventh Century," *Journal of the Warburg and Courtauld Institutes* 19 (1956): 192–258. This scholar stresses that there are in the Alhambra block,

even outside the "ḳaṣaba," walls which emphasize the mode of building in the era of the Berber kings.

He assumes that the famous Pool of the Lions was given by Joseph, the location in which it is currently found. The twelve lions are a combination of the twelve oxen of the molten sea in the Temple (1 Kings, 7:25) and of the twelve lions before the royal throne of Solomon (1 Kings, 10:20), and the replacement of the oxen by lions symbolized that the dynasty of Joseph was more exalted than the preceding dynasties. It is Bargebuhr's opinion that Samuel and his son were influenced by the messianic idea and thought the messiah of the House of Levi would emerge from their family.

H. Schirmann has already noted that there is no connection between the Ibn Gabirol's poem and the structures erected by the *nāgīd* Joseph in the Alhambra area, inasmuch as the poet died a few years before the last days of Joseph (twelve years earlier, in my opinion see below p. 000). On the other hand, the Arabic author who discusses this matter explicitly states that Joseph was then occupied in their construction to prepare a refuge for himself, see in *Kirjath Sepher* 33:256. On the basis of this information, it must be assumed that Joseph did not succeed in finishing the construction of the magnificent palace and adorning it with *objets d'art*.

Bargebuhr's conjecture of the messianic dreams of Samuel ha-lēvī and his son is based on an error in one of Goldziher's articles: "Renseignements de source musulmane sur la dignité de Resch-Galuta," *REJ* 8:125. It is stated there that according to Ibn Ḥazm, Samuel, in a controversy with him, held that the verse in Genesis 49:10—The sceptre shall not depart from Judah, nor the ruler's staff from between his feet—was fulfilled in him. But in Goldziher's article in (Kobak's) *Jes'hurun*, where he published the text (see above note 35) which Bargebuhr had not seen, this passage does not appear. In truth, Ibn Ḥazm did not attribute this argument to Samuel ha-lēvī; see in his work, *Al-Fiṣal*, 1, pp. 152ff. However, Schirmann followed Goldziher and writes that according to Ibn Ḥazm, the *nāgīd* stated "that the verse concerning Shiloh referes to him," see "Samuel Hannagid, the Man, the Soldier, the Politician," *Journal of Jewish Studies* 13 (1951):101.

278. Memoirs of 'Abdallāh, loc. cit.
279. Op. cit., p. 49.
280. The poem was published with a French translation by Dozy, *Recherches*, 1, p. 282, and appendix xxvi (the French translation only is in his *Histoire*, 3, pp. 71–72) and later by García Gómez in his collection of poems: *Abu Isḥaq de Elvira, texto árabe de su "Diwan"* (Madrid, 1925), no. 25.
281. Regarding Joseph's hiding place, preference should be given to 'Abdallāh's account, p. 54, in which it is asserted that he fled to the king's palace. According to Ibn 'Idhārī Joseph hid in his home.

The date of the riots—Saturday, 9 Tēbhet, 4907, i.e., December 30, 1066—is supplied in authentic Jewish sources: Abraham b. Dā'ūd, p. 27; *Shīrat Yisrāel*, p. 69; 20 Tēbhet is an understandable scribal error with the shape of the Hebrew letters in mind. Ibn 'Idhārī, pp. 266–75, gives the date 459 of the *hidjra* (beginning November 22, 1066), and similarly

Ibn Khaldūn, 4, pp. 160–61. Ibn Ḥayyān, who speaks of Samuel ha-lēvī but means Joseph, gives the date: the second decade of the month of Muḥarram 459 (December 2–December 11, 1066), see *Al-Iḥaṭa,* p. 447, whereas 'Abdallāh, loc. cit., states that this was on Saturday, the tenth of Ṣafar (without mentioning the year). But the tenth of Ṣafar 459 was on Sunday, December 31, 1066, and it must be assumed that he well remembered the day in the week and erred concerning the day in the month; we thus find that his testimony corresponds with that of Abraham b. Dā'ūd. That date—10 Ṣafar 459—is also found in an abridgement of *Al-Iḥāṭa,* see Dozy, *Recherches,* 1, appendix xxvi. Along-side the correct date, i.e., 459 of the *hidjra,* there are in the Arabic sources—even in those that give the correct date—erroneous dates: 465 or 469 of the *hidjra* (1072/1073 or 1075/1076), see *A'māl al-a'lām,* p. 267; 480 of the *hidjra* (1087/1088) in *Al-Iḥāṭa* according to the text in Dozy's introduction to *Al-Bayān,* pp. 83–84 and apparently it should read 458 inasmuch as there also exists the version فى سنة ثمان , see *al-Iḥāṭa,* p. 442, in the notes. Here the word خمسين no doubt was omit-ted and it appears that the reference is to 1066.

According to the account by 'Abdallāh—which is the most authentic source—the riots began on the night of the Sabbath, but since the other sources—and the Jewish sources primarily—do not state that the riots occurred at night, it can be concluded that Joseph was slain that night and the riots took place the next day.

According to Ibn 'Idhārī, pp. 275–76, the number of slain amounted to three hundred; and according to *Dhakhīra,* 1, 2, p. 272, four thousand. Abraham b. Dā'ūd asserts that the entire Granadan community was slain, whereas the author of *Shēbheṭ Y'hūda* puts it at more than fifteen hundred families, see ed. *Shōḥaṭ,* p. 22 and cf. his notes, p. 169. It is beyond any doubt that all of these accounts are grossly exaggerated.

CHAPTER THREE

1. Schirmann, *Shīrīm ḥadāshīm min ha-g'nīta,* pp. 190–91.
2. *Shībheṭ Y'hūdā* (ed. Shoḥaṭ), p. 22; cf. the editor's notes, p. 169.
3. Memoirs of 'Abdallāh, p. 55.
4. *Shīrat Yisrāel,* p. 105 and cf. Schirmann in *Sēfer Assaf* (Jerusalem, 5713), p. 498. It should not be assumed that what is meant is the conflict between King 'Abdallāh and the Jews of Lucena about which he tells in his book of memoirs, pp. 130ff. This dispute was connected with the outlays involved in the erection of fortifications with which 'Abdullāh was occupied after the siege of the fortress of Aledo, p. 131, 1, 4; and cf. pp. 114ff., and 120. This siege occurred in the summer of 1088 and the erection of the fortifications began in the summer of 1089, see A. Huici, "El sitio de Aleda," *MEAH* 3:42–46. Especially note that R. Isaac Ibn Gayyāt died in 4849 (1089), see Abraham b. Dā'ūd, p. 60 (the month is not mentioned), and according to the account by R. Moses Ibn Ezra (quoted above) of Ibn Gayyāt planned to write of the tribulations which befell Alyusāna (Lucene) "and what God had brought to pass there-after."

5. Al-Maḳḳarī 2, p. 263. A satirical poem in which, it seems, an enemy of the Jews expressed his rejoicing over the calamity which befell them, is included in the book of Ibn Ṣā'id, *Al-Mughrib fī ḥula al-Maghrib* 2, p. 115. The Arabic author who ascribed the poem to Joseph's son (he interchanged him, incidentally, with his father), understood the poem in literal terms and believed that it was an elegy—which it is not—see S.M. Stern in the memorial volume of H. Peri, *Romanica et Occidentalia,* p. 257.
6. Abraham b. Dā'ūd, p. 60; *Shīrat Yisraēl,* p. 68.
7. Abraham b. Dā'ūd, pp. 44ff. Not only Jews fled from Granada at the time of the riot, but also others who were intimates of Joseph, see, e.g., in the Memoirs of 'Abdallāh, p. 66, concerning the Christian official, Abu 'r-Rabī'.
8. Responsa Alfasi, no. 228.
9. Op. cit., no. 131.
10. Documentos, no. 4. As was already noted by Schechter, *JQR* 12:112, the three signatures on the document indicate that they are the signatures of members of the court, and from this it is reasonable to surmise that the man went there in a matter concerning a levirate marriage.
11. Dubler, pp. 34, 60, 61; and see also Serjeant, *Ars Islamica* 15/16; 35.
12. See Ibn Bashkuwāl, 1, pp. 107, 114, 123, 286, 294.
13. Concerning the conquest of Morón see in Anonymous, p. 296, and for the conquest of Arcos see Ibn 'Idhārī, pp. 271ff., cf. with Anonymous, p. 294. It is true that Anonymous maintains that this occurred in 461 of the *hidjra.* On the other hand, he writes that this principality was established in 402 and lasted fifty-six years, from this the date given by Ibn 'Idhārī, i.e., 458 (1066), is correct.
14. See my article "The Number of Jews in Moslom Spain, *Zion* 28:53–54.
15. See Munk, *Notice,* p. 97.
16. No. 29:25, 55.
17. Ibn 'Abdūn, p. 239.
18. Simonot, pp. 655ff.
19. Abraham b. Dā'ūd, p. 63. To be sure, the Jewish historian speaks of Ibn 'Abbād (thus, and not Abū Abbād), but there is almost no doubt that the reference is to al-Mu'taḍid and not to his father, the kadi. Those who supported Boluggīn had fled from Granada in 1039 and the kadi, the first of the Banū 'Abbād dynasty, died shortly thereafter, in 1042.
20. Al-Djāḥiz, "At-Tabaṣṣur fi 't -tidjāra," *RAAD* 12. Although this treatise dates from his time, it is erroneously ascribed to al-Djāḥiz (i.e., the ninth century).
21. Ibn 'Abdūn, loc. cit. The question of whether it is permissible to eat meat slaughtered by Jews is one which Moslem jurists of the Mālikite school discussed in the first half of the ninth century; the mention of the matter in two treatises on the ḥisba, which were written in Moslem Spain in that epoch, proves that the reference is to a practical problem.
22. T.-S. 13 J 17[4], see Mann, *Jews* 2, p. 100 and cf. Goitein in his article in *Studia Islamica 12:*32.
23. Ibn 'Abdūn, p. 248.
24. Ibid.
25. *Shīrat Yisraēl,* p. 69. In the opinion of Simḥōnī, *Ha-T'kūfa* 10, p. 174, he

is the same Abūn who is mentioned in a poem by Ibn Gabirol, part 1, no. 28, 1:8, and also by al-Ḥarīzī, *Taḥk'mōnī,* p. 40, cf. p. 475. This is a reasonable conjecture because of the closeness to Samuel ha-lēvī which is alluded to in these works.

26. See in the fragments from al-Bakrī which Lévi-Provençal published as an appendix to the translation of *Ar-Rauḍ al-mi'ṭār,* pp. 250–51.
27. No authentic information concerning the location of the Jewish neighborhood in Ronda has been discovered. According to what is told, it was in the northeast section of the city, between the inner and outer walls which surrounded the suburbs, at a site currently known as the San Miguel quarter, and the remains of an old Arab bathhouse are thought to have been the structure of a synagogue; cf. Torres Balbás, "La necrópolis musulmana de Ronda," *Al-Andalus* 9:475.
28. It should be this and not 1058, as Dozy 3, p. 63, writes; see Ibn 'Idhārī, pp. 242–43 where the year given is 446 which ended on April 1, 1055, and see op. cit., pp. 230–31, which tells that al-Ḳāsim reigned six years; on the other hand, it is certain that his father died in 1049 since it is stated there that he was chosen to be the caliph in 439 and died eighteen months later.
29. Documentos, no. 6.
30. See in Schirmann, "Méshōrérīm," *Y'dī'ōt ha-makhōn* 6:259–60 and cf. Schirmann, "Ḥayyē Jéhūda Halevi," ha-levī *Tarbīṣ* 9:224 and see in addition *Diwan Jehuda ha-Levi,* part 2, notes, p. 262.
31. The development of these matters is so reported by Ibn al-Abbār; see Dozy, "Notice sur les Becrites, seigneurs de Huelva," *Recherches* 1:287, and also Ibn 'Idhārī, p. 193.
32. *España Sagrada* 12:70.
33. Responsa Alfasi, ed. Bilgoraj, no. 139.
34. A. Delgado, "Bosquejo histórico de Niebla," *BAH* 18:539.
35. See Serjeant, in *Ars Islamica* 15/16:39.
36. In the first Privilege accorded the city in 1254, the statute of the Jews was fixed in keeping with accepted traditions, see *Collecçao de ineditos de historia portugueza,* 2a ed. [5] (Lisboa, 1926) pp. 475, 520. Cf. M. Kayserling, *Geschichte der Juden in Portugal,* p. 2.
37. Exceptional importance need not be ascribed to what was, supposedly, written in that letter which Saadya Gaon had addressed to the communities of Spain and among others to "Mérida the great city and to all the Jewish cities surrounding it" see in Abraham b. Dā'ūod, p. 59. On the one hand this author did not see the letter but reports what R. Meir b. Bibas, who saw it, told him; on the other hand, proof based on the rhetoric ascribed to Saadya is not admissible, although one can rely on the names mentioned in the text. In any event, the non-mention of these communities in the books of Abraham b. Dā'ūod, R. Moses Ibn Ezra, and other sources can serve as evidence.
38. For the rule of Banū Ibn al-Afṭas see M.J. Hoogvliet, *Diversorum scriptorum loci de regia Aphtasidarum familia et de Ibn-Abduno poeta* (Leiden, 1938); Dozy, "Examen de l'ouvrage de M. Hoogvliet sur l'histoire des Afṭasides et sur la vie du poète Ibn-Abdoun," *Recherches* 1:151–237; A.R. Nykl, "Die Afṭasiden von Badajoz," *Der Islam* 36:16–48; Lévi-Provençal, "Af-

ṭasides," *Encyclopedia of Islam*² 1:249. To be sure, even as in the writings of the Arabic historians, there are many errors in these studies and it should be especially noted that Dozy is defective, since he did not know of the inscriptions on the monuments of this dynasty.

39. For the various forms of spelling of the name, see Matías Ramón Martínez, *Historia del reino de Badajoz durante la dominación musulmana* (Badajoz, 1905), pp. 80–81.
40. T.-S. 13 J 23[22], a letter to Abu 'l-Faradj Yéshū'a b. Samuel; T.-S. 8 J 25[6], a letter from Aleppo to Nahrai b. Nissīm; T.-S. 10 J 5[12], a letter from Tyre to the same wherein he tells of a journey from Lattakia to this city he made by sea, of his future journey to Jerusalem, and of the trade in Persian silks in which he engaged; T.-S. 13 J 28[11], a letter from Jerusalem to the same.
41. Al-Maḳḳarī 2, p. 303; Ibn al-Abbār, "Ḥullat as-siyarā in Dozy," *Recherches* 1:176; Corrections, p. 103. Bearing in mind what the Arabic historians tell of the relations between al-Mutawakkil and his brother Yaḥyā, it can be assumed that the meeting, in consequence of which he wrote these verses, occurred in the 1070s.
42. The Jews of Santarem are mentioned in the Privilege granted the city in 1095 by Alfonso VI, see *Portugaliae Monumenta Historica* 1 (Olisipo, 1856), p. 349. cf. Kayserling, *Geschichte der Juden in Portugal,* pp. 1–2.
43. Dubler, p. 19.
44. J.A. Pereira, "Antiguedades de Santarem," *O Panorama* 2 (1954):263–64; A. Soares d'Azevedo Barbosa de Pinho Leal, *Portugal antigo e moderno* 8, (Lisboa, 1878), p. 574. However, João de Sousa, *Vestigios de lingoa arabica em Portugal* (Lisboa, 1830), p. 22, states that the site of the Jewish neighborhood is called Alboram which is the same word (this passage is explained, erroneously, by Kayserling as if the reference were to the first synagogue in all of Portugal).
45. See Julio de Castilho, *Lisboa antiga,* 2e ed., 9 (Lisboa, 1937), pp. 231ff., and in particular A. Vieira de Silva, *A Cerca moura de Lisboa* (Lisboa, 1899), pp. 29–39.
46. See A. Vieira de Silva, *As Muralhas de ribeira de Lisboa,* 2a ed., (Lisboa, 1940–1941), pp. 5ff. (and cf. in first ed., Lisbon, 1900, at the beginning of the book). The erudite author here refutes the widespread view (which he himself expressed in earlier works, e.g., the Moslem wall, mentioned above, p. 16) that the lower area of the city was then still covered by the sea.
47. Concerning the Jewish quarter south of the Moslem city, see the same author, *A Cerca moura de Lisboa,* p. 40; for the large neighborhood in the lower city, his treatise, "A Judiaria velha de Lisboa," which was published in the periodical *O Archeologo Portugues* 5 (1899–1900):305–26. However, his precise study calls for some emendation and, through conjecture, it would appear that the description given above may explain the development of the Jewish settlement in accordance with topographical discoveries.

The establishment of two Jewish quarters in the days of Moslem rule, Vieira de Silva assumes, of course, results from the narrowness of the site between the wall and the waters of the bay. It is certain that the new settlers sought a vacant area for the establishment of the new quarter, and one not surrounded by members of another faith. Vieira de Silva concludes, that since the churches surrounding the Jewish neighborhood in the lower city are mentioned in documents from the thirteenth century, that earlier, in the Moslem era, Christians dwelt there. If this conjecture were correct, the Jews would surely not have maintained their neighborhood in the center of the baixa, but at its extremities. However, the very data on which the Portuguese scholar relies refute his assumption. He alludes to the well-known report of the crusader Osborn on the conquest of Lisbon by the Christians in 1147 during which the inhabitants of the suburbs fought bravely against the Christians who besieged the city.

48. J. de Castilho, *Lisboa antiga* 9:131.
49. Ibn 'Idhārī, pp. 269, 283; Anonymous, pp. 311–12; *A'māl al-a'lām,* pp. 271ff.; Ibn Khaldūn in *Abbad.* 2, p. 216.
50. An authentic description of the fortifications of Carmona in the Middle Ages is given by J. Hernández Díaz, A. Sancho Corbacho, and F. Collante de Terán, *Catálogo arqueológico de la ciudad de Carmona,* and according to this "Catalogue," in a memorandum of the municipality of the year 1962; see also *Ar-Rauḍ al-mi 'ṭār,* p. 109, and M. Fernandez Lopez, *Historia de la ciudad de Carmona* (Sevilla, 1886), pp. 277ff.
51. Concerning the Carmona family, see *The Jewish Encyclopedia,* 3, col. 581.
52. See my article "The Number of Jews in Moslem Spain," *Zion* 28:55.
53. Responsa Alfasi, no. 279, and there the name of the city is Carṭōna (in the MS. of the British Museum, Add. 26, 977, where it is no. 272, "a certain town" is written in place of the name), but the letters *ṭet* and *mem* could readily be interchanged by a copyist unversed in the geography of Spain—the proof is that the name of the city to which the lender went is Seville, which is near Carmona.
54. Cf. Fernandez Lopez, pp. 81–82 and 344–45, who justifiably observes that there is no basis for the tradition that the Church San Blas, which is west of the Jewish quarter, was built on the site of a synagogue; and see also Fita, *BAH* 10:333. Fernandez Lopez speaks of "the Jewish courtyard" and the "farm of Dona Esther," but when I visited the city in October 1962, the inhabitants of the Juderia pointed to a house in the plazā of the quarter which is marked Jose Ara 1 as "casa de la juderia" and apparently they meant to say that a synagogue had been there.
55. In Seville also this tendency of the masses was one of the reasons for the crowning of Hishām II. According to what al-Marrākushī reports, p. 58, the kadi gave consideration to the desires of the common people.
56. *Dhakhīra* 1, 2, p. 176; al-Maḳḳarī 1, p. 320.
57. See in Reifmann, "M'faaneaḥ Ne'elāmīm," *Ōṣār ṭōbh* (5642–5643):7–8.
58. See below.
59. Abramson in *Sh'ēlōt u-t'shūbhōt ha-Ramban 3,* pp. 169–70; perhaps this is the same Moses b. al-Ḳurtubī, see *Tarbīṣ* 35:194.
60. See my article in *Zion* 28:50–51.
61. Nos. 3, 16, 25. Concerning the friendship which prevailed from the days of youth, see no. 16:9; his forbears—nos. 3:25–28, 16:6, 25:5, and the

superscription. In the poem, no. 3, his name, ben Samuel, is mentioned in 1:22; Harkavy, p. 46, and Sassoon in the introduction, p. xx, already conjectured that these poems were intended for one man. But Harkavy, Sassoon, and Haberman (the latter in his notes to part 2, p. 156) all expressed the opinion that also no. 30 which addresses itself to R. Joseph, see there 1:17, is designated for R. Joseph b. Samuel. However, in the three poems the *nāgīd* stresses his authority and his position as a judge, but this is not the case in this poem, and see note 133 in chapter 2. On the other hand, Harkavy does not believe that poem no. 16 was sent to Joseph b. Samuel.

62. For the astrolabe made by Muḥammad Ibn aṣ-Ṣaffār in 1029, see Woepke, *Über ein . . . arabisches Astrolabium* (Math. Abh. Akad.: Berlin, 1858), pp. 1–31; L.A. Mayer, *Islamic Astrolabists* (Genève, 1956), p. 75. The Hebrew inscription "Toledo" is found on table 13 (according to Woepke's numeration) and that of "Cordova" on table 14. For the astrolabe made by Muḥammad Ibn aṣ-Ṣaffār in Cordova in 1026 (which was acquired by the Edinburgh Museum after Mayer wrote his book), see R.W. Plenderleith, "Discovery of an Old Astrolabe," *The Scottish Geographical Magazine* 76 (1960): 25.

The names "Cordova" and "Toledo" are to be found on the astrolabe of the year 1029 above the names of these cities in Arabic letters written by the master craftsman to mark the latitude for which the table was designated. It can of course be assumed that the table which its owner needed was marked with Hebrew letters. It should be added that in the table designated for Cordova, as well as on other tables, there are Hebrew names for astronomical concepts also in the circles surrounding the table.

63. Cf. vol. 1, pp. 231–32.

64. The name Perigors appears in the Jerusalem Talmud, *T'rūma* 11:2, as the name of a rabbi in Caesarea and is also found on a Jewish inscription in Latin in Narbonne, dating from the end of the seventh century, see Reinach, "Inscription juive de Narbonne," *REJ* 19:75ff. This is apparently a Greek translation of "M'naḥēm": Παρήγορος which, in Latin, was pronounced "paregorus." In the eleventh, twelfth, and thirteenth centuries the name was widespread among the Jews of Germany, see Zunz, "Namen der Juden," *Ges. Schriften* 2:16, 34. However, the name also points—as Reinach p. 78, had already noted—to an origin in a French city. In the province of Dordogne, there is a district called Périgord which is divided into Périgord *blanc* and Périgord *noir.* The chief city of Périgord blanc is Périgueux. Because of geographic proximity, this differentiation is probably preferable.

65. Abraham b. Dā'ūd, pp. 58ff., "Ḳiryat sēfer" by Isaac Lattes in Neubauer, *Med. Jew. Chr.*, 1, pp. 234–35. Abraham b. Dā'ūd's account is seemingly self-contradictory: He reports at first that Isaac took it upon himself to supply all of Perigors' needs and later that the *nāgīds* in Granada supported him. In order to explain the contradiction, apparently it must be assumed that poor in his youth, the *nāgīd* gave aid to R. Perigors through intercession in his behalf, see Dā'ud, note 8 of chapter 6.

66. See vol. 1, p. 300.
67. R. Abraham bar Ḥiyya, *Sefer ha-'ibbūr* (Lyck, 1874), p. 10b; Isaac Israēlī, *Y'sōd 'Ōlām* (Berlin, 1846–1848) part 2, (fourth article), p. 6, col. a.
68. *Shīrat Yisrāel,* p. 72; *Taḥk'mōnī,* p. 39.
69. Abraham b. Dā'ūd p. 59; M'naḥēm ha-Me'īrī's "Bēt ha-b'ḥīra" in Neubauer, op. cit., 2, p. 228; Saadya b. Danān, p. 29b.
70. Some of them were included in the *Maḥzōr Siftē r'nānōt* and cf. Dukes Litbl. des Orients 5, col. 346; Schirmann 1, p. 327.
71. Abraham b. Dā'ūd, p. 75. According to Brody, he is that Joseph to whom R. Moses Ibn Ezra dedicated his *Poetica;* see *Drei unbekannte Freundschaftsgedichte des Josef ibn Zaddik* (Prag, 1910), p. 8. But in the ediction of his *Diwán,* he no longer expresses this view, see in the explanations to poem no. 223.
72. Abraham b. Dā'ūd, p. 73. Brody and Schirmann conjecture that they were brothers, see Brody loc. cit., *The Jew. Enc.,* 6, p. 538, and Schirmann loc. cit. This is a reasonable surmise for it is hard to assume that at that very time there were in Andalusia two families "b. Mē'īr ha-nāsī," both families of standing and producing writers. The poems of Ōhēbh b. M ē'īr were published by Schirmann in his study, "Ha-M'shōr'rīm . . . ," in the *Y'dī'ōt ha-mākhōn* 4, pp. 278ff. and in the new collection *Ha-Shīra ha-'ibhrīt bi-S'tārāc u-be-Provence* 1, p. 328. There is thus no room for the doubts entertained by M. Steinschneider in whose opinion Abraham b. Dā'ūd had in mind one person, see *MGWJ* 42:365.
73. For the history of the family in the days of the caliphs see D.M. Dunlop, "The Dhunnunids of Toledo," *JRAS* (1942): 77–96.
74. *A'māl al-a'lām,* p. 204; Ibn 'Idhārī, p. 276.
75. See op. cit., and cf. Prieto, p. 52 and in addition Dunlop, "Notes on the Dhunnunids of Toledo," *JRAS* (1943):17.
76. Cf. Dunlop, *JRAS* (1942):83 (1943):17.
77. Ibn al-Athīr 9, p. 203; an-Nuwairī p. ٨٧ and cf. Dozy, *Recherches* 1, p. 238.
78. Ibn 'Idhārī, pp. 277ff.
79. Abraham b. Dā'ūd, p. 53.
80. See below.
81. Abraham b. Dā'ūd, p. 68
82. Al-Fiṣal 1, p. 99. His comment on this matter is contained in a passage printed by Poznanski in his article, "Ibn Ḥazm über jüdische Section," *JQR* 16:267.
83. See my article in *Zion* 28:39–40.
84. See González Palencia, nos. 80, 429, 639, 648, 669, 674, 720, 970, 1137. These documents do indeed belong to a period after the Christian conquest, but it cannot be assumed that the occupational stratification had changed and that previously the Jews of Toledo did not engage in all these trades.
85. Op. cit., nos. 391, 539.
86. See op. cit., nos. 80, 970, and see also the bill of sale of a vineyard on the bank of Tagus, published by Assaf in *Zion* 4:34ff.
87. See Baer, *Urkunden* 2, p. 16.
88. Regarding the travels of Jewish merchants from Toledo to Egypt, see

T.-S. 10 J 5^{12}, T.-S. 13 J 23^{22} and cf. note 40 above, note 119 below. Concerning the landed property of Toledo's Jews, see in González Palencia's collection of documents where there are many of the bills of sale of rural estates which Jews sold to Christians in the period subsequent to Toledo's capture by the Castilians: no. 6 of a. 1110, no. 11 of a. 1119, no. 151 of a. 1181, no. 175 of 1185, no. 258 of a. 1194, etc. Of course, one must consider that the Christian conquerors also apportioned land to the Jews, but one should not presume that in the twelfth century all of this vast landed property was acquired by the Jews either in its entirety or in its greatest part.

89. At times the spelling "Sāsōn" appears and this is apparently the same name, see Cantera-Millás, p. 142.
90. No. 93 and in the introduction, p. xxiii, Sassoon conjectured that he was a scion of that family.
91. S. Bernstein, "S'rīdīm mi-shīrē S'fārād," *Ḥōrēbh 2* (5695/5696):253–55. In a manuscript, the poem is ascribed to Isaac Ibn Gayyāt and in the opinion of the editor it is his, except that its marking is that of Isaac ha-lēvī and it therefore belongs to another poet. Moreover, the poem is metered and it is known that R. Isaac Ibn Gāyyāt generally did not write metered poems.

    The word *shōshān* appears in the very first stanza in line 2: *u-l'ḥayyō shōshān,* and then in the second stanza: *u-sh'tōt'alē shōshān v neta'ne'emān,* etc. Therefore Bernstein already judged that the name of the family of the wealthy man was Shōshān. In the sixth stanza it is stated: *he l'khā n'gīd haēl, t'shūrat m'halēl.* The fact that the name Saadya Ibn Shōshān does not appear in the numerous inscriptions and family documents which were preserved from the era of Christian rule is important proof that the man lived in the eleventh century. Perhaps the poem "shōshān 'alē s'īf" was written in honor of one of the members of the family who lived in the middle of the eleventh century, see the *Diwan of Ibn Gabirol,* part 1, no. 122.
92. In the twelfth century, Solomon Ibn Shōshān was the *nāsī* of the Jews of Toledo and after him his son Joseph b. Solomon who died in 1205, *Ha-Manhīg,* 1b. The inscription on Joseph's monument is in the book *Abhnē Zikkārōn,* no. 75 (Cantera-Millás, no. 25).
93. Cf. volume 1, p. 321.
94. González Palencia, nos. 674, 1146, 1147, 1148, 1151. The name of this David's father was Abraham, see no. 1151. According to I. Cagigas, it is not customary in the cities of North Africa (which preserve the Hispano-Moslem tradition) to name a street for a person who merely dwelt or sojourned there, but only for houseowners on that street, see Adarve, *Rev. de Filología Esp.* 23 (1936):65 and cf. Torres Balbás, "Adarves de las ciudades hispano-musulmanas," *al-Andalus* 12:177, but in some documents published by González Palencia, it is expressly stated that in Spain streets indeed were named for men who dwelt in them, see nos. 603, 609, 653, 997.
95. See in González Palencia, p. 192.
96. Op. cit., no. 1.
97. *P'ēr ha-dōr,* no. 211. Mentioned there, in addition, are the wife of Joshua

b. Isaac Saidōn who is called Djamīla and their daughter Ṣéṭōla who was married to Isaac bar Jacob Ḳamaniel.

98. *Abhnē Zikkārōn,* no. 44. From among the many documents relating to this family, in connection with this early epoch it is worthwhile to note González Palencia, no. 175, from the year 1185, where Mē'īr b. David Ibn Naḥmias is mentioned as a witness and no. 673, from the year 1248, in which a number of generations are referred to. This is a bill of sale by Abū 'Āmir Yūsuf b. ash-shaikh Abū Sulaimān David b. Abī 'Amr Ibn Naḥmias. (Although the name is written 'Umar, without a *waw* at the end, I believe it should be read 'Amr, since Jews probably did not call themselves by the name of this caliph.) See also no. 1002, a document relating to him from the year 1254.

99. In a letter cited below.

100. See González Palencia, nos. 1147, 1149, 1151: Jacob he-ḥazzān b. Isaac, a judge in 1282. At that time Moses Ibn Falcón was a tax farmer of the king of Castile, see M. Gabrois de Ballesteros, *Historia del reinado de Sancho IV de Castilla* (Madrid, 1922–1928) 1, p. 62 lix, clviii, clix, clxviii: 2, p. 311. Abraham b. Moses Ibn Falcón died ca. 80, in 1349, see *Abhnē Zikkārōn,* no. 53. Moses bar Solomon was a judge in Toledo at the end of the fourteenth century, see González Palencia, nos. 1138, 1140. Falcón was a common name among the Christians, see the documents cited by me in Documentos, note 48.

101. Mann, *Texts* 1, p. 321.

102. See in González Palencia the documents from the end of the thirteenth century, nos. 677, 690, 711, 1089 and *Abhnē Zikkārōn,* nos. 40, 62, 63, 64, 65, 66, 71, 72.

103. See González Palencia, no. 1150 from the year 1205; among the witnesses, Solomon b. Padanc is a signatory, and no. 1143, from the year 1254, where property of Isaac b. Padanc is mentioned.

104. Documentos, no. 2.

105. See his book, p. 87.

106. *Yĕsōd 'Ōlām* by Isaac Israelī, part 2, f. 11a, col. b.

107. Ibn Khaldūn, see in ed. *Quatremère* 3, p. 107, and cf. the note in his translation 3 (*Notices et extraits* 21), p. 149.

108. Cf. the conclusions of Vallecilo Avila, pp. 62–63.

109. In the year 1130 the privileges of the inhabitants were fixed insofar as Jews and Moslems in the city were concerned, see in Baer, *Urkunden* 2, p. 11.

110. See Garciás Fernandez, *Historia de la villa de Talavera,* ms. of the National Library in Madrid 1722, ff. 4a, 6a f., 13a–b and also Cosme Gomez Tejada de los Reyes, *Historia de Talavera antigua,* ms. in the same library 8396, f. 8b and in addition the treatise of Anonymous, "Historia de la muy noble e insigne villa de Talavera," ms. of the library, 1729, f. 17a, and especially Ildefonso Fernandez y Sanchez, *Historia de Talavera de la Reina* (Madrid, 1896), pp. 165ff.

111. Attesting to this is that Talavera is the only town about which there are several documents in the collection published by González Palencia cf. Baer in *Tarbīṣ* 5:236.

112. See my article in *Zion* 28:40–41.

113. Al-Fiṣal 1, p. 99; about his visit to the city, 4, p. 180; and cf. Asín 1, p. 188.
114. Fernandez y Sanchez, p. 43, who apparently relies on the local tradition; see also the decisions of the municipality from the year 1450, which impose upon the Jews, the Moslems, and the Christians of the district of the Church San Salvador to guard the Puerta de la Miel, at F. Fita, Documentos ineditos anteriores al siglo XVI sacados de los archivos de Talavera de la Reina," *BAH* 2:317.

In truth, the Church of San Salvador is found outside the first wall of the city, at the end of Luis de Jiménez St., in the vicinity where the tradition of Talavera's inhabitants locates the Jewish neighborhood. Thus we have two kinds of evidence—oral and written—which support one another. On the other hand, it is unlikely that these places of residence were established for the Jews after the city was conquered by the Christians. As is known, the conquerors lacked settlers and it therefore was against their interest to expel the Jews from the town surrounded by a wall.

It should also be noted that in the eastern part of the city there is a quarter to this day named Barrio Nuevo which consists of three narrow and crooked streets called Calle de Barrio Nuevo, Entrada Barrio Nuevo, and Travesía Barrio Nuevo—a quarter called by the name given to the Jewish neighborhoods after the expulsion. But as the document published by Fita demonstrates, it is not possible to conclude from these names that the Jewish neighborhood was located there (if we do not assume that in the second half of the fifteenth century the Jews' residences were shifted from the west of the city to its eastern section). It is clear that the old Jewish neighborhoods were not always called Barrio Nuevo.

116. See Fernandez y Sanchez, p. 43.
117. See in the letter quoted above, p. 141, and cf. González Palencia, no. 1142.
118. This is the opinion of Oliver Asín who wrote a comprehensive study about Madrid in Moslem times: J. Oliver Asín, *Historia del nombre de Madrid* (Madrid, 1959); see especially pp. 279ff. The author concludes, also from various sources, that there existed a suburb (ash-Sharḳīya) east of the city and that there were markets in front of the gates, see pp. 333, 341–42. According to the opinion accepted before Oliver Asín, the city was much smaller in Moslem days and was identical with the citadel.
119. See the letter quoted above, p. 1, and see T.-S. 13 J 23[22]. The appelative with which the letter writer of 1053 designates the Madrid Jew who went to Palestine may indicate the smallness of the Jewish settlement and is a sign of the scarcity of Jews from Madrid. During the later Middle Ages the Jews of Madrid dwelt in de la Fe Street, which was then called the Street of the Synagogue, near the San Lorenzo Church. See Antonio Capmani y Montpalau, *Origen histórico y etimológico de las calles de Madrid* (Madrid, 1863), p. 201, and cf. F. Fita, "La Juderia de Madrid en 1391," *BAH* 7:440, but it is commonly accepted that during Moslem rule this quarter was far from the city and one cannot assume that the Jews dwelt during that period in a border city—such as Madrid—outside the walls.

120. Torres Balbás, "Estudios de arqueologia e historia urbana," *BAH* 144:158ff.
121. A description of the fortress is in Torres Balbás, art. cit., pp. 170ff.
122. Eulogius, who visited the city, states that he "descended" to it, and from this it follows that he meant a city located in a valley on the bank of the river, see M. de Portilla, *Historia de la ciudad de Compluto* (Alcalá, 1725)1, p. 113; Rodrigo Amador de los Rios, "Memorias arabigas de Alcaláde Henares," *RABM,* 3a época, 3:653.
123. Baer, *Urkunden* 2, no. 20.
124. R. Santa Maria, "Edificios hebreos en Alcalá de Henares," *BAH* 17:184ff.
125. See my article in *Zion* 28:41–42.
126. Francisco de Torres, *Historia de Guadalajara;* ms. of the National Library in Madrid, no. 1689, Cf. 36b. and also Alonso Nuñez de Castro, *Historia eclesiástica y seglar de la muy noble y muy leal civdad de Gvadalaxara* (Madrid, 1653), p. 30. (The actual author of this book was Hernando Pecha, see T. Muñoz Romero, *Diccionario bibliográfico-histórico* (Madrid, 1858), p. 135.
127. *Diwan Jehudn ha-Leri,* part 1, no. 102 and cf. Baer, "ha-Maṣabh ha-polīṭī shel y'hūdē S'fārād be-dōrō shel Y'hūda ha-lēvī," *Zion* 1:17–18. But Baer reads there the verse: "And in the tower of strength he let stay ten men of the nation in flight" and he therefore speaks of Jewish refugees who were gathered within the city, that is, Jews from outside Guadalajara; however, see Brody who reads "as he was hurrying" and in his commentary, p. 258, explains that that noble, in the poet's words, was mightier and faster than all others and when he hurried, he caught ten of them. Indeed in his book, *Tōl'dōt ha-y'hūdīm bi-'fārād ha-Nōṣrīt,* p. 40, Baer made an emendation in conformity with Brody's explanation.
128. For data concerning the location of the synagogue and cemetery, see Antonio Pareja Serrada, *Guadalajara y su partido* (Guadalajara, 1915), p. 59.
129. Baer, *Urkunden* 2, no. 19.
130. See Cantera, *Sinagogas,* pp. 304ff.
131. Menéndez Pidal assumed that Soria belonged to the kingdom of Saragossa (see the map of Spain in the year 1050 at the end of the second volume of *España del Cid*). He surely reached this view on the assumption that the dominance of the kings of Toledo did not extend beyond the large chain of mountains; but Soria *is* mentioned among the cities that the last Moslem king of Toledo offered the king of Castile in exchange for his aid, see *Abbad.* 2, p. 17. From this, Lévi-Provencal did indeed conclude that Soria was one of the cities which belonged to the kingdom of Toledo, see *Hespéris* 12:45.
132. Miguel Martel, *De la fundación de Soria, del origen de los doze linages y de las antiguedades desta çiudad,* ms. of the National Library in Madrid, 3452, 4a f.
133. Neubauer, no. 1.
134. See Torres Balbás, Soria, "interpretación de sus origenes y evolución urbana," *Celtiberia,* no. 3 (Soria, 1952), pp. 11–13, 23, 26.

135. M. Asín Palacios, *Contribución a la toponimia árabe de España* (Madrid, 1940), p. 64; *Madoz* 2, p. 13.
136. Duchesne, *Historiae francorum scriptores 4* (Paris, 1641), p. 96.
137. L. Duchesne, "Saint Jacques en Galice," *Annales du Midi* 12 (1900):145ff.
138. Vázquez de Parga-Lacarra 1, pp. 39–51.
139. Al-Makkarī 1, p. 270.
140. *España Sagrada* 2, p. 350.
141. Vázquez de Parga-Lacarra 1, pp. 255ff., pp. 401ff.
142. Op. cit., 1, pp. 293ff.; 2, p. 20.
143. See op. cit., 1, p. 465, and also J. Bédier, "La chronique de Turpin et le pèlerinage de Compostelle," *Annales du Midi* 24(1912):28ff; E. Lambert, "Ordres et confréries dans l'histoire du pèlerinage de Compostelle," *AM* 55 (1943):369–403.
144. *Le Guide du Pèlerin de Saint-Jacques,* éd. Jeanne Vieillard, 2e éd. (Maçon, 1950), p. 33.
145. "Epistola Hermanni Abbatis S. Martini Tornacensis," *Analecta Bollandiana* 2 (1883):246; and see J.M. Lacarra, "La repoblación del camino de Santiago," in *La reconquista española y la repoblación del país* (Zaragoza, 1951), pp. 221–32; "A propos de la colonisation 'franca' en Navarre et en Aragon," *AM* 65 (1953):331–42; *Valdeavellano* 2, pp. 342ff.
146. Also Lacarra assumes that the merchants who engaged in trade along the road of the pilgrims were "Francos" and Jews, see Vázquez de Parga-Lacarra 1, p. 468.
147. For the migration of Moslem intellectuals from southern Spain to the Ebro region in the eleventh century, which paralleled the migration of the Jews, see J. Bosch Vilá, *El oriente árabe en el desarollo de la cultura de la Marca superior* (Madrid, 1954), pp. 32ff.
148. See in Torres Balbás, *Al-Andalus* 18:166–67.
149. *Cortes de Cataluña* 1 (Madrid, 1896), p. 23 rub. 64; p. 46 rub. 150; A. de Capmany, *Memorias historicas sobre la marina: comercio y artes de la antigua ciudad de Barcelona* (Madrid, 1779–1792)1, p. 21; 2, p. 22.
150. *Mansi* 19:788.
151. F. Fita, *Roncesvalles, poema historica, estudios historicos* 1 (Madrid, 1884), p. 68, lines 12–14.
152. The document is in the cathedral of Huesca and is cited by Ricardo del Arco, "La judería de Huesca," *BAH* 66:321–22. Since the documents from the period before the bishop moved from Jaca to Huesca are documents that were also brought from there, this, then, is a document from Jaca.
153. See Baer, *Urkunden* 1, no. 6.
154. Op. cit., no. 568.
155. Op. cit., no. 11. A Jew from this village is also mentioned in a document from the beginning of the twelfth century, see below.
156. Op. cit., no. 12. An indirect proof for the relative importance of the Jewish settlement in Monclús is the document from the days of King Sancho Ramirez (1063–1094) which notes the sale of a piece of land by the "Christian community" of Monclús, from which it can be inferred

that there existed alongside it a sizable Jewish community, see J.F. Yela, *El cartulario de Roda* (Lerida, 1932), p. 93.

157. Baer, *Urkunden* 2, no. 15.
158. Op. cit., p. 9. Cantera infers, from a document of the year 1098, that Jews dwelt in the city of Calahorra, at that time, see his study "La Juderia de Calahorra," *Sefarad* 15:353. However, in the document itself, which he published in *Sefarad* 16:73, reference is made to Zaheid (Zaid'.) b. Zofar and there is no certainty that he is a Jew.
159. See F. Fita, "Primer siglo de Santa María de Nájera," *BAH* 26:244ff. It is not indicated that Ḥasan is a Jew, but Fita rightly assumed that he was. However, it is doubtful that Sancho Ayyūb is Jewish—as Fita supposes.
160. Art. cit., p. 253.
161. See, for example, the name Keya which appears as witness in a document of the year 1069 in L. Serrano, *Becerro gotico de Cardena* (Valladolid, 1910), p. 234 and the name cia vita (from the village of Biescasa in Aragon in a document from the year 1069, in Ibarra, *Documentos correspondientes al reinado de Sancio Ramireç T. 2* (Zaragoza, 1908), no. 66, and perhaps he was a grandson of that çia Vita who is mentioned in a document from the year 1036, see note 24 to chapter 1. It is, however, also possible that this is the name of the place called Chia. In a document from the year 1099 the village is mentioned as Gia, see Ubieto Arteta, *Colección diplomatica de Pedro I de Aragon* (Zaragoza, 1951), p. 297, cf. p. 92 there.
162. Baer, *Urkunden* 1, p. 44.
163. J. Bosch Vilá, "Escrituras oscenses en aljamía hebraicoárabe, 3," *Homenaje millás Vallicrosa* 1:192.
164. Art. cit., no. 6:195.
165. Baer, *Urkunden* 1, no. 577[8] and perhaps that man was also the owner of the mill in Tudela which was sold by a deed from the year 1152, see Lacarra 3, no. 373.
166. Baer, *Urkunden* 2, no. 11; and see Fita in his article quoted in note 159, pp. 232, 238, cf. note 19 to chapter 1.
167. See in Fita, p. 238, and also Cantera, *Sinagogas,* pp. 252ff.
168. H. López Bernal, *Apuntes históricos de Belorado* (Estepa, 1907), p. 130; L. Huidobro–F. Cantera, "Juderiás burgalesas," *Sefarad* 13:51.
169. See Cantera, "La Judería de Burgos," *Sefarad* 12:59ff. On the other hand the Jewish neighborhood of Sahagún, for some reason, was outside the city on the north side; see J. Rodriguez, "Judería de Sahagun," *Archivos Leoneses* 7, no. 14:41–42.
170. J.J. Landazuri, *Historia civil, eclesiastica, politica y legislativa de la m. n. y m. l. ciudad de Victoria* (Madrid, 1780), p. 98; see also pp. 112ff. The first document in which the Jews are mentioned in the city is from 1276, see op. cit., pp. 95ff.
171. See Cantera, *Sefarad* 22:15–16.
172. J.A. Gaya Nuño, "La muela de Agreda, restos de la Almedina fortificada y de la Aljama hebrea," *BAH* 106:271ff.
173. J.M. Lacarra, "Desarollo urbano de Jaca en la edad media," *EEMCA* 4:147ff.
174. Gómez, Fr. J., *Apuntes históricos de Logroño* 1 (Logroño, 1943), pp. 70–71.
175. See below.

176. Baer, *Urkunden* 2, no. 6.
177. Op. cit., no. 7; and see A. Ubieto Arteta, *Cartulario de Albelda* (Valencia, 1960), pp. 140–41.
178. T.-S. 12.532 which I published as no. 1 of Documentos.
179. J. Salarullana, *Documentos correspondientes al reinado de Sancio Ramirez* (Zaragoza, 1907), p. 70.
180. See Fita, art. cit. p. 254. Certainly what Fita says about the name of García Sanger—that it is a compound of a Romance name (García) and a Hebrew name (Sanger)—is incorrect. Sanger is not a Hebrew name.
181. Cartulario de San Millán de la Cogolla (por L. Serrano (Madrid, 1930), no. 287.
182. This is the first document in which the place is called Villa nueva de los judios; a second document in which this name appears is from the year 1134. The latter was printed first by Fita, see "Canonización del Abad San Iñigo," *BAH* 27:95, and then by Juan del Alamo, *Colección diplomática de San Salvador de Oña* (Madrid, 1950), no. 177. In his book, *El Obispado de Burgos* 1, p. 266, Serrano states that in the days of King García (1035–1054), the "Villa nueva de los judios" passed into the hands of the monastery of Oña which demonstrates that the village was thus named even then, whence L. Huidobro, "La Judéria de Pancorbo," *Sefarad* 3:160. However, the appelative "of the Jews" is absent from documents prior to 1097, see in the collection of Juan del Alamo, no. 35, from the year 1048, and no. 99 from the year 1092, and this does point precisely to the increase of the Jews in this region in the last third of the eleventh century.
183. J.F. Yela, *Cartulario de Roda* (Lérida, 1932), pp. 116, 117. The name inscribed in the Latin documents, Caleph, is the Arab name خلف, which was current with the Jews; see in González Palencia, no. 258. The name Ferro was current among members of various faiths including Moslems, see J. F. Yela, "Documentos reales del antiguo archivo de Roda," *Memorias de la facultad de filosofía y letras de Zaragoza* 1 (1923):334. In Hebrew this Monclús Jew was probably called Barzilai.
184. Op. cit., pp. 118, 121. For the name Mascarel, which is common in that region to this day, cf. the name Ascarel in Baer, *Urkunden* 1, p. 55. In a deed of gift from the year 1132, op. cit., p. 119, there is mention of the tower over (the house of) Khalaf. As for ownership of land, see an additional document from the year 1052, published by Fita in his study on Nájera, pp. 230ff., mentioned in it are a vineyard and a house which had belonged to Jews and which were given as a gift to the cathedral, after they passed to the king.
185. Vázquez de Parga-Lacarra 1, p. 476.
186. The superiority of the Somport route over the Ibañeta Pass was emphasized by the archeologist E. Lambert in various writings, see E. Lambert, "Roncevaux et ses documents," *Romania* 61 (1935):17ff., 19ff.; "Le livre de Saint-Jacques et le route de pèlerinage de Compostelle," *Revue géographique des Pyrénées et du Sud-Ouest* 14 (1943):5ff.; *Les relations entre la France et l'Espagne par les routes des Pyrénées occidentales au Moyen âge: France méridionale et pays ibériques, Mélanges géographiques offerts en hommage à Daniel Faucher* (Toulouse, 1948), 1, p. 319ff.

187. The description of the development of the government in Saragossa in that era as it is presented in the Arabic sources is confused and because of this, Dozy, in the two first editions of his research into this chapter of Moslem-Spanish history gave various surveys which contradicted each other until, in the third edition, he reached the conclusions summarized above; see "Essai sur l'histoire des Todjibides," *Recherches 1,* pp. 211ff.
188. Ibn Ḥayyān, op. cit., in the appendices, p. xlii; cf. Menéndez Pidal 2, p. 735.
189. According to the accounts of Arabic historians, Sulaimān Ibn Hūd partitioned his kingdom, see Ibn 'Idhārī, p. 222. However, Prieto, p. 45, properly noted that the name of Aḥmad al-Muḳtadir appears on the coins of Saragossa only from the year 441 of the *hidjra* (1049/1050) onward, whereas on the coins minted there in 440 and even in 441 (no doubt in the first half), the name of another prince is mentioned, i.e., Tādj ad-daula Sulaimān; cf. also G. Miles, *Coins of the Spanish Mulūk al-Ṭawā'if* (New York, 1954), p. 89. Prieto even rejected the account of the partition of the kingdom by Sulaimān Ibn Hūd on the assumption that Aḥmad al-Muḳtadir's rule in Saragossa was no more than the result of his victory in the struggle with his brother. The Spanish scholar ignored the fact that Aḥmad's name is mentioned on the coins of Sulaimān Ibn Hūd, beginning in 432, an indication that he was designated as the heir-apparent, see his book, pp. 199–200.
190. Ibn Ḥayyān in Ibn 'Idhārī, p. 176.
191. See my article in *Zion* 28:42–43.
192. See Kayserling, *REJ* 28:117 and the item Saragossa, *The Jewish Encyclopedia,* 11, pp. 52ff.
193. Ibn Ṣā'id, p. 89; Ibn Abī Uṣaibi'a 2, p. 50 (a word-for-word copy from the first-mentioned writer). The name Ibn al-Fawwāl is a widespread family name among the Jews of Aragon; see Baer, *Urkunden* 1, p. 1099. In addition see Bosch Vilá in the jubilee book for Millás 1, p. 193 (no. 4: the name of a physician, Abu 'l-Ḥasan Ibn al-Fawwāl), and also p. 195.
194. Al-Maḳḳarī 1, p. 350, 2, p. 276; cf. Cagigas 2, pp. 452ff. However, al-Maḳḳarī does not indicate that the vizier maintained the Christian faith.
195. D.M. Dunlop, A Christian mission to Muslim Spain in the eleventh century, *Al-Andalus* 17:260–310; J. Bosch Vilá, "A propósito de una misión cristiana a la corte de al-Muqtadir Ibn Hūd," *Tamuda* 2 (1954): 97–105.
196. Annali Compostellani, *España Sagrada* 23:319.
197. *Diwan Ibn Gabirol,* part 1, no. 22; cf. Brody in *Ha-Shilōaḥ* 25:556.
198. See *Diwan Ibn Gabirol,* part 1, no. 23, lines 149, 631–34, 651–66.
199. Our information concerning the history of Y'ḳūtiēl derives primarily from the poems of Ibn Gabirol which Graetz first explained in his article, "Jekutiel und Joseph Ibn Migasch," *MGW* 7:453–59. Only the name Y'ḳūtiēl appears in these poems, but R. Moses Ibn Ezra who cites them, speaks of the laudatory poems for Ibn Ḥassān, see *Shīrat Yisrāēl,* p. 194 and see there, too, p. 187 (and cf. Schirmann in *Tarbīṣ* 7:294, 314), a verse from a poem written in his honor by Isaac Ibn Khalfōn and there, too, R. Moses Ibn Ezra speaks about Ben Ḥassān. The name of his

father, Isaac, is mentioned in no. 22, 1:4, whereas one reads in the superscription to no. 20 in one ms. ולה ימדח אבא אסחאק בן חסאן.

Geiger identified Y'ḳūtiēl with the astronomer Ḥasān b. Mar Ḥasān because Solomon Ibn Gabirol, in a poem, part 1, no. 17, 1:43, refers to his greatness in "astronomy" (according to another version—his "sagacity" and see below). Relying upon the appelative the "old one" which Abraham bar Ḥiyya applies to Ḥasān b. Mar Ḥasān in his *Sēfer ha-'ibbūr,* Geiger argued that there is no chronological difficulty, see *ZDMG* 13:514ff. David Kahana maintained this view by referring to an old Jewish saying in which the science of astronomy is identified with *t'bhūna* (sagacity) and cited a verse in the poems of Ibn Gabirol, part 1, no. 23, 1:169 in which there is a reference to the old age of Y'ḳūtiēl. According to Kahana, Y'ḳūtiēl—Ḥassān b. Mar Ḥassān—is identical with Abba Ḥasān in whose honor the nāgīd wrote a song of friendship, no. 9, and who dwelt in Cordova (or elsewhere) far from Saragossa, see his article: "Ḥayyē Sh'lōmō Ibn g'bhīrōl," *Ha-Shilōaḥ.* 1:231–33. Egers also expressed the opinion that the verse in Ibn Gabirol's poem which mentions the old age of Y'ḳūtiēl suggests his identity with the Cordovan astronomer, see M. Steinschneider, *JQR* 10:537. On the other hand, Derenbourg, because of the chronological difficulty, tended to believe that Y'ḳūtiēl was the son of Ḥasān b. Mar Ḥasān; see *MGWJ* 29:156.

But the identification of Y'ḳūtiēl with Ḥasān b. Mar Ḥasān is refuted not only because of the chronological difficulty, but also because of the difference between the names. After the discovery that his father's name was Isaac, it is impossible to identify him with the astronomer from Cordova, inasmuch as a Jew whose name is Isaac would, of course, be called Isḥāḳ in Arabic, cf. Brody in *Ha-Shilōaḥ* 35:556ff. Further, the family name of the Cordovan astronomer was Ibn Mar Ḥasān, and Y'ḳūtiēl, never called "Ibn Mar Ḥasān" in the sources we have, is always "ben Ḥasān."

Another opinion about the origin of Y'ḳūtiēl was expressed by H. Schirmann in his study, "L'ḥēḳer ḥayyar shel Sh'lōmō Ibn Y'bhīrōl," *K'nēset* 10 (5707):245ff. Since above some of the poems in honor of Y'Ḳūtiēl (poems in which this name is mentioned), "Ibn Ḥasān," is written in the manuscript whereas in others, in the manuscript, there are superscriptions which are in honor of al-Mutawakkil Ibn Ḳaprōn, Schirmann assumes that "Ḥasān" was the name of his *grandfather* and that he was a scion of the renowned Ibn Ḳaprōn family, especially since the Arabic name "al-Mutawakkil" corresponds properly with the name Y'ḳūtiēl as it was explained in the Middle Ages.

Against this conjecture, a number of assertions can be advanced: For example, Moses Ibn Ezra customarily refers to persons by the family name (and not by the name of their father) whenever he mentions them briefly and he does refer to the benefactor of Solomon Ibn Gabirol as having the name Ibn Ḥasān (see above). From this it can be assumed that this was his family name.

From the words of the Hebrew poet cited above, Graetz concluded that Y'ḳūtiēl was, to be precise, the vizier of the king of Saragossa. The fact that the Arabic writers do not mention him, invalidates the conjecture of Graetz who placed too much reliance upon the poetic hyperboles of Solomon Ibn Gabirol. However, it seems that even Wilensky was unjustified in depicting Y'ḳūtiēl as a government-designated rabbi. If this were his position, he would not have had a seat in the King's Council and Y'ḳūtiēl would not have been slain with the other nobles who were close to the king.

According to the explanation Graetz gave to Ibn Gabirol's elegy, part 1, no. 23, Y'ḳūtiēl was slain together with the last of the Tudjībids, the kings of Saragossa. Graetz speaks of the slaying of King Yaḥyā, but the reference is to Mundhir II. Graetz's error is explained by his use of the first edition of Dozy's *Recherches* in which he expressed the opinion that only two kings from this dynasty reigned in Saragossa, the second being Yaḥyā. Again, note should be taken of the chronological difficulty offered by Graetz in the explanation of Ibn Gabirol's elegy. Ibn Gabirol states that Y'ḳūtiēl and the other nobles were slain in the month of Nisan 99—which should, of course, be 489 (1039), see part 1, no. 23, lines 87, 111, and also 95–96. However, according to the Arabic historian, Ibn Ḥayyān, who was a contemporary, Mundhir was slain on the first of Dhu'l-Ḥidjdja 420 (August 24, 1030), see Ibn 'Idhārī, p. 178. But Lisān addīn asserts that this happened on the tenth of Dhu 'l-Ḥidjdja, see Dozy in the edition quoted by Graetz, p. 52. Perhaps this contradiction can be solved by the conjecture that the Arabic historians erred regarding the month and it is also possible to separate the slaying of Y'ḳutiēl from that of the king, that is, to assume that these incidents did not occur at the same time despite the connection between them (both were the result of political tension and a struggle for dominance between two factions). This latter assumption is preferable. This interpretation of the data in the writings of the Arabic historians and Ibn Gabirol's poetry does not prevent us from concluding from the poet's words that Y'ḳūtiēl was a dignitary in the government of the king of Saragossa, since the poet speaks of the nobles who were slain together with him (i.e., simultaneously), see in the elegy, part one, no. 23, 1:21ff. It is likely that the slaying of Y'ḳūtiēl resulted from slander. At all events, it is not to be assumed that Y'ḳūtiēl, the strong supporter of Ibn Gabirol (Ibn Ḥas ān), did not dwell in Saragossa, or to doubt this, as is done by Schirmann in *Kirjath Sepher* 22:126. On the one hand, Ibn Gabirol tells of his downfall together with that of a group of nobles in the spring of 1039 and the Arabic historians report on the murder of the king of Saragossa in the summer of that year, and on the other hand it is known that the poet then lived in Saragossa.

200. Concerning him, see *Sēfer ha-riḳma,* p. 319; *Shīrat Yisrāēl,* p. 29, where it is stated that he sojourned in "eastern Spain" and indeed among the Arabs of Spain the Ebro region was called the eastern part of the country, see Dozy, *Recherches* 1, p. 29.

"Ha-Shīra ha-y'tōma" was printed on the title page of the poem, pp. 27ff., in the *Diwan of Samuel ha-lēvī,* no. 99 and there—no. 100—is the *nāgīd*'s reply. The two poems together were published with an introduction by A. Zak, *Ṣ'bhī ḥēn wi-y'fat mar'e* (Tel Aviv, 5706). For more about *Ha-Shīra ha-y'tōma*, see Schirmann 1, pp. 172ff., and see there, p. 171, his explanation of the name *y'tōma;* cf. Munk, *Notice*, p. 206.

R. Moses Ibn Ezra calls Abū 'Amr b. Ḥasdai the author of *Ha-Shīra ha-y'tōma* and states that he lived in eastern Spain, but one reads in *Sēfer ha-riḳma* that Abū Yūsuf b. Ḥasdai came to Saragossa and therefore Wilensky, in a note to this passage, disagrees on the identification of Abū'Amr and this man. In the *Taḥkemōnī*, p. 40, however, it is expressly stated that Joseph b. Ḥasdai is the author of *Ha-Shīra ha-y'tōma.* Further, in the passage in which he speaks about Abū 'Amr b. Ḥasdai, Moses Ibn Ezra also mentions his son, Abu'l-Faḍl; in the biography of this intellectual from Saragossa which his friend Ibn Ṣā'id included in his book, he calls him: Abu'l-Fadl Ḥasdai b. Yūsuf b. Ḥasdai. As for Moses Ibn Ezra's observation that Abū'Amr dwelt in "eastern Spain," see above. There is, then, no doubt that the passage in *Sēfer ha-riḳma* refers to the same man, since it is unlikely that there were two scholars in Saragossa, at the same time, interested in the principles of the Hebrew language, and each having the name of Ibn Ḥasdai. It seems that the author of *Sēfer ha-riḳma* erred, writing only Abū Yūsuf b. Ḥasdai instead of Abū 'Amr Yūsuf b. Ḥasdai. In the edition of Sassoon, his name is given as Joseph b. Ḥasdai; in that of Jarden, p. 161, as Abū 'Amr b. Ḥasdai.

Regarding the time the poem was composed, see 1:37, which mentions Joseph, the *nāgīd*'s son, who "finds delight in the Mishna." It is well known that boys began to learn Mishna at the age of ten; Joseph was born in Tishrī 4796 (at the end of 1035).

According to Graetz 6, pp. 43–44, the poem was written as an expression of thanks to Samuel ha-lēvī for the help he rendered to the author's two brothers, but according to Schirmann, it was to plead *for* help. In fact, Joseph Ibn Ḥasdai had both in mind. See 1:46: "And if your shadow were not stretched over them, they would have wandered to the ends of the earth"; and see the *nāgīd*'s reply, 1:66: "And know that I esteemed them as my sons" and 1:70: "And I did yet more, because of an inner feeling of friendship going beyond cavil." From this it is to be inferred that the *nāgīd* had already helped them; and see there 1:44: "And I am committed into your hand," that is, the poet seeks the *nāgīd*'s help. On the same line, the verse refers to "two brothers" without stating that they are his brothers, whereas the *nāgīd,* in his reply, 1:65, speaks of "the sons of a brother." It is certain that the grammarian Abu'l-Walīd Ibn Ḥasdai was not the brother of the author of the "Unusual Verse," as was already noted by Wilensky; cf. vol. 1, p. 310. However, it is possible that they were members of one family, as was conjectured by Bacher in the introduction to *Sēfer ha-Shōrāshīm,* p. xi.

Concerning Joseph Ibn Ḥasdai's service at the royal court of Saragossa, see *Dhakhīra,* 3, 125a (where it should be amended to read "Banū Tudjīb"). It can also be understood from this that Samuel ha-lēvī addresses him in his poem, no. 100:27 as "the prince of my people" and his statement there, line 32, "and yours is the inheritance and possession of greatness."

According to Harkavy, p. 46, the *nāgīd*'s poem, no. 16, is intended for Joseph b. Ḥasdai.

201. The treatise in which he criticizes the *Halākhōt g'dōlōt* is cited in *Ha-Shīṭa ha-m'ḳubeṣer* for the tractate Baba Meṣia, f. 104b, (ed. Warsaw, 5660 [*Asefat z'kēnīm*], p. 432). A part of the book dealing with oaths was published by Friedländer under the heading, "Residua of the *Sefer ha-niḳādōn*" in *Tif'ērōl-Yisraēl (Festschrift, Israel Lewy)*, Hebrew section, pp. 60ff; and see S. Assaf, "Sēfer Mishp'ṭē sh'bhū'ōt of R. David b. Saadia," *Kirjath Sepher* 3:295–97. The quotation from the words of R. David b. Saadia which was printed in *Tōrātan shel rīshōnīm,* part 2, p. 36, does not belong to the response of R. Isaac b. Baruch Ibn Albālia, but is an appendix to his response. In this text are mentioned the *P'sīḳōt* of David b. Saadia and this may be the title of his great work. But Assaf properly concluded, from the citing of his words with the addition of the eulogy for the dead, that he lived in the first half of the eleventh century.

202. Lacarra 2, no. 589.

203. See his personal testimony in his translation of Ḥayyudj's writings in Nutt, *Two Treatises on Verbs Containing Feeble and Double Letters by R. Jehuda Ḥayug of Fez* (London-Berlin, 1870), pp. 2^{9}, 23^{28-29}, 98^{26}, 120^{21}.

204. S. Poznanski, *Mose b. Samuel Hakkohen Ibn Chiquitilla* (Berlin, 1895), pp. 8–9; Bacher, *REJ* 31:309.

205. R. Moses Ibn Ezra says: "*'alā lautha kānat bihi wa-akhallat bi-markazihi fī marātib al-djazāla*"; see *CB* 1819 (it is true that the ms. has the expression "*al-dja'la,*" but it should no doubt be amended to read "*al-djazāla*") and its translation is: "In spite of his emotionalism which impaired his standing in the ranks of the speakers." The meaning of the word جزالة is both "munificence" and "power of expression," and since it is close to the word for "standing," its meaning here is: "power of expression." If the matter referred to here were a malady, it would disturb him everywhere.

206. See in his introduction in Nutt's edition, p. [1]: "However the majority of the French who dwell in the country *(bi-g'bhūl)* of our kinsmen, the sons of Esau [the Christians], are not familiar with the Arabic language. . . ." The *Sār'far* referred to here is actually France. To be sure, it is initially possible that *Ṣār'fat* is a translation of Frandja (meaning Catalonia), in accordance with the linguistic usage of the Arabs in Spain, but the observation that the majority of the Jews do not understand Arabic there, is more applicable to France and surely not the city of Saragossa, which spoke Arabic (as is the opinion of Graetz 6, p. 69); the men of France who dwell "*bi-g'bhūl*" of our kinsmen, the sons of Esau" does not mean that they dwell on the border, as was Poznanski's opinion in his book, p. 12, but in the land under Christian dominance. The Jews of Spain used the word *g'bhūl* to translate the Arabic word *naẓar* in the sense of "district" and continued this usage long after Spain ceased, for the greatest part, being Arabic speaking; see *Abhnē Zikkārón,* no. 35 and cf. Cantera-Millás, no. 65 and see above, note 37 to chapter 2.

For the appendices which Moses Ibn Djiḳatilya added to the books he translated, see Poznanski, *ZAW* (1895):133 and also Bacher, *REJ* 31: 312, and additionally in Nutt, p. 133, regarding his notes to the *Sēfer ha-niḳḳūed of Ḥayyūdj.*

207. Fragments from this book were published by Kokowzow, pp. 59–66; N.

Allony, "S'rīdē Sēfer 'al lāshōn zākhār we-lāshōn n'ḳēbha" *Sinai* 24: 33–67, and cf. R. Abraham Ibn Ezra, *Sefer Mōznayyīm* (Offenbach, 5551), 13b: "*Ha-gādōl she-ba-m'daḳd'ḳīm*" (The Greatest Grammarian), and also in *Sēfer Ṣāḥōt* he cites him as an important grammarian.

208. See Derenbourg, *Opuscules*, p. cxx.

209. Remnants of his poems were collected by Brody, "mi-Shirē R. Moses ha-Kōhēn Ibn Djiḳaṭilya," *Y'di'ōt ha-Mākhōn* 3 (5697):67–90, and thereafter, Ratzaby, "Piyyūṭ l'Rabbi Mōshē Ibn Djiḳaṭilya," *Sinai* 24:288–89, and in addition see Schirmann 1, pp. 295–97. Two poems were translated into Spanish by Millás, *Poesía Sagrada,* pp. 228ff. For an evaluation of his poetry see *Shīrat Yisrāel,* p. 69 and *Taḥk'mōnī,* p. 39: "And not like the poems of R. Mōshē ha-kōhen "*atīḳīm,*" and for the meaning of the word "'*atīḳīm*" see Bacher, *REJ* 31:311.

210. See Poznanski, "Aus Mose ibn Chiquitilla's arabischem Psalmenkommentar," *Zeitschrift f. Assyr.* 26:38–60; N. Allony, "Ḳ'ṭa'īm mi-p'rūshē R. Mōshē Ibn Djikaṭilya," *Sinai* 24:138–47, Finkel, "Pērūsh Rabbi Mōshē b. Sh'muēl ha-kōhēn Ibn Djiḳaṭilya 'al L'hillīm," *Ḥōrebh* 3 (5696–5697):153ff. In the ms., Bodleiana, Neubauer 135 (which contains a translation of and commentaries on the Book of Job), aside from R. Saadya Gaon, only Moses Ibn Djiḳaṭilya is mentioned; see Ewald, *Beiträge* 1:78–115 and then Bacher, "An Arabic Translation of the Book of Job with an Arabic Explanation," *Festschrift Harkavy,* Hebrew section (St. Petersburg, 5669), pp. 221ff. On the other hand, Poznanski doubted this conjecture, arguing that this ms. contained a compilation of various commentaries; thereafter Finkel demonstrated that under no circumstances was it to be assumed that this ms. contains only some of the commentaries of R. Saadya Gaon and Moses Ibn Djiḳaṭilya; see art. cit. pp. 153ff.

211. Saadya Gaon in *Kitāb al-Amānāt* (ed. Landauer), p. 247; Abraham b. Dā'ūd, p. 74. Until now, no passages have appeared in the quotations from the commentaries of Moses Ibn Djiḳaṭilya in which he cites the words of Karaite commentators, referring to them by name, cf. Bacher, *REJ* 31:309. But, generally, he rarely acknowledges his sources, as Poznanski indicated in *Zeitschrift f. Assyr.* 26:52.

212. See Poznanski, op. cit., p. 32.

213. See Poznanski, *Zeitschrift f. Assyr.* 26:57ff. Among others, he cites the translation of Psalms by Ḥafṣ b. Albār (Alvaro) al-Ḳūṭī whom Steinschneider, for some reason, held to be a Jew, see *Ar. Lit.* no. 66, despite the surname "Ḳūṭī," which is the Arabic designation for the Visigoths and points to a Mozarab author. Regarding this Hispano-Christian writer who translated the Psalms in 989, see D.M. Dunlop, "Ḥafṣ, b. Albār, the Last of the Goths," *JRAS* 1954:137–51.

214. Lacarra 2, no. 194.

215. Op. cit. 1, no. 90. The seller may have dwelt in Saragossa; cf. Baer, *Urkunden* 1, no. 47.

216. Op. cit. 2, no. 220.

217. See my article in *Zion* 28:43.

218. No. 84. There are, to be sure, several cities called ḳal'a, (e.g., Ḳal'at Ḥammād in Morocco, Ḳal'at Banī Sa'īd in the district of Granada), see

al-Maḳḳarī 1, pp. 188–89, and Calatrava in the vicinity of Ciudad Real. But the *nāgīd*'s words leave no room to interpret that any of these cities is intended. There is no suggestion whatsoever that the sea lies between him and his friend M'bhōrākh nor is it possible that the reference is to a city close to Granada. In lines 14–15, the *nāgīd* says: "And you plotted against your friend and companion/Who had lovingly bound you on his very heart/Who sent you every year his peace greetings, many as sand of the sea/Yet received no peace from your town." It is clear from these verses that the *nāgīd*'s friend dwelt in a faraway city because he found the opportunity to send him regards only once a year. Nothing is known about a Jewish settlement in Calatrava during this period; however the *nāgīd*'s complaint voices his suspicion that his friend is siding with his opponents, whose center was in Saragossa, near Calatayud; see chapter 1.

219. Al-Idrīsī, p. 189; *ar-Rauḍ al-mi'ṭār*, pp. ٧٦ / ٧٧
220. Baer, *Urkunden* 1, no. 22, cf. no. 572.
221. See José Beltrán, *Historia de Daroca* (Zaragoza, 1954), pp. 24–25. Actually, the fortress on Mt. San Jorge is called the fortress of the Jews for the first time (as far as we know) in a document from the year 1337, see Toribio del Campillo, *Documentos historicos de Daroca y su communidad* (Zaragoza, 1915), serie 2, no. 418. But it can be assumed that the Jewish neighborhood was located there in the days of Moslem rule, even though Toribio del Campillo believes that there was no settlement, aside from the city on Mt. San Cristóbal, at the time of the Christian conquest. See additionally, op. cit., no. 380, for mention of the Street of the Ironmongers (Herreria) of the Jews.
222. Dubler, p. 117.
223. See in the book *Ḥudūd al-'ālam* which was written in 982–983, ed. Minorsky, p. 155.
224. See Dozy, *Recherches* 1, p. 203.
225. The conjectures of Codera on this were confirmed through the publication of Ibn 'Idhārī's history, see F. Codera, "Reino arabe de Tudela según las monedas," *BAH* 5:354–61. Cf. Ibn 'Idhārī, p. 22, and see also Prieto, p. 210.
226. J. Bosch Vilá, *El Oriente arabe en el desarollo de la cultura de la marca superior*, pp. 23–24.
227. The Moslems did this in Granada also where they built the mosque in an area which they annexed to the city and which was still sparsely settled; see p. 137, this volume.
228. Fray José Vicente Díaz Bravo, *Memorias históricas de Tudela* (Pamplona, 1956), p. 82.
229. Various opinions have been expressed about the site of the Christian quarter in Moslem Tudela, and since the matter touches upon the chronology of the Jewish settlement as against the history of the entire settlement, it is important to note particular conclusions: No one disputes that the Church of Santa Magdalena was a Mozarab church, see Diáz Bravo, loc. cit., and it follows from this that Christians dwelt near it; *Madoz* 15, p. 176, indeed expresses the view that the neighborhood of the Mozarabs was located there. Lacarra argued that Mozarabs dwelt

in the heart of the city near the current cathedral which was then also in Christian hands, see "La restauración eclesiástica en las tierras conquistadas por Alfonso el Batallador," *Revista Portuguesa de Historia* 4 (1949):269, and this by his relying on the conclusions of Pascual Galindo in his introduction to Fr. Fuents, *Catálogo de los archivos eclesiasticos de Tudela* (Tudela, 1944), p. vii. However, later Lacarra was of the opinion that the Mozarab neighborhood was on San Julián Street, and its vicinity, in the southwest of the city, see *El desarollo urbano de las ciudades de Navarra y Aragon en la edad media* (Zaragoza, 1950), p. 8, map 10. In a study published in 1951, he returned to his earlier view that the Mozarabs dwelt near the cathedral, see *La reconquista y repoblación del valle del Ebro,* p. 72, and this is also the opinion of Torres Balbás in his article, "Mozarabías y juderías," *Al-Andalus* 19:182.

But the documents Galindo cites to prove that, indeed, even under Moslem dominance the Christians held the great house of worship in the center of the city, are unconvincing. Gomez Moreno, on the other hand, showed by decisive proof, from the plan of the present structure, that it served as a mosque and was altered in the manner of other mosques which were turned into churches, see M. Gomez Moreno, "La mezquita mayor de Tudela," *Principe de Viana 6* (1945): 9ff. The mere fact that in 1121 the house of worship was dedicated anew as a church demonstrates that it was formerly a mosque. Thus, the opinion that near it was the Mozarab neighborhood is refuted. Prof. Lacarra did indeed tell me, in a conversation in October 1959, that he had again changed his mind and agrees that their neighborhood was located near the Church of Santa Magdalena. The result, for us, is that the Mozarab neighborhood was inside the city which the first wall surrounded.

230. See the document published in Lacarra 3, no. 373.

231. The Jewish neighborhood remained in the same place until 1170 when the Jews sought to transfer their dwellings to the fortress. Its location in the days of Moslem rule can be determined from documents dating from the beginning of Christian rule: (a) Garcia, king of Navarre, in 1135, gave the church of Tudela a garden inside the city which was surrounded by a wall and near the Jewish neighborhood, see *España Sagrada* 50:395; (b) In 1177, Domingo Albarden and his sons sold to the prior of the church a field, (which had formerly belonged to the physician, Jacob Shu'aib) which abutted on one side, the Jewish house of worship and from the other side, on the garden of the cathedral, see Lacarra 2, no. 274; (c) In 1233, Sancho "the Strong," king of Navarre, bought houses in the cathedral's district *(parroquia)* which abbutted, as stated in the bill of sale, on one side onto the street of the (old) Jewish neighborhood, and from the other, onto the street of the "King's garden," see *Colección diplomática del rey Don Sancho VIII de Navarra,* (D. Carlos Marichalar Pamplona, 1934), p. 246; (d) In the next year the king bought additional houses in the "old Jewish neighborhood" and the bill of sale stated that they abut, on one side, on the "street of the city wall," see op. cit., p. 229. From document (b) it can be deduced that the Jewish neighborhood extended to the cathedral, from document (c), that it extended to the garden Huerta del rey which is near the eastern wall,

and from document (d) that it extended to the southern wall. Document (a) also proves that the Jewish neighborhood was near the city wall.

232. See my article in *Zion* 28:44–45.
233. See Lacarra 1, no. 62.
234. Op. cit. 2, no. 134 from the year 1127: "filio de Lalahcin." I do not believe that he should be identified with Abu 'l-Ḥasan cited in documents from the years 1142–1190, see Baer, *Urkunden* 1, no. 577, and one should also add Lacarra 2, no. 232 from the year 1143. The identification is not reasonable both chronologically and on the basis of the names themselves. Among all the documents which Baer collected the letter *bēt (b)* "Abū" was not omitted, but the document of the year 1127 implies by means of the ī that the man was called Ibn al-Ḥassān and not Ibn al-Ḥasan (and it is a likely conclusion from the pronunciation of his name, i.e., the pronunciation of the long Arabic aleph *(ā)* as an ī that he was by origin from Andalusia, see Steiger according to note 10 to chapter 2). This Abu'l-Ḥasan signed, among other witnesses, the document of King Garcia Ramirez in 1146, see Lacarra 3, no. 359, and he was an agent of the king of Navarre, see the document of the year 1169 in Baer loc. cit., paragraph 13. There is therefore good reason to believe that he was not a veteran inhabitant of Tudela, but had settled there after its conquest by the Christians.
235. Al-Maḳḳarī 1, p. 103, and cf. Lévi-Provençal in his commentaries to *ar-Rauḍ al-mi'ṭār,* p. 150.
236. A document from 1123 bears testimony to its existence at that time. In this document the conqueror of the city, Alfonso el Batallador, gives a tithe from the taxes and customs of the Christians, Jews, and Moslems to the bishop, see Baer, *Urkunden* 1, no. 16.
237. See my article in *Zion* 28:43–44.
238. J. M. Sanz Artibucilla, *Historia de la fidelísima y vencedora ciudad de Tarazona* (Madrid, 1929–1930) 1, pp. 207–11.
239. *Sefarad* 4:73–74.
240. The wall is mentioned in various documents from the end of the eleventh and the beginning of the twelfth century, as, for example, in a document from the year 1094, see J. M. Quadrado, *Aragón* (Piferrer, *España, sus monumentos y artes:* Barcelona, 1844), p. 142, and likewise in a document of 1110, see below, note 244. It is also mentioned in a document of the year 1097, Juan Briz Martinez, *Historia de la fundación y antiguedades de San Juan de la Peña* (Zaragoza, 1620), pp. 638–39. This latter document is forged, see A. Ubieto Arteta, *Colección diplomatica de Pedro I de Aragon y Navarra,* pp. 70–71, 262, but the topographical details mentioned therein are no doubt correct (and especially, whatever is asserted about this wall) since they correspond with the data in other documents. The ms. of the document is from the twelfth century, see ibid.
241. F. Balaguer, "La Muerte del rey Sancho Ramirez y la poesía epica," *Argensola* 4:199.
242. According to *ar-Rauḍ al-mi'ṭār,* p. 190, there were no Arabs in Huesca, but see Ibn Bashkuwāl 1, pp. 163–164, and also the documents pub-

lished by J. Bosch Vilá, "Los documentos árabes del archivo catedral de Huesca," *RIEEI* 5:15–16.

243. F. Balaguer, "Notas documentales sobre los mozárabes oscenses," *EEMCA* 2:379ff., 401ff.

244. The document was published by Quadrado, p. 166. There is no basis for the assumption that only then was this site fixed as the Jewish quarter —as is done by Ricardo del Arco, *Huesca en el siglo XII* (Huesca, 1921), p. 9 and by Balaguer, see in his article cited in note 241, p. 200. As becomes clear from various documents (see below), the number of Christian settlers who came to the city after its conquest by the king of Aragon was not so large that they should clear the Jews from the inner city, nor did they have any reason of security for this, cf. J.M. Lacarra, *El desarollo urbano de las ciudades de Navarra y Aragon en la edad media,* pp. 16–17.

245. R. del Arco, "La Aljama judaica de Huesca," *Sefarad* 7:273.

246. R. del Arco-F. Balaguer, "Nuevas noticias de la aljama judaica de Huesca," *Sefarad* 9:351–52; R. del Arco, *Huesca en el siglo XII,* p. 27.

247. R. del Arco, "Ordenanzas inéditas dictadas por el consejo de Huesca, 3a época," *RABM* 17:435ff.

248. See my article in *Zion* 28:45–46.

249. R. del Arco, *Huesca en el siglo XII,* appendix xi (pp. 130ff.).

250. Op. cit., appendix xvi (pp. 134–35).

251. Lacarra 2, no. 108; R. del Arco-F. Balaguer, "Nuevas noticias," *Sefarad* 9:353–54. (In the document one reads Zebri Ybenhamar and it should no doubt be amended to Zecri, and cf. Zegri in the document of 1151 which del Arco-F. Balaguer published in art. cit., pp. 378–79.)

252. In 1149, his son Joseph leased a field from the prior of San Pedro, see del Arco-F. Balaguer, *Sefarad* 4:378. De Ruesta appears here as a family name. If it were not so, three generations would not have given themselves this name, hence the reference is to an old family in the city.

These are the first known documents which mention the Jews of Huesca. (Some of the documents which del Arco published in his writings and which supposedly belong to this early period, are, in fact, unrelated to the days of Moslem rule; see in his studies, *La Judería de Huesca: Revista de historia y genealogia española 1* (1912), pp. 461ff; "La Judería de Huesca," *BAH* 66 (1915):321ff.) They are: (a) a document from the cathedral archives of the year 1068, but all the documents from these archives which are before 1096 originate from the city of Jaca which was the bishop's see in that district until the conquest of Huesca; (b) The will of Asuero Fafilaz, 1106, in favor of the cathedral. However, this document does not state that this was an apostate Jew—as del Arco thought—and there is no proof whatever for this, as Baer had already noted in his collection of *Urkunden* 1, p. 29; moreover, the document was put into writing in 1126 and not in 1106, i.e., thirty years after the termination of Moslem rule, see Ubieto Arteta, *Colección diplomatica de Pedro I,* 55; (c) Permission to sell a field to a Jew of Huesca which was given by the person in charge of the cathedral in 1087. On a visit to the archives of the cathedral on October 15, 1959, the learned priest Don

Duran Gudiol and I investigated the document, and we were convinced that the date is 1487.

253. R. del Arco, "La Aljama judaica de Huesca," *Sefarad* 12:286.
254. See Ubieto Arteta, *Colección diplomatica de Pedro I,* no. 55. It would seem that this man should not be identified with the one who bore the title mentioned in the Tudela document of 1127 (see p. 260 and p. 268, note 234) because of the distance in time and place.
255. R. del Arco-F. Balaguer, "Nuevas noticias," *Sefarad* 9:357, 359; R. del Arco, *Archivos históricos del Alto Aragon fasc. 2* (Zaragoza, 1930), p. 57.
256. R. del Arco, "La Aljama judaica de Huesca," *Sefarad* 7:288.
257. Al-Makkarī 2, pp. 355–56.
258. According to Raimundus Martinus he was a "great rabbi," but it would appear that his words are not to be taken literally, see *Pugio fidei* (ed. Leipzig, 1687), p. 685. As for his being well versed in Karaite doctrine, see the end of note 261.
259. He himself mentions the date and site of the baptism and his age at that time in the introduction to his *Dialogi.* It is true that he referred to King Alfonso by the title "Imperator," and writers of the Middle Ages and scholars of modern times therefore have been misled into thinking that the reference was to Alfonso VI (then the sole ruler in Spain to bear the title "Imperator"); as an outgrowth of this error, they also referred to Pedro Alfonso as a Castilian. However, the authoritative Aragonese historian, Zurita, plainly states that the sponsor of the baptism was the king of Aragon, see Zurita, *Anales lib.* 1, cp. 36 (in the ed. Saragossa, 1610, 1, p. 35a). Ricardo del Arco searched the minutes of the cathedral for a record of the baptism, and not finding anything, he expressed the opinion that it was indeed a Jew who had become a convert in Castile, see his writings, "La Judería de Huesca," *BAH* 66:322; *Huesca en el siglo XII,* pp. 59ff. Nevertheless, what the convert himself tells about his conversion in Huesca is to be preferred over all other testimony. Huesca was then the capital of Aragon and it may therefore be assumed that the title "Imperator" with which Pedro Alfonso designates the Christian ruler was merely a title of distinction which he accorded him.

    There is no trace in that introduction to the *Dialogi* of his birthplace nor is it in the other writings (see below) of Pedro Alfonso. The majority of historians fix his birthplace as Huesca, see a writer of the sixteenth century, Viencio Blasco de Lanuza, *Historias eclesiásticas y seculares de Aragon* (Zaragoza, 1622) 1, p. 560; *Alfonso Iudio de la ciudad de Huesca* (and note there that this occurred in 1100), whereas Joseph Rodriguez de Castro, *Biblioteca Española* (Madrid, 1781–1786) 1, p. 19, states plainly that he was born in Huesca. The apostate himself only tells that he grew up among the Moslems, see *Dialogi* in Migne 157, col. 597. From his own statement one can apparently conclude that he was a Huescan for, if not, what reason would he have to move to this city? In relation to Toledo, Barcelona, and the other principal cities of Christian Spain, Huesca was small and poor even after it became the capital of Aragon. Further, there is no proof that he then (before he became a Christian) had any status in the court of the king of Aragon.

260. See in the work of a fifteenth century writer, Alfonso de Spina, *Fortalitium*

fidei (Nürnberg, 1494), f. 28a. According to Nicolas Antonio, of the seventeenth century, he was his physician even earlier, see Nicolas Antonio, *Bibliotheca Hispana vetus* (Madrid, 1788) 2, p. 10.

261. The book was first printed in Cologne in 1536, and later in *Bibliotheca Veterum Patrum* (Cologne, 1618) 12, pp. 358–404; *Bibl. Vet. Patr.* 21 (Lyon, 1677), pp. 172–221; Migne 157, cols. 535–671. The date of the work is given in conversation b (in Migne, col. 572) where he states that 1,040 years had passed since the destruction of the Temple. From this it can be deduced that the book was written in 1108, two years after he became a Christian. As for its being a source for Christian authors who wrote against the Jews, see S. Lieberman, *Sh'ḳīīn* pp. 19ff. and 27ff. The description of Mohammed and his religion, contained in this book, is perhaps the first one in Latin which is realistic.

262. The book was first published in Paris in 1824 with an old French translation and therefrom in Migne 157, cols. 671–706, and later by Schmidt, Berlin, 1827. Ultimately a scientific edition based on 73 mss. was published by Hilka-Söderhjelm (*Acta Societatis scientiarum Fennicae* T. 38, nos. 4–5 (Helsinki, 1911–1912). Recently a new English translation has been published by Eberhard Hermes. As for the book's influence on the literatures of Europe, see Chauvin, *Bibliographie des ouvrages arabes,* fasc. 9 (Liège, 1905), pp. 8ff; see also the similar list in the edition of the book with Spanish translation by González Palencia, Madrid, 1948, p. xxviff., and in particular, the study by H. Schwarzbaum about the motives, sources, and influence of this collection, "International folklore motifs in Petrus Alphonsi's 'Disciplina Clericalis'," *Sefarad 21:*267ff., 22, 17ff. Chapters 2 and 3, whose theme is friendship, were translated into Hebrew under the title of *Sēfer Ḥānōkh* and were printed in a collection in Constantinople in 1516, Venice in 1544, and again there in 1605; with a French translation by A. Pichard, Paris, in 1838, and with a Portugese translation by Moses b. Shabbat Amzalak, *Da amizade, ou Livro de Henoch* (Lisbon, 5688).

263. Ch. H. Haskins, *Studies in the History of Mediaeval Science,* 2nd ed. (Cambridge, 1927), p. 119.

264. See Millás, "'Abhōdātō shel Mōshē S'fārādī 'al ḥokhmat ha-t'khuna," *Tarbīṣ* 9:55–64, and his study in Spanish: "La aportación astronómica de Pedro Alfonso," *Sefarad* 3:65–105.

265. Lạcarra 1, no. 20; Millás, "Un nuevo dato sobre Pedro Alfonso," *Sefarad* 7:136–37.

266. Haskins, p. 118; Millás, "La aportación astronómica," *Sefarad* 3:81–83.

267. A map drawn according to this notion is to be found in the Bibliothèque Nationale in Paris in the ms. of the *Dialogue, Script. Lat.* 1218. Whereas in similar maps—maps of the climates—the center of the world, which is called "Arin," is described as an uninhabitable zone and the seat of the devil, a big city appears in the central zone of this map; see C. R. Beazley, *The Dawn of Modern Geography* 2 (New York, 1949), pp. 575–76 where the map is copied. However, according to the spelling, this is a thirteenth-century ms. and there is thus no proof that Pedro Alfonso really drew it, see Millás, *Sefarad* 3:85.

268. See Ibn 'Idhārī, p. 253; Dozy, *Recherches* 2, p. 336.

269. *Libro de Cadena* (Cathedral archives in Huesca), p. 201; cf. A. Bielsa, "Notas sobre la repoblación de Barbastro," *Argensola* 12 (1961): 208. See also Baer, *Urkunden* 1, nos. 23, 31 (p. 21), 46a.
270. See S. Lopez Novoa, *Historia de muy noble y muy leal ciudad de Barbastro* (Barcelona, 1861), p. 38, where there is reference to Calle del Palacio, but currently the place is called Plaza del Palacio.
271. One should approach with great care the placing of the site of the Jewish neighborhood as given by Lopez Novoa, who relies on the local tradition. It is true that in Calatayud (and also in Cordova) the Jewish neighborhood was near the chief mosque; however, according to this tradition, the Jewish quarter was open in more than usual measure toward the place of Moslem gatherings. Perhaps it is preferable to assume that the Jewish quarter was in proximity to the place, e.g., in the street continuing toward the east or in one of the streets ascending from the Plaza del Palacio. For the extent of the city, see *España Sagrada* 48:6.
272. A. Bielsa, loc. cit., but customarily, the Jews had stores outside their neighborhood.
273. Baer, *Urkunden* 1, p. 34.
274. See Dozy, *Recherches* 2, appendix viii and see Ibn 'Idhārī, pp. 223ff.
275. *Ar-Rauḍ al-mi'ṭār,* p.
276. Pleyan de Porta, *Apuntes de historia de Lérida* (1873), p. 117.
277. See my article in *Zion* 28:46.
278. See in Pleyan de Porta, op. cit., pp. 135ff., p. 400, and also in his book *Guia-Cicerone de Lérida* (Lérida, 1877), pp. 83–84. The extent to which tanning was a typically Jewish occupation in northern Spain also can be deduced, among other things, from the fact that to this day the old Jewish quarter in Miranda del Ebro is called "de los Judíos" or "las Tenerias," see Cantera, *Sefarad* 22:16.
279. J. Lladonosa, *Divulgaciones leridanas* (Lérida, 1950–1951), p. 113.
280. Baer, *Urkunden* 1, p. 21.
281. *Ar-Rauḍ al-mi'ṭār,* p.
282. After the capture of the city by the Christians in the twelfth century, the area between the walls was broadened and thereafter the wall went up from the Gardeny Gate to the site of the San Lorenzo Church; therefore documents of that era speak of the "old wall" (in contrast to the new), see Lladonosa, *Divulgaciones,* p. 20 (there it is asserted that the city was widened in the final days of Moslem rule; however, as Mr. Lladonosa informed me when we met in Lérida in September 1962, he changed his mind, and it is indeed a more reasonable view that the urban area between the walls was enlarged at the time of the "repoblación" in the twelfth century).
283. The Cuiraça is mentioned in documents from the second half of the twelfth century—a short time after the town was taken by the Christians, see J. Miret Sans, *Les Cases de Templers y Hospitalers en Catalunya* (Barcelona, 1910), p. 140; J. Ayneto, *La reconquista de Lérida y su virgen blanca* (Lérida, 1919), pp. 86, 141, and cf. Lladonosa, op. cit., p. 19. In addition see Baer, op. cit., no. 43. The Jewish quarter is mentioned in other documents of that time: in a document of the year 1158, in connection with a house in the parish of San Andres (north of the Cuiraça) which

abutted upon the houses of the Jews, Miret, op. cit., p. 74, and in a similar document from 1173, according to J. L. de Moncada, *Episcopologia de Vich,* p. 489, in Baer, p. 22, and see there also p. 55. For the meaning of the word Cuiraça see R. Ricard, "Couraça et coracha," *Al-Andalus* 19:149ff. In the opinion of Lladonosa, it is a corruption of a Latin word meaning "a workshop for tanners," and he bases himself on findings from 1949, when the seminary was razed and, according to him, remains of a workshop, dating from Roman times, were found, see "La Cuiraça y la juderia leridana," *Divulgaciones leridanas,* pp. 111ff. But this local historian, who was unaware of Ricard's study, himself assumed that the wall there had a bulge. At any rate, Ricard's explanation is to be preferred.

284. Lladonosa, op. cit., p. 114.
285. Arch. cap., reg. 21, census 1382, f. 139: "un alberch en la Cuiraça en lo carrer dels pergaminers"; arch. cap., census S. Andres 1429, f. 67: "en la juheria en lo carrer apellat dels Pergaminers"; Lladonosa, p. 113.
286. The *cuesta* (slope) was thus called for a Christian whose name was Juan (in Catalan, Jan) de San Clement, as it is stated in a document from 1429, (cited in the preceding note), and see arch. cap., census S. Andres 1429, f. 68: "l'altra ab la cuiraza e de l'altra ab lo carrer de la juheria que hix devant lo portal del alberch de mossen de Sent Climent," and further arch. cap., reg. 21, census 1382, f. 74v (indicating) that the *cuirasola* is to be found "en la costa Jan." Concerning the gate near the *cuesta,* see Lladonosa, p. 110.
287. D. Romano, "Restos judíos en Lérida," *Sefarad* 20 (1960):50ff. About the discovery of a ring inscribed with Hebrew letters, the burial of bodies in an easterly direction, and a document from 1206 which place the Jewish cemetery at this site, see P. Sanahuja, *Lerida en sus luchas por la fé* (Lérida, 1946), pp. 23–24. All these artifacts leave no doubt that there was a Jewish cemetery at this site and thus, again, it is additional proof that Jews dwelt in the western sector of the city from ancient times, whereas the cemeteries of the Romans and Christians, from the early Middle Ages, were east of the city.
288. In the opinion of a historian of the nineteenth century, the conquest took place in about 1068, see D. Monfar y Sors, *Historia de los condes de Urgel* (Barcelona, 1853) 1, pp. 336, 350–57.
289. Baer, *Urkunden* 1, no. 10.
290. Abraham bar Joseph Cavaler (perhaps the son of Yūsuf mentioned above) sold and let houses in Barcelona from his ownership in 1092–1093 and 1094; Moses, as well as his other sons, also owned property, according to documents from the years 1121, 1133–1134. A document from 1142 speaks of property which had formerly belonged to Abraham Cavaler, see Miret Sans, "Documents sur les juifs catalans aux XIe, XIIe, et XIIIe siècles, no. 8," *REJ* 68:66ff. In the above-mentioned document from 1094, the eulogy of the dead was not added to his name; and see also a document dealing with a land sale by Abraham Cavaler in 1104, in Schwab-Miret Sans, "Nouveaux documents de juifs barcelonnais au XIIe siècle," *BAH* 68:572ff., and there, p. 564, a document from 1113 concerning his sons.

291. J.M. Pou i Marti, *Historia de la ciutat de Balaguer* (Manresa, 1913), p. 47.
292. Op. cit., p. 62.
293. Baer, *Urkunden* 1, no. 14.
294. See p. 88.
295. Different dates for these events are given in Arabic sources: Ibn 'Idhārī, p. 252—the year 455 of the *hidjra* (1063) and al-Maḳḳarī 2, pp. 748ff. —the following year, but according to Anonymous, it is 1065, see the appendix to Ibn 'Idhārī, p. 303, and so too Ibn al-Abbār, see according to Dozy in the study cited below. In Christian sources one finds the date 1065, see *Historia Silense,* ed. Santos Coco, pp. 89–90; Lucas Tudensis, "Chronicon mundi," *Hispaniae illustratae* 4:97 and cf. Dozy, "Histoire de Valence depuis 1061," *Recherches,* 1st ed., pp. 308ff.; on the other hand, Menéndez Pidal 1, p. 151.
296. In Ibn 'Idhārī, pp. 160ff.
297. In the coins of 442 and 443 of the *hidjra* (1050, 1051), the official Ibn Gomez is mentioned, i.e., a member of the Mozarab community, see Prieto, p. 184, and see also G. Miles, *Coins of the Spanish Mulūk al-Ṭawā-'if,* p. 46.
298. Ribera, "La Xarea de Valencia musulmana," *Disertaciones* 2, pp. 326ff.; Lévi-Provençal, "Notes de toponomastique hispanomaghribine," *AIEO* 2:222ff.; Torres Balbás, " 'Muṣalla' y 'Sarī'a' en las ciudades hispanomusulmanas," *Al-Andalus* 13:173ff.
299. It is recorded in *Repartimiento,* p. 274, that two Jews, Solomon and Yaḥyā, receive *"domos"* in *"calle judeorum quas tenent ante balneum de Almeli"*; cf. pp. 217, 229, 244, 257, 290.
300. The boundaries of the Jewish neighborhood are given in *Repartimiento,* p. 290, except that the streets and houses mentioned in that passage are, for the greatest part, unknown to us; see at length J. R. Pertegás, "La judería de Valencia," appended to J. Sanchis y Sivera, *La iglesia parroquial de Santo Tomás de Valencia* (Valencia, 1913), pp. 243ff.
301. M.A. de Orellana, *Valencia antigua y moderna* (Valencia, 1923–1924) 1, pp. 505ff.
302. Pertegás, pp. 255–56, 260, 265ff.
303. *Repartimiento,* pp. 255, 256.
304. R. Isaac Alfāsī, Responsa, no. 132.
305. See my article in *Zion* 28:49, where a printing error occurred: 479 should be 974.
306. Documentos, no. 7., Piṭbōn was a male name, see T.-S.18.24: Isaac bar Abraham Séfaradī, known as Pīṭbōn, gives a guarantee on the payment of the debt of Menasseh bar David. This is a document from the 1020s.
307. See Ibn 'Idhārī, pp. 224, 250; the passages from the books of Ibn Khaldūn and Lisān ad-dīn which Prieto cites, p. 37, and the coins he lists, pp. 188ff. His conjectures regarding two periods of rule by Nabīl are without foundation, as is shown by the passages, noted earlier, from Ibn 'Idhārī's book of which this scholar had no knowledge.
308. Simonet, p. 654; Bayerri, *Historia de Tortosa* 6, pp. 715ff.
309. The Arabic story is copied from *Al-Bakrī* in *Ar-Rauḍ al-mi'ṭār,* p. ٤٢ . The count of Barcelona is Ramon Berenguer I, called "the

Old" (1035–1076) who married Almodis in 1053 after having repudiated his second wife Blanca. However, Almodis was not from Narbonne but was the wife of Pons, the count of Toulouse, see in detail Pr. Bofarull, *Los condes de Barcelona vindicados* (Barcelona, 1836) 2, pp. 29ff.

310. Cf. Baer, *Urkunden* 1, no. 28 and see Kayserling in *The Jewish Encyclopedia* 12, p. 202.
311. See vol. 1, pp. 395–96.
312. *Shīrat Yisrāel,* p. 69, and see Schirmann 1, pp. 169–70; and cf. *Y'dī'ōt ha-mākhūn* 4 (5698):254, 276.
313. See my article in *Zion* 28:48–49.
314. After the conquest of Tortosa by the Catalan Count Ramon Berenguer IV, the Jews were given the shipyard area (dār aṣ-ṣinā'a) on condition that they would erect there a quarter of sixty houses. The Jews did indeed settle on that site which was southwest of the city (near the present market), and for two or three generations this constituted the Jewish quarter of Tortosa. They later moved from there and returned to the quarter in the north of the city. In the later Middle Ages, because of these changes, the neighborhood near the market was called Call vell (the old Jewish neighborhood) and the neighborhood in Remolins, Call nou (the new Jewish neighborhood), see Fr. Carreras y Candi, *L'Aljama de juhéus de Tortosa: Memorias leidas en la Real Academia de buenas letras de Barcelona IX,* fasc. 3 (Barcelona, 1928), and in particular, p. 15. However, the text of the document in which Ramon Berenguer granted the Jews the shipyard area shows clearly that he gave them a stretch of (fortified) land which they had not previously held, in the manner of the Christian conquerors-colonizers who endeavored to attract settlers to the cities they conquered. But one cannot conclude from this document that Jews formerly dwelt on that site. The fact that they moved, at a much later period, to the quarter which lay in the northern part of the city is proof that they had a historic link with it.

    One can assume, however, that after the conquest of the city by the Catalans, they did *not* sell their fields and their homes—were this not so, how could they return there? And, too, the fact that the Jewish cemetery was on the other side of the northeast wall of the city—see Cantera-Millás, p. 276—apparently proves that the Jews of Tortosa did earlier dwell in the Remolins quarter.
315. Cf. Ramon O'Callaghan, *Algunos apuntes de los anales de Tortosa* (Tortosa, 1911), p. 44.
316. Pastor y Lluis, "La judería de Tortosa," *Boletin de la Sociedad Castellonense de Cultura* 2:327.
317. F. Pastor y Lluis, "La judería y su sinagoga," *Boletin de la Sociedad Castellonense de Cultura* 2 (1921):131; "La judería de Tortosa," ibid., pp. 327–31.
318. See Bayerri 6, pp. 712ff.
319. *Ar-Rauḍ al-mi'ṭār,* p.   , and this passage is no doubt taken from *Al-Bakrī.* The words of al-Idrīsī, p. 191, cf. vol. 1, p. 341 concerning Tarragona, the "Jewish city," can possibly be explained only if, in that period, all the Moslems left the city and only the Jews remained. This

explanation is perhaps preferable on the assumption that the Arabic geographer had an earlier period in mind; this was a Roman city in ancient times.

320. For proof that after the Christian conquest there was at times a larger community in Tarragona than in Tortosa, see in Kayserling, *The Jewish Encyclopedia* 12, p. 64.

321. R. Chabas, *Historia de la ciudad de Denia,* 2a ed. (Alicante, 1958) 1, p. 185.

322. *Diwān of Samuel ha-lēvī,* no. 67 and there it is al-Dītī; and cf. Schirmann 1, p. 276; Mirsky, in the introduction to the *Diwān of Ibn Khalfōn,* p. 16.

323. Bodleiana 2877[31].

324. T.-S. 10 J 14[16b] and see below regarding a ship that came to Alexandria from Denia. Also see the letter of Ismā'īl b. Faraḥ to Yūsuf b. 'Ēlī al-Fāsī in Tyre, T.-S. 13 J 16[19], and this is a letter from the second half of the eleventh century, inasmuch as Nahrai b. Nissīm, living in that period, is mentioned there; cf. *JQR* 19:737, *REJ* 56:234. In addition see Alfāsī's *Sefer Sh'ēlōt u-t'shūbhōt,* no. 132. See also Goitein, Letters, p. 319.

325. Responsa Alfāsī, ms. Bodleiana 2794, no. 11.

326. Documentos, nos. 8, 9.

327. T.-S. 10 J 16[17], cf. S.D. Goitein, *Tarbīṣ* 28:352. For the various forms of this family's name, see Goitein, *PAAJR* 28:43.

328. See Goitein in *Tarbīṣ* 24:139.

329. *Shīrat Yisrāēl,* p. 111 (the Arabic text is in Steinschneider, *ZDMG* 8:551 and also in Derenbourg, *Opusc.* p. xix); Ibn Abī Uṣaibi'a II, p. 50, and see also Dukes, N'ḥal Ḳ'dūmīm, p. 11. "Saḳṭār" is merely a corruption of Ḳasṭār which means a moneychanger, a banker. See Steinschneider, op. cit.

330. R. Abraham Ibn Ezra in the introduction to *Sēfer ha-moznayim.* He is cited as the author of *Sēfer ha-diḳdūḳ,* see Dukes, *Litbl. des Orients* 9, col. 509. The book called *Kitāb at-Taṣārīf* which Neubauer found in a ms. in St. Petersburg and from which Derenbourg first published fragments, op. cit., pp. xx–xxi, is not from Ibn Yashūsh, see Fuchs in his study on Ibn Bal'am, pp. 12ff. From the biography in *Ibn Abī Uṣaibi'a,* one cannot deduce that Ibn Yashūsh wrote treatises on the Hebrew language.

331. R. Abraham Ibn Ezra quotes his words in the *Sēfer ha-Yiṣḥāḳī* and refutes them in his commentary to Genesis 36:31–32, Hosea 1:1 and Job 42:16 and refers to him as "ha-mahbhil" (the vaporizer, the generator of nonsense) whose "book deserves to be burned," and see too in *Sēfer ha-shīm* (ed. Lippman) 3b. On the other hand, Ibn Ezra cites Ibn Yashūsh in the first commentary on Genesis 1:31 (ed. M. Friedländer in an appendix to "Essays on the Writings of Abraham Ibn Ezra," *Ibn Ezra Literature* 4, p. 33). But the reference is no doubt to the same person. Carmoly, in the periodical *Zion* (of Jost-Creizenach) 1 (5601):46, cited the passage from the Mishna commentary of Joseph b. Eleazar Ṭōbh 'Elem who identifies Ibn Yashūsh as the author of *Sēfer ha-Yiṣḥāḳī.* Despite this, it is not to be assumed that there were two writers at the same time whose names were Yiṣḥāḳ, and who engaged in the same field of research utilizing the identical liberal approach. On the one hand, R. Abraham Ibn Ezra explicitly calls the author of *Ha-Yiṣḥāḳī* "Yiṣḥāḳ" and on the other hand, an Arabic writer (see below) who knew him person-

ally states that he was "well-versed in their history" (the history of the Jews). If this were not Yiṣḥāḳ Ibn Yashūsh, his memory would surely have been preserved in one of the literary sources. Bacher, in *Winter-Wünsche* 2, p. 262, held the view that the reference is to one person, but Harkavy was uncertain; see "Ḥadāshīm gam y'shānīm 7" (appendix to Graetz-Shefer 4), p. 15.

As for the assumption that words may be changed in the text of the Bible—a practice which Abraham Ibn Ezra condemns with caustic language—see his commentary on Exodus 19:12, his brief commentary on Exodus 21:8, and his commentary on Daniel 1:1, *Sāfa k'rūra* (ed. Lippman) 9b, cf. David Ḳimḥī on Jeremiah 33:26, and especially *Sēfer Ṣāḥōt* (Berlin, 1768) f. 52a f., and cf. Abu'l-Walīd in *Sēfer ha-riḳma,* p. 309; see also Geiger, *Litbl. d. Or.* 1, col. 348 who believes that this is the method of Abu 'l-Walīd in his *Sēfer ha-riḳma* and see as against him [Fürst] in the same periodical cols. 807ff., whose view is the same as Lippman's, and especially D. Herzog, "Die 'Wortvertauschungen' im Kitāb al-Luma' des Abulwalīd Merwān Ibn Gānāḥ v. in den Schriften Abraham Ibn'Esra's," *MGWJ* 53:708–19; 54:82–102; 55:213–40, who proves clearly that this is not the opinion of the grammarian from Saragossa and arrives at the conclusion that this is that of Ibn Yashūsh.

332. Ibn Ṣā'id, p. 89 (and from him, Ibn Abī Uṣaibi'a), the English translation in Finkel, *JQR* n.s. 18:52. The year of his death is 448 of the *hidjra* (March 23, 1056–March 9, 1057).

333. Documentos, nos. 8, 9.

334. *Diwān,* no. 74, and see the emendation of Sassoon xxiii and see there lines 16–18.

335. This should be his name. It is true that in the first printing of Abraham b. Dā'ūd (ed. Neubauer, p. 75; ed. Cohen, p. 61), his name is Ibn Sakhnī, but Neubauer, in his edition, p. 75, prefers the version, Ibn Sukkarī; Saadya b. Danān calls him Ibn Safrī, see p. 30b. "Sakhnī" has no meaning whereas Sukkarī means a seller of sugar or a sugar manufacturer; and see Poznanski, "Les cinq Isaac," *REJ* 65:312 and cf. Steinschneider, *JQR* 11:320.

336. Poznanski and Mann hold that this occurred in approximately 1070, see *Texts* 1, pp. 207, 212.

337. See the Geniza fragment published by Mann, "Glanures de la Gueniza," *REJ* 74:175ff. in which is given his explanation of a passage in Tractate Shabbāt, f. 8a.

338. Abraham b. Dā'ūd, p. 62; *Bēt ha-b'ḥīra* by M'nahēm Mē'īrī, in Neubauer, *Med. Jew. Chr.* 1, p. 228.

339. In the introduction, the translator states that he performed his work in 1078 when he was thirty-five years old. (The translation was first printed in Venice in 5362.)

340. See *Shīrat Yisrāēl,* pp. 72–73 and *Taḥk'mōnī,* p. 41. The first printing was in Venice, 5353, cf. *CB,* pp. 1148ff. There should be added the commentary *N'tībh miṣvōtēkha* of Samuel b. Mūsā ha-Kōhēn which is also a commentary on the Azhārōt of Solomon Ibn Gabirol.

341. A *s'līḥa* which begins: "*Paḥad'ti mi yōṣ'ri*" was printed in *Ōṣār Neḥmad* (Vienna, 5617), pp. 188ff. and thereafter in *Sefer Rabbēnu B'khōr Shōr,* part

1 (Jerusalem, 5716, f. [1bf.]). For other poems see Brody, *Mibhḥar ha-shīra,* pp. 121ff; Shirmann, *Shīrīm hadāshīm,* p. 196ff. There is a Spanish translation of one poem in Millás, *Poesía Sagrada,* pp. 241ff. and in addition, cf. *The Jewish Encyclopedia* 6, p. 629, Zunz, "Litgesch. d. syn. Poesie," p. 201.

342. Al-Idrīsī, p. 197, cf. al-Maḳḳarī 1, p. 102. Al-Idrīsī is speaking here about the eleventh century.
343. Torres Balbás, "Almería islámica," *Al-Andalus* 22:429ff.
344. See *Ar-Rauḍ al-mi'ṭār* ١٨٣ f.; Torres Balbás, art. cit., pp. 434ff.
345. See Torres Balbás, art. cit., p. 452.
346. Torres Balbás, art. cit., p. 438, who relies on local tradition.
347. Cf. art. cit., p. 441 and see, in his drawing alongside p. 428, the Puerta del socorro.
348. Al-Idrīsī, p. 196.
349. See my article in *Zion* 28:50.
350. Aḍ-Ḍabbī, *Bughyat al-multamis* (Madrid, 1885), pp. 332–33.
351. *Ṭauḳ al-ḥamāma,* p. 48. It is true that Ibn Ḥazm was also in Almería in 1038, see Ibn 'Idhārī, p. 171, but this book was written in 1027 and the book al-Fiṣal in which he mentions his debates with Ismā'īl (see below) was written in 1027–1030; their meeting should therefore be ascribed to the 1020s.
352. T.-S. 8 J 18^2.
353. Al-Fiṣal 5, p. 120. The passage was given its printing by Schreiner in *ZDMG* 42:657, and cf. there pp. 616–17, and see too Steinschneider, *Ar. Lit.,* no. 87. (Steinschneider is incorrect in concluding from the text that the reference there is to a literary work for which reason he included Ismā'īl b. Yūnus's name in his book.) See also *JQR* (n.s.) 40:280f.

INDEX OF PERSONS AND PLACES

Names beginning with al-, an-, ar-, as-, az-, are listed under the second element of the name